BOOK II
ORGANIZING THINKING
GRAPHIC ORGANIZERS

SANDRA PARKS AND HOWARD BLACK

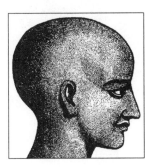

© 1990

CRITICAL THINKING PRESS & SOFTWARE

P.O. Box 448, Pacific Grove, CA 93950
Phone 800-458-4849 • FAX 408-393-3277
ISBN 0-89455-355-0
Printed in the United States of America

ABOUT THE AUTHORS

HOWARD BLACK received an M.A. in Physics from Indiana State University and did doctoral studies at both Indiana State and Michigan State universities. He taught physics at Indiana State for 28 years and in 1978 received the Distinguished Teaching Award from that university. He currently teaches math and general studies at Bethune-Cookman College, Daytona Beach, Florida, where he was given the 1990 Award for Excellence in Teaching.

SANDRA BLACK received an M.A. in Curriculum from the University of South Florida and did doctoral studies at Indiana State University. She is an educational consultant to schools throughout the country, as well as a consultant on several projects for the Regional Laboratories for Educational Improvement in the Northeast and the Islands. She conducts annually the National Curriculum Study Institute for the Association for Curriculum Development. Sandra Black is the founding president of the Indiana Association for the Gifted.

ACKNOWLEDGMENTS

The authors appreciate the cooperation of administrators, teachers, and students in the academic excellence programs of Dade County (Florida) Public Schools. The students and teachers at South Miami Heights Elementary School contributed to the classroom effectiveness of *Organizing Thinking* by field-testing these lessons.

The authors extend their thanks to editors Donna Grace, Barbara Mitchell, and Brian Langlois for their assistance in preparing the complex graphics and specialized text of this manuscript.

The authors gratefully acknowledge the assistance of Dr. Robert Swartz of the University of Massachusetts at Boston, co-director of the Center for Teaching Thinking of the Regional Laboratory for Educational Improvement for the Northeast and the Islands. Dr. Swartz advised the authors regarding metacognition and the appropriate explanation of critical thinking principles.

TO

DEAN CLEO HIGGINS
BETHUNE-COOKMAN COLLEGE
DAYTONA BEACH, FLORIDA

CONTENTS

INTRODUCTION

COMPONENTS OF ORGANIZING THINKING

ORGANIZING THINKING provides:

prepared lessons (student materials and lesson plans) for infusing thinking skills instruction into content learning.

suggestions for class discussion topics on content lessons and thinking processes.

identification of numerous content objectives for applying thinking skills instruction across the curriculum.

master graphics to prepare a transparency collection for explaining concepts and guiding classroom discussion.

tools for process writing instruction.

ORGANIZING THINKING

Organizing Thinking is a handbook of lessons to integrate the teaching of thinking skills into elementary school instruction. Central to all lessons is the use of graphic organizers to illustrate how information is related. These graphic organizers depict key skills (compare and contrast, sequence, part/whole relationships, classification, and analogy) and involve students in active thinking about textual information to promote clearer understanding of content lessons. Diagrams serve as "mental maps" to depict complex relationships in any subject and at any grade level. Thus, graphic organizers become a metacognitive tool to transfer the thinking processes to other lessons which feature the same relationships.

The use of graphic organizers encourages students to see information as components of systems or as contrasting concepts, rather than as isolated facts. Once information and relationships have been recorded on graphic organizers, students then use the pictorial outline to form more abstract comparisons, evaluations, and conclusions. These "diagrammatic outlines" help students organize their thinking for writing, for oral or visual presentations, and for problem solving.

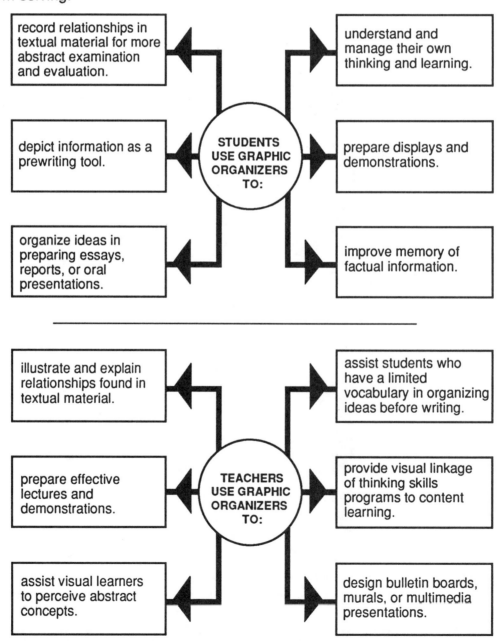

record relationships in textual material for more abstract examination and evaluation.

understand and manage their own thinking and learning.

depict information as a prewriting tool.

prepare displays and demonstrations.

STUDENTS USE GRAPHIC ORGANIZERS TO:

organize ideas in preparing essays, reports, or oral presentations.

improve memory of factual information.

illustrate and explain relationships found in textual material.

assist students who have a limited vocabulary in organizing ideas before writing.

prepare effective lectures and demonstrations.

provide visual linkage of thinking skills programs to content learning.

TEACHERS USE GRAPHIC ORGANIZERS TO:

assist visual learners to perceive abstract concepts.

design bulletin boards, murals, or multimedia presentations.

 © 1990 MIDWEST PUBLICATIONS • CRITICAL THINKING PRESS & SOFTWARE • P. O. Box 448, Pacific Grove, CA 93950

Lessons in *Organizing Thinking* are designed to supplement text material and to accompany corresponding content objectives. *Organizing Thinking* features graphs and diagrams of relationships commonly employed in language arts, mathematics, social studies, science, art, and music instruction. Each lesson includes a lesson plan, background information which can be reproduced for student use, and the completed graphic organizer containing suggested answers. Since a photocopy machine will not reproduce light blue print, the completed graphic organizer also serves as a blank graphic organizer for student use.

LESSON PLAN FORMAT

THINKING SKILL: Identifies the thinking process employed in the lesson so that teachers and students use appropriate terms.

CONTENT OBJECTIVE: Identifies the content objective of the lesson. *Organizing Thinking* lessons supplement the corresponding content lesson and are taught as the lesson appears in course outlines or text material. Some lessons are appropriate to introduce concepts; others are designed to review or extend content lessons.

DISCUSSION: Suggests techniques for using graphic organizers in discussion, provides dialogues to explain, model, or extend lessons, and summarizes inferences, interpretations, or conclusions which result from discussion.

WRITING EXTENSION: Provides suggestions for essay questions, summary writing, or creative writing tasks. Questions may also be used as essay items on unit tests or as a class Think/Pair/Share activity.

THINKING ABOUT THINKING: Provides suggestions to help students reflect about their own thinking and learning. THINKING ABOUT THINKING questions may be used for class discussion or as a Think/Pair/Share activity.

SIMILAR CONTENT LESSONS: Identifies other lessons in the same content area which feature the same thinking process and the same graphic organizer.

COMPLETED GRAPHIC: Provides answers for the lesson.

TEXT PASSAGE AND WORKSHEET: Provides lesson material (background information and a blank graphic) to be reproduced for student use.

SUGGESTIONS FOR CLASS DISCUSSION

The discussion section of each lesson suggests techniques for using the graphic organizer in classroom discussion, dialogues to clarify key concepts within the lesson, and results of the discussion (interpretations, inferences, or conclusions). The class discussion is guided by using a transparent graphic organizer on an overhead projector. The TECHNIQUE of visually guided discussion focuses students' attention on the information and relationships in the lesson. It becomes a visual tool for recording student responses, picturing the content of the lesson and recording each individual's contribution to the discussion.

DIALOGUE suggestions offer models for expressing thought processes when discussing key concepts. Sample dialogues appear in "screened" bold type. The WRITING EXTENSION and metacognitive questions (THINKING ABOUT THINKING) may also be used to stimulate class discussion or as a Think/Pair/Share activity. Dialogues extend students' understanding of the content beyond the given lessons and prompt them to form interpretations, inferences, or conclusions.

The purposeful use of graphic organizers should lead students to understand significant factors in a lesson. The RESULT paragraph expresses the main point of the discussion: a clarification, interpretation, inference, or conclusion drawn from the lesson.

USING GRAPHIC ORGANIZERS AS A PREWRITING TOOL

Graphic organizers are helpful for organizing ideas prior to answering essay questions or doing expository writing assignments. Thus, the lessons in *Organizing Thinking* are designed to teach students the process of writing effective essays, accurate descriptions, persuasive arguments, or poems. Students follow these steps in each lesson:

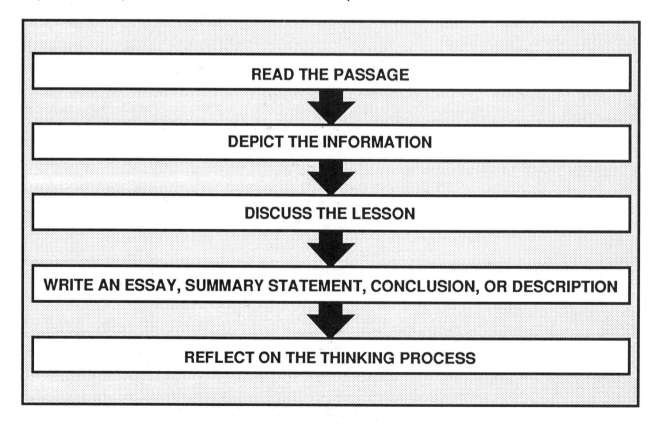

READ THE PASSAGE

↓

DEPICT THE INFORMATION

↓

DISCUSS THE LESSON

↓

WRITE AN ESSAY, SUMMARY STATEMENT, CONCLUSION, OR DESCRIPTION

↓

REFLECT ON THE THINKING PROCESS

Students should transfer information from texts or research notes to a graphic organizer. The graphic organizer serves as a "visual outline" of information for descriptive, expository, persuasive, or creative writing passages. Provide a blank graph for the prewriting step until students are confident enough to identify the analysis relationship independently. Students should write brief, concise passages, which should contain all the significant information recorded on the graphic organizer and which should state clearly how that information is related. Encourage students to draw their own organizational graphs and diagrams. To reinforce student use of the graphic organizers, ask students to identify sections from a text that can be illustrated on a transparency of a graphic organizer. In addition to the writing component of each lesson, a series of ORGANIZING THINKING FOR WRITING lessons provides direct instruction in common forms of writing.

Introduce one type of graphic organizer at a time. Include essay questions on your unit tests. Use a completed graph as your answer key to help score essay tests quickly. Don't hesitate to give language-limited students essay questions. Critical thinking is significant for all students and can be demonstrated by well-organized essays whatever the individual's level of language proficiency.

METACOGNITIVE QUESTIONS

Metacognition refers to knowledge about, awareness of, and control over one's thinking and learning. Metacognitive questions, labeled THINKING ABOUT THINKING, are designed to help students become more aware of their thinking processes, and more deliberate and reflective about how well the process works. According to Swartz and Perkins (*Teaching Thinking: Issues and Approaches*) metacognitive strategies include:

1. Awareness of the thinking process
   - Using thinking terms—e.g., "predicting," "uncovering assumptions,"—to mark the presence of these thinking activities

2. Strategic use of the thinking process
   - Providing a list of components or a series of steps for students to follow in doing a certain type of thinking
   - Verbal prompting of students to go through a series of steps in their thinking
   - Asking students to describe retrospectively what they did in thinking about a particular issue or problem
   - Having students "think out loud" while another student records the thinking processes going on

3. Reflective use of the thinking process
   - developing rules for good thinking
   - recommending to others ways to think
   - correcting ineffective thinking

Metacognitive questions prompt students to make their thinking processes explicit and to evaluate the effectiveness of the process. Metacognition facilitates transfer and promotes the clear understanding of the lesson. In *Organizing Thinking* these questions refer primarily to the use of graphic organizers as a thinking strategy and as an effective tool in comprehending information. For additional background and examples of metacognitive questioning in creative thinking, critical thinking, and decision making, see *Teaching Thinking: Issues and Approaches* (Swartz and Perkins, 1990).

Teachers find that students recognize the usefulness of graphic organizers easily and use them independently. Metacognition about this technique is best reflected in students' design of their own graphic organizers, specialized to the particular task. Encourage students to develop graphic organizers for *Organizing Thinking* lessons and text lessons.

The Think/Pair/Share lesson in the study skills chapter illustrates the value of metacognitive discussion between students. This peer-teaching technique improves the quality and frequency of student participation in class discussion, models reflective, self-correcting thinking, and can be used with any lesson for clarity and understanding. The WRITING EXTENSION and THINKING ABOUT THINKING questions in each lesson may also be used as a topic for a Think/Pair/Share discussion.

CURRICULUM APPLICATIONS

Each *Organizing Thinking* lesson plan features numerous examples of lessons in each discipline in which the same thinking process and graphic organizer can be used to clarify the content. Teachers and thinking skills curriculum committees may use these application references in identifying curriculum opportunities for the meaningful integration of thinking skills instruction.

DIRECTIONS FOR PREPARING AND USING MASTER GRAPHS

Blank master graphs may be reproduced as student worksheets and used in several ways.

- If you are working with students who have a limited attention span or who require considerable reinforcement and practice, you may direct students to fill in their worksheets as you develop the lesson on the transparency.
- You may use the worksheet as a note-taking guide for students as you explain a lesson without the use of a transparency.
- Students may use the graphs as a study tool, to prepare oral presentations or position papers, and to examine complex passages.

To prepare a transparency which you may reuse often, reproduce the master graph on acetates with your photocopy or transparency master machine. Remember to use washable markers when recording information for each lesson. To reuse the transparency, wipe off the markings with a damp cloth. Store your "library" of transparencies in pocket folders in a ringed notebook.

To prepare your own infusion lessons, examine your texts for examples of the relationships depicted on the graphs: compare/contrast, part/whole, sequence, classification, analogy. Select the appropriate graphic organizer and write in expected answers to create an answer key. Use the blank lesson plan form on the following page to prepare your lesson plan. (It is not necessary to represent every example of the relationships in this fashion, since over-using any technique becomes less effective.) Graphic organizers are especially effective for complex lessons that contain significant, but possibly unclear or confusing, concepts to students.

As graphic organizers become a familiar visual outline for organizing information, use them as a basis for bulletin board design. Such displays offer students a colorful reminder of current lessons and the thinking processes involved. Students may also use the graphic organizers in design projects, displays, media presentations, science fair exhibits, report writing, and speech preparation. Place a file of blank graphs where students may take them as needed.

BRIDGING *BUILDING THINKING SKILLS*® TO CONTENT OBJECTIVES

For teachers who use *Building Thinking Skills*® (Midwest Publications • Critical Thinking Press) or other thinking skills programs, *Organizing Thinking* links thinking skills instruction to specific content lessons. Each graphic organizer can be used to teach a *Building Thinking Skills*® lesson and, subsequently, to apply the same process to teach a content lesson. The graphic organizer serves as a visual cue to remind students of the thinking process and to transfer that process to a particular content application.

BIBLIOGRAPHY

Swartz, Robert J. and D. N. Perkins, *Teaching Thinking: Issues and Approaches* (Pacific Grove, CA: Midwest Publications • Critical Thinking Press,1990).

CHAPTER 1 – BLACKLINE MASTER GRAPHS

LESSON PLAN FORM		COMPARE AND/OR CONTRAST DIAGRAMS
	INTERVAL GRAPHS	
TRANSITIVE ORDER GRAPHS		FLOWCHART DIAGRAMS
	CENTRAL IDEA GRAPHS	
BRANCHING DIAGRAMS		CLASS RELATIONSHIPS DIAGRAMS
	MATRIX DIAGRAMS	

LESSON PLAN FORM

TITLE

THINKING SKILLS _____

CONTENT OBJECTIVE _____
_____

DISCUSSION _____
_____
_____
_____
_____
_____
_____
_____
_____
_____
_____
_____
_____
_____

WRITING EXTENSION _____
_____
_____
_____
_____

THINKING ABOUT THINKING _____
_____
_____
_____

SIMILAR CONTENT LESSONS _____
_____

COMPARE AND/OR CONTRAST DIAGRAMS

TWO PEOPLE

- Backgrounds
- Historical periods
- Achievements
- Ideals
- Challenges
- Life stages
- Contribution effects

TWO SOLUTIONS

- Goals
- Options
- Plans
- Actions
- Outcomes
- Criteria

TWO THINGS

- Parts
- Measurements
- Kinds
- Uses
- Origins
- Operations
- Significance

TWO ORGANISMS

- Phyla
- Habitats
- Life requirements
- Physiological function
- Structures

USE COMPARE AND/OR CONTRAST DIAGRAMS TO EXAMINE

TWO STORIES

- Significant characteristics
  - Conflicts
  - Ideals
  - Characters
  - Styles
  - Organization
  - Significance of titles
  - Novelty

TWO PLACES

- Locations
- Land forms
- Significance
- Natural resources
- Development

TWO EVENTS

- Participants
- Leaders
- Significance
- Causes
- Consequences
- Historical periods

TWO CULTURES

- Geographic locations
- Histories
- Economic systems
- Political systems
- Leaders
- Technologies
- Values
- Art

TWO IDEAS

- Effects
- Assumptions
- How developed
- Leaders
- Significance
- Implications

USING COMPARE AND CONTRAST DIAGRAMS

RATIONALE FOR COMPARE AND CONTRAST ACTIVITIES

The compare and contrast process is a helpful technique for clarifying and understanding concepts. Concepts may include objects, organisms, people, places, institutions, or ideas. The comparison step (HOW ALIKE?) allows learners to relate a new concept to existing knowledge. The more similarities the learner can identify, the more clearly the new concept will be understood and remembered. The contrast step (HOW DIFFERENT?) allows learners to distinguish the new concept from similar concepts. This promotes clear understanding and memory by eliminating confusion with related knowledge.

The compare and contrast process should become a regular habit for students and teachers when examining new vocabulary words. After a student gives a definition, the teacher may ask, "How is that like…," followed by "How is that unlike…." This completes clarification in three steps:

1. Definition of the concept.
2. Identification with a similar concept that the student already knows.
3. Distinction from the concept in step two.

The number of responses in the HOW ALIKE or HOW DIFFERENT steps will vary. Each lesson may not contain the same number of similarities and differences contained on the master graph. Several blanks are provided on the diagram to encourage students to consider as many similarities or differences as possible.

NOTE: The Class Relationships Diagrams (pages 37–39) may also be used to describe similarities and differences.

USE THE COMPARE AND CONTRAST DIAGRAM TO:
- Compare and contrast two terms or ideas.
- Organize thinking to prepare essay questions.
- Clarify the meaning of terms in reviewing for a test.

TO USE THE COMPARE AND CONTRAST DIAGRAM:
1. Write the two concepts in the blanks at the top.
2. Discuss with students the definition and significant characteristics of each concept as you record it. This discussion confirms that students have sufficient background to make the rest of the exercise meaningful.
3. Record phrases which express similarities on each HOW ALIKE line. Note that these phrases commonly begin with "both," confirming that the characteristic is shared by the concepts.
4. Record phrases which express differences on each HOW DIFFERENT line. Each difference between the two concepts should relate to the same quality, but should point out the difference between the two terms. Establish this pattern:

    "**With regard to** (quality), (concept one and its distinctions), **but** (concept two and its distinctions)."
5. Ask students to explain what the distinction between the two concepts means or how the concepts will be used differently.

COMPARE AND CONTRAST DIAGRAM

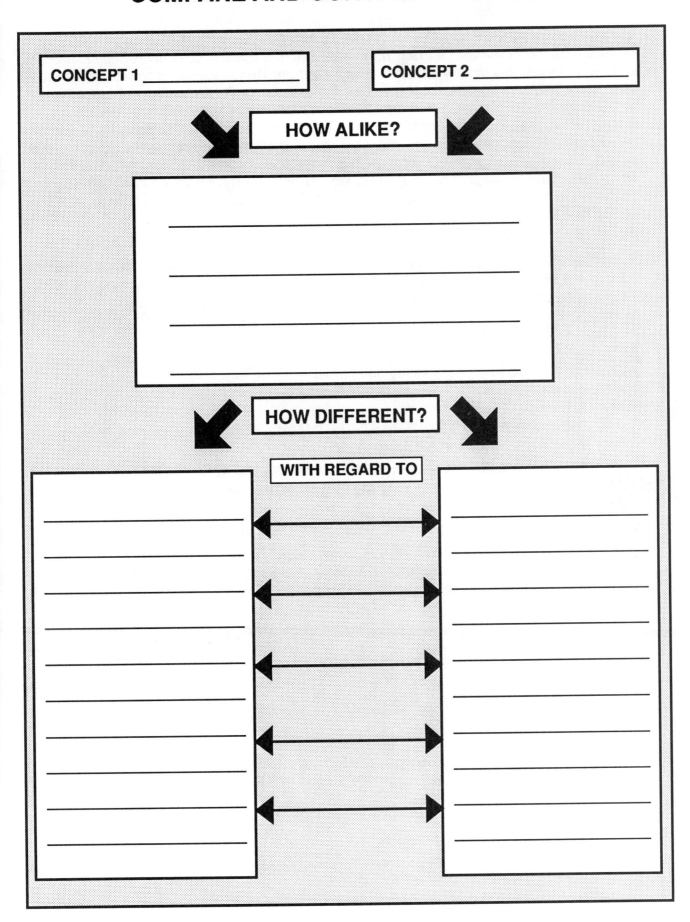

CONCEPT 1 _____

CONCEPT 2 _____

HOW ALIKE?

HOW DIFFERENT?

WITH REGARD TO

USING COMPARE OR CONTRAST DIAGRAMS

RATIONALE FOR COMPARE OR CONTRAST ACTIVITIES

Use the compare or contrast diagram when only one of the two processes is significant. To compare concepts, use the diagram to emphasize shared traits, such as showing analogous relationships between figures of speech. Use the diagram to illustrate many characteristics which two objects, organisms, or ideas share and how each expresses that characteristic. Students recognize that many connections are being expressed in a few metaphoric words.

To contrast concepts, use the diagram to emphasize differences and to eliminate confusion by separating a new term from similar ones. "Contrast" emphasizes subtle differences which might otherwise be overlooked. For clarity, begin each discussion by identifying the characteristics being differentiated. Then describe how that characteristic is different for each term. Establish this pattern:

"**With regard to** (quality), (concept one and its distinctions), **but** (concept two and its distinctions)."

The number of responses in the HOW ALIKE or HOW DIFFERENT steps will vary. Several blanks are provided on the diagram to encourage students to consider as many similarities or differences as possible.

USE THE COMPARE OR CONTRAST DIAGRAM TO:
- Compare or contrast two concepts.
- Organize thinking to prepare essay questions.
- Analyze metaphors.

TO USE THE COMPARE OR CONTRAST DIAGRAM:
1. Write the two terms in the blanks at the top.
2. Identify the characteristic being compared or contrasted. Write it in the center column.
3. Discuss how that characteristic applies to the first term and write the answer in the left column.
4. Discuss how that characteristic applies to the second term and write the answer in the right column.
5. Encourage students to draw inferences about the significance of the differences between these two terms or concepts.

COMPARE OR CONTRAST DIAGRAM

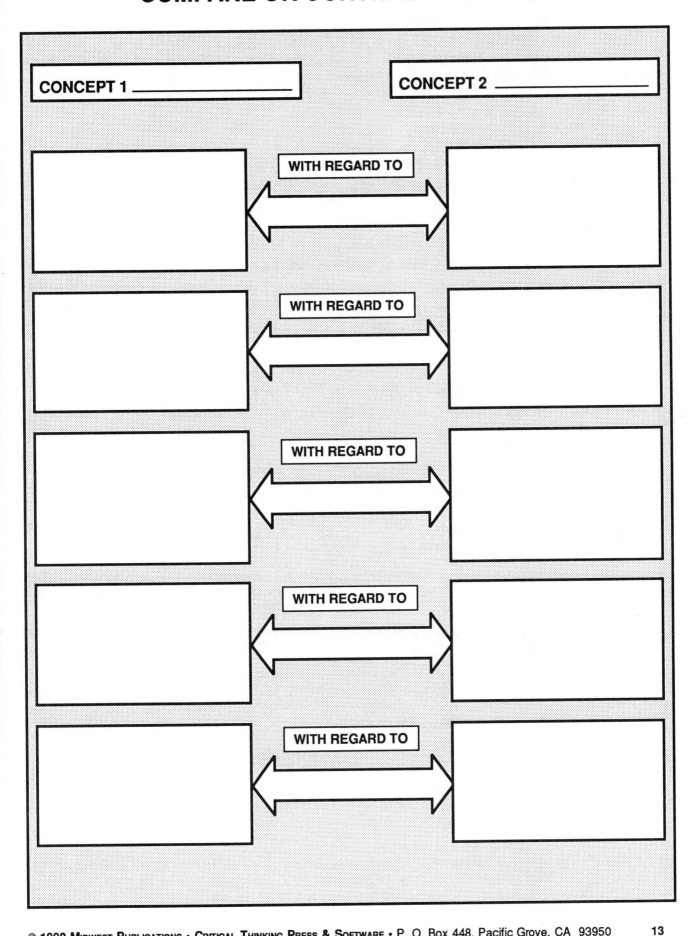

CONCEPT 1 _____

CONCEPT 2 _____

WITH REGARD TO

WITH REGARD TO

WITH REGARD TO

WITH REGARD TO

WITH REGARD TO

INTERVAL GRAPHS

CHRONOLOGICAL ORDER

- People (life events)
- Countries (history)
- Cultures (development)
- Geologic eras

NUMBER VALUE

- Relative number values
- Inequalities

USE INTERVAL GRAPHS TO DEPICT

PARALLEL EVENTS

- Complex plots in fiction
- Biographical data
- Record events for writing narratives

GRAPH INFORMATION

- Bar graphs
- Scattergrams
- Cartesian coordinates

USING INTERVAL GRAPHS

RATIONALE FOR USING INTERVAL GRAPHS
Interval Graphs can be used to depict sequence and order in a variety of forms. For example, time lines are frequently featured in text materials to show events in chronological order. Number lines are used to explain positive and negative number values.

Since interval graphs are primarily used to record quantitative data, students may use the information on the graphs to interpret trends, correlations, or simultaneous values. To depict two trends or to correlate a series of events, use a parallel interval graph to organize information. To depict simultaneous values of two variables, use a grid graph with perpendicular scales.

USE THE INTERVAL GRAPH TO:
- Record and correlate events with given dates.
- Depict positive and negative number values.
- Depict correlations or parallels between events occurring at the same time.
- Depict simultaneous values of two variables.

TO USE THE INTERVAL GRAPH:
1. Select the appropriate type of interval graph: time line, parallel interval graph, or grid graph.
2. Decide the range (years, values, etc.) that the total graph should cover and select appropriate intervals. (The master graph contains ten intervals.)
3. Label the lines of the graph.
4. Record the data.
5. Interpret significant trends or conclusions suggested by the data .

TO DESIGN AN INTERVAL GRAPH WITH OTHER THAN TEN INTERVALS:
1. Determine the range of dates or values and mark at each end of the graph.
   Example: *To record events from 1775 to 1800, record 1775 at the left end and 1800 at the right end of the line.*
2. Subtract the smaller value from the larger value to calculate the range value.
   The range value of this example is determined by 1800 – 1775 = 25 years (range).
3. Decide the practical number of intervals for this data.
   For this example, five intervals should be sufficient. Note that six marks are needed to produce five intervals.
4. Divide the range value by the number of intervals to get the interval value.
   25 years ÷ 5 intervals = 5 years per interval (interval value).
5. Add the interval value to the smaller limit of the range to determine the value of the second mark.
   1775 + 5 = 1780 value (year) of the second mark.
6. Repeat this process until you have labeled all the marks on the graph.

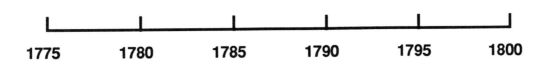

| 1775 | 1780 | 1785 | 1790 | 1795 | 1800 |

TIME LINE INTERVAL GRAPH

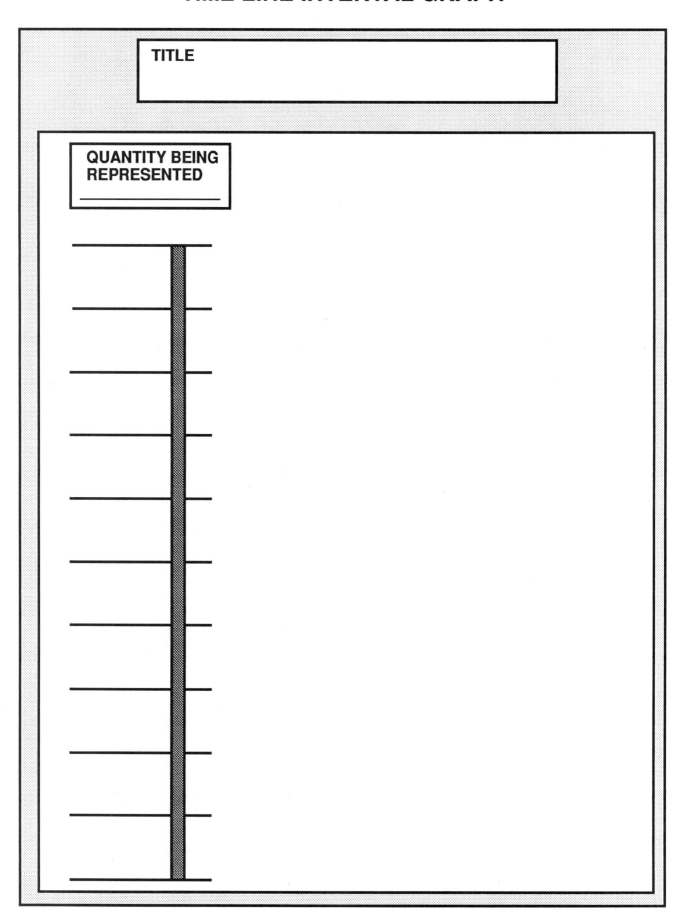

TITLE

QUANTITY BEING
REPRESENTED

© 1990 MIDWEST PUBLICATIONS • CRITICAL THINKING PRESS & SOFTWARE • P. O. Box 448, Pacific Grove, CA 93950

PARALLEL INTERVAL GRAPH

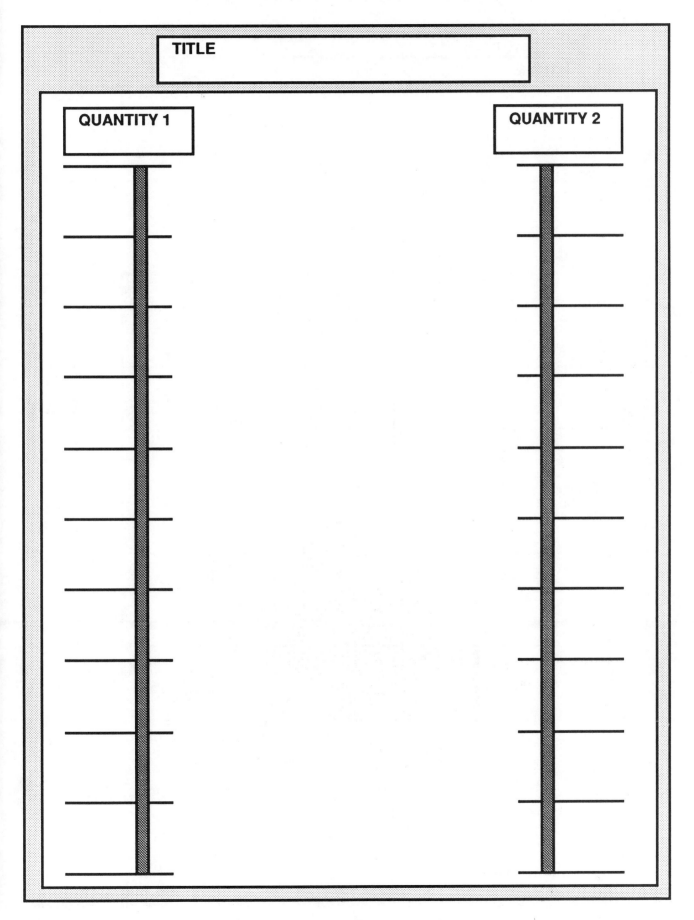

TITLE

QUANTITY 1

QUANTITY 2

GRID GRAPH

TITLE

ITEM OR INTERVAL

ITEM OR INTERVAL

TRANSITIVE ORDER GRAPHS

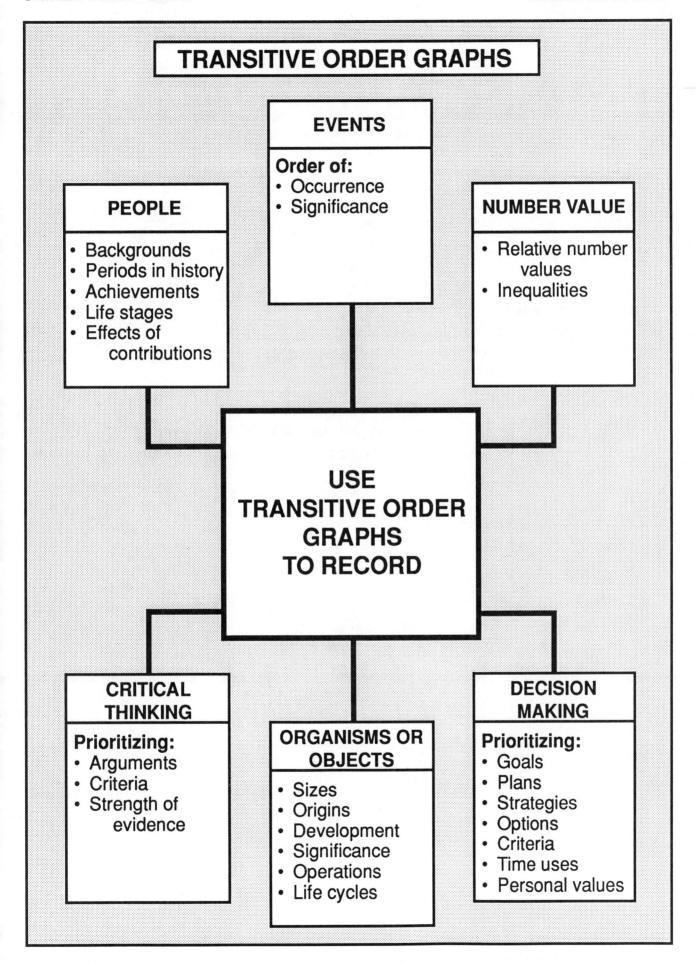

EVENTS

Order of:
- Occurrence
- Significance

PEOPLE

- Backgrounds
- Periods in history
- Achievements
- Life stages
- Effects of
  contributions

NUMBER VALUE

- Relative number
  values
- Inequalities

USE
TRANSITIVE ORDER
GRAPHS
TO RECORD

**CRITICAL
THINKING**

Prioritizing:
- Arguments
- Criteria
- Strength of
  evidence

**ORGANISMS OR
OBJECTS**

- Sizes
- Origins
- Development
- Significance
- Operations
- Life cycles

**DECISION
MAKING**

Prioritizing:
- Goals
- Plans
- Strategies
- Options
- Criteria
- Time uses
- Personal values

USING TRANSITIVE ORDER GRAPHS

RATIONALE FOR USING TRANSITIVE ORDER AND CYCLE GRAPHS

Transitive order graphs are useful for recording inferred order from written passages. Readers can use the graph to keep track of relative position, rank, order, or quantity. Since this graph is used to record the information given, an item's relative position may change as the text identifies intervening items. Thus, using a pencil or erasable marker is recommended.

Cycle graphs are transitive order graphs which depict repeating chronological order or interrelationship. Cycle graphs are useful in recording information to show time or direction cycles or to emphasize the repetitive characteristic of a trend. The directional arrows in the diagram may point in either direction to depict a relationship.

USE THE TRANSITIVE ORDER GRAPH TO:

• Record order by inference from text materials.

TO USE THE TRANSITIVE ORDER GRAPH:

1. Indicate the factor or characteristic being ranked.
2. Indicate the direction of the transitive order and list the limits; i.e., youngest to oldest, earliest to latest, largest to smallest.
3. Enter items on the lines as information is given in the written passage. Use a pencil or erasable marker in order to change answers easily.
4. Change item order, if necessary, as text material identifies intervening items.
5. You may use the margin to record proposed position, until text information confirms the relative order.

USE THE CYCLE GRAPH TO:

• Record cyclical occurrences.
• Depict interrelationship.

TO USE THE CYCLE GRAPH:

1. Divide a circle into the number of parts in the process to be shown.
2. Enter events in order.
3. Use arrows to indicate the direction of flow .
4. Interpret significant trends or conclusions that the information suggests.

TRANSITIVE ORDER GRAPHS

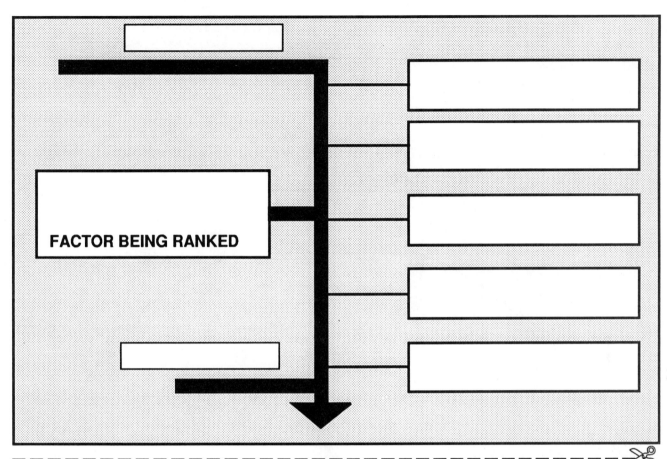

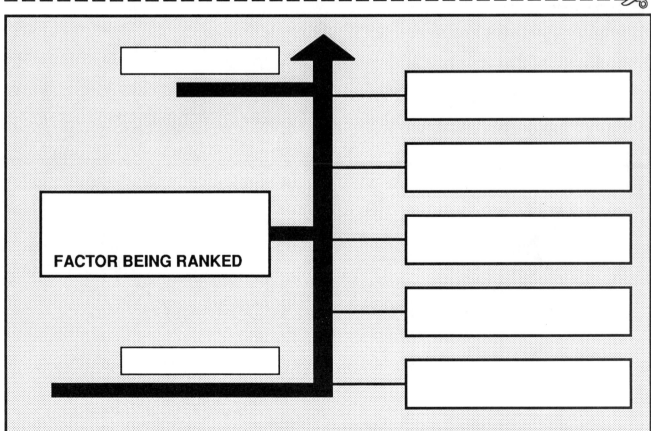

CYCLE GRAPH

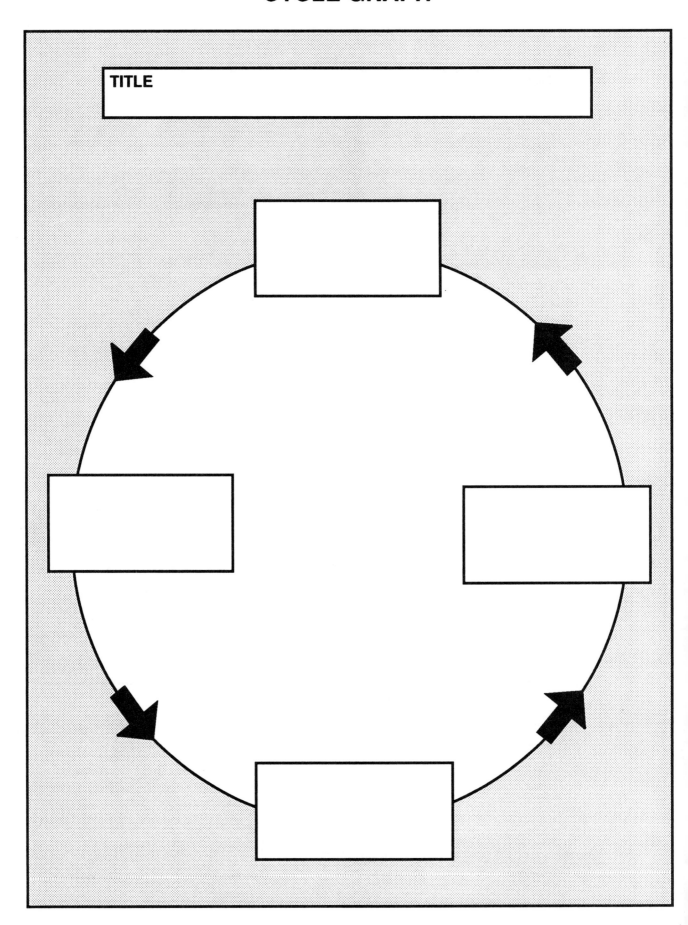

TITLE

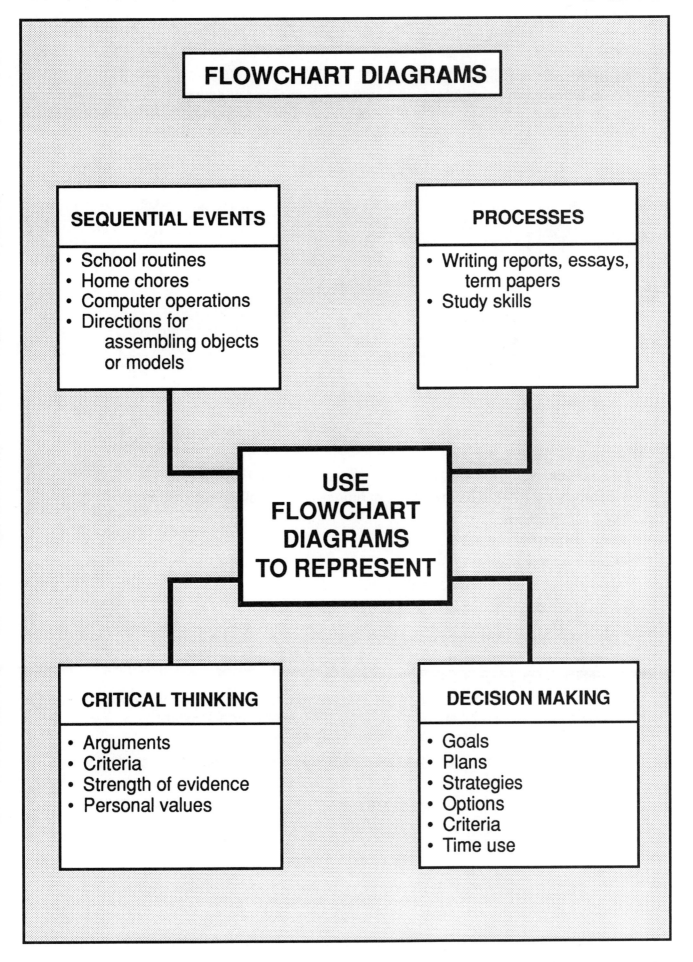

FLOWCHART DIAGRAMS

SEQUENTIAL EVENTS

- School routines
- Home chores
- Computer operations
- Directions for
    assembling objects
    or models

PROCESSES

- Writing reports, essays,
    term papers
- Study skills

USE FLOWCHART DIAGRAMS TO REPRESENT

CRITICAL THINKING

- Arguments
- Criteria
- Strength of evidence
- Personal values

DECISION MAKING

- Goals
- Plans
- Strategies
- Options
- Criteria
- Time use

USING FLOWCHART DIAGRAMS

RATIONALE FOR USING FLOWCHARTS
A flowchart diagram is useful for representing a sequence of events, actions, or decisions. Flowcharts have also become a useful tool for computer programmers. Programmers use a standard set of symbols so that the reader may quickly understand the **flow** of thought represented by the **chart**.
    Flowchart symbols include:

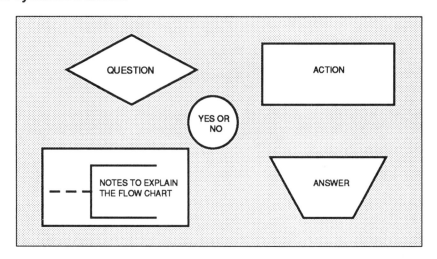

USE THE FLOWCHART TO:
 • Sequence events in plots, historical eras, or laboratory instructions.
 • Picture stages in the development of organisms, social trends, or legislative bills.
 • Write instructions.
 • Depict social or natural cycles.
 • Plan a course of action.
 • Solve mathematics and scientific problems.
 • Depict the consequences of decisions.

TO USE THE FLOWCHART:
 1. Reproduce the decision diagram and flowchart template to create enough symbols to depict the steps or decisions in a lesson.
 2. Cut apart the reproductions of the master graphic. Rearrange the symbols to form a flowchart with careful attention to decisions, actions, and answers.
 3. Label each symbol to show the steps or decision points.
 4. Leave some symbols blank to lead students to predict decisions, consequences, or alternatives.
 5. Use the open rectangle to write notes explaining that step or decision point.

STEPS

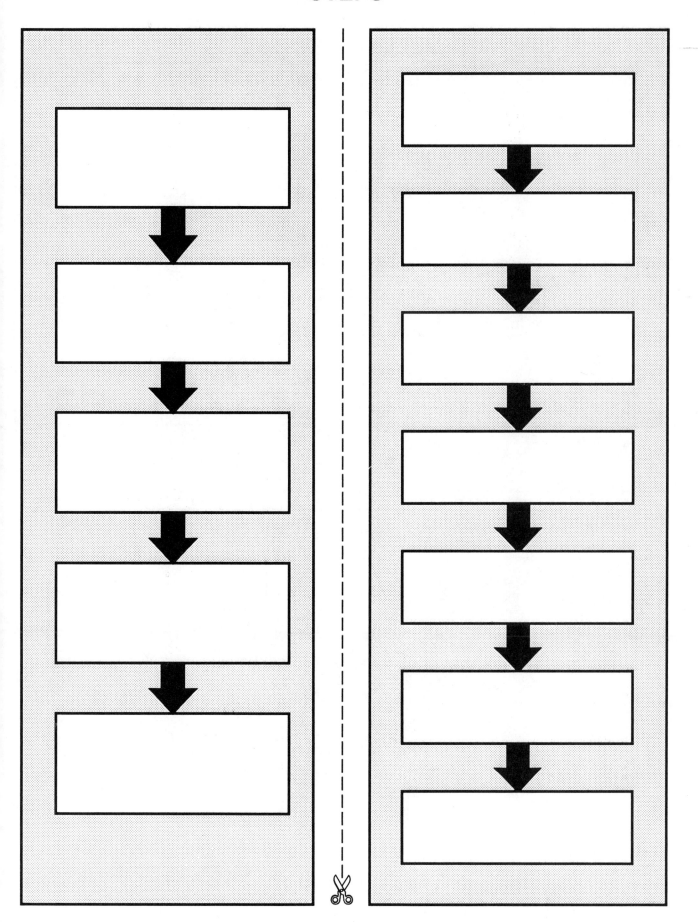

DECISION DIAGRAM/FLOWCHART TEMPLATE

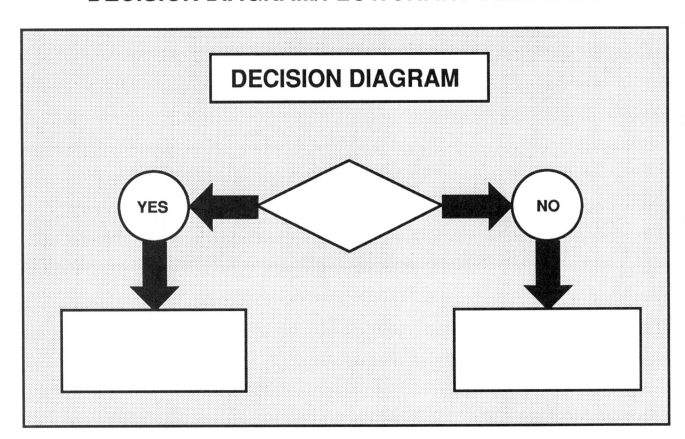

DECISION DIAGRAM

YES   NO

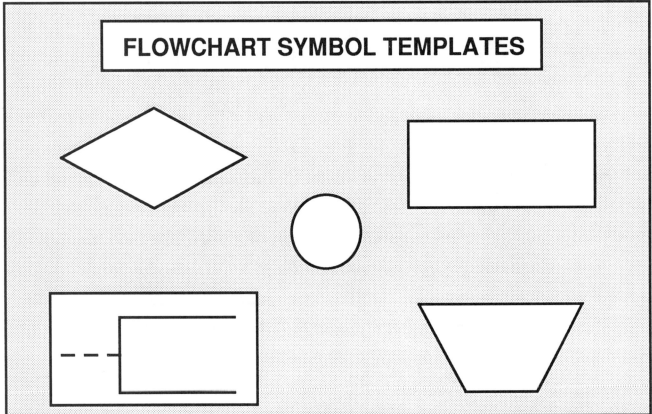

FLOWCHART SYMBOL TEMPLATES

CENTRAL IDEA GRAPHS

PEOPLE
- Backgrounds
- Historical periods
- Achievements
- Ideals
- Challenges
- Life stages
- Contribution effects

PLACES
- Locations
- Land forms
- Significance
- Natural resources

THINGS
- Parts
- Measurements
- Kinds
- Uses
- Origins
- Operations
- Significance

ORGANISMS
- Structures
- Phyla
- Habitats
- Life requirements
- Physiologies

USE CENTRAL IDEA GRAPHS TO DESCRIBE

STORIES
- Significant characteristics
  - Conflict
  - Ideal
  - Character
  - Title
  - Style
  - Organization
  - Novelty

EVENTS
- Participants
- Leaders
- Significance
- Causes
- Consequences

DECISIONS
- Goals
- Options
- Plans
- Actions
- Outcomes
- Criteria

CULTURE
- Geography
- History
- Economic system
- Political system
- Leaders
- Technology
- Values
- Art

IDEAS
- Assumptions
- How developed
- Leaders
- Significance
- Implications
- Effects

USING A CENTRAL IDEA GRAPH

RATIONALE FOR CENTRAL IDEA ACTIVITIES

The central idea graph (sometimes called a "web" diagram) is used to depict the parts of, results of, or contributors to a central theme. Students often perceive the supporting points as disconnected fragments of information, rather than as a conceptual whole. Use this graph to prompt students that supporting data are not isolated facts and are related to the central idea. For example, in a classroom discussion of the United Nations, students will probably recognize that the General Assembly and the Security Council are divisions of the United Nations. As the discussion proceeds to include the Trusteeship Council or the International Court of Justice, use the central idea graph to remind students that these agencies are divisions of the United Nations, not separate institutions.

Central idea graphs are useful as a reading comprehension tool, a review aid, or a guide for designing exhibits or displays. In creative thinking and decision making activities, use them to depict alternatives, consequences, or related terms. These graphs can be used to depict a variety of relationships: part/whole, events/consequences, causes/effects, class/subclass, and concepts/examples. Because this graph is so versatile, it is commonly used as a prewriting tool. Several variations of the central idea graph are featured in the ***Thinking for Writing*** lessons.

The number of arms will vary. Four to six blanks have been provided to encourage students to consider as many divisions, examples, or alternatives as possible.

USE THE CENTRAL IDEA GRAPH TO:

- Depict a main idea and supporting details.
- Depict parts of a given object, system, or concept.
- Depict general classes and subclasses of a system.
- Depict factors leading to or resulting from a given action.
- Narrow or broaden proposed topics for a paper or speech.
- Organize thoughts in writing essay questions or in preparing a speech.
- Depict alternatives or creative connections in decision making and creative thinking.

TO USE THE CENTRAL IDEA GRAPH:

1. Write the central idea in the circle. Write each supporting detail on an arm of the diagram. Each arm may also branch to illustrate examples or subcategories.

2. To depict factors contributing to or resulting from a given event, mark each arm as an arrow. Direct the arrows toward the central idea to illustrate multiple causes; direct them away to illustrate multiple consequences or effects.

3. In decision making, enter the issue in the circle and brainstorm with students as many options or alternatives as they can suggest. Use the same graph to generate criteria that should apply to the most desirable solution. Examine each alternative regarding the proposed criteria.

4. To generate creative images or applications, write the subject in the circle. Brainstorm related ideas and record them on the arms. Each arm may branch to generate new connections. Examine the richness of ideas that the connections bring to the central idea. Select arms which are unusually imaginative or descriptive and use the ideas recorded there to create metaphors.

CENTRAL IDEA GRAPHS

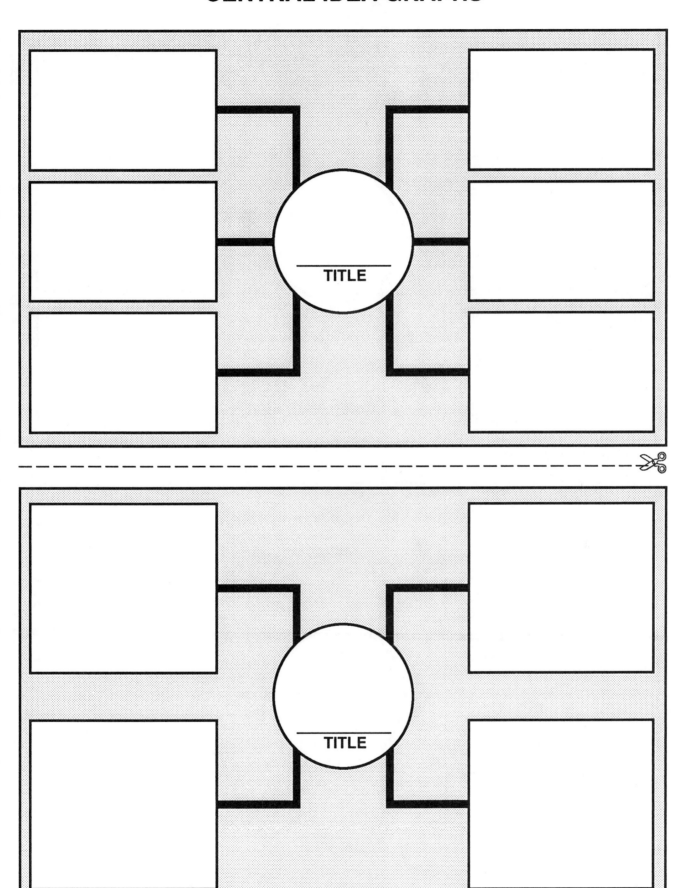

TITLE

TITLE

CENTRAL IDEA GRAPHS

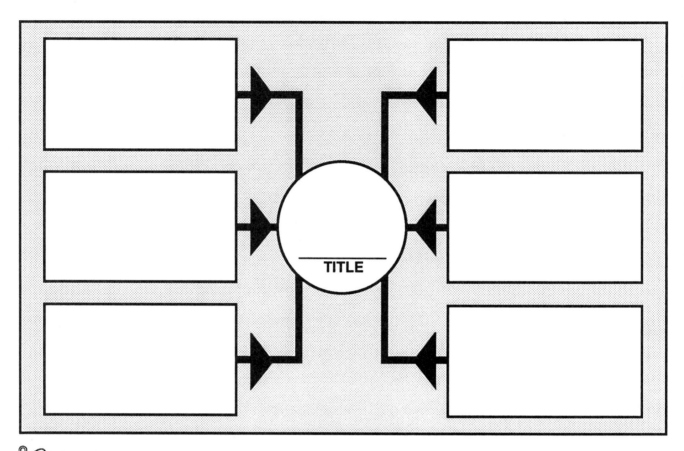

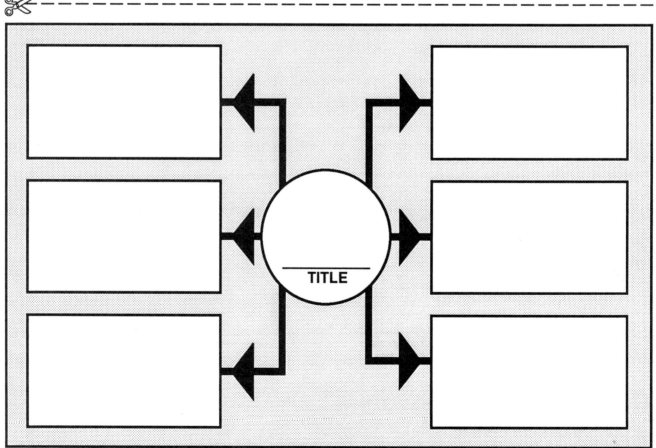

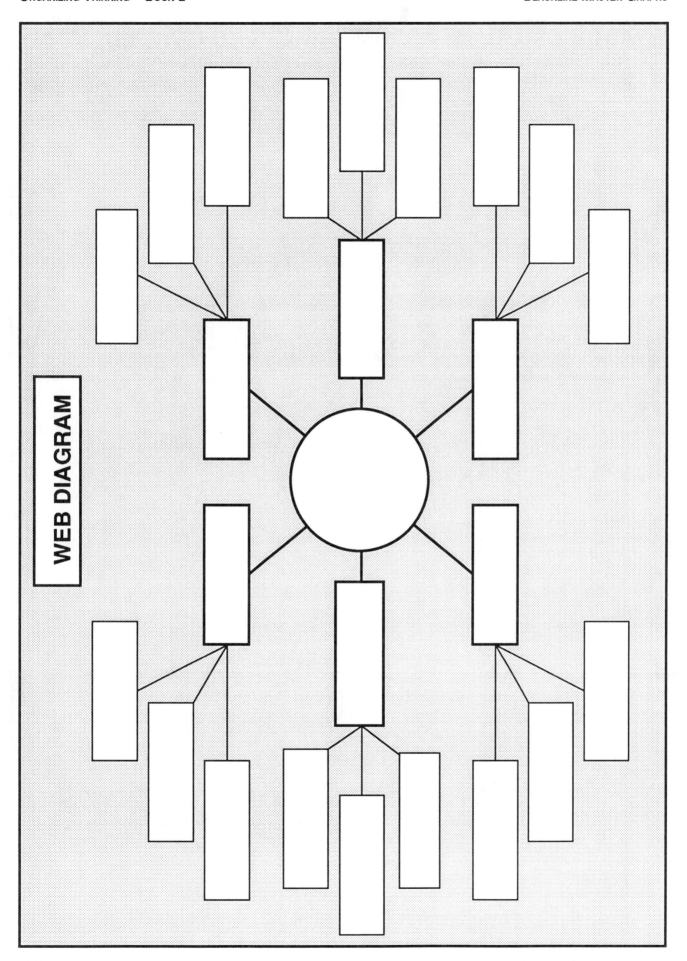

WEB DIAGRAM

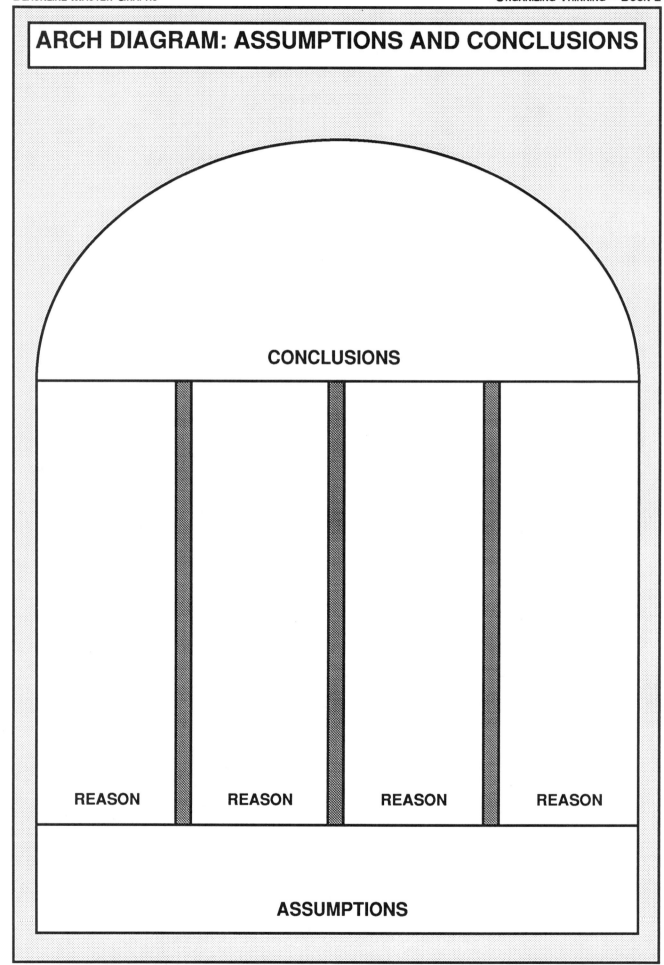

ARCH DIAGRAM: ASSUMPTIONS AND CONCLUSIONS

CONCLUSIONS

REASON   REASON   REASON   REASON

ASSUMPTIONS

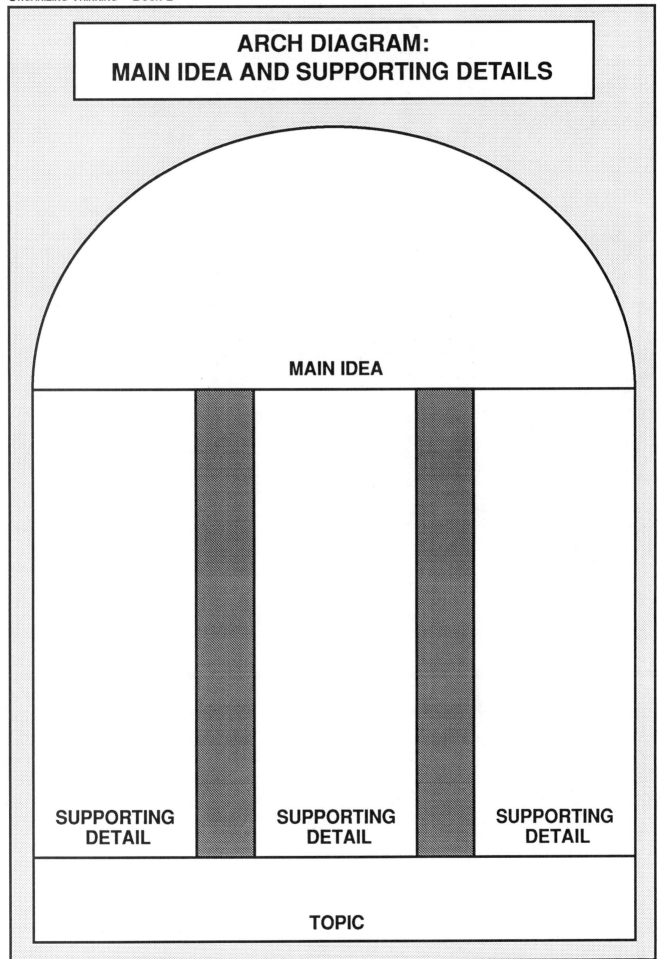

ARCH DIAGRAM:
MAIN IDEA AND SUPPORTING DETAILS

MAIN IDEA

SUPPORTING DETAIL **SUPPORTING DETAIL** **SUPPORTING DETAIL**

TOPIC

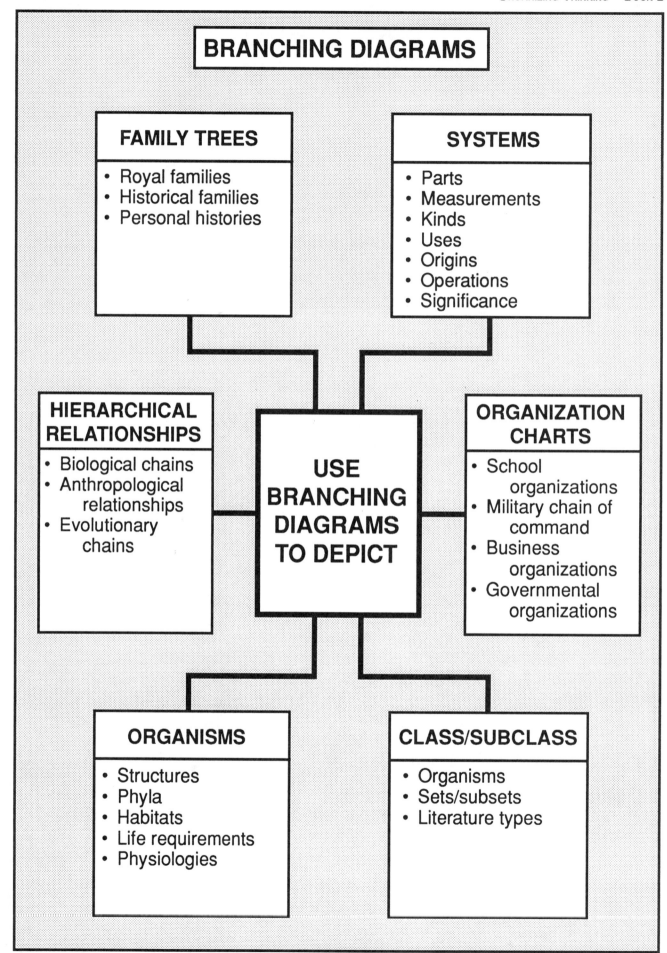

BRANCHING DIAGRAMS

FAMILY TREES
- Royal families
- Historical families
- Personal histories

SYSTEMS
- Parts
- Measurements
- Kinds
- Uses
- Origins
- Operations
- Significance

HIERARCHICAL RELATIONSHIPS
- Biological chains
- Anthropological relationships
- Evolutionary chains

USE BRANCHING DIAGRAMS TO DEPICT

ORGANIZATION CHARTS
- School organizations
- Military chain of command
- Business organizations
- Governmental organizations

ORGANISMS
- Structures
- Phyla
- Habitats
- Life requirements
- Physiologies

CLASS/SUBCLASS
- Organisms
- Sets/subsets
- Literature types

USING BRANCHING DIAGRAMS

RATIONALE FOR BRANCHING ACTIVITIES

Branching diagrams are useful when recording information about class and subclasses, hierarchical relationships, family trees, and complex systems. They allow elaborate relationship systems to be represented visually.

These diagrams, like the others in this series, prompt students to depict complex relationships as they read texts, newspapers, and magazines. In this way students learn the content and the technique simultaneously. Many textbooks give students the completed diagram as a quick and effective means of illustrating complex relationships. However, providing the completed diagram for the learner does not offer the student the opportunity to recognize complex relationships in a passage without assistance. A student who completes the diagram independently is more likely to learn to identify complex relationships in a passage.

Use a branching diagram to depict many subdivisions or subclasses of a broader category. A central idea graph, on the other hand, should be used to describe individual terms or categories which are not further subdivided.

USE THE BRANCHING DIAGRAM TO:

- Break categories into smaller classes.
- Depict family trees and hierarchical relationships.
- Illustrate systems.

TO USE THE BRANCHING DIAGRAM:

Note: The master graphs contain two or three subdivided classes. To create additional master graphs with a different number of subdivisions, use the blank graph most similar to what you need (having the correct number of subdivisions in the correct locations). Use correction fluid to white out unneeded labels, branches, or boxes. Draw additional branches and boxes by tracing others.

1. Start with the broadest category and the classes into which it can be sorted.
2. Draw a branching diagram, labeling boxes containing the broad category.
3. Determine the characteristic for dividing each class of the broad category.
4. Determine the number of subclasses required by that division.
5. Draw and label each subclass of each category.
6. Determine whether each class can be subdivided and draw appropriate branches.

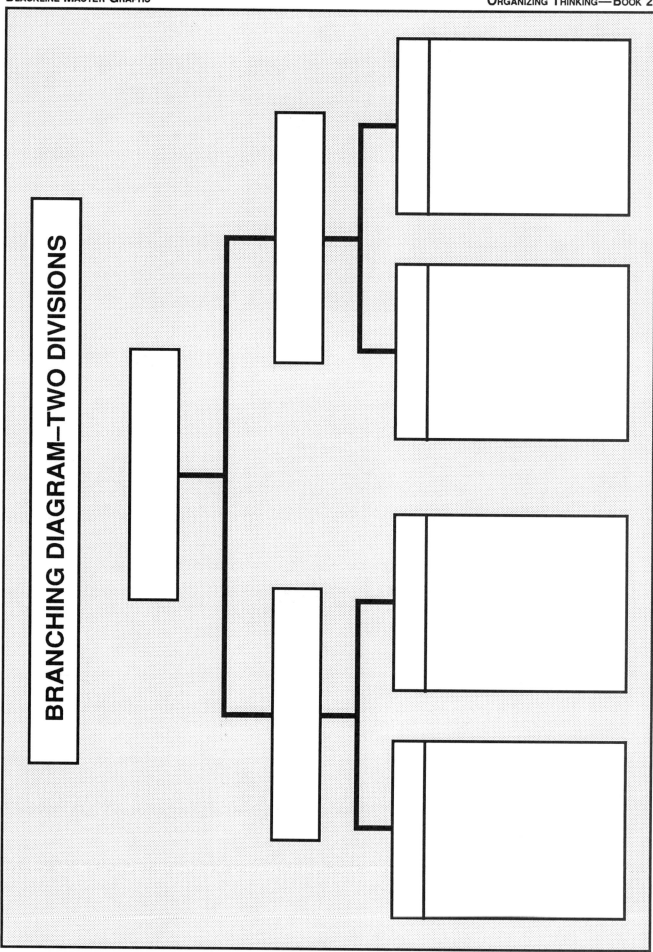

BRANCHING DIAGRAM–TWO DIVISIONS

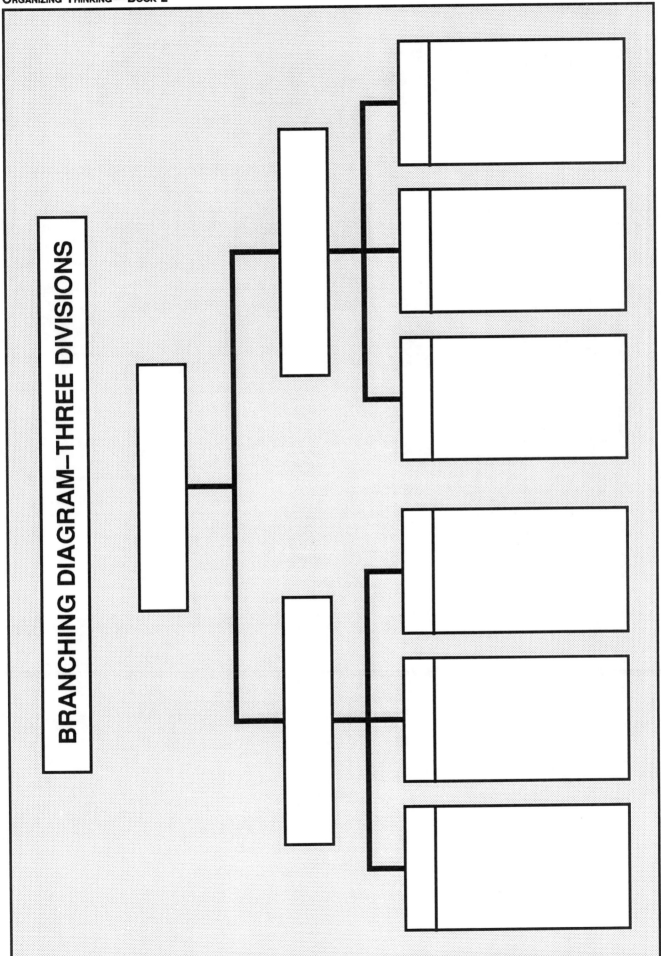

BRANCHING DIAGRAM—THREE DIVISIONS

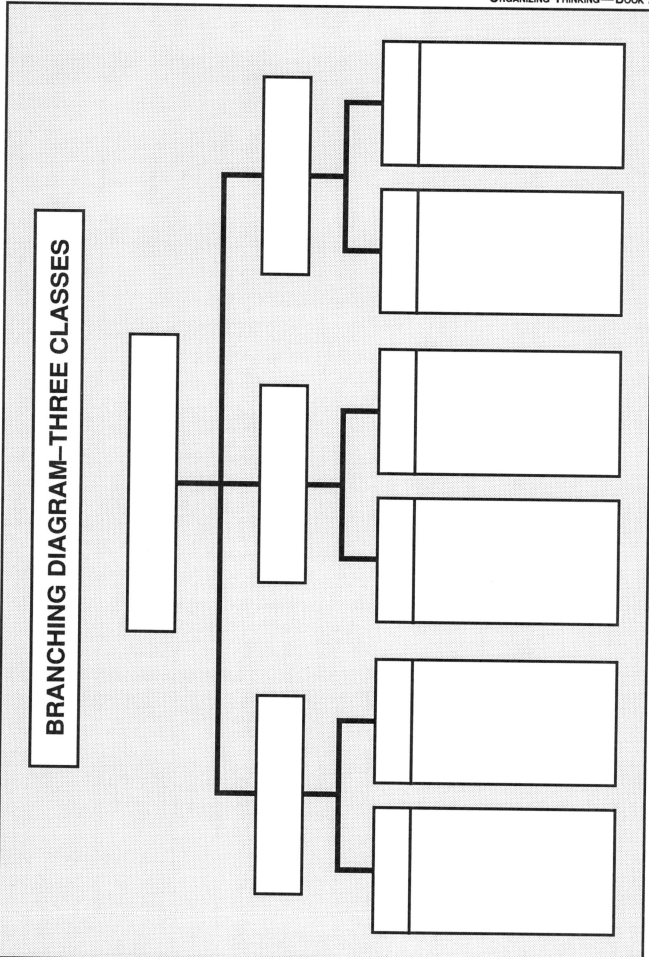

BRANCHING DIAGRAM–THREE CLASSES

CLASS RELATIONSHIPS DIAGRAMS

LOGICAL-REASONING CONCEPTS

- Connectives (*and, or, not,* and *if...then*)
- Quantifiers (*all, none,* and *some*)
- Class arguments

CLASS RELATIONSHIPS

- *Includes* or *is included in*
- *Some...are*
- *No (none)...are*

USE CLASS RELATIONSHIP DIAGRAMS TO ILLUSTRATE

COMPARISON RELATIONSHIPS

- People
- Places
- Things
- Organisms
- Cultures
- Ideas
- Stories

MATHEMATICS CONCEPTS

- Factoring
- Least common multiple
- Greatest common factor
- Types of polygons
- Set theory

USING CLASS RELATIONSHIPS DIAGRAMS

RATIONALE FOR CLASS RELATIONSHIPS ACTIVITIES

Class relationships diagrams (also called Venn diagrams or Euler circles) are used to illustrate the relationship between or among classes. These diagrams are also used to show the union of two sets, to demonstrate the meaning of logic connectives (*and, or, not,* and *if...then*) and to depict class membership in arguments involving class logic.

Using class relationships diagrams involves two steps. First, use the diagram to illustrate relationships in content (from a passage to a diagram). Then, translate the relationship into English sentences using the logic connectives *and, or, not,* and *if...then* and the logic quantifiers *all, some,* and *none.*

USE THE CLASS RELATIONSHIPS DIAGRAM TO:

• Depict class membership.

• Depict class logic arguments.

• Depict the union of two or more sets.

• Depict comparison and or contrast of two things, organisms, people, or ideas.

TO USE THE CLASS RELATIONSHIPS DIAGRAM:

1. Clarify the characteristics of the compared sets.
2. Decide which of the following class relationships diagrams illustrates the relationship of the compared sets.

RELATIONSHIPS INVOLVING TWO CLASSES

Target Diagram

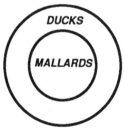

a. If one class *includes* or *is included in* another class, then a target diagram expresses that relationship. For example, to compare the class "mallards" to the class "ducks," you would use a target diagram. The outer circle would represent "ducks" and the inner circle "mallards." This relationship can be stated "All mallards are ducks."

b. If *some,* but *not all,* members of one class are also members of another, then an overlapping diagram expresses that relationship. For example, to compare the class "wild birds" to the class "ducks," you would use an overlapping diagram. One circle would represent "wild birds" and the other "ducks." This relationship can be stated several ways; e.g., "Some ducks are wild birds." "Some wild birds are ducks." "Some ducks are not wild birds." "Some wild birds are not ducks."

Overlapping Diagram

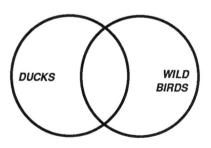

Disjoint Set Diagram

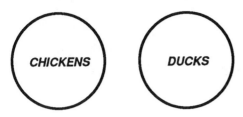

c. If *no* members of one class are members of another, then a disjoint set diagram illustrates that relationship. For example, to compare the class "chickens" with the class "ducks," you would use a disjoint set diagram. One circle would represent the class "chickens" and the other the class "ducks." This relationship can be stated two ways: "No ducks are chickens" or "No chickens are ducks."

RELATIONSHIPS INVOLVING THREE CLASSES

d. Complex target diagrams are used to depict class arguments. For example:

All ducks are wild birds.
All mallards are ducks.
Therefore, all mallards are wild birds.

There are three classes included in the argument (*ducks, mallards,* and *wild birds*). To illustrate the argument, use a target diagram to show that all mallards must be included in the larger class "ducks," which in turn is entirely within the larger class "wild birds."

Complex Target Diagram

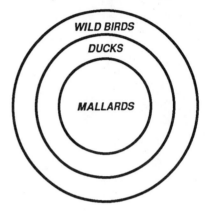

Three-set Overlapping Diagram

e. A three-set overlapping diagram expresses relationships between and among three classes if some, but not all members of one class are members of one or both of the others. For example, to depict the classes "land animals," "water animals," and "flying animals," you would use the three-set diagram to show characteristics of the animals. A duck is described as a land animal **and** a water animal **and** a flying animal.

© 1990 MIDWEST PUBLICATIONS • CRITICAL THINKING PRESS & SOFTWARE • P. O. Box 448, Pacific Grove, CA 93950

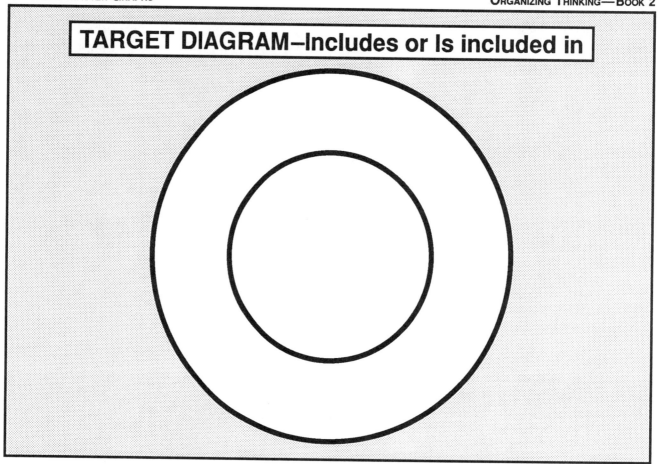

TARGET DIAGRAM–Includes or Is included in

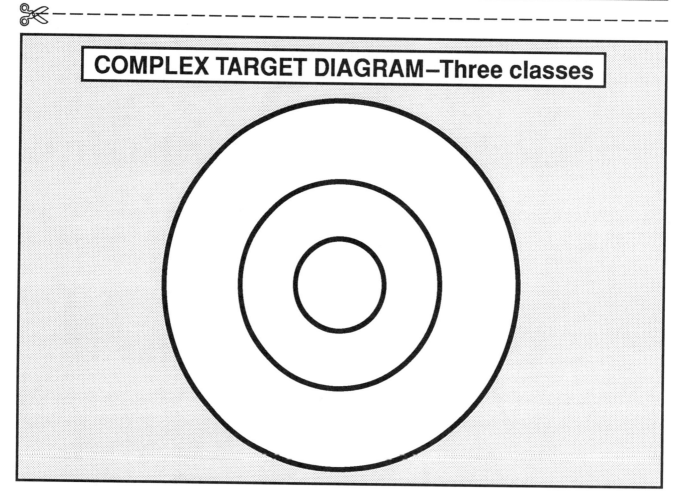

COMPLEX TARGET DIAGRAM–Three classes

OVERLAPPING CLASSES–Some...are

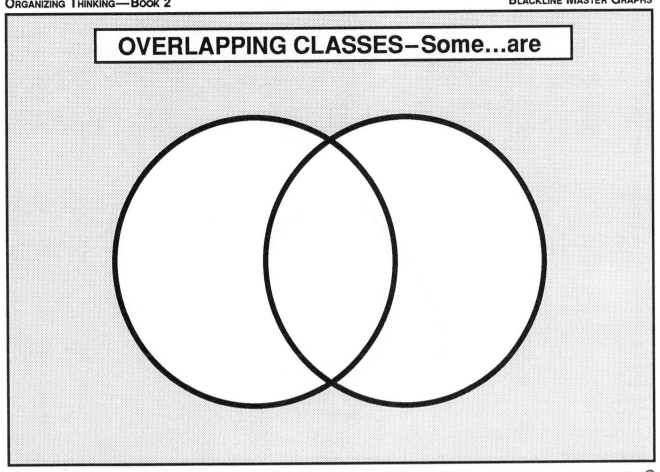

DISJOINT CLASSES– Is separate from

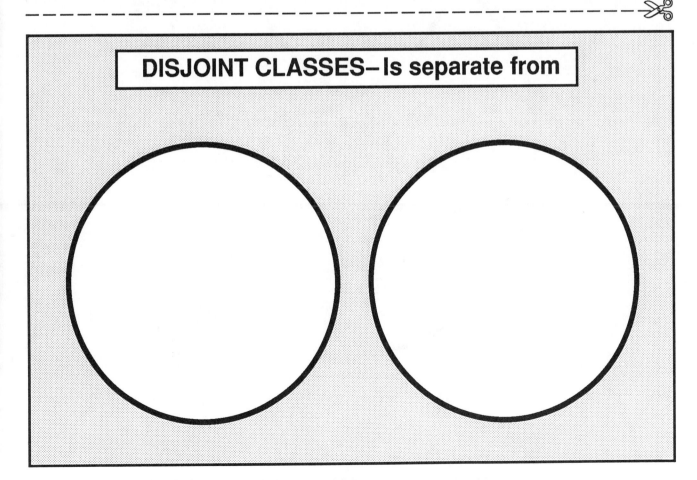

OVERLAPPING CLASSES–Three classes

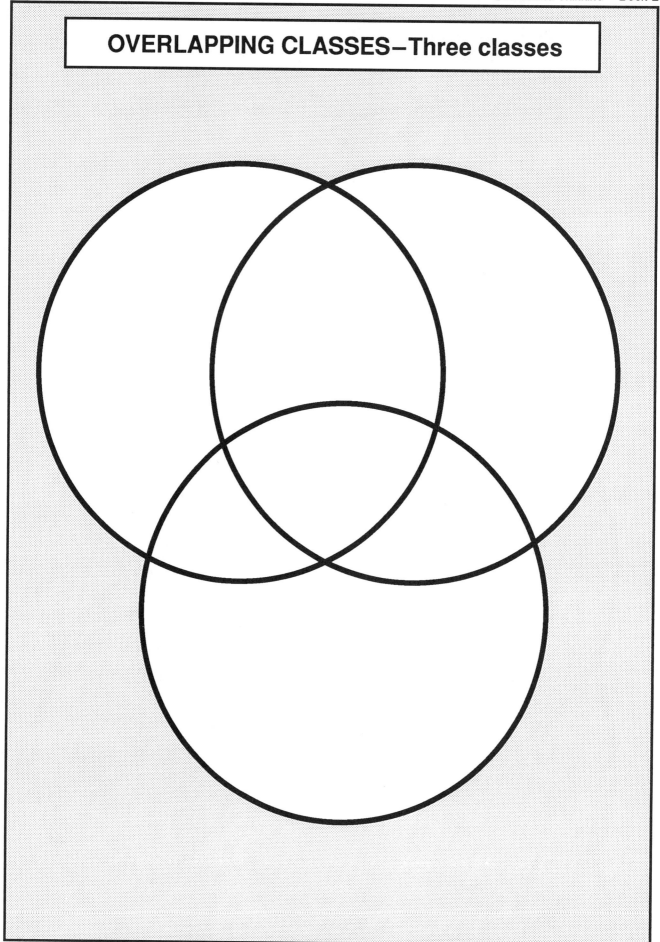

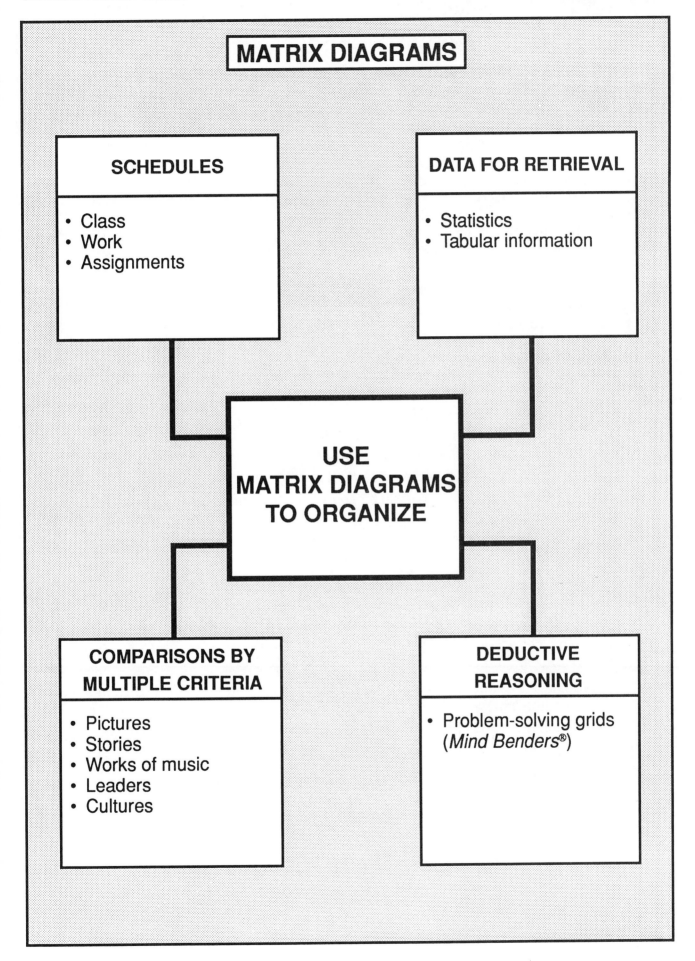

MATRIX DIAGRAMS

SCHEDULES

- Class
- Work
- Assignments

DATA FOR RETRIEVAL

- Statistics
- Tabular information

USE MATRIX DIAGRAMS TO ORGANIZE

COMPARISONS BY MULTIPLE CRITERIA

- Pictures
- Stories
- Works of music
- Leaders
- Cultures

DEDUCTIVE REASONING

- Problem-solving grids (*Mind Benders®*)

USING MATRIX DIAGRAMS

RATIONALE FOR MATRIX ACTIVITIES

Matrix diagrams are used to record and cross-reference information by two characteristics. Common matrices include bus, train, and airline schedules, mileage charts, class schedules, and statistical reports. These diagrams allow data to be quickly and easily understood.

Matrix diagrams allow students to organize information from written passages and to record inferences from pictures, passages, or artifacts. The learner may then examine significant similarities and differences and draw defensible conclusions from the information. The matrix diagram is also useful when applying the same criteria to compare several pictures, pieces of music, stories, historical events, or leaders.

Students may use a completed matrix diagram as a guide to prepare a descriptive speech or paper. The debate lessons include the use of a matrix to organize claims and evidence for debate arguments.

In most of the lessons in this handbook, students complete a matrix diagram from information given in written passages. Many textbooks give students the completed matrix, a quick and effective means of illustrating complex relationships. However, providing the completed diagram for the learner does not train the student to recognize and interpret complex relationships solely from written material.

USE THE MATRIX DIAGRAM TO:

- Record information by two characteristics.
- Report information in schedules, charts, or tables.
- Organize information in order to draw inferences or to form generalizations.
- Compare literary or artistic works by several characteristics.
- Compare historical figures or events by several characteristcs.
- Illustrate number patterns or functions.

TO USE THE MATRIX DIAGRAM:

NOTE: The matrix diagram may have as many vertical and horizonal squares as the characteristics of the data require. The master graphs contain a 3 x 3 and a 4 x 4 matrix, since these are the most common formats. To create diagrams containing different numbers of squares, use copies of master graphs which come closest to containing the correct number of squares. Use correction fluid to white out unneeded labels or boxes. Additional boxes may be drawn by tracing others.

1. Determine the number of horizontal and vertical squares needed to represent the concepts and criteria.
2. Label each row and column.
3. Record information in each square.
4. Draw comparisons or conclusions from the information.

MATRIX DIAGRAM – 3 x 3

MATRIX DIAGRAM – 4 x 4

CHAPTER 2–LANGUAGE ARTS LESSONS

NOUNS AND PRONOUNS (Compare and Contrast Diagram)		DESCRIBING PRONOUNS (Matrix Chart)
	PARTS OF SPEECH (Branching Diagram)	
DEWEY DECIMAL SYSTEM (Transitive Order Graph)		HISTORY OR FICTION? (Class Relationships Diagram)
	WHAT KIND OF BOOK DO YOU WANT TO READ? (Flowchart)	
AESOP'S FABLES (Flowchart)		LAURA INGALLS WILDER (Interval Graph)
	CHARLOTTE'S WEB (Central Idea Graph, Arch Diagram)	
DESCRIBING A STORY (Central Idea Graph)		"FOG" (Compare or Contrast Diagram)
	DESCRIBING A GOOD SPEECH (Branching Diagram)	
DESCRIBING CLASS RELATIONSHIPS (Class Relationships Diagram)		MAIN IDEA AND SUPPORTING DETAILS (Arch Diagram)
	DEBATE (Compare and Contrast Graph, Flowchart, Matrix Chart)	

NOUNS AND PRONOUNS

THINKING SKILL: Compare and Contrast

CONTENT OBJECTIVE: Students will use the compare and contrast diagram to differentiate between nouns and pronouns.

DISCUSSION: TECHNIQUE—Use a transparency of the diagram to record student responses regarding nouns and pronouns. Encourage your students to identify additional similarities or differences between nouns and pronouns.

DIALOGUE—As students report differences between nouns and pronouns, discuss those differences by naming the quality that is different. Establish this pattern: "**With regard to** (quality), (item one and its distinction), **but** (item two and its distinction)." For example,

"**With regard to capitalization, proper nouns are always capitalized, but pronouns are capitalized only at the beginning of a sentence**."

RESULT—Pronouns depend on noun antecedents for their meaning. A listener or reader may be confused regarding who is included in "we" or "they" if the listener is unsure to whom the pronoun refers. There may also be confusion regarding whether "you" refers to one person or to a group "you" in which that person belongs.

WRITING EXTENSION
- **Describe how nouns and pronouns are alike and how they are different.**
- **Explain why a listener or reader may be confused if the noun to which a pronoun refers is unclear. What can a writer or speaker do to prevent that confusion?**

THINKING ABOUT THINKING
- **How did using the diagram help you understand the differences between nouns and pronouns? How did it help you organize your thoughts before you began to write?**
- **Suggest another lesson in which comparing and contrasting would help you understand what you are learning.**
- **Design another diagram that would help you distinguish between nouns and pronouns.** (Students may find that the overlapping classes diagram depicts the difference between nouns and pronouns easily.)

SIMILAR LANGUAGE ARTS LESSONS
- To compare fiction and nonfiction, types of narratives, types of nonfiction, types of periodicals, types of nonprint media, and forms or types of poetry.
- To compare parts of speech, figures of speech, types of sentences, active and passive verbs, plural and singular forms, or common and proper nouns.
- To compare denotation and connotation, fact and opinion, or premises and conclusions.
- To compare characters within or between novels, short stories, or plays; to compare plots or styles of writing between novels, short stories, or plays.
- To clarify terms in vocabulary enrichment lessons (synonyms and antonyms).
- To prepare speeches, essays, debate topics, or persuasive arguments.
- To organize information in order to examine ethical issues in different situations or conflicts.

NOUNS AND PRONOUNS

DIRECTIONS: Use the diagram to record how nouns and pronouns are alike and how they are different.

Nouns refer to people, places, things, or ideas. Common nouns are general categories and are capitalized only as the first word in a sentence. Proper nouns are names of specific people, places, or things and are always capitalized. Because names are proper nouns and we don't know every person's name, nouns are too numerous to be counted.

Pronouns serve as a substitute word for a person, place, thing, or idea which has already been mentioned in a sentence or paragraph. A pronoun is capitalized only if it is the first word in a sentence. There are fewer than fifty pronouns in the English language.

Both nouns and pronouns usually change spelling to form plural or possessive forms.

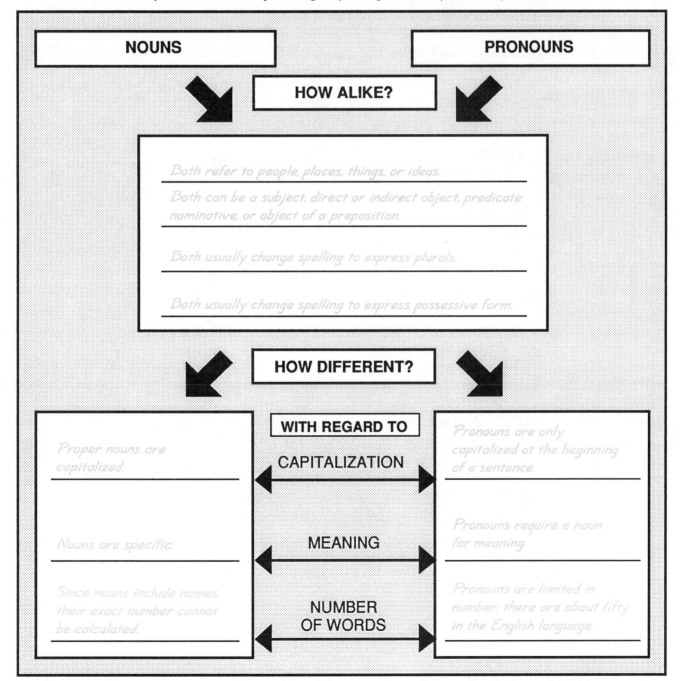

NOUNS

PRONOUNS

HOW ALIKE?

Both refer to people, places, things, or ideas.

Both can be a subject, direct or indirect object, predicate nominative, or object of a preposition.

Both usually change spelling to express plurals.

Both usually change spelling to express possessive form.

HOW DIFFERENT?

WITH REGARD TO

Proper nouns are capitalized.

CAPITALIZATION

Pronouns are only capitalized at the beginning of a sentence.

Nouns are specific.

MEANING

Pronouns require a noun for meaning.

Since nouns include names, their exact number cannot be calculated.

NUMBER OF WORDS

Pronouns are limited in number; there are about fifty in the English language.

DESCRIBING PRONOUNS

THINKING SKILL: Cross-classification

CONTENT OBJECTIVE: Using the matrix diagram, students will differentiate between singular and plural pronouns and between first, second, and third person pronouns.

DISCUSSION: TECHNIQUE—Use a transparency of the matrix to record student responses as the class reviews singular and plural forms of pronouns. As students report their answers, ask each student to use the pronoun in a sentence.

DIALOGUE—You may use this opportunity to distinguish nominative, objective, possessive, and reflexive forms of pronouns.

"You" and "your" are the same in singular and plural form. How might that create confusion in speaking or writing?

Remind students that there is sometimes misunderstanding if it is unclear to whom a pronoun refers. Ask students to relate personal experiences of misunderstanding because the listener or reader was uncertain who is meant by "we," "you," or "they."

RESULT—A listener or reader may be confused regarding who is included in "we" or "they," if the listener is unsure to whom the pronoun refers. There may also be confusion whether "you" refers to one person or to a group "you" in which that person belongs.

WRITING EXTENSION

- **Describe what "first person," "second person," and "third person" mean. How does "person" make a difference in using pronouns?**
- **Explain why listeners or readers get confused if they don't understand what is meant by "we" or "you."**

THINKING ABOUT THINKING

- **How did using the diagram help you understand the kinds of pronouns? How did using it help you remember the kinds of pronouns?**
- **Suggest another lesson in which using a diagram like this would help you understand what you are learning.**
- **Design another diagram that would help you organize nouns and pronouns.** (Students may find that the branching diagram illustrates types of pronouns easily.)

SIMILAR LANGUAGE ARTS LESSONS

- To illustrate works of fiction and nonfiction, types of narratives, types of periodicals, types of nonprint media, and forms or types of poetry.
- To illustrate parts of speech, figures of speech, types of sentences, active and passive verbs, plural and singular forms, and common and proper nouns.
- To illustrate types of novels, short stories, or plays.
- To classify styles of writing or elements of literary works (main character, point of view, symbolism, etc.).
- To solve deductive-reasoning problems (*Mind Benders®*).
- To use true-false tables to determine truth value in statements.
- To classify languages, grammatical structures, punctuation or spelling rules.

DESCRIBING PRONOUNS

DIRECTIONS: Decide whether each of the following pronouns is singular or plural and whether it refers to me, to you, or to others. Write each pronoun in the box of the matrix that best describes it.

he	it	our	they
her	its	ourselves	us
hers	itself	she	we
herself	me	their	your
him	my	them	yourself
himself	myself	themselves	yourselves
his			

	SINGULAR	PLURAL
I	me my myself	our ourselves us we
YOU	your yourself	your yourselves
OTHERS	he her hers herself him himself his it its itself she	their them themselves they

PARTS OF SPEECH

THINKING SKILL: Hierarchical classification

CONTENT OBJECTIVE: Students will use the branching diagram to identify parts of speech. *NOTE: This lesson is intended to review an instructional unit on parts of speech. It presents too much information to be used as an introductory lesson.*

DISCUSSION: TECHNIQUE—Use a transparency of the branching diagram to record student responses as the class reviews parts of speech. In this lesson the branching diagram is used to illustrate classes and subclasses of parts of speech. This may also serve as a poster or bulletin board design. As the various parts of speech are explained over several sessions, add the appropriate label to the diagram, forming a visual summary of the unit. Encourage your students to use the diagram as a memory tool to review for a test.

DIALOGUE—Encourage students to describe the significant characteristic by which categories are subdivided.

How do we describe different kinds of nouns? (Common nouns describe general categories; proper nouns describe names of specific people, places, or things.) **What characteristic is being described by "common" or "proper"?** (Whether the noun describes a group or an individual.)

RESULT—The different functions and different forms distinguish the different types of parts of speech. Clarifying functions and forms is the key to understanding, identifying, and remembering parts of speech.

WRITING EXTENSION
• **Define the eight parts of speech and explain their use.**

THINKING ABOUT THINKING
• **How did using the diagram help you understand the parts of speech clearly? How did using it help you remember the information more accurately?**
• **Suggest another lesson in which using a diagram like this would help you understand what you are learning.**
• **Design another diagram that would help you understand and remember the parts of speech.**

SIMILAR LANGUAGE ARTS LESSONS
• To illustrate class/subclass relationships: figures of speech, parts of speech, types of literature, types of books or reference sources.
• To illustrate headings and subheadings in an outline.
• To depict the family relationships of kings, mythological characters, or characters in books or plays.

PARTS OF SPEECH

DIRECTIONS: Read the passage carefully to identify parts of speech. Record the information on the diagram.

Our English language has eight basic kinds of words. These are called **parts of speech.** **Nouns** are words which name people, places, things, or ideas. There are two types of nouns: common nouns and proper nouns. Common nouns name types of objects and are not capitalized. Proper nouns name a specific item and are always capitalized. A **pronoun** (such as *he*, *she*, or *it*) may be substituted for a noun that has been named previously in the thought or paragraph.

Verbs are words which describe action or link words in the predicate back to the subject. **Linking** verbs include forms of the verb "to be": *is, are, was, am*, etc. There are two types of **action** verbs—active verbs and passive verbs. Active verbs are used when the subject of the sentence does the action. Passive verbs are used when the subject of the sentence receives the action.

Words which describe what something is like or how it works are called **modifiers. Adverbs** are modifiers that tell how, when, or where something happens. **Adjectives** are modifiers that describe nouns (color, size, or shape) or determine a particular object (such as the articles *a* and *the*, demonstrative words like *these* and *those*, words that show numbers like *three* or *first*, and possessives like *my* and *your*).

Interjections include cries or shouts (such as "Oh!" or "Ah!"). Words which join parts of a sentence are **connectives**. Connectives that show location, position, or relationships of nouns (such as *behind, near, of*, and *for*) are called **prepositions**. Connectives such as *or, but*, or *and* join words or phrases within the sentence. These are called **conjunctions**.

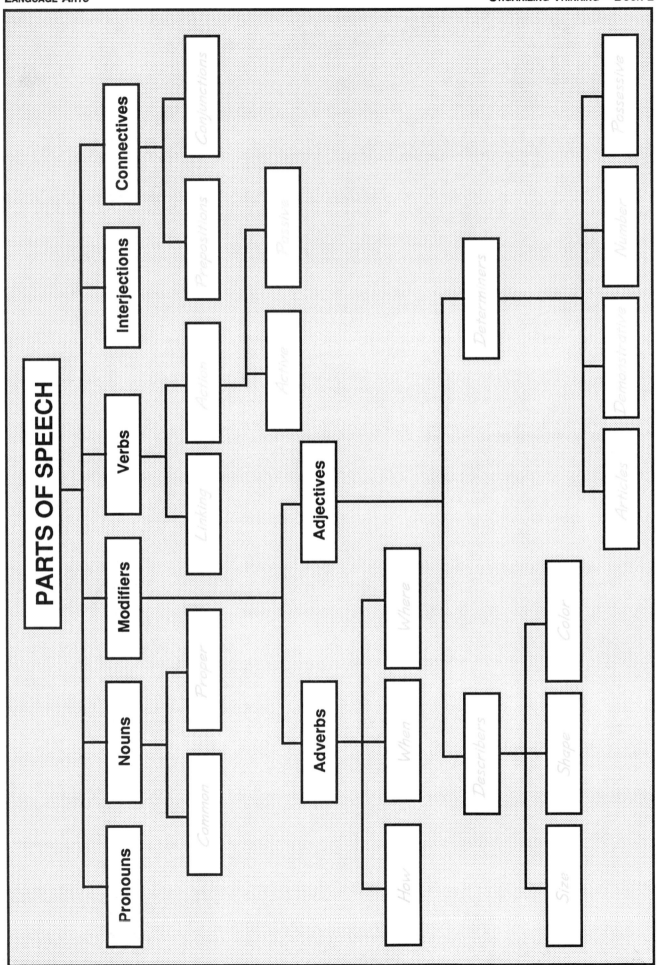

DEWEY DECIMAL SYSTEM

THINKING SKILL: Transitive order, classification

CONTENT OBJECTIVE: Students will use the transitive order graph to organize book titles according to the order in which they can be found in a library.

DISCUSSION: TECHNIQUE—Use a transparency of the graphic organizer to record students' identification of each book with its type. Students must infer the type of book from the title. Direct students to write a title by each category. List each title on the transitive order graph in the order that it is found in a library.

Encourage students to examine many different kinds of books by extending this lesson during a library visit. Give students an additional blank worksheet and direct them to identify one book for each category. Use the graph as a record of student book reports, demonstrating the value of reading a variety of books.

DIALOGUE—Encourage students to explain how they classified each book.

RESULTS—By understanding and following the order in which objects or concepts are arranged, we can locate them quickly and easily.

WRITING EXTENSION

• **How does the Dewey Decimal System make it easier to find what you want to read?**

THINKING ABOUT THINKING

• **What clues did you use to decide what kind of book each title suggested? Why do you have to classify before you can list the books in order?**

• **What pattern of organization do you see in the Dewey Decimal System? Explain.**

• **How did using the graph help you understand how the library was organized?**

• **Suggest another lesson in which listing things in order would help you do tasks more quickly or easily.**

• **Design another graphic organizer that would help you organize your library selections.** (Students may find the branching diagram helpful in depicting many selections for each type of book.)

SIMILAR LANGUAGE ARTS LESSONS

• To record complex plots of novels or plays.

• To record biographical data.

• To record events for writing narratives.

• To organize information for writing letters, term papers, biographies, or stories.

• To depict degree of meaning in superlative forms: adjectives, nouns, or verbs which show degree.

DEWEY DECIMAL SYSTEM

DIRECTIONS: Suppose that you want to locate nonfiction books in the library according to the order in which they are organized on the shelves. Read each title and decide which type of book it is. Write the number range beside each title. Use the transitive order graph to record the titles of the books in the order in which you will locate them.

000–099: References, Encyclopedias
100–199: Philosophy, Psychology
200–299: Religion, Church History
300–399: Sociology, Politics, Law
400–499: Languages
500–599: Mathematics, Sciences
600–699: Technology, Medicine, Agriculture, Computers
700–799: Art, Music, Crafts, Sports
800–899: Literature
900–999: Geography, History

NUMBER RANGE	BOOK TITLES
600-699	*The Creative Kid's Guide to Home Computers*, Fred D'Ignazio.
900-999	*Explorations of America*, Franklin Folsom.
000-099	*Firsts, Facts, and Feats*, Bill Adler.
100-199	*Memory: How It Works and How to Improve It*, Ray Gallant.
700-799	*Soccer for Juniors: A Guide for Players, Parents, and Coaches*, Robert Pollock.
800-899	*Stories from Shakespeare*, Marchette Chute.
300-399	*The Story of the U.N.*, Katherine Savage.
400-499	*The Story of Writing*, William and Rhoda Cahn.
500-599	*The Sun and Its Family*, Irving Adler.
200-299	*The World's Great Religions*, Time/Life.

DEWEY DECIMAL SYSTEM

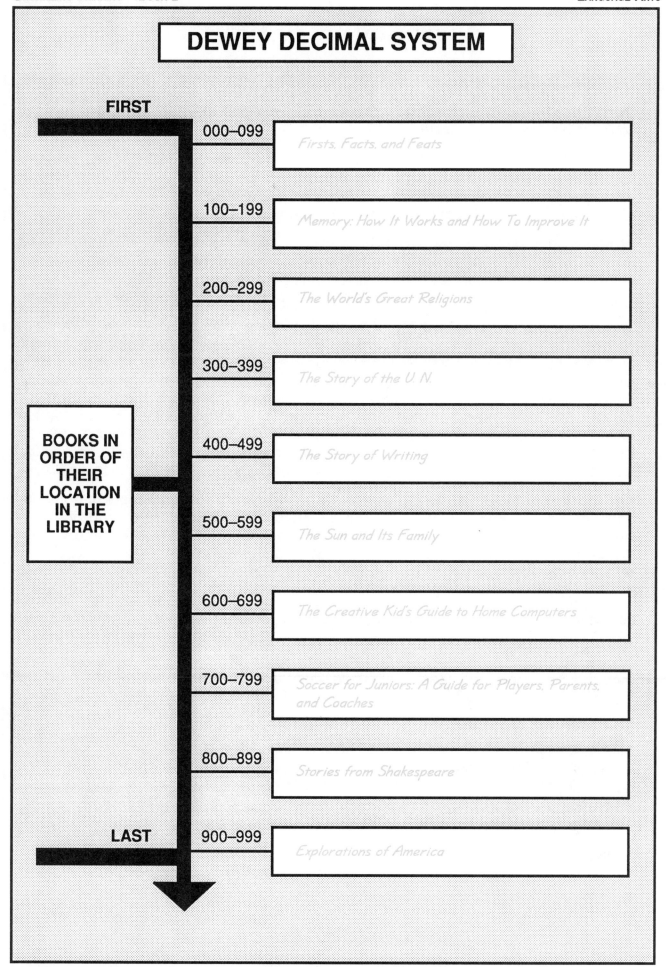

FIRST

000–099   *Firsts, Facts, and Feats*

100–199   *Memory: How It Works and How To Improve It*

200–299   *The World's Great Religions*

300–399   *The Story of the U. N.*

BOOKS IN ORDER OF THEIR LOCATION IN THE LIBRARY

400–499   *The Story of Writing*

500–599   *The Sun and Its Family*

600–699   *The Creative Kid's Guide to Home Computers*

700–799   *Soccer for Juniors: A Guide for Players, Parents, and Coaches*

800–899   *Stories from Shakespeare*

LAST   900–999   *Explorations of America*

HISTORY OR FICTION?

THINKING SKILL: Class relationships

CONTENT OBJECTIVE: Students will use a class relationships graph to classify types of books as history, fiction, or both.

DISCUSSION: TECHNIQUE—Use a transparency of the class relationships graph to record responses as students discuss each type of book.

DIALOGUE—Encourage students to describe these relationships using the words *some*, *all*, *and*, and *not*. Sample translations of the diagram using logic quantifiers might be:

All comic books are fictional. (A possible exception might be comic books that are designed to teach history.) **All diaries are historical, and not fictional. All fairy tales are fictional, and not historical. All history textbooks are historical, and not fictional. All legends are somewhat historical and somewhat fictional. All myths are fictional, and not historical.**

Discuss how a legend and a myth are alike and how they are different. The Funk and Wagnall's *Standard Dictionary* describes a **legend** as "an unauthenticated story from earlier times, preserved by tradition and popularly thought to be historical." A **myth** is "a traditional story focusing on the deeds of gods or heroes, often in explanation of some natural phenomenon." A myth makes no claim to be an historical account; a legend, though embellished, is believed to represent some historical occurrence. For example, legends about the Trojan War are rooted in history, but myths about the birth of gods or goddesses are fictional. Identify examples of each type of story from reading assignments. Help the students examine the value and appeal of historical novels, such as *Johnny Tremain* or *Little House on the Prairie.*

How does their historical setting add to the story? How does the appeal of the story encourage us to know more about the historical event? How are our purposes in reading history, historical novels, and general fiction different? Why is the information in history books more reliable than information in fiction? How could one find out how reliable the information in either history books or fiction really is?

RESULTS—Some story types do not fit neatly into history or fiction categories. Information in history books is usually more reliable than that from fiction, legends, or historical novels.

WRITING EXTENSION
- **How does a reader decide whether a book is history or fiction?**
- **What are some stories that don't fit clearly in either history or fiction?**

THINKING ABOUT THINKING
- **Why does it matter to the reader whether a story is history or fiction?**
- **Design another graphic organizer to distinguish between history and fiction.** (The compare and contrast graph depicts the difference between history and fiction.)
- **How does the graph help you understand how to use *some, all, and*, and *no*? Identify another example in which it is important to use these terms correctly.**

SIMILAR LANGUAGE ARTS LESSONS
- To compare characters within or between novels, short stories, or plays.
- To illustrate class relationships in an article, report, or presentation.
- To interpret claims in advertising on television or in magazines and newspapers.
- To interpret arguments containing class relationships.

HISTORY OR FICTION?

DIRECTIONS: Use the class relationships graph below to classify each of the following kinds of literature.

comic book, diary of a president, fairy tale,
historical novel, history textbook, legend, myth

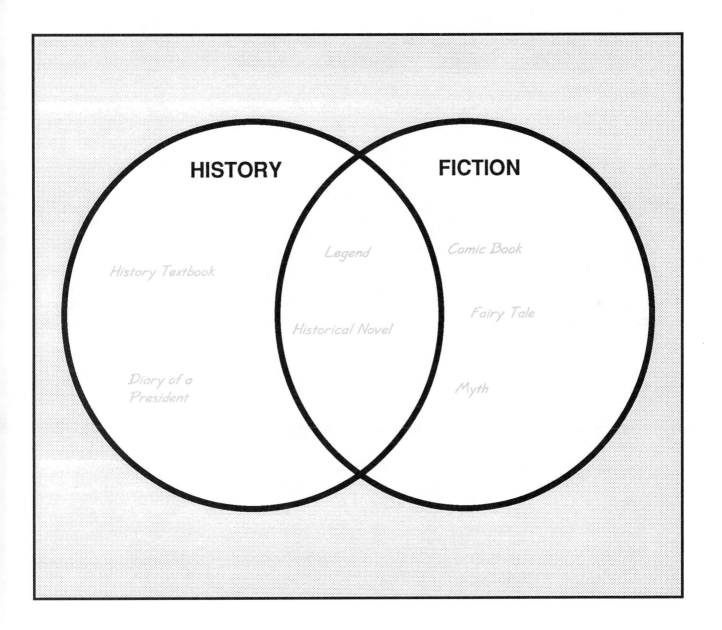

WHAT KIND OF BOOK DO YOU WANT TO READ?

THINKING SKILL: Flowcharting, classification

CONTENT OBJECTIVE: Students will use a flowchart to identify types of books by their distinguishing characteristics.

DISCUSSION: TECHNIQUE—Use a transparency of the flowchart to record responses as students answer the question that appears in each diamond. To simulate the process in the library, ask students to write a selection for each type of book.

DIALOGUE—This lesson clarifies the significant characteristics of different types of books. Discussion of the answers should model the process on the flowchart.

If you need short facts about a real topic, which types of book on our list provide that? (Dictionaries, encyclopedias, atlases.) **If you need a broader background about real people's lives, what kinds of books do you need?** (Biographies and autobiographies.) **What real things other than people might you need information about?** (Places, objects, systems, organisms, or ideas.)

This line of questioning demonstrates the significance of naming key attributes of types of books and verbalizes the metacognitive process of deductive decision making. You may also take this opportunity to introduce additional language terms which are featured in this lesson.

Do you want to read about a real topic? (Use the terms *nonfiction* and *fiction*.) **Is this a story?** (Use the term *narrative*.) **Is it a long story?** (Review the characteristics of a short story.) **Is it intended for individual reading?** (Clarify that, although we may read plays individually, they are intended for performance for a large audience.) **Do you need short facts?** (Discuss other types of references.)

If a student does not want to read about places, you might discuss nonfiction books that are about neither people nor places; i.e., sports, personal appearance and development, hobbies, computers, or social science.

RESULTS—By knowing the characteristics of books we like to read and other kinds of books that are similar, we can broaden our book selections by reading new kinds of books.

WRITING EXTENSION
• Describe the criteria that people use in selecting books?

THINKING ABOUT THINKING
• Why does it matter what kind of book a person reads?
• What other decisions and alternatives can be pictured this way?
• How did using the flowchart show you the differences in types of books?
• Design a graphic organizer that shows how people select different types of books?

SIMILAR LANGUAGE ARTS LESSONS
• To depict the steps in information retrieval, directions, or study skills procedures.
• To depict the plot of a narrative.
• To depict the steps in independent study or the preparation of a term paper.
• To depict rules of punctuation, spelling, grammar, or capitalization.

WHAT KIND OF BOOK DO YOU WANT TO READ?

DIRECTIONS: Complete the flowchart to answer the series of questions about choosing a book. In each rectangle of the flowchart, record the type(s) of books which belong in that category. To save space, use the following abbreviations.

Adventure (Ad)	**General Fiction (GF)**
Atlases (At)	**History (Hi)**
Autobiography (Au)	**Philosophy (Phy)**
Biography (Bio)	**Poetry (Pty)**
Dictionary (Dty)	**Science Books (SB)**
Drama (Dr)	**Science Fiction (SF)**
Encyclopedias (En)	**Short Story (SS)**
Fantasy (Fa)	**Travel (Trv)**

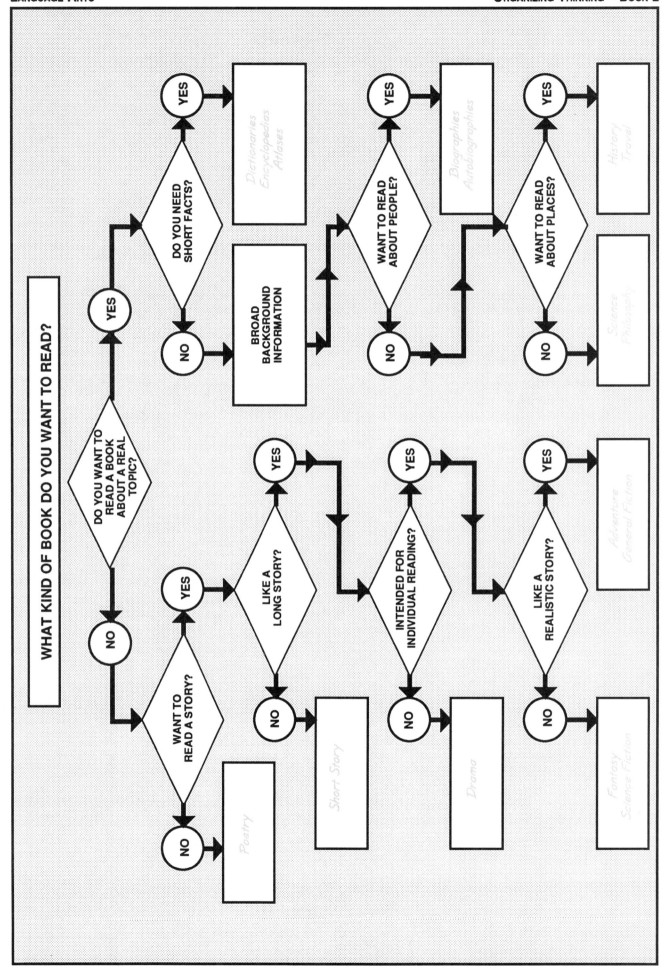

WHAT KIND OF BOOK DO YOU WANT TO READ?

DO YOU WANT TO READ A BOOK ABOUT A REAL TOPIC?

DO YOU NEED SHORT FACTS?

YES — Dictionaries Encyclopedias Atlases

NO — BROAD BACKGROUND INFORMATION

WANT TO READ ABOUT PEOPLE?

YES — Biographies Autobiographies

WANT TO READ ABOUT PLACES?

YES — History Travel

NO — Science Philosophy

WANT TO READ A STORY?

LIKE A LONG STORY?

NO — Poetry

INTENDED FOR INDIVIDUAL READING?

NO — Short Story

LIKE A REALISTIC STORY?

NO — Drama

YES — Adventure General Fiction

NO — Fantasy Science Fiction

AESOP'S FABLES

THINKING SKILL: Identifying reasons, decisions, results, and conclusions in parallel plots; generalizing a moral

CONTENT OBJECTIVE: Students will use the parallel flowchart to depict similar themes, reasons, decisions, results, and conclusions in two fables.

DISCUSSION: TECHNIQUE—Use a transparency of the parallel flowchart to record significant features of two Aesop's fables: similar themes, reasons, decisions, results, and conclusions. Because fables are short, simple, interesting to children, and contain significant moral teachings, they are a valuable source for the teaching of critical thinking, moral values, and decision making to elementary students. This activity demonstrates the comparison of two literary works. By analyzing two stories with similar conflicts and conclusions, students examine two samples instead of drawing inferences from one story. Students find it interesting that the same themes and conclusions can be present in stories that have different characters and plots. Students may need an explanation of the significance of conflict or theme in a story.

DIALOGUE—Encourage students to identify other Aesop's Fables in which greed leads the main character to lose what he already has. ("The Goose That Laid the Golden Egg," "The Lion and the Hare," "The Tortoise and the Eagle"). Encourage students to identify parallel conflicts, plots, and conclusions in other Aesop's fables. Other fables which have parallel plots leading to the same moral lesson include:

Honesty is the best policy: "Mercury and the Woodman," "The Wolf in Sheep's Clothing"
Pride goes before a fall: "Mice and the Weasels," "The Eagles and the Cock," "The Ass Carrying the Image," "The Wolf and His Shadow," "The Gnat and the Lion"
Look before you leap: "The Bat and the Weasels," "The Fox and the Goat," "The Frogs and the Well"
Performance is better than appearance: "Mice and the Weasels," "The Peacock and the Crane," "The Horse and the Groom," "The Olive Tree and the Fig Tree," "The Stag at the Pool," "Brother and Sister," "The Rose and the Amaranth"
Don't be fooled by flattery: "The Fox and the Crow," "The Dog, the Cock, and the Fox," "The Grasshopper and the Owl," "The Fox and the Grasshopper," "The Lion and the Bull"
Don't try to be what you're not: "The Ass and the Wolf," "The Monkey and the Camel," "The Eagle, the Jackday, and the Shepherd," "The Crow and the Raven"
If you choose bad companions, others will think that you are bad, also: "The Farmer and the Stork," "The Ass and the Purchaser," "The Rivers and the Sea," "Hercules and Plutus"
You can't please everyone: "The Miller, the Son, and the Ass," "Father and Daughter"
Prepare now rather than later: "The Wild Boar and the Fox," "The Grasshopper and the Ants"
There is strength in unity: "The Lion and the Boar," "The Man and his Sons," "The Lion and the Three Bulls," "The Ass and the Mule," "The Belly and the Members"
Deeds count more than words: "The Boasting Traveler," "Two Soldiers and the Robber"
Stay away from danger and treachery: "The Wolf and the Goat," "The Wolf and the Lamb," "The Archer and the Lion"

The parallel flowchart can also be used as a writing tool. List a selected story down the left side of the graphic organizer, and use the right side to develop an original story having the same conflict or theme and conclusion.

RESULT—Stories which portray different decisions, actions, and results can express the same moral. Moral principles can be expressed effectively in fables.

WRITING EXTENSION

- Select two of Aesop's Fables with the same issue and the same moral. How are the decisions, actions, and results different for the main character in each story?
- Write a fable using the parallel flowchart. Outline an existing fable down the left side. Create a story with a similar theme and conclusion. Develop the plot by filling in the right side. Write the story from the flowchart.

THINKING ABOUT THINKING

- Design another graphic organizer to depict the conflict, decisions, actions, results, and moral of a story.
- Design another graphic organizer to compare similar conflicts, decisions, actions, results, and morals of two stories.
- How did using the graphic organizer help you understand the conclusions of the two stories?
- How did using the graphic organizer help you organize your thoughts before you began to write?
- Why was it easier to identify the moral in two stories than to infer the conclusion from just one?
- Suggest another pair of stories that could be understood more clearly if they were compared this way.

SIMILAR LANGUAGE ARTS LESSONS

- To compare complex plots of novels or plays.
- To compare biographical data.
- To record events for writing narratives.
- To organize information for writing letters, term papers, biographies, or stories.

 © 1990 MIDWEST PUBLICATIONS • CRITICAL THINKING PRESS & SOFTWARE • P. O. Box 448, Pacific Grove, CA 93950

AESOP'S FABLES

DIRECTIONS: Read the two fables carefully. Identify the main character in each fable and write its name in the character box on the diagram. Decide what conflict, theme, or situation led to the character's reasons and actions. Identify the conclusion that is suggested by the actions and the results. Use the parallel flowchart to show the themes, reasons, decisions, results, and conclusions in the two fables.

MERCURY AND THE WOODMAN

A woodman was chopping down a tree on the bank of a river when his ax fell out of his hands and into the water. As he stood by the water's edge, upset over his loss, Mercury appeared, dived into the river and brought up a golden ax. Mercury asked him if that ax was the one that he had lost. The woodman replied that it was not. Mercury dived a second time, brought up a silver ax, and asked if it was his. The woodman replied that it was not. Once more Mercury dived into the river and brought up the missing ax. The woodman was overjoyed at recovering his property and thanked Mercury warmly. Mercury was so pleased with the woodman's honesty that he made him a present of the other two axes.

When the woodman told his story to his companions, one decided to try his luck for himself. He went to the bank of the river, chopped down a tree, and let his ax drop into the water. Mercury appeared as before, dived into the river and brought up a golden ax. Without waiting to be asked whether it was his or not, the excited fellow stretched out his hand crying, "That's mine! That's mine!" Mercury was so disgusted at his dishonesty that he refused to give him the golden ax or to recover the one that he had let fall into the stream.

THE DOG AND THE SHADOW

A dog with a piece of meat in his mouth was walking on a log over a stream when he saw his own reflection in the water. He thought it was another dog with a piece of meat twice as big. He let go of his own meat and charged at the other dog to get the larger piece. Of course, all that happened was that he got neither. One was only a reflection and the other was carried away by the current.

COMPARING PLOTS IN TWO STORIES

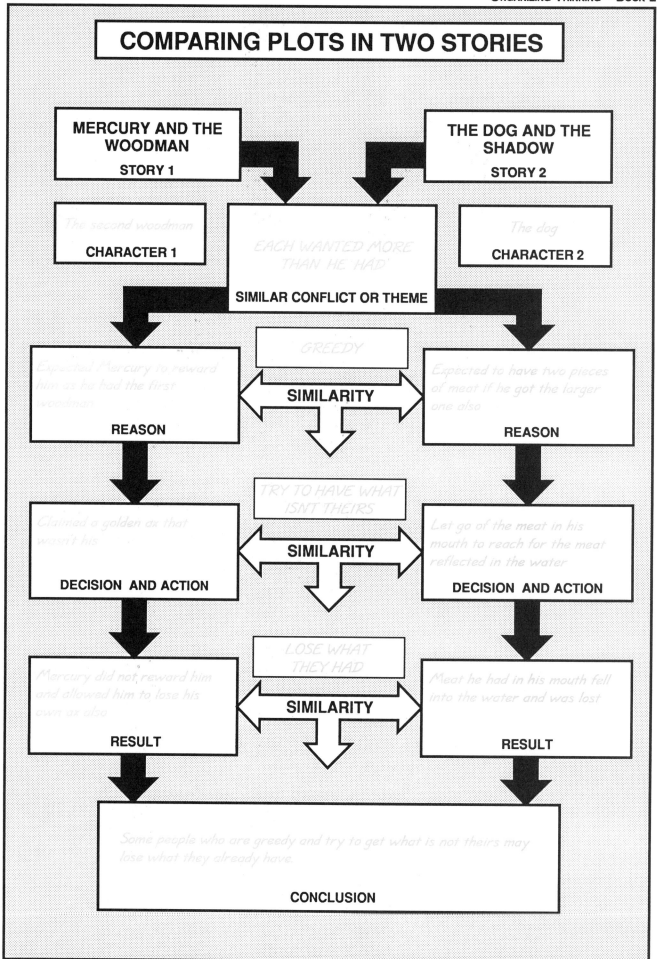

MERCURY AND THE WOODMAN

STORY 1

THE DOG AND THE SHADOW

STORY 2

The second woodman

CHARACTER 1

EACH WANTED MORE THAN HE HAD

SIMILAR CONFLICT OR THEME

The dog

CHARACTER 2

GREEDY

Expected Mercury to reward him as he had the first woodman

REASON

SIMILARITY

Expected to have two pieces of meat if he got the larger one also

REASON

TRY TO HAVE WHAT ISNT THEIRS

Claimed a golden ax that wasn't his

DECISION AND ACTION

SIMILARITY

Let go of the meat in his mouth to reach for the meat reflected in the water

DECISION AND ACTION

LOSE WHAT THEY HAD

Mercury did not reward him and allowed him to lose his own ax also

RESULT

SIMILARITY

Meat he had in his mouth fell into the water and was lost

RESULT

Some people who are greedy and try to get what is not theirs may lose what they already have.

CONCLUSION

LAURA INGALLS WILDER

THINKING SKILL: Chronological order

CONTENT OBJECTIVE: Students will use the parallel time line to relate an author's works to biographical data.

DISCUSSION: TECHNIQUE—Use the transparency of the parallel time line to record student responses as they review the life and works of Laura Ingalls Wilder. Encourage students to raise questions regarding how her books reflect the events of her life.

DIALOGUE—Students must relate the significance of events in Laura Ingalls Wilder's life to the order in which she wrote her books. Check a biography of Mrs. Wilder to determine the order in which the books were written and to identify interesting experiences in her adult life.

Does the order in which she wrote the books indicate what she thought was significant and dramatic in her childhood? Since her series stops at her life as a young adult, what books might have been written about her later years? Why are the "Little House" books so popular? (Historical fiction, particularly autobiographical novels, are appealing because they show the human drama of historical events.) **How do the experiences of the Ingalls and the Wilder families** (Westward movement, natural disasters, primitive living conditions, the deaths and serious illnesses of children) **relate to what was happening in our country in the period from 1865 to 1895?** (Use the parallel time line to relate the Ingalls' experiences to historical events of this period.) **Did Mrs. Wilder realize as she was growing up that the experiences of her family illustrated a significant era in the history of our country? Did she realize that these experiences would be interesting to readers a hundred years later? Why do you think so?** (Students may consider the stories of the Ingalls family to be heroic or adventurous. They may not understand that the Ingalls' daily life and hardships were common experiences of pioneer families of that period.) **What other authors can you think of who drew on their childhood experiences to write books describing significant trends or events in the history of our country? What experiences has your family had that someone living a hundred years from now might find interesting?**

RESULTS—Childhood experiences can be reflected in works of fiction. An author's systematic and accurate memory of childhood conditions add detail and interest to writing.

WRITING EXTENSION

- **Describe how events in Laura Ingalls Wilder's childhood are expressed in her books.**
- **To extend this lesson as an autobiographical writing assignment, see WRITING AN AUTOBIOGRAPHY in Chapter 3.**

THINKING ABOUT THINKING

- **How did using the graph help you connect the events in Laura Ingalls Wilder's life to the contents of her books?**
- **How would using the parallel flowchart help you remember events in your life?**
- **Suggest another lesson in which showing time connections would help you understand what you are learning.**

SIMILAR LANGUAGE ARTS LESSONS

- To record complex plots of novels or plays, especially those featuring flashback episodes.
- To record biographical data.
- To organize information when writing letters, term papers, stories, or biographies.

LAURA INGALLS WILDER

DIRECTIONS: Read the passage carefully to determine the order in which the events occurred. Write the events in the life of Laura Ingalls Wilder beside the correct year on the time line to the left. Write the names of the books which contain those events beside the time line to the right.

Laura Ingalls Wilder began writing her "Little House" books when she was sixty-three years old. The titles of her books contain the events and locations of her childhood. Her works include:

By the Shores of Silver Lake *On the Way Home*
Little House in the Big Woods *The First Four Years*
Little House on the Prairie *The Long Winter*
Little Town on the Prairie *These Happy Golden Years*
On the Banks of Plum Creek

In 1867 Laura Ingalls was born in a log cabin in Pepin, Wisconsin. Three years later the Ingalls family packed their belongings into a covered wagon and traveled to Independence, Kansas, where her sister Carrie was born in a *Little House on the Prairie*. The next year the Ingalls family moved back to Pepin, the location of the *Little House in the Big Woods*.

In 1873 the Ingalls family moved to a sod dugout house near Walnut Grove, Minnesota, where Laura attended school. This was the site of *On the Banks of Plum Creek*. Swarms of grasshoppers wiped out the family crops in 1876. Also in that year, Laura's infant brother Freddy died and the family moved to Burr Oak, Iowa.

In 1879 Laura's sister Mary lost her eyesight. Later that year the family moved to the Dakota territory and helped found the town of DeSmet, South Dakota. DeSmet was the setting for *By the Shores of Silver Lake* and *Little Town on the Prairie*.

The family spent *The Long Winter* of 1880 in a railroad surveyor's hut and then moved into a store. As Laura grew to adulthood, the family's experiences were described in *These Happy Golden Years*. Laura married Almanzo Wilder in 1885. Their life in a hut two miles north of DeSmet is described in *The First Four Years*. Eleven years later the Wilder family moved to Mansfield, Missouri, the location of *On the Way Home*.

LAURA INGALLS WILDER

| EVENTS IN THE LIFE OF LAURA INGALLS WILDER | | RELATED BOOKS |

1865   **1865**

1867–Laura Ingalls born in Pepin, WI

1870   **1870**
1870–Sister Carrie born in KS   LITTLE HOUSE ON THE PRAIRIE
1871–Ingalls family returned to Pepin   LITTLE HOUSE IN THE BIG WOODS
1873–Family moved to a sod dugout   ON THE BANKS OF PLUM CREEK
house in MN

1875   **1875**
1876–Grasshoppers destroyed crops;
Freddie died; family moved to IA.

1879–Mary lost her sight; family   BY THE SHORES OF SILVER LAKE
moved to SD   LITTLE TOWN ON THE PRAIRIE
1880 1880–Family spent a hard winter in a   THE LONG WINTER   **1880**
surveyor's hut

                                                           THESE HAPPY GOLDEN YEARS

1885   **1885**
1885–Laura married Almanzo Wilder   THE FIRST FOUR YEARS

1890   **1890**

1895 1896–Wilders moved to Mansfield, MO   ON THE WAY HOME   **1895**

CHARLOTTE'S WEB: DESCRIBING A CHARACTER

Note: The following three lessons are developed from the first chapter of **Charlotte's Web**. *Since these lessons are substantial and lengthy, one lesson per class session is recommended. Each lesson is based on the same text (see page 77) and involves critical reading, class discussion, and a writing application.*

THINKING SKILL: Describing attributes; characterizing or drawing characterizations from examples; identifying the short- and long-term consequences of a personal trait

CONTENT OBJECTIVE: Students will use a central idea graph to identify characteristics and give examples of words, actions, or situations to illustrate each characteristic.

DISCUSSION: TECHNIQUE—As students identify Fern's characteristics, record their ideas on a transparency of the graph. Ask students for an example or quotation which illustrates each characteristic they identify.

DIALOGUE—To arrive at an informed understanding of what the author intended us to believe about a character, we must base our interpretations on specific examples and quotations. Students may follow two approaches as they examine characteristics and examples: they may identify an incident and suggest a characteristic reflected in the incident, or they may identify a characteristic and look for an incident that illustrates it. To prompt students in either process, ask for a characteristic and an example.

Why it is important to support our character interpretations by citing examples? How might our understanding of Fern be different if we didn't use examples?

Students may find additional characteristics to describe Fern.

*   Inquisitive: "Where's papa going with that ax?"
*   Speaks frankly: "Do away with it? You mean kill it?"
*   Puts ethical values before courtesy: "It's a matter of life and death and you talk about controlling myself."
*   Thinks for herself: Challenges her parents' reasons for killing the pig and confirms what she believes to be true.

Encourage them to examine whether Fern's characteristics are positive, negative, or neutral. For example, "inquisitive" tends to suggest a positive quality; "asks questions" tends to be neutral; "butts in" or "nosey" tends to suggest a negative quality. Discuss positive and negative connotations of each characteristic, then discuss the students' overall impression of Fern.

Do you think that a characteristic is positive or negative? What are the short-term effects of that characteristic in this situation? What might the long-term effects of that characteristic be for Fern? What might the long-term effects be if other people had the same characteristic? Do Fern's qualities that might seem to be negative have negative effects in the story? Would you like Fern? Would you respect her? What, if any, is the difference between "liking" and "respecting" someone?

RESULT—Examples should be given for each trait inferred about a character. Before deciding whether a characteristic ascribed to a person is positive or negative, examine whether the short- and long-term results are positive or negative.

WRITING EXTENSION

*   **Describe Fern's character. In each sentence state one of her characteristics and give an example that illustrates that trait.**
*   **Using the same graph, write a description of Mr. Arable.**

THINKING ABOUT THINKING
- **How did using the graph help you understand character description?**
- **How did using the central idea graph help you organize the paper?**
- **Suggest another lesson where using the central idea graph would help you understand a character.**

SIMILAR LANGUAGE ARTS LESSONS
- To illustrate factors leading to or resulting from a turning point in a narrative or biography.
- To illustrate a topic sentence and its supporting statements.
- To illustrate headings and subheadings in an outline.
- To record examples of figures of speech and types of literature, writing, or books.

CHARLOTTE'S WEB: CHARACTER ANALYSIS

NOTE: This is the second of three lessons in a series based on the same excerpt from the first chapter of **Charlotte's Web** *(see page 77). The three lessons should be taught sequentially.*

THINKING SKILL: Identifying character attributes

CONTENT OBJECTIVE: Students will use a central idea graph to describe Fern's character in terms of qualities that readers look for in any character, supporting their descriptions by citing specific actions from the text.

DISCUSSION: TECHNIQUE—Use a transparency of the central idea graph to record comments as students describe Fern by identifying her significance in the story. In each box write an example or explanation of the trait specified on the arm of the graph.

    DIALOGUE—The second character description exercise involves analyzing the significance of the character to the novel, requiring more abstract inferences about Fern than the character/example description in the last lesson. This exercise identifies how the character relates to others, moves the plot along, and conveys important ideas in the story.

Let's examine why each characteristic is important in understanding Fern's significance in the story. Personal character: How would one describe her personal character regarding honesty, sense of responsibility, awareness of others, self-reliance, sense of fairness, dependability, etc.? Relationship to others: How does Fern treat the people and the animals in the story? (If Fern had not saved Wilber's life, there would be no story. Fern treats animals as if they have the same motives, feelings, values, and problem solving skills as humans, the view that the author takes in the rest of the book.) **Ideals: What are Fern's beliefs and ideals? How do her ideals relate to the author's? To the beliefs of others in the story? To the reader's ideals? Why are a character's ideals important in a story? Positive qualities: Does Fern demonstrate any positive qualities? Are they important to the story? How? Negative qualities: Does Fern demonstrate any negative qualities? Are they important to the story? How? Significance in the action of the story: How do her decisions move the story along? How would the story have changed if she had acted differently?**

    RESULT—To describe the significance of a character in a novel, examine both the personal characteristics and the importance of that person to the plot.

WRITING EXTENSION
- **Describe Fern's significance in** *Charlotte's Web.*

THINKING ABOUT THINKING
- **How did using the graph help you understand how to describe the significance of a character to the plot of a story?**
- **Suggest another lesson where using the graph would help you understand the significance of a character in the plot of a story.**

SIMILAR LANGUAGE ARTS LESSONS
- To illustrate factors leading to or resulting from a turning point in a narrative or biography.
- To illustrate a topic sentence and its supporting statements or outline headings and subheadings.
- To record examples of figures of speech, types of literature, types of writing or books.

CHARLOTTE'S WEB: ASSUMPTIONS, REASONS, AND CONCLUSIONS

*NOTE: This is the third of three lessons in a series based on the same excerpt from the first chapter of **Charlotte's Web** (see page 77). The three lessons should be taught sequentially.*

THINKING SKILL: Identifying assumptions, reasons, and conclusions.

CONTENT OBJECTIVE: Students will use the arch diagram to identify assumptions, reasons, and conclusions for and against killing the runt pig in *Charlotte's Web.*

DISCUSSION: TECHNIQUE—Students will use the argument diagram to describe the assumptions, reasons, and conclusions which the Arables and Fern believe regarding the life of the pig. Ask students to write the conclusion in the arch of each diagram. While we commonly look first for reasons and then the conclusion, in this case the Arables' and Fern's conclusions are stated first. Students should turn their papers sideways and write the exact reasons that each character gives for his or her conclusions about the life of the pig. As students record quotations from the passage in each "reason" column, encourage them to write in parentheses what inferences they can draw from these about the value of the pig's life.

DIALOGUE—In introducing this lesson, it is important to familiarize students with the "structure" of an argument represented by the diagram.

An *assumption* is what someone believes to be true. Assumptions may or may not be stated by the person. We can understand what a person believes to be true by looking for similar ideas in his or her reasons. Our assumptions form the foundation of our thinking. Our reasons "grow out of" or "rest upon" what we assume to be true. Like the foundation which supports a building, our assumptions must be firm enough to support our reasons and conclusions. If we are unclear about our assumptions, or if our assumptions are untrue, then our conclusions may not be good ones. Our reasons "hold up" our conclusions in much the same way that columns or walls hold up a roof. Without good reasons our conclusions "fall" down because they are not "supported" by good explanations or sufficient evidence.

This passage from *Charlotte's Web* provides one of the most eloquent examples of persuasive argument, unstated assumptions, and inferences in children's literature. The argument represents a transition from an adult, pragmatic view of a pig to a childlike, personified view of a pig—which is the point of view the author maintains through the rest of the book. The following questions will encourage students to examine the text carefully and identify assumptions, reasons, and conclusions.

What is the person trying to convince us to believe? How do we know what a person's conclusions are? (actions, statements, or attitudes) What words signal a person's conclusions? ("decided," "so," "therefore") How does a person explain his thinking? (appeal to authority, practical considerations, humanitarian considerations, appeal for justice, analogous reasons, appeal to emotion) Describe different types of reasons that people may give for their thinking. What is a person likely to believe if he gives the reasons and the conclusions that he expresses? What does he take for granted?

Students may find other reasons why the Arables believe that killing the pig is the more reasonable choice. For example:
• Mr. Arable: "I know more about raising a litter of pigs than you do." (He has more experience and authority in deciding what is best.)

- Mr. Arable: "A little girl is one thing, a runty little pig is another." (The pig's life is not as valuable as human life.)

Students may also find additional reasons why Fern believes that killing the pig is unjust:

- Fern: "Just because it's smaller than the others." (Comparing the runt to other pigs should not be sufficient reason for its death.)

The key concept in this chapter is the difference between the Arables' and Fern's assumptions regarding the value of the pig's life. The Arables view the pig as a commodity, an organism that does not express the characteristics that we attribute to humans: intelligence, emotion, personality, spirit, motive, humor, compassion, planning, and problem-solving abilities. Fern attributes these human-like characteristics to the pig. For the rest of the novel, pigs, spiders, and other barnyard animals exhibit these characteristics in a funny and poignant fable of compassion and self-sacrifice. Encourage students to read the entire novel, a masterpiece of humor, allegory, creative and critical thinking.

RESULT—To understand an individual's point of view, note his conclusions, his reasons, and the assumptions behind his thinking. Determining assumptions from one or two reasons is not as strong as having more reasons, taken together, to suggest his underlying beliefs.

WRITING EXTENSION

- How did Fern's assumptions about the pig's life differ from that of her parents?
- Why do you think Mr. Arable changed his mind about killing the pig? Give reasons from the story to support your opinion.
- Use the two diagrams to depict a difference of opinion (assumptions, reasons, and conclusions) that a boy or girl might have with someone else. Write a short story that illustrates their difference of opinion.

THINKING ABOUT THINKING

- How did using the arch diagram help you understand what Fern and the Arables assume to be true?
- Suggest another lesson where using the arch diagram would help you understand an issue.
- How did the diagram help you understand the structure of an argument (assumptions, reasons, and conclusions)?
- Why is it important to identify the assumptions in an argument?
- Do you feel confident about suggesting an assumption that is based on one or two reasons? Are you more confident if it is based on many reasons? Explain.

SIMILAR LANGUAGE ARTS LESSONS

- To describe arguments or generalizations in news reports, speeches, or in the plots of short stories, novels, and plays.
- To describe scientific research and laboratory demonstrations.
- To prepare arguments or generalizations in debate.

CHARLOTTE'S WEB

"Where is Papa going with that ax?" said Fern to her mother as they were setting the table for breakfast.

"Out to the hoghouse," replied Mrs. Arable. "Some pigs were born last night."

"I don't see why he needs an ax," continued Fern, who was only eight.

"Well," said her mother, "one of the pigs is a runt. It's very small and weak, and it will never amount to anything. So your father has decided to do away with it."

"Do *away* with it?" shrieked Fern. "You mean *kill* it? Just because it's smaller than the others?"

Mrs. Arable put a pitcher of cream on the table. "Don't yell, Fern!" she said. "Your father is right. The pig would probably die anyway."

Fern pushed a chair out of the way and ran outdoors. The grass was wet and the earth smelled of springtime. Fern's sneakers were sopping by the time she caught up with her father. "Please don't kill it" she sobbed. "It's unfair."

Mr. Arable stopped walking. "Fern," he said gently, "you will have to learn to control yourself."

"Control myself?" yelled Fern. "This is a matter of life and death, and you talk about *controlling* myself!" Tears ran down her cheeks as she took hold of the ax and tried to pull it out of her father's hand.

"Fern," said Mr. Arable, "I know more about raising a litter of pigs than you do. A weakling makes trouble. Now run along!"

"But it's unfair," cried Fern. "The pig couldn't help being born small, could it? If *I* had been very small at birth, would you have killed *me?*"

Mr. Arable smiled. "Certainly not," he said, looking down at his daughter with love. "But this is different. A little girl is one thing, a runty pig another."

"I see no difference," replied Fern, still hanging onto the ax. "This is the most terrible case of injustice I ever heard of."

A queer look came over John Arable's face. He seemed almost ready to cry himself. "All right," he said. "You go back in the house and I will bring the runt when I come in. I'll let you start it on a bottle, like a baby. Then you'll see what trouble a pig can be."

CHARLOTTE'S WEB: DESCRIBING A CHARACTER

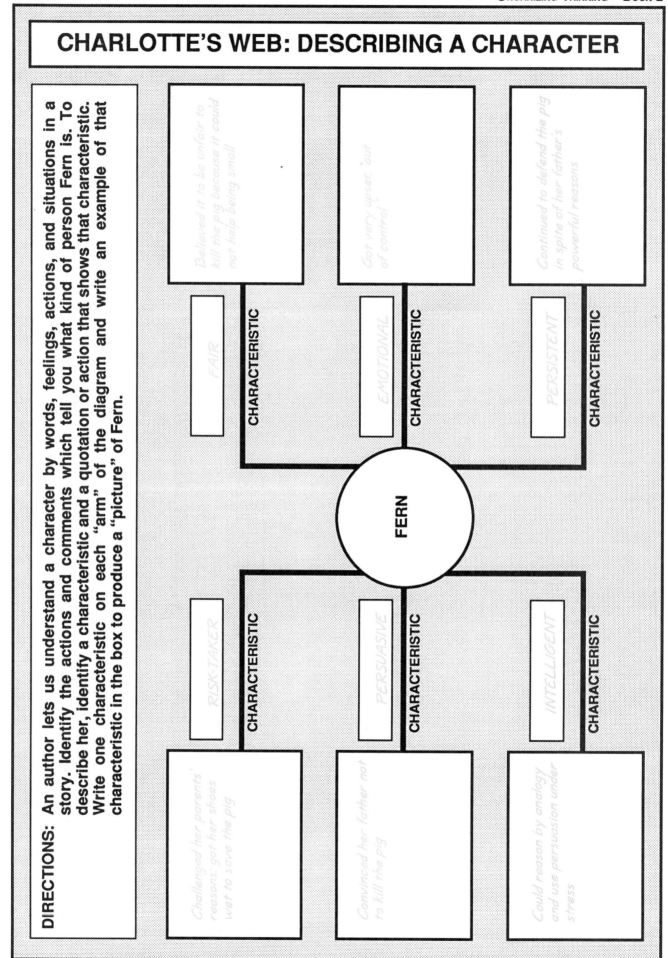

DIRECTIONS: An author lets us understand a character by words, feelings, actions, and situations in a story. Identify the actions and comments which tell you what kind of person Fern is. To describe her, identify a characteristic and a quotation or action that shows that characteristic. Write one characteristic on each "arm" of the diagram and write an example of that characteristic in the box to produce a "picture" of Fern.

Believed it to be unfair to kill the pig because it could not help being small

Got very upset, "out of control"

Continued to defend the pig in spite of her father's powerful reasons

FAIR
CHARACTERISTIC

EMOTIONAL
CHARACTERISTIC

PERSISTENT
CHARACTERISTIC

FERN

RISK-TAKER
CHARACTERISTIC

PERSUASIVE
CHARACTERISTIC

INTELLIGENT
CHARACTERISTIC

Challenged her parents' reasons; got her shoes wet to save the pig

Convinced her father not to kill the pig

Could reason by analogy and use persuasion under stress

CHARLOTTE'S WEB: CHARACTER ANALYSIS

DIRECTIONS: Review the passage on page 77. Identify the characteristic written on each "arm" of the diagram. Write a quotation or action to illustrate that characteristic in each box.

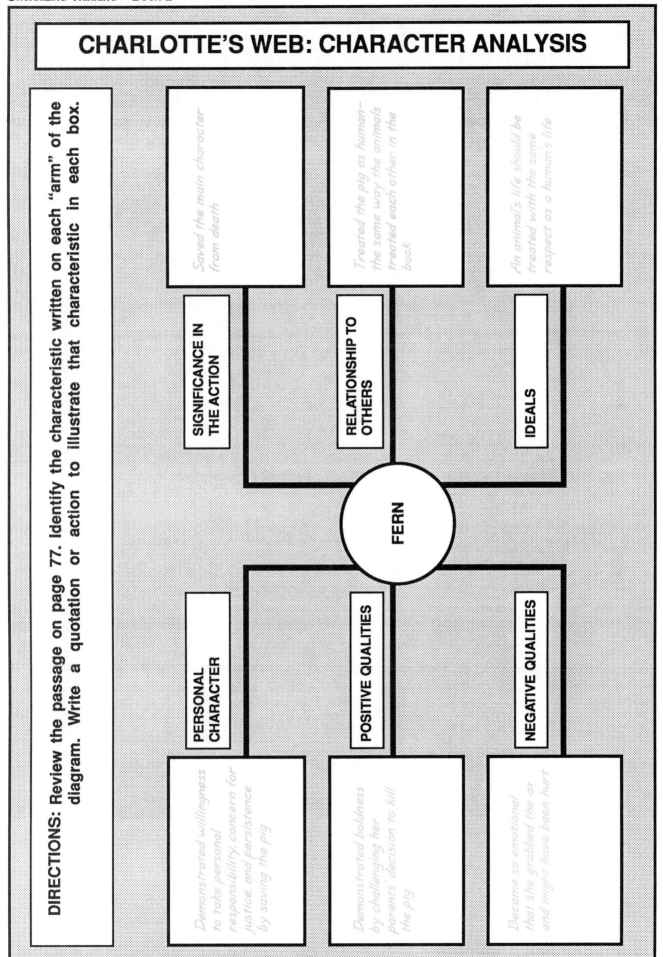

Saved the main character from death

Treated the pig as human— the same way the animals treated each other in the book

An animal's life should be treated with the same respect as a human's life

SIGNIFICANCE IN THE ACTION

RELATIONSHIP TO OTHERS

IDEALS

FERN

PERSONAL CHARACTER

POSITIVE QUALITIES

NEGATIVE QUALITIES

Demonstrated willingness to take personal responsibility, concern for justice, and persistence by saving the pig

Demonstrated boldness by challenging her parents' decision to kill the pig

Became so emotional that she grabbed the ax and might have been hurt

CHARLOTTE'S WEB:
ASSUMPTIONS, REASONS, AND CONCLUSIONS

DIRECTIONS: An assumption is what someone believes to be true. Assumptions may or may not be stated by the person. We can understand what someone believes to be true by looking for similar ideas in their reasons for reaching a conclusion.

In the "arch" of the diagram, write Mr. and Mrs. Arable's conclusion regarding the pig. Turn the page sideways and write their exact words in each "reason" column. In parentheses write what their words suggest about the life of the pig. From the reasons given by the Arables for killing the runt pig, determine what they assumed to be true about the value of the pig's life. Write these assumptions at the base of the diagram.

Follow the same process in the second diagram to describe Fern's conclusions, reasons, and assumptions about the value of the pig's life.

CHARLOTTE'S WEB:
ASSUMPTIONS, REASONS, AND CONCLUSIONS

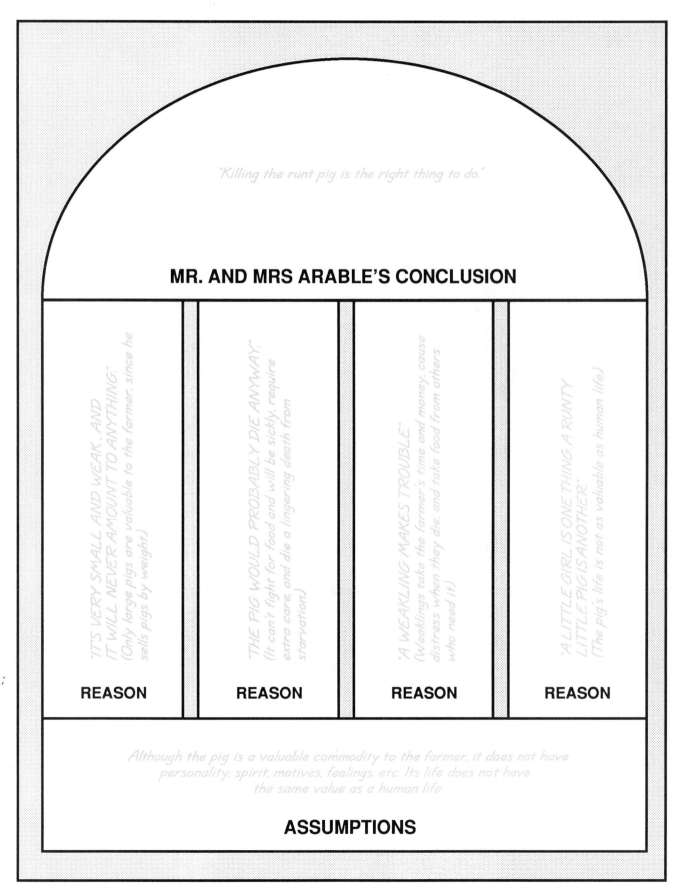

"Killing the runt pig is the right thing to do."

MR. AND MRS ARABLE'S CONCLUSION

"IT'S VERY SMALL AND WEAK, AND IT WILL NEVER AMOUNT TO ANYTHING."
(Only large pigs are valuable to the farmer, since he sells pigs by weight.)

REASON

"THE PIG WOULD PROBABLY DIE ANYWAY."
(It can't fight for food and will be sickly, require extra care, and die a lingering death from starvation.)

REASON

"A WEAKLING MAKES TROUBLE."
(Weaklings take the farmer's time and money, cause distress when they die, and take food from others who need it.)

REASON

"A LITTLE GIRL IS ONE THING; A RUNTY LITTLE PIG IS ANOTHER."
(The pig's life is not as valuable as human life.)

REASON

Although the pig is a valuable commodity to the farmer, it does not have personality, spirit, motives, feelings, etc. Its life does not have the same value as a human life.

ASSUMPTIONS

CHARLOTTE'S WEB:
ASSUMPTIONS, REASONS, AND CONCLUSIONS

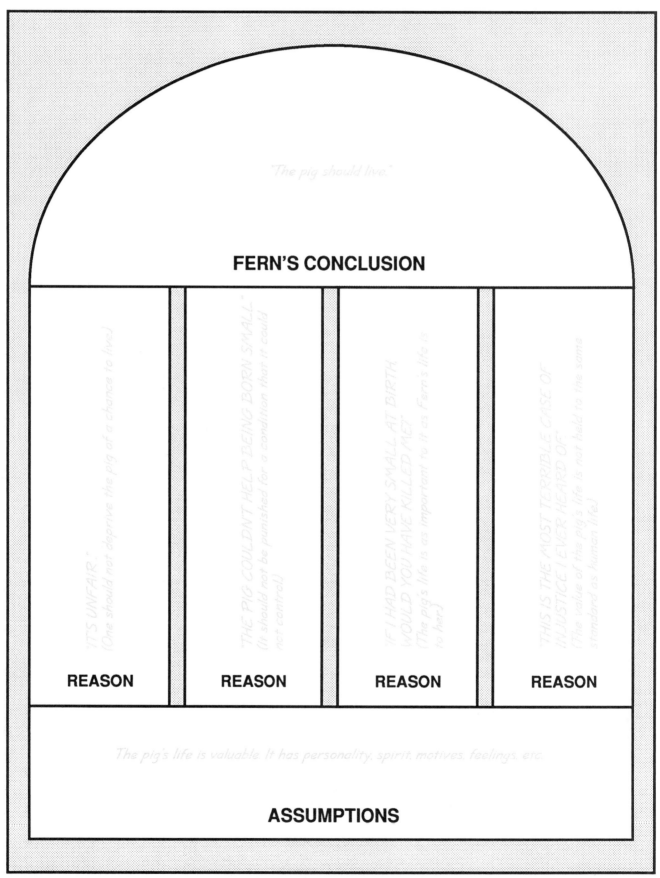

FERN'S CONCLUSION

"The pig should live."

"IT'S UNFAIR."
(One should not deprive the pig of a chance to live.)

"THE PIG COULDN'T HELP BEING BORN SMALL."
(It should not be punished for a condition that it could not control.)

"IF I HAD BEEN VERY SMALL AT BIRTH WOULD YOU HAVE KILLED ME?"
(The pig's life is as important to it as Fern's life is to her.)

"THIS IS THE MOST TERRIBLE CASE OF INJUSTICE I EVER HEARD OF."
(The value of the pig's life is not held to the same standard as human life.)

REASON   **REASON**   **REASON**   **REASON**

The pig's life is valuable. It has personality, spirit, motives, feelings, etc.

ASSUMPTIONS

DESCRIBING A STORY

THINKING SKILL: Describing attributes

CONTENT OBJECTIVE: Students will describe the characteristics of a work of fiction.

DISCUSSION: TECHNIQUE—When writing an essay or book report, students may not know how to identify the important parts of a story. This lesson features the letters in the word "fiction" as a mnemonic device for describing a narrative. After students have completed the diagram from the written passage, give them a blank diagram to describe a story that you have recently read as a class.

DIALOGUE—Discuss the details for describing each characteristic of a story.

"F"—Friction (conflict). Resolving a conflict or problem makes a story interesting and worthwhile. If there is no conflict, there is no reason for a story.

Is a conflict or problem necessary in a story? Can you think of an interesting and significant story that contains no conflict or problem?

"I"—Ideal (message). The ideal or message is the point or purpose of a story. If there is no ideal, there is no point to a story. Examine popular television shows for the ideal that is being conveyed. In some shows, publications, movies, and song lyrics designed for young people, the ideal may not be a positive one. Students in the upper elementary and middle school grades should learn to recognize ideals and to distinguish positive and negative ones. Such clarification reduces the influence of unexamined messages and ideals.

Why is an ideal or message significant in a story? Can you think of an interesting and significant story that contains no ideal or message?

"C"—Characters. Students' discussion of characters is often limited to statements of taste— whether they like a character or not. Use the suggestions on describing a character in the *Charlotte's Web* lessons to expand the discussion of characters that you have recently read about in your language arts program.

Think about a character in one of the stories we have read together. How realistic was the character? Did you admire the character? Why or why not? How did he or she relate to others in the story? How did that character give meaning or purpose to the story?

"T"—Title. Students should look at the title in relation to the main idea of the story. Emphasize the necessity of selecting a few words that will convey the sense of the book.

How does the title fit the story? How does it relate to the characters, actions, or ideals of the story? Can you think of any other title that might have been better suited to the events and characters? What steps do you follow to decide whether a title is a good one for the story? (Read the story carefully; think about the main idea; decide if the title refers to the main idea or action and whether it attracts the interest of a reader.)

"I"—Imitate. It is much easier for elementary students to describe "who" (characters) or "what" (plot), than it is to describe "how" (style). Expand the discussion of style presented in this lesson to include aspects you have addressed in your language arts program: humor, detail, imagery, or tone.

If you were going to write a book like this one, what would it be like? What kind of characters or actions would you select? How would the characters talk? If you read the story out loud, what effect would the words suggest?

"O"—Organization. Organization is also frequently obscure to young readers. Most children's stories are written in simple chronological order and told from a single point of view. Identify stories which you have read in class that feature different organizational patterns, such as stories within a story, stories told from different viewpoints, stories told in flashbacks, etc.

"N"—Newness (novelty). Discuss why novelty (uniqueness) is important in a story.

Why is the uniqueness of a book important to a reader? Why is it important that we read many types of books? Identify a book that is so different that it encouraged you to read a type of book that you don't usually select. Why is uniqueness important to the success of a book? What "reading ruts" have you gotten into, such as reading only mysteries or science fiction? Think of an example of a book that sparked your interest in selecting a type of book different from the type you usually read. How does a unique and interesting book encourage you to expand the kinds of books you read?

Use **F.I.C.T.I.O.N.** in book reports, essay questions, library displays, bulletin boards, and descriptive speeches. Encourage students to examine the personal confidence that comes from knowing that now they can easily remember how to describe a story.

RESULT—One can understand and describe a work of fiction more adequately by reading systematically to examine significant characteristics.

WRITING EXTENSION
- What characteristics can one discuss when describing a story or play?
- Use the F.I.C.T.I.O.N. concept to write a review of a short story, novel, television show, or drama.

THINKING ABOUT THINKING
- How did using the graph help you describe a story?
- Suggest another lesson where using this graph would help you understand what you are learning.
- F.I.C.T.I.O.N. is a mnemonic—a catchy code that helps someone remember something more easily. How does using FICTION help you remember what to say about a story?
- Suggest another mnemonic that will help you understand or remember something that you are learning.
- Design another graph that you can use to describe a story.
- How does looking for the characteristics in FICTION help you more fully appreciate and understand the significance of a book?

SIMILAR LANGUAGE ARTS LESSONS
- To record examples of figures of speech, types of literature, types of writing, or types of books.
- To make up mnemonics to help cue other analysis tasks.

DESCRIBING A STORY

DIRECTIONS: Read the passage carefully. Identify the characteristic of a story that relates to each of the letters F.I.C.T.I.O.N. Write the word for each characteristic next to the letter on the graphic. Write a phrase to remind yourself what you should say about that characteristic of a story.

Have you ever forgotten what you are supposed to talk about when someone asks you to describe a story? The word **"fiction"** itself contains a letter for some characteristics you need to think about when you are describing a play, a novel, or a short story.

"F" stands for the **"friction"** or conflict in a story. Most good stories involve a difficult situation or conflict for the main character. The conflict may be between the character and nature, as in *Call It Courage.* The conflict may occur between characters, such as the disagreement between Fern and her parents in *Charlotte's Web.* There may also be a conflict of values within the character, as in *The Wizard of Oz* when Dorothy's loyalty to her dog conflicted with her family's reluctant agreement to get rid of it.

"I" stands for the **"ideal"** of the story, the message that the story relates. The ideal in *The Wizard of Oz* is that we already have the abilities that we think we lack.

"C" stands for the **"characters."** Are they realistic? Are they people that you admire? How do they relate to each other? How do they give meaning and purpose to the story? For example, each of the four major characters in *The Wizard of Oz* represents a characteristic we all value and can demonstrate: love, wisdom, courage, and security.

"T" stands for the significance of the **"title."** *A Wrinkle in Time* tells the reader how time travel takes place. *Charlotte's Web* identifies the device that saved Wilbur's life and illustrated the compassion, resourcefulness, and purposefulness of animals.

"I" stands for how you would **"imitate"** the book. This refers to the style in which the book was written. Does the author write about everyday situations or characters to help us see them with humor, as in the *Encyclopedia Brown* series? Does the author describe the surroundings with considerable detail, as in *Call It Courage*? Does the author use humor and compassion to describe unusual qualities in people or animals, such as the way the author describes Wilbur and Charlotte in *Charlotte's Web*?

"O" stands for how the plot is **"organized."** Is the story told sequentially, as in *A Wrinkle in Time*? Is it a story within a story, as in *The Arabian Nights*? Is the story told in flashbacks or from different points of view?

"N" stands for what makes the story **"new"** or **"novel"** (different). *Charlotte's Web* is different because we become sympathetic and loving toward a creature we might normally fear, a spider. *Call It Courage* is "novel" because a young person overcomes the forces of nature.

Now you have a tool to describe any story: F.I.C.T.I.O.N.

What is the Friction?

What is the Ideal?

What are the Characters like?

What is the significance of the Title?

How would you Imitate it? What is the author's style of writing?

How is the story Organized?

How is the story New or Novel?

DESCRIBING A STORY

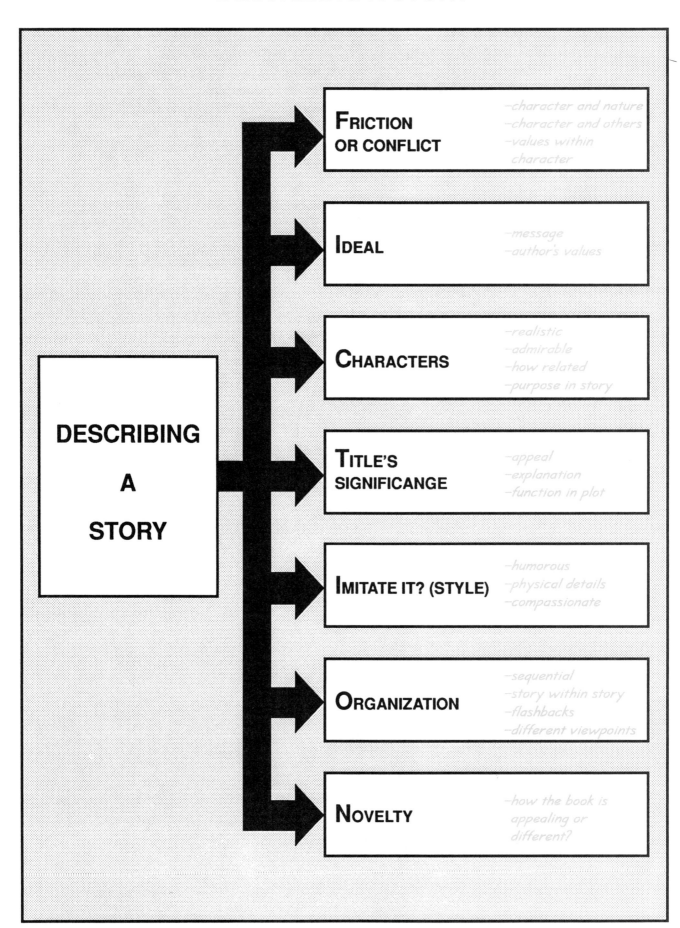

DESCRIBING A STORY

FRICTION OR CONFLICT
– character and nature
– character and others
– values within character

IDEAL
– message
– author's values

CHARACTERS
– realistic
– admirable
– how related
– purpose in story

TITLE'S SIGNIFICANCE
– appeal
– explanation
– function in plot

IMITATE IT? (STYLE)
– humorous
– physical details
– compassionate

ORGANIZATION
– sequential
– story within story
– flashbacks
– different viewpoints

NOVELTY
– how the book is appealing or different?

"FOG"

THINKING SKILL: Verbal analogies; interpreting figurative language; comparison

CONTENT OBJECTIVE: Students will use the compare or contrast graph to identify analogous characteristics between cats and fog. They will use the information to interpret the metaphor in Carl Sandburg's "Fog." Students will perceive that the poet uses economy of language to convey many images, characteristics, and implications in the use of a simple metaphor.

DISCUSSION: TECHNIQUE—Use a transparency of the compare or contrast graph to record responses as students examine the similarities between a cat and fog. Encourage students to identify a characteristic that applies to both a cat and fog and to write it on the central arrow. Prompt students to identify many adjectives, nouns, and verbs that describe that characteristic of cats. Record the class's combined descriptors of a cat on the left side of the graph and the descriptors of fog on the right.

When students have generated a long list of comparisons, make a copy of Carl Sandburg's poem "Fog" available for them. (The poem is included in many anthologies.) Circle all student-generated comparisons that Sandburg applied to the image of fog as a cat.

The poem modeled by the blanks in the exercise follows the same pattern as "Fog." Encourage students to compare their poems to Sandburg's classic and to identify the many connections between a cat and fog suggested in their poems and in Sandburg's.

DIALOGUE—Students may suggest implications or motives for cats or fog that may not be intended in the poem. After they have generated a long list of comparisons, examine each regarding its suitability to the poet's tone and purpose. Suppose, for example, that students suggest a sinister characteristic of a cat and fog. Encourage them to state reasons for the sinister interpretation. Don't superimpose any characterization until students' reasons have been examined for plausibility.

Use the same examination process for other figures of speech: simile, personification, and hyperbole. The process of making correlations is a rigorous form of comparison and is the primary thinking skill goal of the lesson. Metaphors are a natural and dramatic context to help students do this kind of thinking. Using the process to interpret the cat metaphor in "Fog" is the content goal. Teaching students to interpret the poem using the thinking process of comparison allows them to understand the meaning of the poem more fully. Examining the poem as analogy allows them to clarify the comparison process.

RESULTS—Metaphors express ideas richly because they are analogies that let us perceive something better by its similarity to something else. Objects or organisms that have many similar characteristics can be used to describe each other in very few words.

WRITING EXTENSION

- **How are a cat and fog alike?**
- **Poems are expressive because the poet conveys so much meaning in so few words. In Sandburg's "Fog," how does the image of the cat describe fog to you?** (Write a poem, extended description, essay, emotional response, or statement of literary criticism.)
- **If a cat is a good metaphor for fog, our comparison suggests that fog may also be a good image for describing cats. Use the information on your graph to write a cat poem using the descriptors of fog or write a second verse to Sandburg's poem.**
- **What other forms of metaphors do people enjoy?** (Puns, cartoons, commercials, greeting cards, political speeches)
- **What purposes do metaphors serve in language? Why would you use a metaphor rather than describe the same thing literally without the metaphor? Suggest other reasons for using metaphors.**

THINKING ABOUT THINKING

- **How does listing the characteristics of cats and fog on the graph help you "see" the many ways that fog seems to act like a cat?**
- **Describe the steps in your thinking process as you compared fog with a cat.**
- **How did the image of the fog as a cat change after you examined the ways that they are alike?**
- **You could describe the fog as a cat by the process called "analogy." When comparisons are strong between two objects, we can use one object to convey meaning about another. Can you think of other examples of analogy? What effects can an analogy have?** (humor, persuasion, description)
- **Suggest another poem in which using this graph would help you understand its meaning.**
- **Identify an experience in which someone taught you concepts about something that you could not see by comparing it with something that you could see. How did the comparison help you "picture" the new idea?**
- **Why do some people enjoy "playing with words" by using metaphors to explain their thoughts?**

SIMILAR LANGUAGE ARTS LESSONS

- To interpret figurative language.
- To analyze reasoning by analogy.
- To compare characters within or between stories, plays, or novels.
- To compare or contrast two parts of speech or kinds of stories.
- To compare or contrast lives or works of authors, artists, or actors.

 © 1990 MIDWEST PUBLICATIONS • CRITICAL THINKING PRESS & SOFTWARE • P. O. Box 448, Pacific Grove, CA 93950

CATS AND FOG

DIRECTIONS: Use the comparison diagram to identify words that you can use to compare specific characteristics of a cat and fog. Look at the general characteristics shown in the arrow boxes in the center of the diagram. In the box to the left of each arrow, write a few words (adjectives, nouns, and verbs) that describe that particular characteristic in cats. In the box to the right, write a few words that describe that characteristic in fog.

When you have finished the diagram, use the blanks below to create a cat or fog poem. Use words from the comparison chart, if you like. The blanks in each line may represent either words or syllables. Put the title of your poem on the top line.

_____

_____ _____ _____

_____ _____ _____ _____ _____

_____ _____ _____ _____

_____ _____ _____ _____ _____

_____ _____ _____ _____ _____

_____ _____ _____ _____

CATS AND FOG

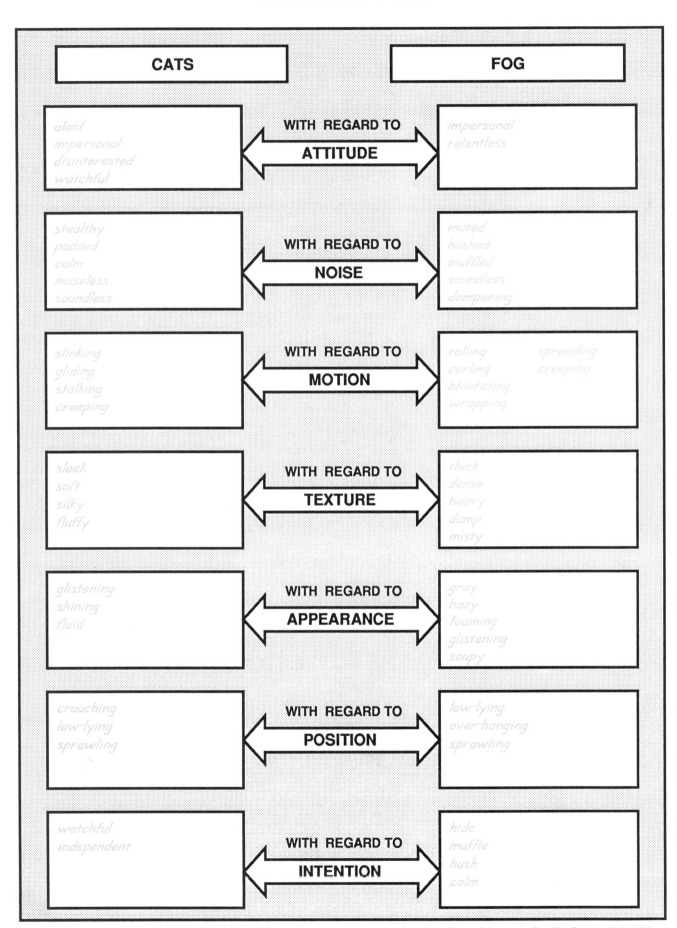

CATS		FOG

	WITH REGARD TO	
aloof *impersonal* *disinterested* *watchful*	**ATTITUDE**	*impersonal* *relentless*

	WITH REGARD TO	
stealthy *padded* *calm* *noiseless* *soundless*	**NOISE**	*muted* *hushed* *muffled* *soundless* *dampening*

	WITH REGARD TO	
slinking *gliding* *stalking* *creeping*	**MOTION**	*rolling* *spreading* *curling* *creeping* *blanketing* *wrapping*

	WITH REGARD TO	
sleek *soft* *silky* *fluffy*	**TEXTURE**	*thick* *dense* *heavy* *damp* *misty*

	WITH REGARD TO	
glistening *shining* *fluid*	**APPEARANCE**	*gray* *hazy* *foaming* *glistening* *soupy*

	WITH REGARD TO	
crouching *low-lying* *sprawling*	**POSITION**	*low-lying* *over-hanging* *sprawling*

	WITH REGARD TO	
watchful *independent*	**INTENTION**	*hide* *muffle* *hush* *calm*

DESCRIBING A GOOD SPEECH

THINKING SKILL: Describing attribute, class/subclass

CONTENT OBJECTIVE: Students will use a branching diagram to identify characteristics of an effective speech. *NOTE: This lesson is intended to review an instructional unit on the characteristics of a good speech. It presents too much information to be used as an introductory lesson.*

DISCUSSION: TECHNIQUE—Use a transparency of the branching diagram to record the characteristics of an effective speech as students discuss information from the written passage. Discuss why each characteristic is important and the effect on the listener if the speaker is not proficient at each aspect of speaking.

    You may also use the matrix diagram as a speech evaluation form which contains each of these characteristics. Reproduce the speech matrix so that each student observes and evaluates each speaker. Direct students to write a phrase in each box that describes that characteristic in the speech. To grade the speech, use a 5-1 rating scale for each characteristic. Add the scores to generate the final grade.

    DIALOGUE—Discuss examples of good speaking.

According to the principles described in this lesson, what factors made this a particularly effective speech? Was there anything the speaker might have done to make the speech more effective?

    Review video tapes of famous speeches as a means of identifying principles of effective speaking. These might include Martin Luther King's "I Have a Dream" speech or John Kennedy's inaugural address. Speakers from the Toastmasters Club, other speaking clubs, or debating teams may also be willing to provide examples of effective speeches, and 4-H clubs often hold speech tournaments.

    Use the branching diagram for a bulletin board design as you develop your speech unit, adding each characteristic to the design as it is discussed in class.

    RESULT—Understanding characteristics of a good speech can improve both speaking skills and appreciation of good speeches.

WRITING EXTENSION

- **Describe the characteristics of a good speech.**
- **Select one characteristic of a good speech and tell how you have used it effectively.**

THINKING ABOUT THINKING

- **How can using the branching diagram help you understand the characteristics of a good speech?**
- **How did using the diagram help you organize thoughts before you started to write?**
- **Suggest another lesson where a branching diagram would help you understand what you are learning.**
- **Which characteristics of a good speech do you already demonstrate well? Which do you expect to improve upon?**
- **When you become aware that you are demonstrating one of these speaking characteristics, what are you thinking that makes it work well? What are you thinking that allows you to adjust what you are doing to keep that high level of performance?**
- **How can the branching diagram help you organize the content of a speech?**

- **Design another diagram that will help you organize a speech.**
- **How does being aware of the characteristics of a good speech change the way that you listen to a speech?**

SIMILAR LANGUAGE ARTS LESSONS

- To illustrate part/whole relationships: parts of a book, parts of a letter, languages contributing to contemporary English.
- To illustrate class/subclass relationships: figures of speech, parts of speech, types of literature, types of books, or reference sources.
- To illustrate a topic sentence and its supporting statements.
- To illustrate headings and subheadings in an outline.
- To depict family relationships of rulers, mythological characters, or characters in literature or dramas.

DESCRIBING A GOOD SPEECH

DIRECTIONS: Read the passage carefully to identify characteristics of a good speech. Record the information on the graphic organizer as you read.

If you want to give a good speech, there are several tips you can keep in mind to help you. A good speech should be about an interesting subject. It should be organized so that the listener can understand it and spoken in a pleasant way. **Selection of the subject** depends upon the speaker's knowledge, how well it fits the audience, and what the audience wants to know.

Use your own **knowledge** to select your speech topic. Include personal experiences, special training, beliefs, or hobbies. Your speech should fit the **background** of the audience. If people listen to ideas they don't understand or already know well, they get bored. Your speech will be more interesting if you use **information** you researched yourself. These might include surveys, observations, research, and interviews that you have conducted on the subject.

The **organization** of the speech allows the listener to follow the speaker's ideas, holds his interest in the topic, and provides him enough information to understand the topic reasonably well. To understand a topic, a thoughtful listener expects you to use good **supporting materials**: background information, examples, quotations, and statistics.

A good speech is well planned; it starts and ends well. A **good start** often contains stories or jokes. Use humor to interest the audience in your topic. For an **effective ending**, review the main ideas of the speech and seek the agreement of the audience.

The way ideas are presented may be as important to the audience as the information being shared. **Presentation** includes the qualities of speaking, as well as the speaker's appearance. Your **voice** should be loud enough to be heard easily, but not shrill. Your pronunciation should be understandable to the audience. Don't speak too slowly or too fast.

Your **general appearance** (grooming, selection of clothes, alertness) is important to your listener's acceptance of the speech. Your **body language** tells your audience how you really feel about speaking or the subject of the speech. "Connect" with the audience by eye contact and facial expressions. A speaker who "won't look the audience in the eye" doesn't seem interested in the audience's understanding or point of view about the subject. Your posture tells the audience how comfortable you are with them and with the subject. Standing rigidly, slouching to one side, leaning on a chair, or rocking back and forth suggests that you are uneasy about the presentation.

Use **gestures** to add to the meaning of the speech. Natural motions emphasize your words and improve the effectiveness of the speech. Fast or jerky motions, however, startle the audience and make them uncomfortable about what is being said. No motion at all suggests that you are not interested in the subject. This reduces the speech's impact on the audience.

Listen to effective speakers to see how these ideas can work together in a good speech. Keep these tips in mind when you give a speech.

DESCRIBING A GOOD SPEECH

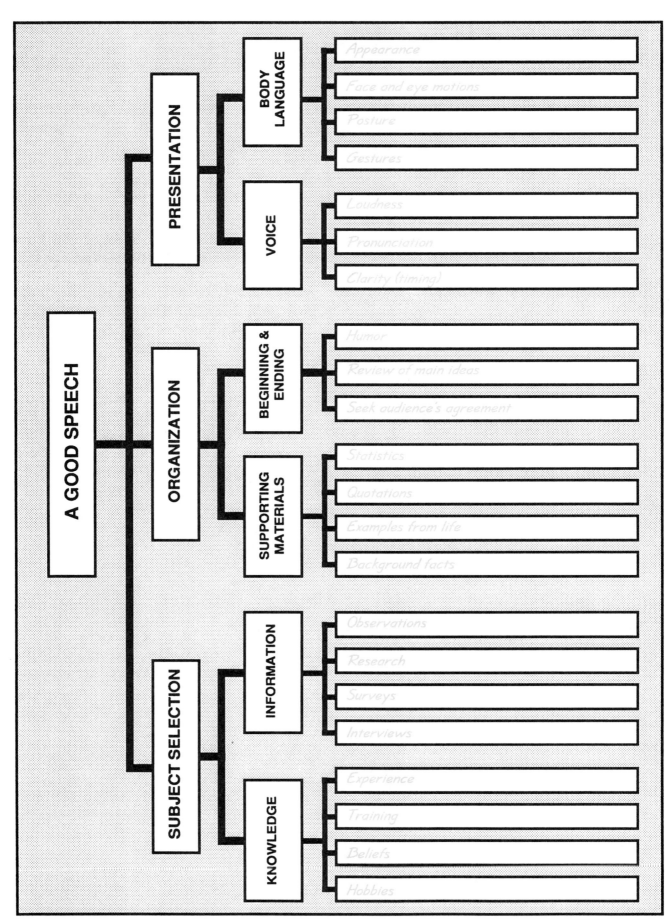

A GOOD SPEECH

PRESENTATION
- BODY LANGUAGE
  - Appearance
  - Face and eye motions
  - Posture
  - Gestures
- VOICE
  - Loudness
  - Pronunciation
  - Clarity (timing)

ORGANIZATION
- BEGINNING & ENDING
  - Humor
  - Review of main ideas
  - Seek audience's agreement
- SUPPORTING MATERIALS
  - Statistics
  - Quotations
  - Examples from life
  - Background facts

SUBJECT SELECTION
- INFORMATION
  - Observations
  - Research
  - Surveys
  - Interviews
- KNOWLEDGE
  - Experience
  - Training
  - Beliefs
  - Hobbies

SPEECH ANALYSIS MATRIX

CHARACTERISTIC	APPLICATION	RATING

Subject Selection
KNOWLEDGE
    hobbies
    beliefs
    training
    experience		

INFORMATION
    interviews
    surveys
    research
    observation		

Logical Organization
SUPPORTING MATERIALS
    background facts
    examples
    quotations
    statistics		

PLANNING
    good start
    effective ending		

Presentation
VOICE
    clarity
    pronounciation
    loudness		

BODY LANGUAGE
    gestures
    posture
    eye contact
    appearance		

DESCRIBING CLASS RELATIONSHIPS

THINKING SKILL: Verbal classifications

CONTENT OBJECTIVE: Students will represent class relationships between words using a number of diagrams. *NOTE: The following three lessons introduce elementary students to class logic. For most classes one lesson per class session is recommended to allow sufficient class discussion.*

DISCUSSION: TECHNIQUE—Use a transparency of the diagram sheet to mark answers as students state the relationships shown in the various diagrams.

DIALOGUE—(FAMILY RELATIONSHIPS) Ask students to use the terms *all, no, not,* and *some* to express the class relationships shown in the first diagram. (This exercise refers only to human mothers; if students refer to animal mothers, accept that comment.)
All **fathers are parents.** *All* **mothers are parents.** *Not all* **parents are mothers.** *Not all* **parents are fathers.** *No* **mothers are fathers.** *No* **fathers are mothers.** *All* **mothers are women.** *All* **female teachers are women.** *Some* **female teachers are mothers.** *Some* **mothers are female teachers.** *Some* **female teachers are not mothers.** *Some* **mothers are not female teachers.** *All* **women are people.** *All* **mothers are people.** *All* **mothers are women.** *Not all* **women are mothers.** *Not all* **people are women.**

Use sentences like the following in the second exercise.
Some living things are plants. Some living things are animals. Some living things are not plants. Some living things are not animals. Some plants are ferns. Some plants are trees. Some plants are not ferns. Some plants are not trees. No plants are animals. No animals are plants. Some animals are vertebrates. Some animals are not vertebrates. Some animals are invertebrates. Some animals are not invertebrates. No vertebrate is an invertebrate. No invertebrate is a vertebrate.

(VEHICLES) Use the terms *all, no, not,* and *some* to describe class relationships.
All planes are vehicles. Some vehicles are planes. Some vehicles are not planes. All jets are planes. Some planes are not jets. Some planes are jets. All cars are vehicles. Some vehicles are cars. Some vehicles are not cars. All station wagons are cars. Some cars are station wagons. Some cars are not station wagons. All convertibles are cars. Some cars are convertibles. Some cars are not convertibles.

(CLASS ARGUMENTS) You may use the "target" diagram to introduce class arguments.
Are the following arguments necessarily true? "All station wagons are cars. All cars are vehicles. Therefore, all station wagons are vehicles." Is there any place on the diagram in which a station wagon is not also a vehicle? (No. The conclusion is true.) **"All cars are vehicles. All planes are vehicles. Therefore, all cars are planes." Is there any place on the diagram in which all cars are inside the region for planes.** (No cars are planes. Therefore, the conclusion is false.) **"All station wagons are cars. All convertibles are cars. All cars are vehicles. Therefore, all station wagons and convertibles are vehicles." Is there any place on the diagram in which a station wagon or a convertible is not also a vehicle?** (No. The conclusion is true.) **"All station wagons are cars. All convertibles are cars. All cars are vehicles. Therefore, all station wagons are convertibles." Is there any place on the diagram in which all station wagons are inside the region for convertibles?** (No station wagons are convertibles. Therefore, the conclusion is false.) **"All jets are planes. All planes are vehicles. All cars are vehicles. Therefore, some jets are cars." Is there any place on the diagram in which any jets are inside the region for cars?** (No jets are cars. Therefore, the conclusion is false.)

(STUDENTS, SOCCER PLAYERS, AND BAND MEMBERS) You may use the terms *and* and *not* to describe the following relationships. In common English usage, *but* is used in place of *and* to indicate that one does one thing and (but) not another.

> **Anita is a girl who plays soccer and is in the band.**
> **Hannah is a girl who does not play soccer and is not in the band.**
> **Jessica is a girl who plays soccer, but is not in the band.**
> **Justo is a boy who plays soccer and is in the band.**
> **Lorenzo is a boy who plays in the band, but does not play soccer.**
> **Marco is a boy who does not play soccer and is not in the band.**
> **Yolanda is a girl who is in the band, but does not play soccer.**

RESULT—One can clarify the meaning of statements containing *all*, *no*, *not*, and *some* by picturing their classes. One can depict class arguments to illustrate whether or not conclusions can be verified.

WRITING EXTENSION
• **Describe how logic circles can be used to verify conclusions.**

THINKING ABOUT THINKING
• **Why is it important to understand the effect of *some*, *all*, and *no* on the meaning of the sentence? Identify a situation in which someone was misled because that person was confused or mistaken about *some*, *all*, and *no*. How could you eliminate that confusion?**

• **How do the logic circles help you clarify how things are related? What is it about the use of the circles that helps you keep track of whether *some*, *all*, and *no* statements apply to the objects or ideas you are describing?**

• **Identify other objects or ideas that would be easier to understand if their relationships were described this way?**

• **How do the logic circles help you determine whether a conclusion is valid?**

• **Design another graphic organizer that would help you picture *some*, *all*, and *no* statements.**

SIMILAR LANGUAGE ARTS LESSONS
• To illustrate class relationships in an article, report, or presentation.
• To interpret claims in advertising, television, magazines, and newspapers.

DESCRIBING CLASS RELATIONSHIPS

DIRECTIONS: Draw a line from each group of words to the diagram which pictures the correct relationship. Use the abbreviations in the parentheses to label the diagrams. One example is shown.

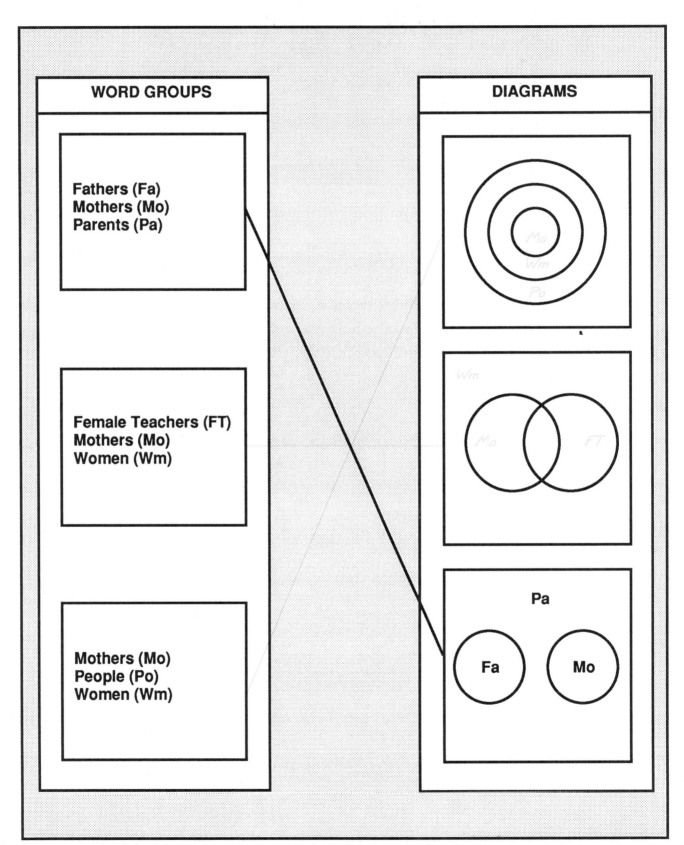

DESCRIBING CLASS RELATIONSHIPS

DIRECTIONS: **Label the following classification diagram to show the relationship among these terms.**

animals, ferns, invertebrates, living things, plants, trees, vertebrates

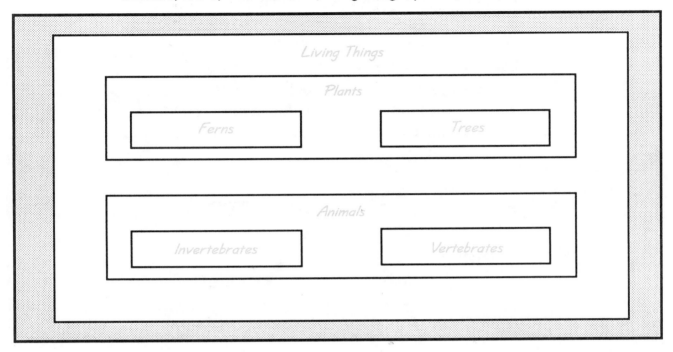

DIRECTIONS: **Label the following classification diagram to show the relationship among these words.**

cars, convertibles, jets, planes, station wagons, vehicles

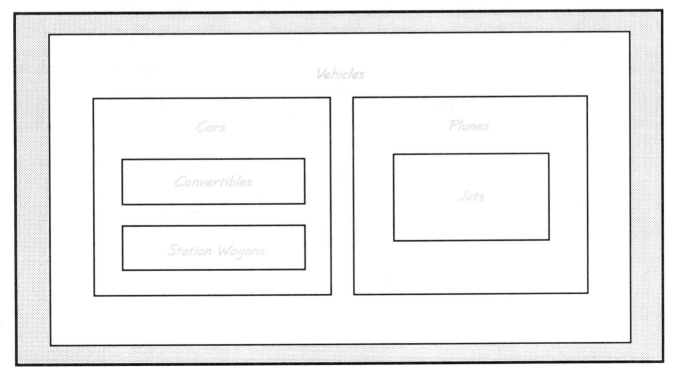

DESCRIBING CLASS RELATIONSHIPS

DIRECTIONS: Label the graph below to describe each of the following individuals.

Anita plays soccer and is in the band.
Hannah does not play soccer and is not in the band.
Jessica plays soccer, but is not in the band.
Justo plays soccer and is in the band.
Lorenzo does not play soccer, but is in the band.
Marco plays soccer, but is not in the band.
Yolanda does not play soccer, but is in the band.

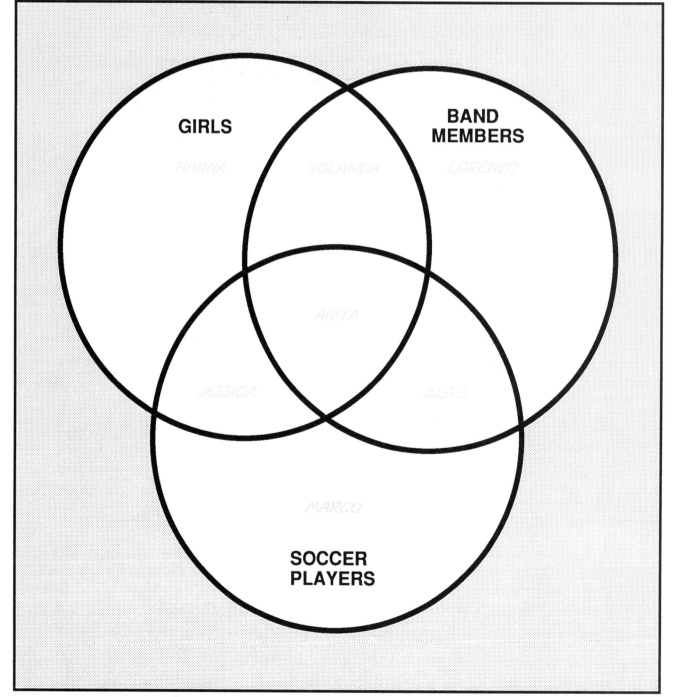

MAIN IDEA AND SUPPORTING DETAILS

THINKING SKILL: Identifying main idea and supporting details

CONTENT OBJECTIVE: Students will use an arch diagram to identify the main idea and supporting details in a given passage.

DISCUSSION: TECHNIQUE—Use a transparency of the graphic to record student responses regarding the main idea and supporting details. In introducing this lesson, it is important to familiarize students with the structure of expository paragraphs. The main idea is the over-arching theme that connects the details together. It is a generalization which summarizes the effect of the many details. The main idea "grows out of" and "rests upon" details which support it. Supporting details clarify, illustrate, provide examples for, or justify the main idea.

Ask students to identify which sentence in the paragraph is the general statement for which the other sentences are examples or reasons. Students should write the main idea in the arch of the diagram, turn the paper sideways and write the sentences providing details and examples in each column.

DIALOGUE—Explain the key characteristics of a main idea.

A main idea statement should have four characteristics:
  1. **It states a point of view.**
  2. **It should be limited to a single idea.**
  3. **It should contain specific language.**
  4. **It should be limited to the supporting details given in the paragraph or passage.**

For this and other main idea/supporting detail lessons, direct students to highlight the main idea with a pink pen and supporting details with a yellow pen. Use the same process as students review each other's expository writing. If a student's writing contains few pink marks, then the student is writing facts with little, if any, interpretation or organization. If a student's writing contains few yellow marks, then the student is expressing generalizations without adequate supporting information. This color coding alerts students to omissions or superfluous sentences in their writing.

To design a bulletin board which illustrates this principle, assemble passages from magazines or newspapers and photo-enlarge them to an appropriate size. Display the passages containing main ideas and supporting details on a bulletin board using the same color coding.

If you wish to illustrate economics principles regarding factors which influence the price of goods, ask students to compare the price per gallon of maple syrup with other food commodities sold by the gallon. They should recognize that the cost of goods includes time, labor, and resource availability. Students should also be familiar with the time and labor involved in processing other food products that are sold by the gallon (milk, orange juice, ice cream, or soft drinks). Students should recognize how much more time- and labor-intensive the production of maple syrup is when compared to the processing of other food products.

RESULT—When reading critically, identify the main idea and the details that support it. The main idea should interpret or summarize what the details mean and should not express more than the details support.

WRITING EXTENSION

• **Select a passage and describe how the main idea fulfills the four characteristics. How do the details in the passage clarify, illustrate, provide examples for, or justify the main idea?**

- **How do you distinguish the main idea from supporting details?**
- **Why must a main idea be limited to a single point of view or idea, contain specific language, and be limited by the information provided in the supporting details?**

THINKING ABOUT THINKING

- **How did using the graphic organizer help you picture the main idea in this passage?**
- **How would using the graphic organizer help you organize your thoughts before you begin to write?**
- **Why is it important to recognize the main idea and supporting details in a passage?**
- **How can recognizing the main idea and supporting details help you understand more clearly what you read?**
- **Design another graphic organizer to illustrate a main idea and supporting details.**
- **Why is it important that supporting details clarify, illustrate, provide examples for, or justify the main idea?**

SIMILAR LANGUAGE ARTS LESSONS

- To illustrate many consequences of a turning point in a narrative or biography.
- To illustrate headings and subheadings in an outline.
- To illustrate assumptions, reasons, and conclusions in arguments.

MAIN IDEA AND SUPPORTING DETAILS

DIRECTIONS: The main idea sentence is a general statement that "grows out of" and "rests upon" the other sentences in the paragraph. It should state a point of view, be limited to a single idea and to the supporting details in the paragraph or passage, and should contain specific language. Supporting details explain, illustrate, provide examples for, or justify the main idea.

Read the following passage carefully. In the "arch" of the diagram, write a main idea statement which summarizes the meaning of the other sentences in the paragraph. Turn the paper sideways and write one supporting detail sentence in each column.

MAKING MAPLE SYRUP

In 1985 a gallon of maple syrup cost about $20.00. The time, labor, and materials required to make pure maple syrup explains its high price. It takes four maple trees six weeks to produce enough sap to make a gallon of maple syrup.

Gathering crews must collect the sap daily during March and April. Forty gallons of sap must be boiled down to make one gallon of syrup. A four-foot log has to be sawed, split, dried, and burned to boil the sap long enough to make one gallon of syrup.

A firing crew must keep the fire going twenty-four hours a day. Other crews must sterilize, filter, grade, and pack each gallon of syrup.

MAIN IDEA AND SUPPORTING DETAILS

"Maple syrup is expensive because
of the time, labor, and materials needed to make it."

MAIN IDEA

TIME: it takes two months for maple trees to produce the
sap and for crews to gather and boil it.

LABOR: workers must gather the sap, chop firewood,
boil the sap, and package the syrup.

MATERIALS: large quantities of firewood are used
to boil forty gallons of sap, which makes one gallon of
maple syrup.

**SUPPORTING
DETAIL**

**SUPPORTING
DETAIL**

**SUPPORTING
DETAIL**

MAKING MAPLE SYRUP

TOPIC

WHAT IS A DEBATE?

THINKING SKILL: Compare and contrast, decision making

CONTENT OBJECTIVE: Students will use a compare and contrast graph to differentiate among a debate, a disagreement, and a discussion. *Note: This lesson is the first in a series of activities to introduce students to the debate process: **the nature of a debate, the steps in preparing a debate, stating debate issues, and organizing arguments.** Several ORGANIZING THINKING lessons can be used to prepare students for debate: recognizing assumptions, reasons, and conclusions; recognizing the main idea and supporting details; writing a compare/contrast essay; and describing speeches.*

DISCUSSION: TECHNIQUE—The purpose of this lesson is to distinguish between different situations in which people express what they believe to be true. People express their ideas in order to arrive at a better understanding of the truth, to assist others who question the same issue, or to persuade people who hold a differing view. The purpose, form, and degree of agreement varies in these types of expression. This lesson involves comparing and contrasting debate, disagreement, and discussion with regard to their purpose, structure, preparation, number of participants, nature of conflict or agreement, and conclusion.

DIALOGUE—Help students discuss how debate differs from other forms of discussion.

What is the purpose of debate? Debates encourage thoughtful people to examine carefully prepared arguments on each side of a significant issue. The purpose of debate is to help the listener make a reasoned decision about a complex issue. This lesson introduces formal debate, although you may also wish to expose students to other debate types, such as broad-topic debates, political debates, and courtroom proceedings.

How is a debate different from the kind of persuasion one may find in letters to the editor, commercials, sermons, monologues, or news articles? In what situations are each of these techniques used? Why are they persuasive? Usually other forms of persuasion offer only one side of an issue. They do not present an opportunity for people who hold different views to challenge claims or evidence point-by-point. These forms of persuasion are not interactive. Debate requires that every claim be supported by evidence and answered by opponents, who also present evidence to support their beliefs.

Why is a debate a stronger, more reasoned type of persuasion than the forms we have just discussed? Debate offers balanced arguments in which the claims, evidence, and discussion time are relatively controlled. Those who listen to a debate expect that arguments will be supported by evidence and challenged by speakers who do not share that point of view. Evidence is limited to certain types of support (facts, statistics, examples, opinions of experts). Less objective appeals (unsupported claims, emotional language, or advertising techniques) may be used in other forms of persuasion, but are not appropriate for debate.

How does a debate model the process of critical thinking? In what settings is formal debate commonly practiced? Why? Emphasize the value of debate in protecting the rights of individuals or companies by fair decisions in court. Emphasize the value of debate in governmental hearings, in making and interpreting laws, and in understanding candidates' qualifications and their positions on significant issues.

What is the difference between "presenting" an argument and "having" an argument? Argument in the casual sense means a disagreement, which may or may not be presented in a reasoned manner. In describing logical reasoning, an argument is a conclusion that is supported by reasons. Debaters "present" an argument; they don't "have" an argument.

Why don't people examine more issues by debate? Are debates what people commonly believe that they are? People sometimes believe that debates are either "no-holds-barred" confrontations or that they "prove" or "decide" an issue. Neither is the case. A debate is a balanced, well-organized, and researched presentation of opposing viewpoints about an issue. The team that offers the stronger debate has not necessarily "proven" its argument, but it has given the listener better information regarding its position on the issue.

It may help students to review a video tape of a debate. Discuss how debates are different in form and purpose from other types of persuasion or discussion. If possible, attend and analyze a court proceeding or government hearing. Encourage students to attend high school debate competitions. There may also be other resources in your community, such as the League of Women Voters, Toastmasters, or 4-H speech tournaments. Discuss the significance of famous debates in history.

RESULT—Although people express their beliefs in debates, disagreements, and discussions, these forms of discussion differ with regard to their purpose, preparation, number of participants, structure, nature of conflict or agreement, and conclusion. We listen to a debate differently than we listen to other kinds of discussion or persuasion.

WRITING EXTENSION
- **How are a discussion and a debate alike? How are they different?**
- **How are a discussion and a disagreement alike? How are they different?**
- **How are a debate and a disagreement alike? How are they different?**
- **How is a debate different from a talk show or other forms of persuasion?**

THINKING ABOUT THINKING
- **How does using the compare and contrast graph help you distinguish among different forms of persuasion? How does it help you stick to what is important?**
- **How does being able to tell the difference between a discussion, a debate, and a disagreement make a difference in the way you pay attention to speeches on television? To talk shows? To conversations among your friends or family? To commercials?**
- **Design another graph that will help you distinguish different forms of persuasion.**
- **How does the active thinking that one would use in listening to a debate differ from the kind of thinking one would do in listening to a story or a commercial?**
- **Which technique (discussion, disagreement, or debate) can best help you decide what to believe or do? Does that choice vary in different situations? Explain why.**

SIMILAR LANGUAGE ARTS LESSONS
- To depict arguments and generalizations in newspaper or television news reporting, short stories, novels, or plays.

WHAT IS A DEBATE?

DIRECTIONS: Read this passage carefully to identify the similarities and differences among discussions, disagreements, and debates. There are three graphs to compare and contrast these types of discussions. Use the first to record how a discussion and a debate are alike and different. The second is to record the similarities and differences between a discussion and an argument. The third graph may be used to record how a debate and an argument are alike and different.

For the next several lessons you will learn how to prepare a special kind of discussion called a debate. Not all discussions are debates. **A discussion is the process by which people talk together to solve a problem or to improve their understanding.** People discuss things to find acceptable solutions, to share information, or to clarify their own thoughts about a concept.

In a discussion, people express what they believe to be true. They will usually give reasons why they believe what they do, and they may or may not express a conclusion about their beliefs. A discussion may express the same or opposing views, but it is informal and largely unplanned. Discussions may be between two people or among large numbers of people.

Not all discussions are disagreements. **A discussion becomes a disagreement when there is a basic difference between the speakers' conclusions, reasons, or assumptions.** In a disagreement people express what they believe to be true and often give reasons why they believe what they do. People usually have arrived at a conclusion that conflicts with someone else's view. The number of people on either side of the disagreement

will vary and will not necessarily be equal. While disagreements may occur between friends, usually there is at least some minor conflict. A disagreement is usually informal and unprepared.

A debate is the process by which individuals take opposing viewpoints in order to persuade others of their particular position. There are many kinds of debates: political debates, balanced discussions about broad topics, team debates, and courtroom debates. Teams debate about a **proposition** which contains suggestions for a change in an action, conclusion, or decision.

A team debate consists of two teams of speakers who present carefully planned and researched speeches containing claims and evidence to support their particular point of view. Debaters do not really clarify ideas or convince each other. They present their arguments to an audience whose agreement they hope to win. Debaters state positions, which they express as true, and take turns explaining why their position is correct and why the opponent's position is wrong. An equal number of people take turns speaking in a given order for an equal period of time.

DISCUSSION AND DISAGREEMENT

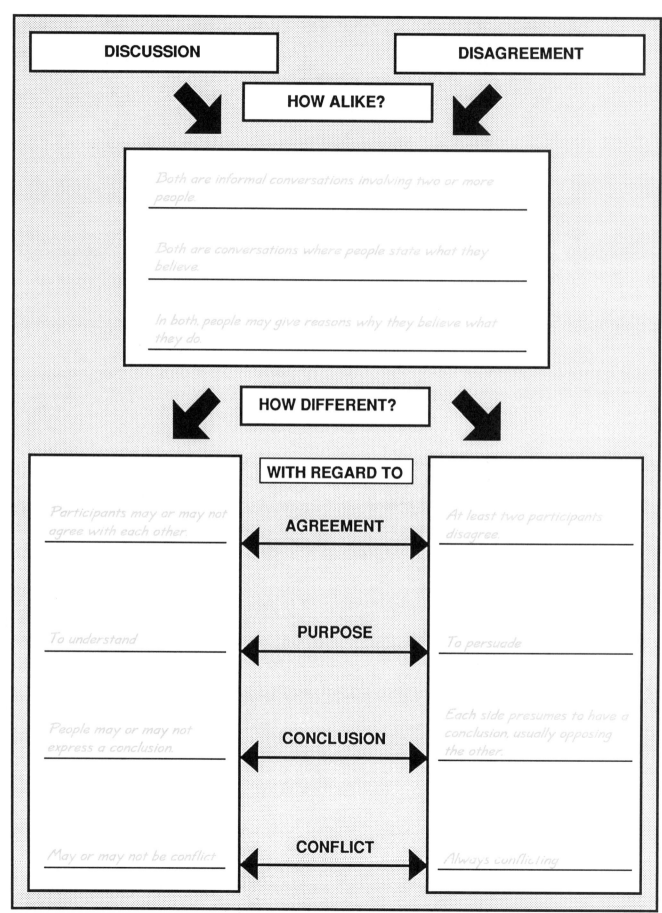

DISCUSSION

DISAGREEMENT

HOW ALIKE?

Both are informal conversations involving two or more people.

Both are conversations where people state what they believe.

In both, people may give reasons why they believe what they do.

HOW DIFFERENT?

WITH REGARD TO

AGREEMENT

Participants may or may not agree with each other.

At least two participants disagree.

PURPOSE

To understand

To persuade

CONCLUSION

People may or may not express a conclusion.

Each side presumes to have a conclusion, usually opposing the other.

CONFLICT

May or may not be conflict

Always conflicting

DISAGREEMENT AND DEBATE

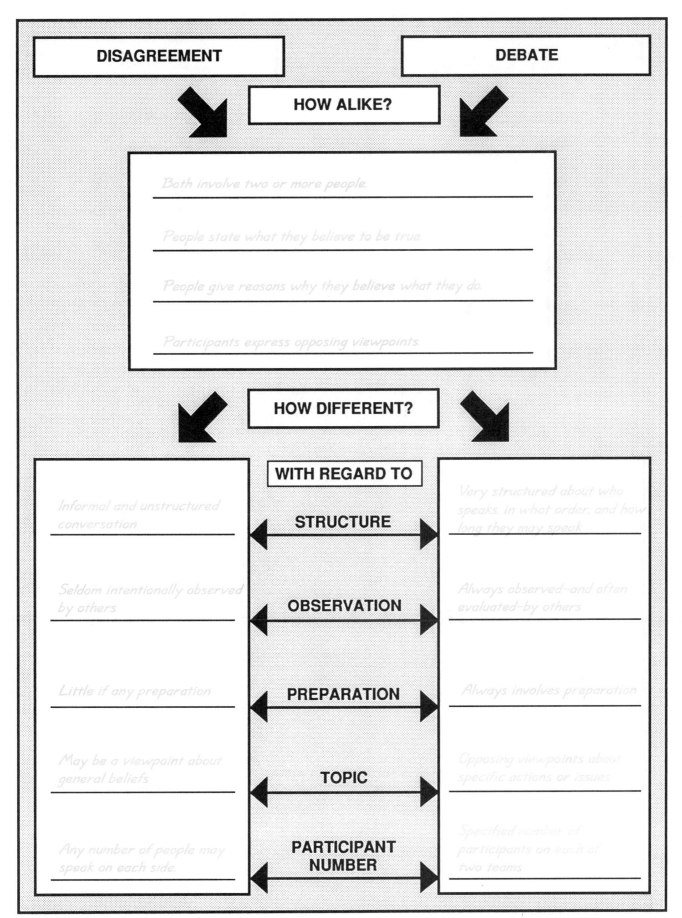

DISAGREEMENT

DEBATE

HOW ALIKE?

Both involve two or more people.

People state what they believe to be true.

People give reasons why they believe what they do.

Participants express opposing viewpoints.

HOW DIFFERENT?

WITH REGARD TO

DISAGREEMENT		DEBATE
Informal and unstructured conversation	**STRUCTURE**	Very structured about who speaks, in what order, and how long they may speak
Seldom intentionally observed by others	**OBSERVATION**	Always observed—and often evaluated—by others
Little if any preparation	**PREPARATION**	Always involves preparation
May be a viewpoint about general beliefs	**TOPIC**	Opposing viewpoints about specific actions or issues
Any number of people may speak on each side.	**PARTICIPANT NUMBER**	Specified number of participants on each of two teams

DISCUSSION AND DEBATE

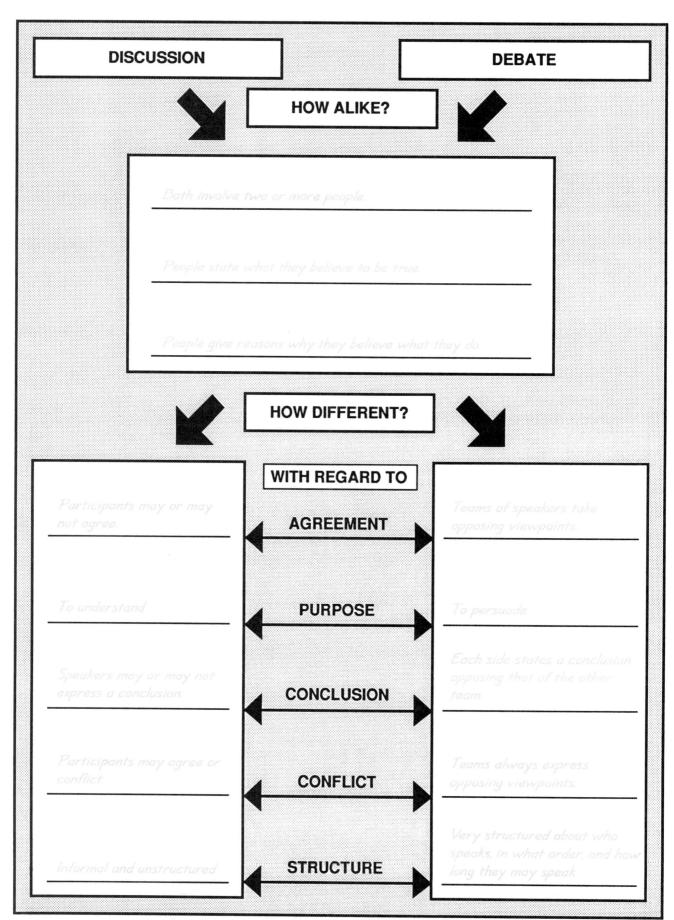

DISCUSSION

DEBATE

HOW ALIKE?

Both involve two or more people.

People state what they believe to be true.

People give reasons why they believe what they do.

HOW DIFFERENT?

WITH REGARD TO

DISCUSSION		DEBATE
Participants may or may not agree.	**AGREEMENT**	Teams of speakers take opposing viewpoints.
To understand	**PURPOSE**	To persuade
Speakers may or may not express a conclusion.	**CONCLUSION**	Each side states a conclusion opposing that of the other team.
Participants may agree or conflict.	**CONFLICT**	Teams always express opposing viewpoints.
Informal and unstructured	**STRUCTURE**	Very structured about who speaks, in what order, and how long they may speak

PREPARING A DEBATE

THINKING SKILL: Verbal sequences

OBJECTIVE: Students will use the flowchart to identify steps in preparing a debate. *Note: This is the second in a series of activities designed to introduce students to the debate process. The sequence of activities includes:* **the steps in preparing a debate, stating debate issues, organizing arguments, and the debate process.**

DISCUSSION: TECHNIQUE—This exercise features the steps in the debate process. The completed *flowchart* shows when the two teams should work together and when they should plan separately. Teachers may use the flowchart to monitor each team's preparations and to confirm with students that each step has been completed properly.

Confirm that students understand that the term "argument" in this lesson, and the remaining ones in this series, refers to a reason to agree with the team's position. Each reason includes a claim that must be supported by evidence. Each argument is usually challenged by the opposing team. Correct any misconception of the casual definition of an "argument" as a disagreement or confrontation.

There are two ways to conduct this lesson: by inference or by critical reading. In the first option, students infer the order of the steps in preparing a debate. Reproduce the matrix which contains the steps of a debate in random order. Students should cut apart the boxes, rearrange them in the order they think appropriate, and record the order on the flowchart. The second option involves careful reading of an explanatory passage and completing the flowchart from the information in the passage.

This lesson introduces the planning of a debate and serves as a guide for managing students' preparation of classroom debates. The directions in this series provide for debate teams of four students each. Additional students may be added to any team to assure that all students in the class have the opportunity to debate. Another variation allows two debaters plus the chairperson on each team, since the chairperson gives the summary argument. This provides for two three-student teams for each debate proposition. Only one debate should be held on the same proposition, since students will lose interest in hearing the same reasons often and will imitate previous teams. Allow some class time each day, for at least a week, for research and team planning for the debate.

DIALOGUE— Encourage students to explain their sequences.

Why is it important for debate preparation to follow a particular order? How does the order of preparing a team debate resemble the process of deciding what to believe? How does it resemble the process of writing a research paper?

Team debate involves presenting opposing viewpoints regarding a proposition (a decision, conclusion, or plan). Students are accustomed to hearing arguments about broad topics. It is important that they distinguish between discussing a topic and debating a proposition.

What is the difference between a topic and a proposition? What is the difference between discussing a topic and debating a proposition? What is significant in selecting a topic? What decisions do you make to narrow a topic to decide on a proposition?

Confirm that students recognize the difference between talking about a topic and debating a proposition. Students must narrow the topic to a statement of an action or decision and then must agree on the wording of the proposition. They must confirm definitions of terms and clarify that both teams understand the action or decision in the proposition.

RESULT—The steps in preparing a debate involve making decisions on clarifying the key issues of large topics, recognizing significant arguments on both sides, researching one's position, and presenting it to an audience.

WRITING EXTENSION

- **Why is it important to prepare for a debate?**
- **Why is it important for each team to follow the steps in preparing the debate?**
- **What is the difference between a proposition and discussing a broad topic?**

THINKING ABOUT THINKING

- **What clues or patterns did you use to determine the order in preparing a debate?**
- **How does knowing the order help you plan your debate?**
- **How is this order similar to other activities involving critical thinking?**
- **How is your thinking different in planning a debate than it is in discussing a broad topic?**
- **Design another graph that would help you prepare a debate.**

SIMILAR LANGUAGE ARTS LESSONS

- To depict the steps in information retrieval or following directions.
- To depict study skills procedures, independent study, or the preparation of a term paper.
- To depict the plot of a narrative.
- To depict steps in a demonstration speech or for assembly instructions.

PREPARING A DEBATE

DIRECTIONS: As you read the passage carefully, record the steps in preparing a debate.

A **debate** is the process by which speakers explain opposing viewpoints in order to persuade others of their particular position. A debate centers on a **proposition** which contains suggestions for a change in an action or decision. A proposition may also be a set of rules or may refer to a particular plan.

First, the class selects an interesting debate topic. The topic should contain decisions, actions, or plans that people do not agree on. Select one decision or action, then state a proposition: an action that should be taken or a decision that should be changed. Some research will be necessary to learn enough about the subject to prepare sound arguments about it.

Next is the selection of teams to speak for or against the proposition. The team that argues for the proposition is called the **affirmative team.** The team that argues against the proposition is called the **negative team.** Appoint two people to the affirmative team and two people to the negative team.

Teams do not share information with each other. Each should select a chairperson to take notes, conduct the rehearsals, and state the team's position in the last argument.

As a team, list the arguments that your team could offer. Predict also the arguments that you expect the other team to raise. Select your team's four strongest arguments and what you believe will be your opponent's four strongest arguments. List each team's arguments from weakest to strongest.

Assign each team member to give two of your team's arguments and to argue against two of the opposing arguments. Research the issue and prepare your arguments. Prepare the summary statement, in which each team reminds the audience of its arguments and its evidence against the other team's arguments.

Rehearse the debate, giving your team's arguments in order from the least important to the most important. Each team member will argue against two of your opponents' arguments. The other team should not hear your rehearsal or your evidence.

On the day of the debate, line up chairs for the two teams and conduct the debate in front of your audience. The audience will record the arguments and decide which team presented the stronger case and most effectively answered the arguments presented by the opposing team.

PREPARING A DEBATE

ASSIGN SPEAKERS

REHEARSE DEBATE

AUDIENCE RECORDS ARGUMENTS

RESEARCH AND PREPARE EVIDENCE

AUDIENCE DECIDES HOW WELL EACH TEAM PRESENTED ITS CASE AND ANSWERED THE OTHER

SELECT STRONGEST ARGUMENTS

CONDUCT DEBATE

SELECT TEAM CHAIRPERSON

LIST ARGUMENTS

SELECT A TOPIC

PREDICT OPPONENT'S ARGUMENTS

SELECT TEAMS

PREPARE SUMMARY STATEMENT

STATE THE PROPOSITION

PREPARING A DEBATE

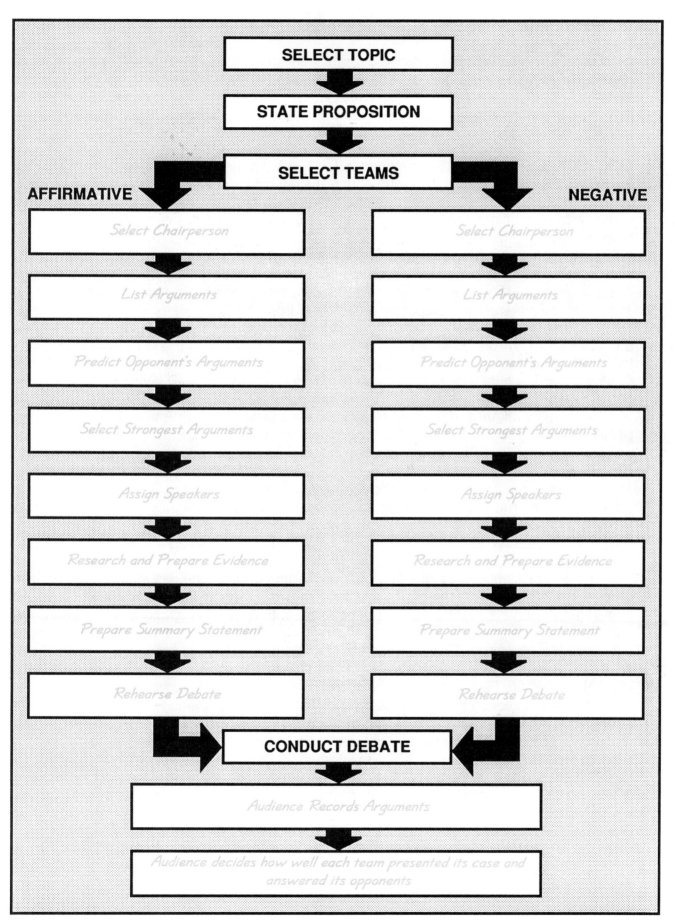

SELECT TOPIC

STATE PROPOSITION

SELECT TEAMS

AFFIRMATIVE

NEGATIVE

Select Chairperson

List Arguments

Predict Opponent's Arguments

Select Strongest Arguments

Assign Speakers

Research and Prepare Evidence

Prepare Summary Statement

Rehearse Debate

Select Chairperson

List Arguments

Predict Opponent's Arguments

Select Strongest Arguments

Assign Speakers

Research and Prepare Evidence

Prepare Summary Statement

Rehearse Debate

CONDUCT DEBATE

Audience Records Arguments

Audience decides how well each team presented its case and answered its opponents

© 1990 MIDWEST PUBLICATIONS • CRITICAL THINKING PRESS & SOFTWARE • P. O. Box 448, Pacific Grove, CA 93950

STATING DEBATE ISSUES

THINKING SKILL: Predicting and prioritizing arguments.

CONTENT OBJECTIVE: Students will use the matrix graph to identify affirmative and negative arguments in preparing a debate. Students will use the transitive order graph to prioritize arguments from weakest to strongest. *Note: This lesson is the third in a series of activities to introduce students to the debate process:* **the nature of a debate, steps in preparing a debate, stating debate issues, and organizing arguments.**

DISCUSSION: TECHNIQUE—In planning the team debate, students raise arguments for the team position and predict the arguments of the opposing team. From this list of arguments, students will research evidence to support their own positions and to answer what they expect will be arguments for the opposing team. Selecting debate topics makes the difference between a lively, interesting exercise and an uninteresting assignment. Topics should be sufficiently controversial to offer contrasting views, but should not be unduly sensitive. Since student research is a key objective of this process, the information should be adequately available in school library resources, or from outside agencies in the immediate community. The class will generate the proposition statement from the topic.

The first step in stating debate issues is a **statement of the proposition. This states the action that should be taken or the decision that should be made or changed**. Don't try to debate about something that should not happen. It becomes too confusing for both the debaters and the audience to remember which side is negative and which is affirmative in debating a negative proposition.

Remind the affirmative team that it is their responsibility to **define the key words in the proposition statement**. They must demonstrate that the **existing situation is not satisfactory** and that **the recommended course of action is workable, practical, and desirable.**

The team that argues against the proposition is called the **negative team.** This team must remember that they are arguing against the change and that they only need to create a reasonable doubt that another action, decision, or plan is better than the existing one. They are not required to put forward an alternative. Avoid getting into a "compare two plans" discussion.

In the first step each team "brainstorms" arguments presented for and against the proposition. It is important that students thoroughly examine the issue, since each team will challenge the other's arguments. If an opponent puts forward a strong argument that the first team has not prepared for, then it is caught by surprise and cannot offer evidence to challenge the argument. This planning step should take a full one-hour class period. Each student will need a copy of the Debate Planning Chart 1. Each team should have one team copy of the Debate Planning Chart 1 to compile the group list of possible arguments.

From the collection of arguments on this matrix planning sheet, the team will select its strongest arguments and predict which of the opposing team's arguments are likely to be the strongest. Students may need some research time on the proposition prior to this step in order to know enough about the issue to suggest arguments.

The second step in the process involves each team prioritizing its arguments and those it expects the opponents will raise. Students will use a transitive order graph to list the strongest four arguments on each side of the issue from least to most significant. Duplicate one copy of the graph for each team member (for individual ranking) and one copy for each team (to record the group decision). Each team should take 30 to 45 minutes to prioritize their arguments and their opponent's arguments. Each team will then designate a member to argue for two of its strongest arguments and to challenge the proposed arguments of the other team. One team member may research one opposing argument, but all members should know all challenge arguments.

DIALOGUE—Help each team examine its arguments for and against its position. Discuss why each team prioritized the arguments as it did.

What did you look for in deciding which was the strongest or weakest argument? Since you are limited to four arguments, what was the basis for your eliminating the other arguments? What makes an argument strong or weak?

Appeal to the audience, the amount of evidence to support it, the significance of the argument to the issue, the practicality of the argument, the clarity of the argument.

RESULT—Debate issues should be stated as an affirmative proposition recommending a change in policy, plan, decision, or method. Considering significant arguments for and against one's own position allows each team the opportunity to research and prepare one's thoughts for presentation. Prioritizing arguments from the weakest to the strongest allows listeners to hear the most persuasive claims last.

WRITING EXTENSION
- **Why is it clearer to debate about an action or decision than it is to argue about a general topic?**
- **Why is it important to predict the opposing team's arguments and to gather evidence that challenges it?**

THINKING ABOUT THINKING
- **How does the preparation of a debate demonstrate critical thinking?**
- **How does the preparation of a debate help you better understand how you reason through a problem or issue?**
- **Why does a debate team present its strongest arguments last?**
- **How does the matrix graph help your team prepare its debate?**
- **How does the transitive order graph help your team prepare its debate?**
- **Design another graph that will help you state a debate issue.**

SIMILAR LANGUAGE ARTS LESSONS
- Comparing points of view, decisions, reasons, or influences between characters in plays, novels, and short stories.
- Comparing advantages and disadvantages of an action, a resource, or a method.

STATING DEBATE ISSUES

DIRECTIONS: Use the matrix graph to list the arguments that you expect each side would raise about the proposition. After everyone has listed arguments, record all the arguments suggested by your team and the arguments you expect the other team will use.

As a team, use the transitive order graph to select the strongest arguments for each side. Decide which team member will present your team's arguments and will research for the evidence which each of you may use to answer the opposing team's arguments.

The first step in stating debate issues is a **statement of the proposition.** The proposition states **the action that should be taken or the decision that should be changed**. Always word the proposition as something which "should" happen or be decided.

The team that argues for the proposition is called the **affirmative team**. It is this team's responsibility to be sure that **the key words in the proposition statement are defined**. Through their arguments they must demonstrate that the **existing situation is not satisfactory** and that **another course of action is workable, practical, and desirable.**

The team that argues against the proposition is called the **negative team.** The negative team must remember that they are arguing against the change. They only need to create a reasonable doubt that the plan suggested in the proposition should be adopted. They are not required to put forward an alternative. Avoid getting into a "compare two plans" discussion.

"Brainstorm" arguments that might be presented for and against the proposition. Do not discuss your planning with the other team. Identify **all the arguments that your team and the other team could raise about the proposition**. Select the four strongest arguments and mark them on the Debate Planning Chart 1 from the strongest (1) to the weakest (4) of the selected arguments.

In a debate, you state your strongest argument last because you want the audience to remember it. Each argument you give should be stronger than the previous one, building to your most persuasive argument. This means that you must rearrange your selected arguments in order from the weakest to the strongest. Use the Significance of Arguments Graph to list your arguments from the weakest to the strongest.

To predict your opponent's arguments, repeat this process for the list of arguments which you expect the other team to give. On Debate Planning Chart 1, number the four strongest arguments in order from 1 to 4. Use the Significance of Arguments Graph to reverse the order of significance from weakest to strongest.

Now that you have predicted the order in which each team will present its arguments, decide which member of your team will present each of your team's arguments. Use the priority listing of the arguments from weakest to strongest to determine the speech order.

DEBATE PLANNING CHART 1
STATING DEBATE ISSUES

PROPOSITION:

POSSIBLE AFFIRMATIVE ARGUMENTS	POSSIBLE NEGATIVE ARGUMENTS

DEBATE PLANNING CHART 1

DEBATE PLANNING CHART 2
SIGNIFICANCE OF ARGUMENTS

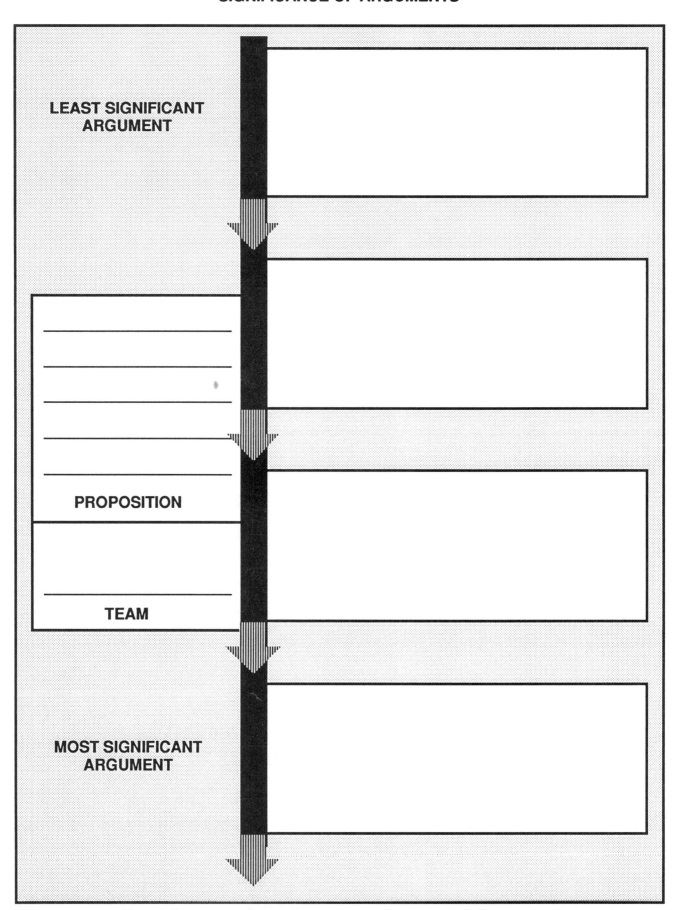

LEAST SIGNIFICANT ARGUMENT

PROPOSITION

TEAM

MOST SIGNIFICANT ARGUMENT

ORGANIZING ARGUMENTS

THINKING SKILL: Recognizing claims and evidence, recognizing strong and weak arguments, summarizing

CONTENT OBJECTIVE: Students will use the matrix graph to organize constructive, challenge, and summary arguments in preparing a debate. *Note:This is the fourth in a series of activities for introducing students to the debate process:* **the nature of a debate, steps in preparing a debate, stating debate issues, claims and evidence, and organizing arguments.**

DISCUSSION: TECHNIQUE—Students are now ready to organize their arguments, to predict opponents' arguments and to plan challenge arguments. In this lesson the matrix graph is used to record claims and evidence and to predict opponents' arguments in a debate. Key concepts in this lesson include:

1. An argument includes claims and evidence.
2. He who claims must prove.
3. The divisions of debate include position arguments, challenge arguments, and summary arguments.
4. Evidence includes facts, statistics, examples, and the opinions of experts.

The concept of an argument (claims and evidence) is a basic one in critical thinking and is not limited to debate. Familiarize students with the common expression of arguments in advertising and personal opinions by asking students to bring in examples of arguments (ads, bumper strips, newspaper stories, letters to the editor). Highlight the claim with a pink pen and the evidence with a yellow pen. Identify and label the type of evidence (facts, statistics, examples, and the opinions of experts).

Assemble an "argument bulletin board" using the same color coding. Select an issue of local or national importance. Then, using news magazines or local newspapers, reconstruct arguments for and against the issue. Include evidence and challenge arguments.

Student research is a key objective in organizing evidence. The facts, statistics, examples, and opinions of experts for students' debate topics should be adequately available in school library resources or from outside agencies in the immediate community.

Encourage students to recognize the importance of thoroughness in examining the issue. Since each team must prepare challenges for the other side's arguments, challenge speakers must have evidence to support their claims rejecting the opponents' position.

The summary arguments highlight each team's arguments and its challenge of the opponent's position. The whole team prepares the summary statement, which should be concise, strong, and clearly presented, since the summary is the last argument the audience will hear.

You can see at a glance how well the team is organizing its presentation by checking each team's debate planning chart. Reproduce the Debate Planning Chart 2 for each member of the class to record the claims and evidence in each argument as the debate is given. This will allow you and the audience to determine which claims were not challenged or whether teams mistakenly offer new arguments or unrelated evidence in challenge arguments.

DIALOGUE—Help the students discuss the significance of claims and evidence in an argument.

Why it is important that, if someone claims something is true, then he or she must offer evidence to support it? How do facts contribute to the strength of an argument? How do statistics contribute to the strength of an argument? What is the difference between a fact and a statistic? How does an example contribute to the strength of an

argument? **How does an opinion of an expert contribute to the strength of an argument? What does one have to know about an expert if that person's opinion is to be used as evidence? What makes evidence persuasive?** (Its reliability, objectivity, relative freedom from bias, and relevance.)

RESULT—Since the goal of debate is to persuade listeners by offering sound arguments, each position must be supported by evidence.

WRITING EXTENSION
- **In what circumstances is it important that one should provide evidence for what he claims? Explain.**
- **Why it is important in a debate that one must provide evidence.**
- **Describe each type of evidence (facts, statistics, examples, and expert opinion) and why each is important in defending a claim.**
- **Why are challenge arguments important in a debate?**
- **Why are summary arguments important in a debate?**
- **Why would a debate be weakened if a team did not plan for the other team's arguments?**

THINKING ABOUT THINKING
- **How does information from the lesson help you think differently about what you read and what you see on television?**
- **As you listen for claims and evidence, what questions would you ask yourself to evaluate the argument?**
- **Suggest another situation in which you believe that listening to arguments for and against an issue will help you understand it better?**
- **Identify situations in which you recognize that an argument (claims and evidence) is presented. Do you listen differently to an argument now than you did before this lesson? Explain.**
- **How does knowing about arguments (claims and evidence) help you understand how people try to persuade each other?**
- **How did the use of the graphic organizer help you understand the debate process?**
- **How did the use of the graphic organizer help you organize your team's speeches?**

SIMILAR LANGUAGE ARTS LESSONS
- To depict arguments and generalizations in newspaper or television reporting of the news, in the plots of short stories, novels, or plays.

ORGANIZING ARGUMENTS

DIRECTIONS: Use the matrix graph to list the arguments that you expect each side to raise about the proposition. In each argument box, write phrases which briefly state the claims and evidence for arguments. In the summary argument box, write a few words to represent the arguments and significant evidence offered by your team's position.

Now you are ready to plan your arguments. Each argument contains two parts: the **claim** and the **evidence**. The claim is **the stated reason to support your position.**

Evidence includes **the facts, statistics, examples, or opinions of experts that support your claim**. A **fact** is a description of an event or object free of interpretation or judgment. A **statistic** is the mathematical reporting of facts (averages, number, size, etc. usually reported on graphs, charts or tables). Statistics may be the result of your surveys or the reports of research agencies. An **example** is a sample which accurately represents the larger group from which it came. An **opinion** is a judgment based on facts; it is only as good as the background of the expert and the reliability of the facts or observations on which it is based.

In the first part of the debate, each team presents **position arguments.** Each speaker should state his or her claims (reasons) and offer evidence to support each claim. Find strong evidence (facts, statistics, examples, and expert opinions) to support your reasons. Be sure to write out the complete evidence statements on index cards and to name the source of your evidence in your speech. Use the *matrix graph* (Debate Planning Chart 3) to record just a phrase to remind you what you will say and what you think the other team will argue to challenge your position.

In the second part of the debate, each team presents **challenge arguments**. Challenge arguments offer claims (reasons) and evidence (facts, statistics, examples, and expert opinions) to reject the other team's arguments. Each team tries to predict the reasons and evidence that the other team will use to challenge their argument. NEVER PRESENT NEW POSITION ARGUMENTS OR NEW EVIDENCE FOR YOUR POSITION DURING CHALLENGE ARGUMENTS. This is the time you offer evidence to reject what your opponents have said in their position or to challenge the arguments they have made.

The third part of the debate is the **summary statement**, which is made for the team by the chairperson. The summary reminds the audience of your arguments and your challenge of the other team's arguments.

Use Chart 3 to record your arguments and what you think the opposing team's arguments will be. Find evidence to challenge your opponents' arguments. Try to guess what your opponents will use to challenge your arguments and find the strongest evidence in support of your position to use in your position arguments.

The completed chart should include your team's position arguments, what you expect may be the other team's challenge of your arguments, what you think the other team's arguments will be, and how your team will challenge their position.

DEBATE PLANNING CHART 3
ORGANIZING ARGUMENTS AND CHALLENGES

PROPOSITION:

	AFFIRMATIVE		NEGATIVE	
POSITION	CHALLENGE	POSITION	CHALLENGE	
CLAIM:		CLAIM:		
EVIDENCE:		EVIDENCE:		
CLAIM:		CLAIM:		
EVIDENCE:		EVIDENCE:		
CLAIM:		CLAIM:		
EVIDENCE:		EVIDENCE:		
CLAIM:		CLAIM:		
EVIDENCE:		EVIDENCE:		
SUMMARY ARGUMENT:		SUMMARY ARGUMENT:		

CHAPTER 3–WRITING

WRITING DEFINITIONS (Central Idea Graph)		**WRITING AN AUTOBIOGRAPHY** (Interval Graph)
	REPORT WRITING: ORGANIZING THE TASKS (Flowchart)	
DESCRIPTIVE WRITING: A COMMON OBJECT (Central Idea Graph)		**EXPOSITORY WRITING: A HISTORICAL EVENT** (Central Idea Graph)
	CREATIVE WRITING: CATS (Web Diagram)	
REPORT WRITING: NARROWING A TOPIC (Central Idea Graph)		**ESSAY WRITING: COMPARE AND CONTRAST** (Compare and Contrast Diagram)

WRITING DEFINITIONS

THINKING SKILL: Verbal classification

CONTENT OBJECTIVE: Students will use a central idea graph to analyze and write clear, concise definitions. They will identify the category to which a term belongs and the characteristic that makes it different from others in its class. *Note: This lesson is a writing extension of the concepts featured in the science lesson **Amphibians and Reptiles** and may be used as a follow-up activity for that lesson.*

DISCUSSION : TECHNIQUE—Use a central idea graph to record student suggestions of qualifiers that distinguish one term from others in the same category. After students have read the description of an appropriate definition and the passage about amphibians and reptiles, they "picture" the information on the graph and organize concise, accurate definitions to describe each term. Draw the central idea graph on the chalkboard, on two sheets of chart paper, or project it from a transparency. Use the graph to record class discussion of the characteristics of amphibians and reptiles. Students then apply the information from the graph to write appropriate definitions.

DIALOGUE—Consider the strong correlation between clear conceptualization and clear expression of that concept by being able to state appropriate definitions.

Why is it important to name the category that something belongs to when you are defining it? Can you think of a time that you misunderstood what somebody was explaining because they used the word in one category and you thought of it in another? For example, "turkey" is a slang term; a person who understands the term literally would think of an animal instead of a person. "Class" is another term which can be used to convey several categories: a group of students, a set that a group of objects belongs to, or a standard of social refinement.

Can you think of a time that you misunderstood what someone was explaining because the idea or thing they were talking about was unclear in your mind? For example, if a teacher uses the term "denominator" and a student does not know which part of the fraction the denominator refers to, the student's understanding of the addition of fractions may become confused.

Why is it important to name the characteristics that make something different from things that are similar to it? Can you think of a time that you couldn't remember clearly what something is because you kept confusing it with other things or ideas in that category? How might a person confuse a reptile with an amphibian if the distinctions were not clear? Students sometimes confuse reptiles and amphibians. They are both cold-blooded vertebrates that lay eggs. Some appear shiny, "slimy," and wet. Although students are usually more familiar with reptiles, they sometimes mistakenly think that the skin of snakes is wet. Key distinctions between amphibians and reptiles include metamorphosis, respiration, and habitat.

Encourage students to use the above criteria for oral and written definitions in all academic areas. Prompt them to include the category and the qualifiers for each term you ask them to define. Emphasize the category and the qualifiers in each definition that you give. Model and insist upon appropriate definitions in explanations, class discussion, oral and written reports, and examinations. Allow ample time for students to explain significant characteristics and to give examples, especially those statements which include "some," "all," and "no."

RESULT—When defining an object, organism, person, process, or idea, one should express clearly the category to which it belongs and the qualifiers that make it different from other things in that category.

WRITING EXTENSION

• Apply this model to definition questions on unit tests.

THINKING ABOUT THINKING

• How does knowing how to write appropriate definitions help you give clearer answers in class and on tests?

• How does this model for writing definitions help you to be sure that you really know what something is?

• How does using the graphic organizer help you write better definitions?

• How does the model definition help you write better definitions?

• How does listening for the category and qualifiers help you understand more clearly what is being said?

• How is knowing the category and characteristics of an idea being discussed a sign of clear thinking?

• Why is it important to know accurate terms for the category to which something belongs? When might you need to know the appropriate category to find what you need? Examples include preparing outlines; finding items in a supermarket, hardware store, mall directory, telephone book yellow pages, or classified ads; using the Dewey Decimal System to locate sources in a library; locating related topics in books, reference sources, or card catalogs; differentiating among tools or utensils for specific jobs.

SIMILAR LANGUAGE ARTS LESSONS

• To organize and write descriptive paragraphs.

• To organize topic or passage outlines.

• To locate related topics in books, reference sources, or card catalogs.

• To describe main ideas and supporting details when preparing speeches or papers.

• To define terms when preparing speeches, papers, or debates.

• To describe artifacts, museum displays, performances, and television shows.

• To describe scientific phenomena, organisms, geographic features, physical science concepts, and astronomical terms.

• To illustrate part/whole relationships: parts of a book, parts of a letter, languages contributing to contemporary English.

WRITING DEFINITIONS

DIRECTIONS: Read the first passage to be sure that you know what the definition of a term should contain. Next read the information about amphibians and reptiles. Identify the category and the characteristics that describe each type of animal. Write the significant characteristics of each on the diagrams. Use the definition model to write a clear definition of each.

A **definition** is a clear, exact statement of the meaning of a word. A good definition lets the reader know precisely what the word means and what makes the word different from other similar terms. A complete definition of a noun should contain the **class** to which the person, place, or thing belongs and the **characteristics** that make it different from similar ones.

Suppose you had never seen a bicycle and someone told you, "A bicycle is something that kids ride to school." The last part of the sentence tells you that the bicycle is a vehicle. The definition doesn't give you enough information to distinguish a bicycle from a bus, subway, tractor, or other vehicles which "kids ride to school."

Suppose someone told you that a bicycle has two wheels, handlebars, and is powered by pedaling with one's feet. This definition gives the characteristics of a bicycle, but you may not know what a bicycle really is. It could be a game, an exercise device, or a generator of electricity.

A clear accurate definition must include:
1. the **class** to which something belongs.
2. the **characteristics** that make it different from others in its class.

EXAMPLE: A bicycle is something people ride on (a vehicle) which has two wheels, is steered by handlebars, and is powered by pedaling with the rider's feet.

AMPHIBIANS AND REPTILES

Amphibians are vertebrates which hatch from eggs. An immature amphibian, such as a tadpole, has gills which are replaced by lungs as it becomes an adult. As a tadpole grows lungs and legs, it is ready to leave the water. Amphibians are cold-blooded and must hibernate in cold climates to survive the winter. Most amphibians have moist, soft skins.

Reptiles are also vertebrates which hatch from eggs. The young look almost exactly like their parents and do not change form as they grow up. Reptiles are also cold-blooded and have dry, scaly, or leathery skin.

WRITING DEFINITIONS

DIRECTIONS: Describe an amphibian on one diagram and a reptile on the other. Write one characteristic on each arm of the diagram and write the details about that characteristic in the box. Use the model sentence to write your definition.

BORN

TEMPERATURE

Hatched from eggs

Cold-blooded

AMPHIBIAN

Change form as they develop, growing lungs and legs

Most have soft skin which must be kept moist

CHANGES FORM

SKIN

An amphibian is a _____*vertebrate*_____ **that** _____*is cold-blooded*_____ ,
　　　　　　　　　　　　　(category)　　　　　　　　　　　　　　　　　　　(characteristic)

_____*hatches from eggs*_____ , _____*changes form as it grows up*_____ ,
　　　　　(characteristic)　　　　　　　　　　　　　　　　(characteristic)

and_____*has soft, moist skin*_____ .
　　　　　　　　(characteristic)

BORN

TEMPERATURE

Hatched from eggs

Cold-blooded

REPTILE

Do not change form as they develop

Most have dry, scaly, or leathery skin

CHANGES FORM

SKIN

A reptile is a_____*vertebrate*_____ **that** _____*is cold-blooded*_____ ,
　　　　　　　　　　　(category)　　　　　　　　　　　　　　　　　　　(characteristic)

_____*hatches from eggs*_____ , _____*does not change form as it grows up*_____ ,
　　　　　(characteristic)　　　　　　　　　　　　　　　　(characteristic)

and _____*has dry, scaly, or leathery skin*_____ .
　　　　　　　　(characteristic)

WRITING AN AUTOBIOGRAPHY

THINKING SKILL: Verbal sequences, recognizing chronological order

CONTENT OBJECTIVE: Students will use a parallel time line to write an autobiography.

DISCUSSION: TECHNIQUE—Students use the parallel time line to record their memories and the key events which serve as milestones for keeping track of chronological order. Each student must decide the range of months or years about which he is going to write and label each mark on both time lines with the same time period.

DIALOGUE—Since few youngsters routinely keep journals or diaries, writing an autobiography can provide a valuable record of each child's experiences. Because writing an autobiography draws on the student's own experiences, it conveys the message that each child's experiences are valuable. Encourage this writing assignment as a family history opportunity by suggesting that students involve older family members in recalling the special events in the life of the child. Help the students appreciate the significance of their childhood experiences by sharing special memories from your own childhood.

What do you remember most from when you were a small child? Think of five experiences that seem important to you. What is it about these experiences that make them stand out in your mind?

Students often identify family milestones that were unusually happy or dramatic. They may also relate incidents that seem ordinary but are common experiences that all people share and value. These situations may be funny, may illustrate growing up or some personal insight about people, or may demonstrate healthy solutions to problems we all face.

Encourage students to read biographies, autobiographies, and autobiographical novels and short stories. Laura Ingalls Wilder is an excellent example of an author who used her childhood experiences as a basis for her books. To follow up this lesson with a reading assignment, see the LAURA INGALLS WILDER lesson in Chapter 2.

RESULT—Our memory for details and order tends to be associated with key events. Remembering the order of key events reminds us of experiences which occurred before, during, or after those events. Similarly, vivid details may help us keep track of the order in which things happen. Recording the important events of our lives chronologically produces a valuable record of our growth.

WRITING EXTENSION
- **Describe how a sequence of events in your childhood developed some talent, good habit, or special quality in you.**

THINKING ABOUT THINKING
- **How did using the parallel time line help you remember events in your life?**
- **How did the connection between your experiences and key events help you remember the details and the order in which things happened?**
- **How does the connection between your memories and the key events affect how you feel and what you understand about the experiences?**
- **Suggest another lesson in which showing the time connection would help you understand what you are learning.**
- **How did remembering the time order help you appreciate how far you've come in doing something that is important to you?**
- **How did identifying why your memories were significant help you understand what you consider to be important?**

SIMILAR LANGUAGE ARTS LESSONS
- To record complex plots of novels or plays.
- To record biographical data.
- To record events for writing narratives.
- To organize information for writing letters, term papers, biographies, or plots.

WRITING YOUR AUTOBIOGRAPHY

DIRECTIONS: Use the parallel time line to record the order of important events in your life. Decide the range of months or years you are going to write about, then label each mark on both time lines with the same time period. Record your important memories on the left side of the parallel time line. Record events that happened in your family or in our country on the right side.

Talk to your friends, your parents, and your grandparents and add events which they think are important to the right side of the time line. Fill in as many details and events as you can recall. Use your personal parallel time line to write your autobiography.

When we remember important things that have happened to us, we tend to recall images or feelings. Remembering our experiences in order may be much harder. We tend to connect our memories to other significant events in our family. Remembering the birth of a new baby, moving to a new place, the death of a relative, receiving or loosing a beloved pet, receiving a special present, experiencing something scary, or a special trip may help us recall our experiences before, during, or after the key event. Simply thinking about the key event may help us remember details of other events we are trying to recall.

Your autobiography is a record that may become precious to you years from now, because what you write today may dim in your memory later. Try to remember as many details and events as you can to put on each side of the parallel time line.

WRITING YOUR AUTOBIOGRAPHY

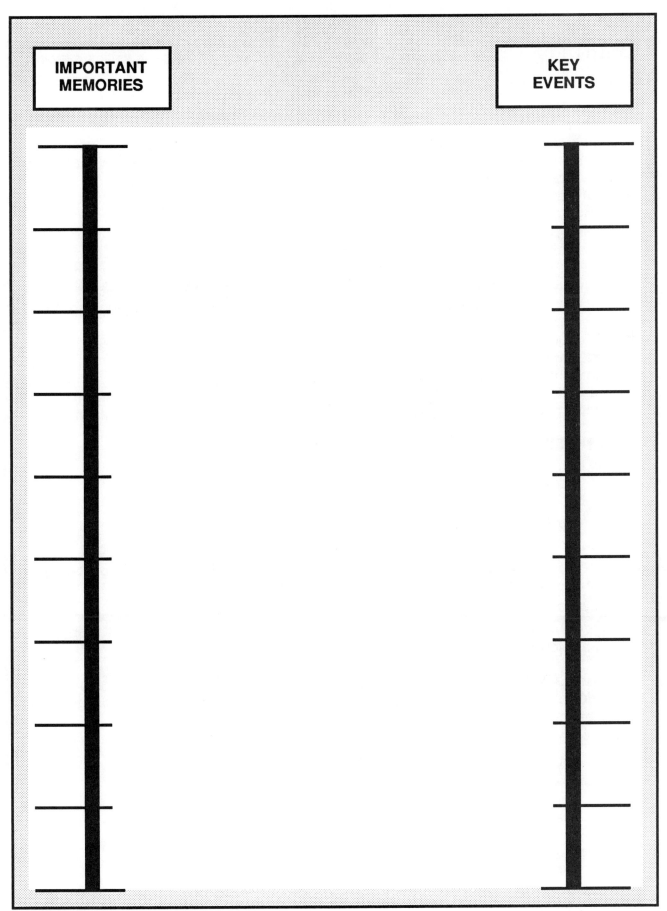

IMPORTANT MEMORIES

KEY EVENTS

REPORT WRITING: ORGANIZING THE TASKS

THINKING SKILL: Verbal sequences, inferential reasoning

CONTENT OBJECTIVE: Students will use a flowchart to identify steps in writing a report.

DISCUSSION: TECHNIQUE—Use a transparency of the graph to record responses as students read the directions for writing a report. Use the steps to record student progress and to monitor students' research and preparation of their papers. The lesson can be conducted by inference or by critical reading.

If the focus is on inferential reasoning, students should arrange in logical order the steps in the process of preparing a report. Reproduce the matrix, which contains the steps, in random order. Direct students to cut apart the boxes and to rearrange them into the order that they think appropriate. Students then record the order on the flowchart to illustrate the process.

In the critical reading option, students read an explanatory passage and then complete the flowchart from information in the passage. You may combine using the paper strips and reading the passage for the students who have difficulty following lengthy directions.

Other graphics may also be useful in helping students organize reports. See the lessons on descriptive writing, expository writing, narrowing a topic, main idea and supporting details, and assumptions, reasons, and conclusions.

DIALOGUE—Encourage students to identify any clues they used to establish the order. The clues will be different if the lesson is taught by arranging the printed steps than if it is taught by identifying the signal-word cues from the passage.

RESULT—Preparing a report is more efficient and effective if carried out according to a sequential plan. The plan follows a logical sequence of decision making and research.

WRITING EXTENSION

• **Why is it important to follow given steps in preparing a report?**

THINKING ABOUT THINKING

• **What clues or patterns did you see that suggested an order to preparing a report?**
• **Is the order similar to any other activities which involve critical thinking?**
• **What do you consider important when selecting a topic? What do you consider important when narrowing a topic?**
• **Design another graphic organizer to help you prepare a report.**
• **Suggest another lesson in which using a flowchart would help you understand what you are learning.**

SIMILAR LANGUAGE ARTS LESSONS

• To depict the steps in instructions, information retrieval, study-skills procedures, or independent study.
• To depict the plot of a story.
• To depict the rules of punctuation, spelling, grammar, or capitalization.

REPORT WRITING: ORGANIZING THE TASKS

DIRECTIONS: Read the following information, then complete the flowchart to show the steps in writing a report.

When you need to write a report about something you are studying, pick a topic that seems interesting to you. Based on what you know now about the subject, decide what you want to find out about that topic. Then go to the library and locate books which give you more information about each idea related to the topic.

As you read, record the important facts and ideas that you expect to include in your paper on index cards. Write the title, the author, and the publisher of each book that you use so that anyone who reads your paper may find out more about the topic.

When you think you have gathered as much information as you need, organize your notes on the index cards in the order in which the facts and ideas should appear in your paper. Arranging the cards this way gives you an idea of how your thoughts will flow, sentence by sentence in each paragraph. You can rearrange the cards easily to make the clearest explanation of your ideas about the topic.

Write the first draft of your paper almost as carefully as you expect the final paper to appear. Leave an extra space between each line of writing. Read the report out loud and listen to yourself. Make changes or corrections by writing them in the extra space between the lines and crossing out the words you want to replace. Discuss your paper with your teacher or with another student. Make any changes which will add to your subject or make it more clear.

Now you are ready to write your final version of the report. Follow your teacher's directions about headings, spacing, references, and appearance.

DISCUSS DRAFT	DECIDE WHAT TO FIND OUT ABOUT THE TOPIC	ORGANIZE NOTES
READ PAPER ALOUD	PICK A TOPIC	WRITE FINAL REPORT
GO TO LIBRARY	WRITE A DRAFT	TAKE NOTES

REPORT WRITING: ORGANIZING THE TASKS

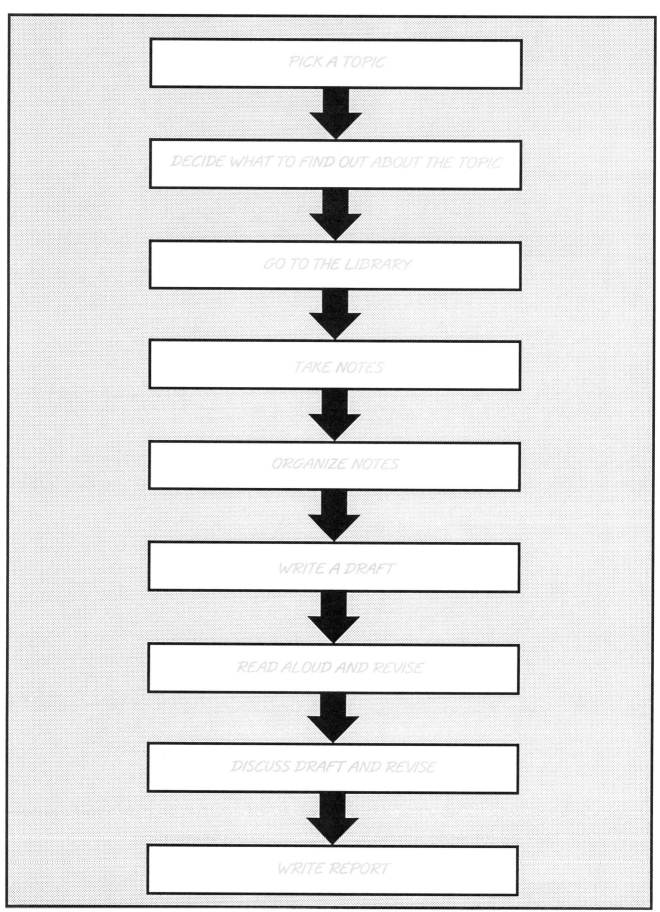

PICK A TOPIC

DECIDE WHAT TO FIND OUT ABOUT THE TOPIC

GO TO THE LIBRARY

TAKE NOTES

ORGANIZE NOTES

WRITE A DRAFT

READ ALOUD AND REVISE

DISCUSS DRAFT AND REVISE

WRITE REPORT

DESCRIPTIVE WRITING: A COMMON OBJECT

THINKING SKILL: Verbal classification, identifying attributes, identifying main idea and supporting details

CONTENT OBJECTIVE: Students will organize information on a central idea graph to help them describe a common object thoroughly. *NOTE: For more "branches," use the diagram in the creative writing lesson. To modify this exercise as a social studies lesson, select a common object from other periods in history and encourage students to describe it thoroughly.*

DISCUSSION: TECHNIQUE—Use a transparency of the central idea graph to record details as students describe a common object. Encourage them to distinguish how one's perception of the same object is different using the various types of graphic organizers.

DIALOGUE—Describing **significant characteristics** of the object gives the reader the best background and overall understanding of it. This technique includes the key concepts in basic description: appearance, purpose, materials, origin, value, and personal significance. Encourage students to research the object using resource books. Good sources include *Why Things Are, What Is It For?, How Things Began* (Simon and Schuster); *Tell Me Why* (Grosset and Dunlop); *Browser's Book of Beginnings* (Ballantine Books).

Describing **details** of the object gives the reader the richest possible image of its appearance. Encourage students to see the object "with new eyes" and to use precise language when describing even the smallest details. Characteristics will include color, shape, size, texture, condition, similes, and metaphors.

Describing the **structure** of the object gives the reader an impression of what it looks like and an idea of how it is manufactured. Encourage students to notice the parts of the object and their function and to use precise language to describe the components. Characteristics will include shape, function, materials, assembly, operation, and manufacture. Helpful resource books include *What's What* (Ballantine Books); *How Do They Do That?* (William Mower Publishers); *How It Works* (Grosset and Dunlop); *How Things Work* (Simon and Schuster); *How To Do Just About Anything* (Reader's Digest).

Describing the **category** of the object gives the reader associations with other similar objects. Encourage your students to notice similar objects and to use precise language in describing the category to which the object belongs, other objects in that same class, and qualifiers that differentiate it from similar items. The object may be in the center of the diagram and subclasses of it on the arms. If the object isn't easily subdivided, it may be a subclass of the larger class. List the object on the arm, the larger class to which it belongs in the center, and other objects that belong in that class on the other arms of the diagram.

When students have completed all four descriptive prewriting diagrams, the writing assignment can proceed two ways. You may ask students to select one of the four types of descriptions which best suits the object and their purpose in writing about it. They would then proceed to write a half-page description of the object. The second variation requires students to use all four diagrams for a detailed, thorough description of the object. This option involves research and results in a longer (one- to two-page) paper.

RESULT—The purpose of describing an object, person, organism, idea, or institution determines which of its characteristics is emphasized.

General understanding—significant characteristics

Mental image—several details

What kind of thing it is—class, subclass, attributes

Structure or operation—components

© 1990 MIDWEST PUBLICATIONS • CRITICAL THINKING PRESS & SOFTWARE • P. O. Box 448, Pacific Grove, CA 93950   137

WRITING EXTENSION

- Select a common object and describe it thoroughly. Can you state the purpose of your description?
- Explain the four ways that something may be described. What characteristics would you include for each way? How is the reader's or listener's understanding different in each type of description?

THINKING ABOUT THINKING

- How did using the diagram help you organize your thoughts about the object?
- How did using all four diagrams help you "see" and describe the object differently?
- Design another diagram that would help you observe or describe an object.
- How does knowing how to describe something help you understand what you observe in science or social studies?
- How has your understanding of describing things changed after doing this lesson?
- What does choosing different ways of describing things tell you about how people perceive (see) the same thing differently?

SIMILAR LANGUAGE ARTS LESSONS

- To organize main ideas and supporting details when preparing speeches or papers.
- To outline classes and subclasses when preparing speeches or papers.
- To describe artifacts, museum displays, performances, or television shows.
- To describe scientific phenomena, organisms, geographic features, physical science concepts, or astronomical terms.
- To illustrate part/whole relationships: parts of a book, parts of a letter, languages contributing to contemporary English.
- To illustrate class/subclass relationships: parts of speech, types of books.
- To illustrate multiple factors leading to a turning point in a narrative or biography. (Each branch should be drawn as an arrow pointing toward the center.)
- To illustrate multiple consequences of a turning point in a narrative or biography. (Each branch should be drawn as an arrow pointing away from the center.)

DESCRIPTIVE WRITING: A COMMON OBJECT

DIRECTIONS: Select an interesting and important object in your house, your school, or your neighborhood. Use each of the diagrams to record all the details and information about the object that would help you explain it to someone who had never seen one.

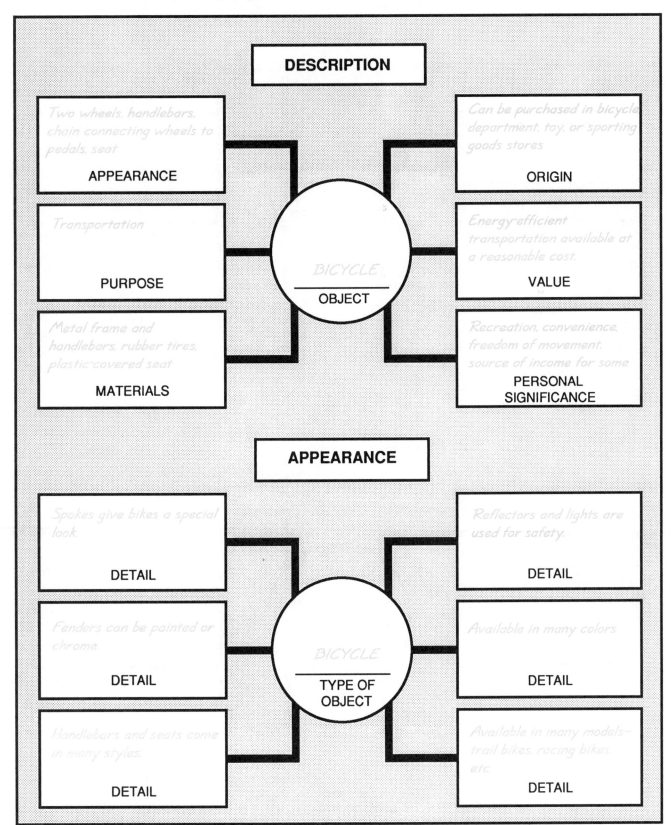

DESCRIPTION

APPEARANCE
Two wheels, handlebars, chain connecting wheels to pedals, seat

PURPOSE
Transportation

MATERIALS
Metal frame and handlebars, rubber tires, plastic-covered seat

BICYCLE
OBJECT

ORIGIN
Can be purchased in bicycle department, toy, or sporting goods stores

VALUE
Energy-efficient transportation available at a reasonable cost.

PERSONAL SIGNIFICANCE
Recreation, convenience, freedom of movement, source of income for some

APPEARANCE

DETAIL
Spokes give bikes a special look

DETAIL
Fenders can be painted or chrome.

DETAIL
Handlebars and seats come in many styles.

BICYCLE
TYPE OF OBJECT

DETAIL
Reflectors and lights are used for safety.

DETAIL
Available in many colors

DETAIL
Available in many models— trail bikes, racing bikes, etc.

DESCRIPTIVE WRITING: A COMMON OBJECT

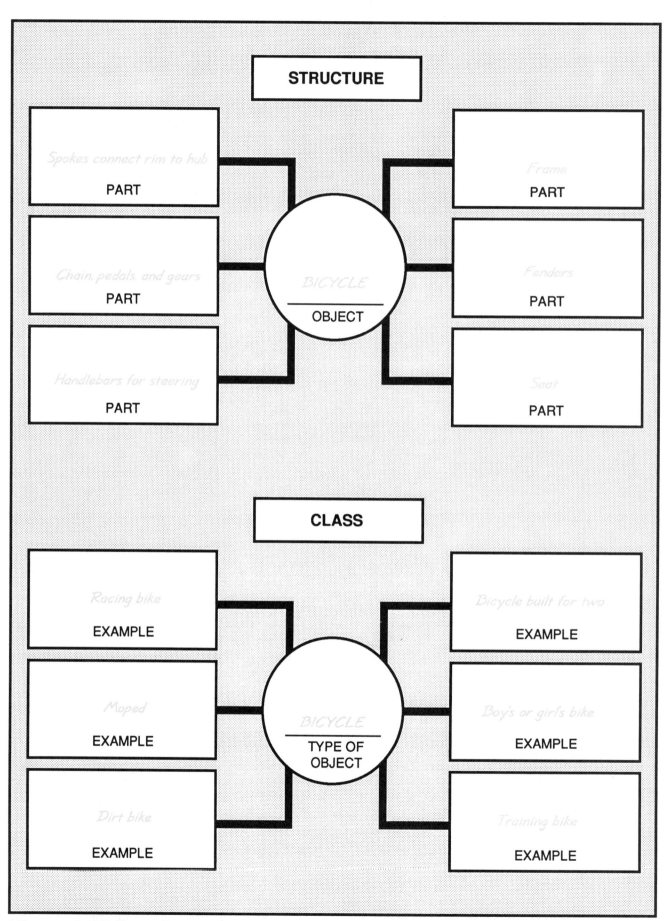

STRUCTURE

Spokes connect rim to hub

PART

Chain, pedals, and gears

PART

Handlebars for steering

PART

BICYCLE

OBJECT

Frame

PART

Fenders

PART

Seat

PART

CLASS

Racing bike

EXAMPLE

Moped

EXAMPLE

Dirt bike

EXAMPLE

BICYCLE

TYPE OF
OBJECT

Bicycle built for two

EXAMPLE

Boy's or girls bike

EXAMPLE

Training bike

EXAMPLE

EXPOSITORY WRITING: A HISTORICAL EVENT

THINKING SKILL: Verbal classification, identifying attributes

CONTENT OBJECTIVE: Students will use the central idea graph to organize information to describe a significant event in history thoroughly.

DISCUSSION: TECHNIQUE—Use a transparency of the central idea graph to help students organize descriptions of a historical event. Show your students that discussing the significant features of an event and the conditions leading to and resulting from it, helps them understand current or past events meaningfully.

To introduce this lesson, reproduce a class set of a current newspaper story. Direct students to use different colored pens to highlight the significant features of the event, the background explaining how the event occurred, and the probable consequences or significance of the event.

You may apply the diagrams to any historical event or you may use the Columbus lesson to introduce the process. The information in the first seven paragraphs explains factors leading to Columbus' crossing the Atlantic Ocean. The next two paragraphs describe the voyage and landing. The last five paragraphs discuss consequences of Columbus' discoveries.

To extend this lesson, encourage students to fill in the diagrams as a critical viewing exercise. Ask students to compare their understanding of an event from the information given in short segments in evening news reports with the extended treatment of the same event in documentary news features or lengthy news accounts, such as the McNeil-Lehrer Report. The more comprehensive the news report is, the more information will be available to fill in the graph. This process may also be used to examine the plot of a story which the class has recently read.

DIALOGUE—Discuss why each element of a journalistic description (*who, what, when, where, why, how*, and *significance*) is important in our understanding of an event.

Why is it important to know who is involved in a news story? What is the effect on the reader if the key people aren't named? (Confusion, uncertainty, mystery.) **In what kind of news stories are the key people not named?** (Crimes involving juveniles, national security, or crimes still under investigation; tragedies when family members have not been notified.)

Why is it important to know the results of an event in a news story? What is the effect on the reader if the results of an event aren't given? Are there some news stories in which the results of an event aren't described? (The results may not be known at the time of the report. Results may be long term and not immediately apparent.)

Also help students discuss the importance of recognizing background situations which contribute to events.

How is our understanding of an event limited if we don't understand what has lead to it? Do factors that lead to an event necessarily cause it to happen? Give some examples of events in which factors leading to it did not cause it to happen. Why is it useful in planning or decision making to recognize what factors contributed to a situation? How is understanding of an event limited by not understanding the consequences of it? Why is it useful in planning or decision making to recognize what factors have contributed to a situation and to predict what the consequences might be?

RESULT—To understand the significance of an event, we must know its key elements, the factors leading to it, and the consequences of it.

WRITING EXTENSION

- Describe a current or historical event. Identify the factors leading to it and its possible consequences.
- Describe a significant event in your family. Identify the factors leading to it and its consequences.
- Describe an important sports event. Identify the factors leading to it and its consequences.

THINKING ABOUT THINKING

- How did using the diagram help you write more clearly?
- Design another diagram to describe an event.
- Suggest another lesson in which describing the key features, the background, and the consequences of an event would help you understand it more fully.
- How does examining events this way change your understanding of them?

SIMILAR LANGUAGE ARTS LESSONS

- To describe the climax or turning point in a story.
- To describe performances, television shows, or current events.
- To describe scientific phenomena and laboratory demonstrations.
- To illustrate part/whole relationships: parts of a book, parts of a letter, the structure of a news story.

DESCRIBING A HISTORICAL EVENT

DIRECTIONS: Read this passage about Columbus' discoveries. Identify the significant information which describes the event, the factors leading to it, and the consequences of it.

COLUMBUS' DISCOVERY OF THE NEW WORLD

How was Columbus able to guide his ship across the Atlantic? Why had other southern European explorers not been able to do it earlier? How did his discoveries change history? Several changes in the 1400's made Columbus' voyage possible and profitable. At that time people in Europe traded with the Middle East, China, and India. Merchants used Middle-Eastern land routes or sea routes through the Indian Ocean to get to China and India. In the 1400's the Arabs took control of both the land routes and the small neck of land between the Mediterranean Sea and the Red Sea entryway to the Indian Ocean. Arab merchants stopped trade completely or required that all goods must be sold or bought through them. This made cotton, silk, spices, perfume, and other needed products very expensive for Europeans.

In 1420 Prince Henry of Portugal started a school to improve sailors' knowledge of maps, ships, sailing, astronomy, geography, and ship building. Prince Henry believed that Europeans could go west across the ocean or south around Africa to get to China. Some of the scientific knowledge developed by this school resulted in better ships, maps, and methods of navigation (steering or guiding a ship by knowing its location and the direction that it must travel to get to its destination).

An explorer crossing the Atlantic Ocean needed strong ships, accurate instruments and maps, and reliable methods of navigating the vast unexplored sea. Until this time, European merchant ships were made of wood and were curved to a point at both ends. They were powered by one square sail supported by a single mast. Now European ship builders began experimenting. They tried using triangular sails, which were lighter and could sail into or with the wind. By flattening the back of the ships, they made them more sturdy and less likely to tip over.

At the time of Columbus, a sailor could use the North Star and a compass to show his direction, but once he was out of the sight of land, he could not tell where he was. Prince Henry's scholars introduced the astrolabe to European sailors. An astrolabe is a device used to measure latitude (the number of degrees above or below the equator).

Many expert map makers went to Portugal to produce better maps for the sailors at Prince Henry's school. They studied Arabic maps and sailors' logbooks to help them fill in details about coastlines they had never seen. Since astrolabes were marked in degrees, map makers began marking their charts in degrees of latitude.

By 1450 scholars knew that the earth was not flat. Previously sailors feared sailing off the end of a flat ocean. In 1492 a young German named Martin Behaim made the first globe—a map shaped like the earth. If the earth was round like a ball, reasoned Columbus and other sailors, Europeans could get to India and China by crossing the Atlantic Ocean. Like other sailors of his time, Columbus thought that the earth was much smaller than it is. He had no idea that the Atlantic Ocean and the Pacific Ocean were not the same body of water and that another continent stood between Europe and China.

King Ferdinand and Queen Isabella had combined their two smaller kingdoms to form the new country of Spain. They recognized that Columbus' plan could bring wealth to their country. First, however, Ferdinand and Isabella had to use their money to gain control of the parts of Spain that were held by Muslims. Columbus waited eight years. When the

Muslims were driven out of Spain in 1492, Ferdinand and Isabella agreed to pay for Columbus' trip.

With three small ships, the *Santa Maria*, the *Pinta*, and the *Niña*, Columbus set sail with a crew of convicts, criminals, and inexperienced sailors. These sailors did not share Columbus' great dream. They were worried about sailing in unknown waters. They wanted to turn back and even plotted to kill Columbus. On October 12, 1492, after 33 days on the open sea, they sighted an island in the Bahamas. Columbus called this island "San Salvador."

Believing that he had reached an island in the Indies near China, Columbus called the native people "Indians." As he explored the nearby islands looking for a continent, one ship was destroyed in a storm. The captain of the second ship refused to go back with Columbus. The little *Nina* headed home to Spain carrying Columbus and the news of his discoveries.

On his second voyage Columbus brought 1500 farmers, craftsmen, soldiers, and priests to settle the islands. Twice more Columbus crossed the ocean. He sailed along the coast of Central and South America and at Panama came within 40 miles of the ocean that stretched to China. Bitter and disgraced at failing to find the mainland of Asia, Columbus died in 1506.

Amerigo Vespucci, an Italian banker who had purchased supplies for Columbus, questioned that the world was as small as Columbus believed. Vespucci reached the islands of the Caribbean in 1494. He made careful notes and drawings of the trees, fruit, flowers, birds, and the appearance and customs of the natives. What he saw did not match travelers' descriptions of China. He reasoned that the large land mass was an unknown continent and called it the New World. North and South America were named for Amerigo Vespucci.

Other Europeans began exploring the New World. In 1497 John Cabot discovered land near Canada. In 1513 Balboa discovered the Pacific Ocean and Ponce de Leon, one of Columbus' officers, discovered Florida. In 1528 Cabeza de Vaca landed on the west coast of Florida, explored the Gulf Coast and Texas, and crossed the American southwest to the Gulf of California.

As early as Columbus' first voyage, native people on the island of Haiti showed explorers trinkets of gold which had come from a large land mass to the west. The crew that Columbus left behind explored for gold. Portuguese sailors visited the coasts of South America and brought back rumors of golden cities hidden in the jungles of the New World. In 1519 Hernando Cortez landed on the coast of Mexico, conquered the Aztec Empire, and sent ships loaded with gold back to Spain. Francisco Pizarro followed rumors of a rich kingdom to the south and, in 1533, captured the capital city of Peru and the Inca treasure houses of gold. In 1540 Coronado set out from the Gulf of California and wandered through the American southwest looking for cities of gold.

Could Columbus have been right? Was it possible to reach China by sailing west? Was there some way to get around the continent that stood between Spain and Asia? In 1519 Ferdinand Magellan traveled west across the Atlantic Ocean and south along the coast of South America. It took more than a year to reach the southern tip of South America. His ships then traveled a thousand miles north along the west coast of South America and crossed the Pacific. In the spring of 1521, they reached the Philippine Islands. A year and a half later, after sailing around the continent of Africa, 18 of the original 280 men returned to the Spanish harbor of Seville. Their voyage had taken over three years and hundreds of lives, but they had proved Columbus' belief that he could reach the East by sailing west.

Columbus had opened the door for Europeans to colonize and develop modern nations in North and South America. European interests in the New World were protected by the Spanish settlement of Saint Augustine in 1565, the English colonies in Jamestown in 1607 and Plymouth in 1620, and the French founding of Quebec in 1607. While he had never found a route to the riches of China, Columbus had opened the New World to those who would follow.

DESCRIBING A HISTORICAL EVENT

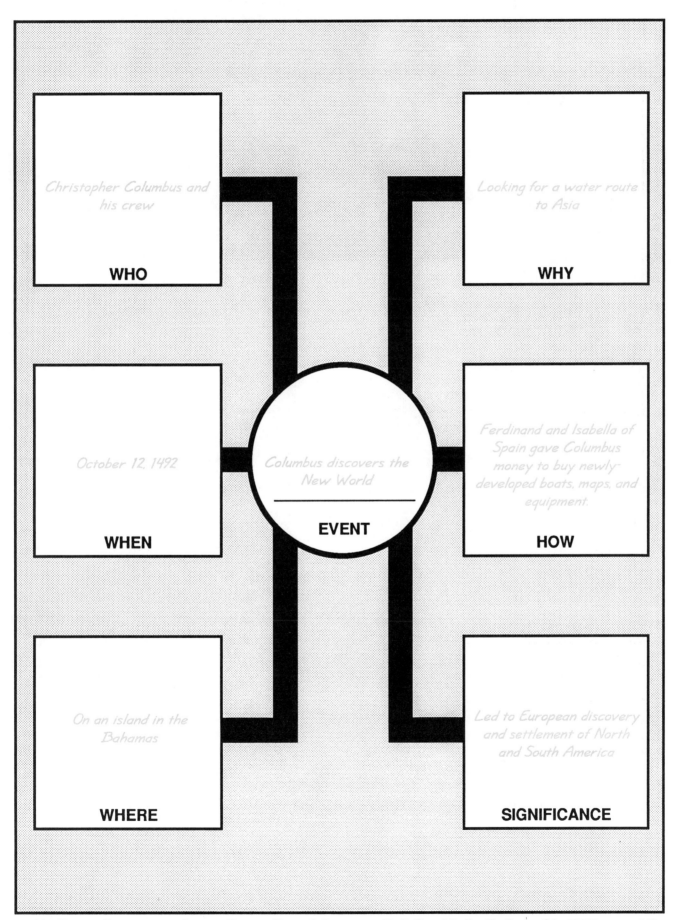

Christopher Columbus and his crew

WHO

Looking for a water route to Asia

WHY

October 12, 1492

WHEN

Columbus discovers the New World

_____

EVENT

Ferdinand and Isabella of Spain gave Columbus money to buy newly-developed boats, maps, and equipment.

HOW

On an island in the Bahamas

WHERE

Led to European discovery and settlement of North and South America

SIGNIFICANCE

DESCRIBING A HISTORICAL EVENT

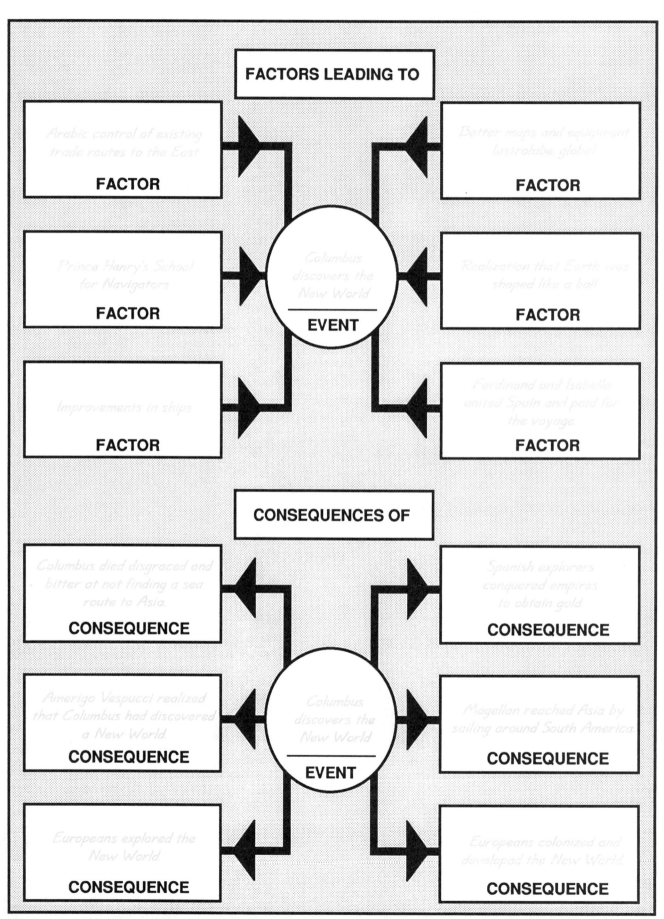

FACTORS LEADING TO

Arabic control of existing trade routes to the East **FACTOR**	*Better maps and equipment (astrolabe, global)* **FACTOR**
Prince Henry's School for Navigators **FACTOR**	*Realization that Earth was shaped like a ball* **FACTOR**
Improvements in ships **FACTOR**	*Ferdinand and Isabella united Spain and paid for the voyage* **FACTOR**

Columbus discovers the New World
___
EVENT

CONSEQUENCES OF

Columbus died disgraced and bitter at not finding a sea route to Asia. **CONSEQUENCE**	*Spanish explorers conquered empires to obtain gold* **CONSEQUENCE**
Amerigo Vespucci realized that Columbus had discovered a New World. **CONSEQUENCE**	*Magellan reached Asia by sailing around South America.* **CONSEQUENCE**
Europeans explored the New World **CONSEQUENCE**	*Europeans colonized and developed the New World* **CONSEQUENCE**

Columbus discovers the New World
___
EVENT

CREATIVE WRITING: CATS

THINKING SKILL: Verbal classification and analogy, identifying attributes and metaphors

CONTENT OBJECTIVE: Students will use the web diagram to form metaphors or similes in creative writing. *NOTE: This lesson extends the concept of metaphor presented in the lesson on "FOG."*

DISCUSSION: TECHNIQUE—To demonstrate the process, write a word associated with "cat" in the box on one of the diagram's arms. In the box on each branch, write a word that you associate with the word in the box. Ask students to continue adding words to arms or branches to produce as many "cat connections" as possible. Students may add additional arms and branches to the diagram to generate more ideas.

After students have completed the diagram individually, compile a class composite "web" of words associated with cat. Because students' ideas will probably exceed the number of branches on the worksheet, a transparency of the diagram will not be adequate for class discussion. Draw a web diagram on the chalkboard and continue to add arms. For the writing exercise students may use their own diagrams or the class composite web for ideas. Ask each student to select three arms and branches and use those associatives on them to write a poem or a paragraph about cats.

Extend this lesson by asking students to find poems, stories, advertisements, and cartoons about cats. Use the web diagram to organize the metaphors and descriptions of cats. Make a bulletin board of "The Cat in Literature and Popular Media." Produce the class composite as a poem, a bulletin board, a mobile, or a slide-tape presentation.

DIALOGUE—Encourage each student who suggests a primary connection to suggest several branches. Allow other students to add branches. Encourage as many students as time and student interest will allow to contribute connections. Not all the associations will result in metaphors. If the concepts of metaphor and simile have been explained in your language arts program, encourage students to select nouns for the boxes on the arms and limit their selections to things or ideas that resemble or can be substituted for cat.

RESULT—Generating connections provides a pool of ideas for creating metaphors or descriptions. Generating many connections produces numerous, interesting descriptions.

WRITING EXTENSION
- Write a poem or essay to describe a cat.

THINKING ABOUT THINKING
- How did using the web diagram help you write about a cat?
- Design another diagram to help you picture connections.
- What did using the web diagram suggest about how people think up new ideas?
- How did using the web diagram help you realize that you know more connections than you thought?
- Suggest another lesson in which using a web diagram would help you understand and write about something that you are learning.

SIMILAR LANGUAGE ARTS LESSONS
- To organize students' creative thinking about images or metaphors for writing speeches, poems, or humor.
- To organize students' creative thinking in order to find creative alternatives or solutions to problems.

CREATIVE WRITING: CATS

DIRECTIONS: In the box on each arm of the circle write a word connected with a cat. In the box on each branch, write another word connected with the word on the arm. Choose the most interesting "cat connections" and use them to write a poem.

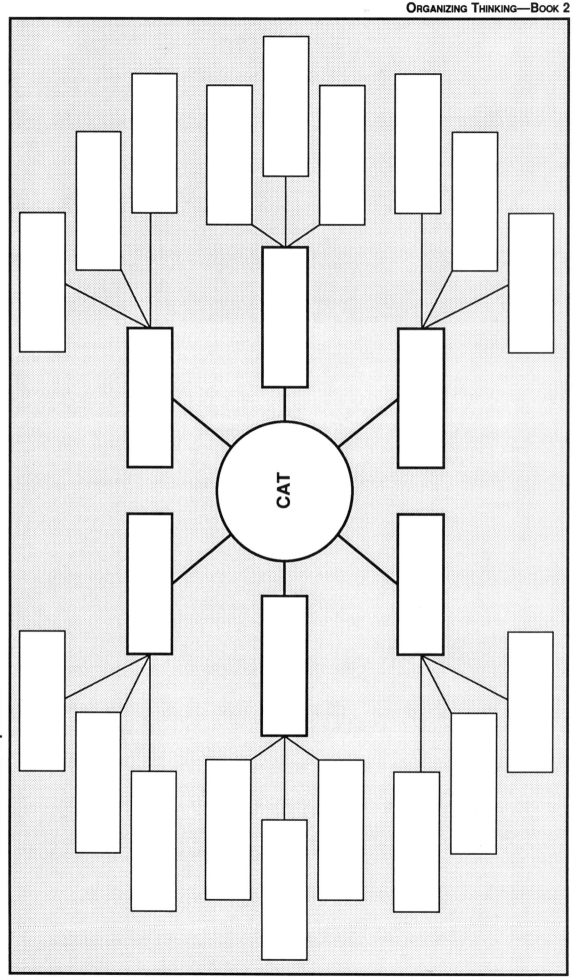

REPORT WRITING: NARROWING A TOPIC

THINKING SKILL: Identifying attributes, parts of a whole, and main ideas and details.

CONTENT OBJECTIVE: Students will use the central idea graph to restrict a proposed, overambitious subject for a report to a more manageable one.

DISCUSSION: TECHNIQUE—Sometimes students propose a report which is too broad or ambitious. The example in this lesson, selecting the Civil War as a subject for a one-page paper, demonstrates this problem. This lesson helps students determine whether a subject is too large for the purpose of their paper and provides them with a technique for selecting a more appropriate one. Help students recognize subjects that are too broad by using a large chalkboard drawing of the central idea graph. Generate a visual outline of all the topics that are important in describing the Civil War. Use the combined background of the students by brainstorming as many significant topics about the subject as time and student interest will allow. Add additional arms and branches, if needed, to create a comprehensive "mental map" of the subject. Most upper elementary and middle schools students have enough background about the Civil War to contribute much more information than could be covered in a one-page paper. If your students are not knowledgeable enough to identify many topics about the Civil War, select a broader subject that is more obvious, i.e., "America" or "man."

DIALOGUE—Discuss with students whether a one-page paper on the Civil War can meaningfully contain information on all the headings shown on the completed graph.

Can a one-page paper contain enough information to describe each of these topics meaningfully? How do you decide if the subject is too large? (Many planning questions may be raised by students to answer that question.) **What is the purpose of the paper?** (The paper may be a summary, new information that the class would not get from textbooks, or some interesting incident or condition that may encourage others to learn more about the subject.) **How much time do you have to plan and research the paper?** (Is there so much information on the subject that you could not read it in time to finish your paper?) **Is the subject appropriate for the background of the reader? How do you decide whether each topic is an important one or not? Would leaving out a topic give the reader a misleading or inadequate understanding of the subject? Could your report assignment be written about any one of the topics in the graph?**

To demonstrate that any one of the topics might be a more appropriate subject for the report, students should select one topic and write it in the circle of the second graph. On each of the arms, they will write a topic about that subject. Answers will vary.

NOTE: This process can be reversed if the proposed subject is too specialized for available reference material. Write the narrow subject on one of the arms and ask the student to identify a broader idea that includes his selection. Write the broader idea in the circle of the graph and encourage the student to generate other topics related to the broader subject.

RESULT—The subject of a paper should be appropriate for the given length, preparation time, and resources. Selecting one topic of a broader subject may result in a more meaningful paper than trying to cover the broader one.

WRITING EXTENSION

• **Why is it important for the subject of a report to fit its length?**
• **Describe how you can narrow or broaden a report subject.**
• **Describe some clues that you can use to decide whether a subject is too broad or too narrow.** (Possible clues might include whether the topic can be described meaningfully

within the assigned length of the paper, researched in the amount of preparation time with locally available resources, and described within the student's background or reasonably acquired knowledge.)

THINKING ABOUT THINKING
- **How did using the central idea graph help you narrow or broaden the subject?**
- **Why is it important for you to be able to judge how broad or narrow the subject of a paper should be?**
- **What other graphs might you use to organize the contents of a report?**

SIMILAR LANGUAGE ARTS LESSONS
- To plan main ideas and supporting details or to illustrate creative alternatives or solutions in the preparation of speeches or papers.
- To illustrate part/whole relationships: parts of a book, parts of a letter, languages contributing to contemporary English.
- To illustrate many factors that lead to or are consequences of a turning point in a narrative or biography.

NARROWING A TOPIC

DIRECTIONS: Suppose you had selected the Civil War as the subject for a one-page report. You turned in the top graph to show the outline of the paper. The teacher asks you to reconsider whether this subject is too large for a one-page report. You must redesign the paper about just one of your original Civil War topics.

Using the second central idea graph, select one topic that could be the subject of a one-page report. Write it in the center circle of the bottom graph. Using your text, encyclopedias, or library books, find out what topics you could use to discuss that subject. List these new topics in the boxes on the arms.

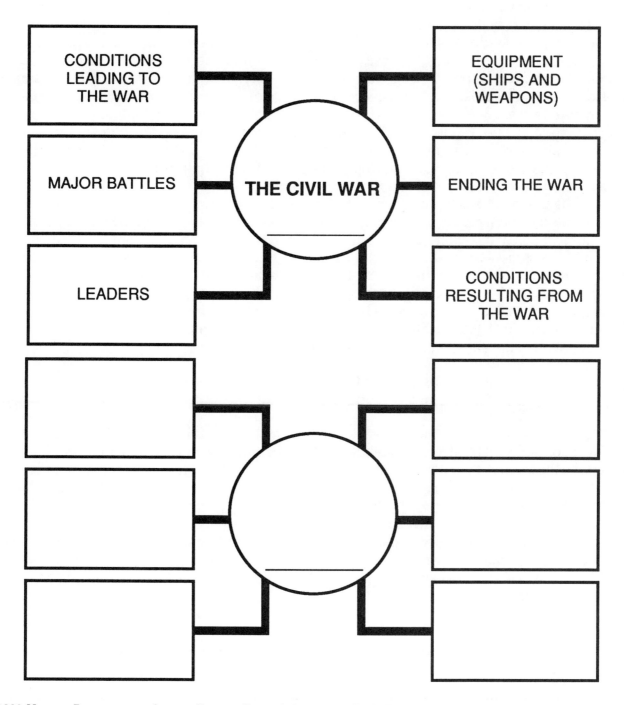

ESSAY WRITING: COMPARE AND CONTRAST

THINKING SKILL: Compare and contrast

CONTENT OBJECTIVE: Students will use an essay form to write essay question answers. *NOTE: Students may use the provided compare and contrast graph about ABRAHAM LINCOLN AND FREDERICK DOUGLASS, or they may use their own completed compare and contrast graphs from any social studies lesson.*

DISCUSSION: TECHNIQUE—Several lessons in **Organizing Thinking** feature compare and contrast writing assignments. This lesson emphasizes the process of writing concise, well-organized answers to essay questions. The purpose of the lesson is to demonstrate how information from an outline, in this case a graphic organizer, can be expressed in essay form.

If students have not written compare and contrast essays in other **Organizing Thinking** lessons, they may need guidance in identifying signal words and sentence patterns that are common in this kind of essay. This technique involves comparing the information on the graph with the wording of a sample essay. (Information from the completed Lincoln-Douglass compare and contrast graph is used in the sample essay.) Ask students to examine the sample essay for signal words that show how comparison and contrast is expressed. As they read the sample essay answer, ask students to highlight the signal words for comparisons in yellow and for contrast in blue. Highlight the introduction sentence and the conclusion sentence about Lincoln and Douglass in pink. This reminds the student that the opening and closing sentences discuss the same thought. Then apply the second technique in this lesson to answer a compare and contrast question about another subject.

The use of an essay model can be demonstrated by applying the information from any completed compare and contrast graph without reference to the Lincoln-Douglass example. Assign an essay question based on information from any completed compare and contrast graph. Ask students to interpret the information on the graph to fit the essay form. Remind them that all the information on the graph may not be necessary in writing their essay answer.

DIALOGUE— In the critical reading portion of this lesson, students highlight information on the graph that is also expressed in a sample essay. All the information on the graph may not necessarily fit the question that the essay asks. Students should recognize that the information in the sample essay expresses significant facts from the graph.

As you look at the similarities and differences between Abraham Lincoln and Frederick Douglass, what conclusions can you reach about the contributions of these two men?

Answers to this question will vary. Although both men came from poor families and had little education, they were able to influence public opinion about improving conditions for black Americans through their determination and leadership. Both men were influential leaders, but Lincoln had fewer obstacles to overcome and more opportunities and civil liberties than Douglass did.

RESULT—Learning how to translate factual information into organized paragraphs guides us in answering essay questions. We express our understanding more fully and with greater confidence when we organize our thoughts before writing essay answers. Being able to organize and express ideas clearly promotes a person's appreciation of himself or herself as a critical thinker.

WRITING EXTENSION

- How does an essay answer express what you have learned in ways that short answers or multiple choice questions do not?

THINKING ABOUT THINKING
- **How did using the compare and contrast graph help you organize your thoughts before you began to write?**
- **How is the sample answer to an essay question like other kinds of critical thinking?** (It is similar to identifying the main idea/ supporting details or assumptions, reasons, and conclusions.)
- **Design another graphic organizer that would help you answer compare and contrast essay questions?** (Students may find that the overlapping classes diagram also illustrates similarities and differences easily. The matrix diagram is helpful in comparing several items by multiple criteria.)

SIMILAR LANGUAGE ARTS LESSONS
- To compare fiction and nonfiction; types of narratives, nonfiction, periodicals, or nonprint media, and forms or types of poetry.
- To compare parts of speech, figures of speech, types of sentences, active and passive verbs, plural and singular forms, and common and proper nouns.
- To compare denotation and connotation in meaning, fact and opinion, and premises and conclusions.
- To compare characters, plots, or styles of writing between novels, short stories, or plays.
- To clarify terms in vocabulary enrichment lessons (synonyms and antonyms).
- To prepare speeches or essays involving comparison or contrast.
- To prepare debate topics or persuasive essays.
- To organize information to examine ethical issues in different situations or conflicts.

ESSAY WRITING: LINCOLN AND DOUGLASS

DIRECTIONS: This lesson will show you how to select words and patterns of sentences to compare and contrast two things, ideas, or people. Use these steps:

1. Compare the information about Abraham Lincoln and Frederick Douglass on the compare and contrast graph with that in the essay answer below. On both the completed graph and the sample essay below, highlight with a green marker all the information on the given compare and contrast graph that is also mentioned in the sample essay answer.

2. Identify what the person who wrote this answer believes to be true about Abraham Lincoln and Frederick Douglass. Highlight those ideas with a pink marker.

3. With a yellow marker, circle or highlight the signal words that remind you how the lives of these two men are alike.

4. With a blue marker, circle or highlight the signal words that remind you how the lives of these two men are different.

SAMPLE ESSAY

COMPARING AND CONTRASTING LINCOLN AND DOUGLASS

Abraham Lincoln and Frederick Douglass contributed to ending slavery in America. Both men were born into very poor families and had very little education. Both leaders used powerful language to influence other people's opinions about legal rights and opportunities for black Americans.

Lincoln and Douglass were not born with the same civil rights. Lincoln was born a free citizen with all the rights guaranteed to Americans, but Douglass was born a slave and denied the basic protections of the Constitution. Since Douglass was black, he did not experience the same opportunities and acceptance that Lincoln did. While Lincoln was a persuasive speaker, Douglass used the power of his newspaper to persuade others. As President of the United States, Lincoln used his war powers authority to free the slaves in the Confederate States and established military opportunities for blacks. Douglass used dramatic descriptions of his life in slavery and strong moral arguments to gain public support against slavery.

By using different methods and taking advantage of opportunities available to them, Abraham Lincoln and Frederick Douglass overcame hardship and limitation to gain the respect of the public. Their leadership contributed to improving opportunities for black Americans.

ESSAY WRITING: COMPARE AND CONTRAST

DIRECTIONS: An essay question is one that asks you to state a conclusion about something you have learned and to use information to explain that conclusion. This lesson shows the steps in writing answers to an essay question that asks you to compare and contrast two things, ideas, or people. Use these steps to write an answer to an essay question your teacher assigns.

1. Use a compare and contrast graph to outline information.
2. Decide why the similarities and differences are important. State a belief that you think the comparison and contrast suggests.
3. Select the information that supports your conclusion.
4. Use the essay form as a guide to organize your sentences.
5. Write your essay as clearly and as briefly as possible. Include only sentences that are necessary to explain your conclusion.

Use the essay model at the bottom of the page to write your answer. Your essay should contain four parts:

A. An opening sentence which introduces your conclusion.
B. Statements that express how the two ideas, things, or people are alike. Use signal words like *both*, *alike*, *similar*, *same*, and *resemble*.
C. Statements that express how the two ideas, things, or people are different. Use signal words like *but*, *although*, *in contrast to*, *unlike*, and *while*.
D. A conclusion sentence that expresses the belief that you have realized from the comparison and contrast of the two ideas, things, or people.

ESSAY MODEL

_____
Introductory sentence

_____. _____
Comparison sentences

_____

_____

_____
Contrast sentences

_____

_____

_____. _____
Conclusion sentences

_____

ESSAY WRITING: COMPARE AND CONTRAST

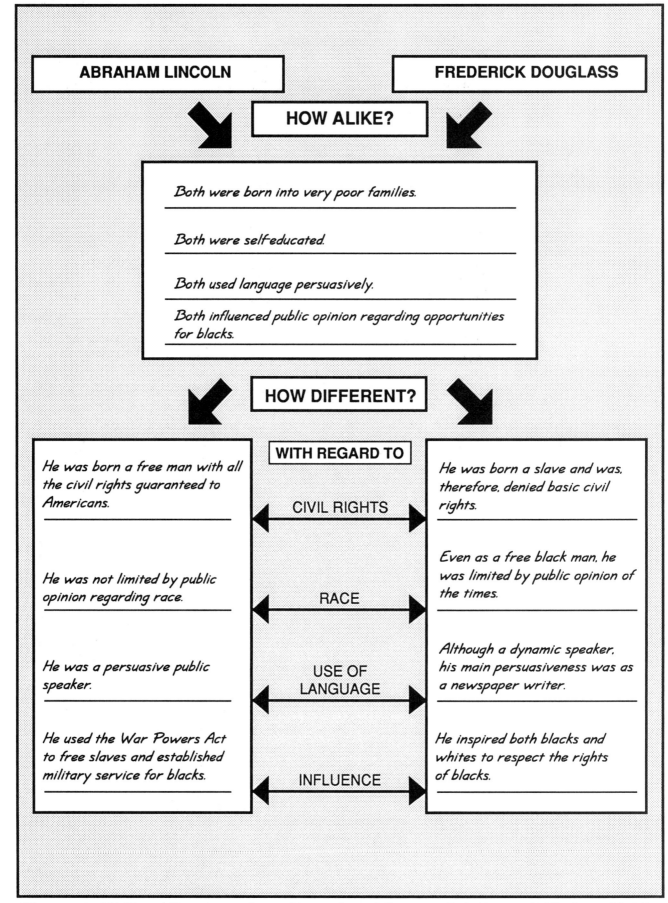

ABRAHAM LINCOLN   FREDERICK DOUGLASS

HOW ALIKE?

Both were born into very poor families.

Both were self-educated.

Both used language persuasively.

Both influenced public opinion regarding opportunities for blacks.

HOW DIFFERENT?

WITH REGARD TO

He was born a free man with all the civil rights guaranteed to Americans.

CIVIL RIGHTS

He was born a slave and was, therefore, denied basic civil rights.

He was not limited by public opinion regarding race.

RACE

Even as a free black man, he was limited by public opinion of the times.

He was a persuasive public speaker.

USE OF LANGUAGE

Although a dynamic speaker, his main persuasiveness was as a newspaper writer.

He used the War Powers Act to free slaves and established military service for blacks.

INFLUENCE

He inspired both blacks and whites to respect the rights of blacks.

CHAPTER 4 – SOCIAL STUDIES

GREAT BRITAIN AND JAPAN (Compare and Contrast Diagram)		LAND FORMS AND BODIES OF WATER (Branching Diagram)
	COLONIAL STOCK COMPANIES (Cycle Diagram)	
EARLY PRESIDENTS (Transitive Order Graph)		LINCOLN AND DOUGLASS: TWO BIOGRAPHIES (Interval Graph)
	LINCOLN AND DOUGLASS: COMPARING LEADERS (Flowchart)	
LINCOLN AND DOUGLASS: CONDITIONS AND CONTRIBUTIONS (Compare and Contrast Diagram)		PETROCHEMICAL PRODUCTS (Branching Diagram)
	NEEDS AND RESOURCES: SURVIVAL AND QUALITY-OF-LIFE NEEDS IN TWO CULTURES (Web Diagram)	
NEEDS AND RESOURCES: THE BUFFALO AS A SOURCE OF SUPPLY (Branching Diagram)		NEEDS AND RESOURCES: COMPARING GOODS (Multiple Diagrams)
	STATE AND FEDERAL GOVERNMENT (Contrast Diagram)	
LOCAL, STATE, AND FEDERAL GOVERNMENT (Matrix Chart)		THE UNITED NATIONS (Central Idea Graph)
	THE DEVELOPMENT OF CIVILIZATION (Flowchart)	

GREAT BRITAIN AND JAPAN

THINKING SKILL: Verbal similarities and differences

CONTENT OBJECTIVE: Students will use a compare and contrast graph to record the similarities and differences between Great Britain and Japan with regard to geography, population density, economic and political institutions. Option: Students will calculate population density and demonstrate the effects of increasing it.

DISCUSSION: TECHNIQUE—Use a transparency of the compare and contrast graph to record student responses as the class discusses characteristics of Great Britain and Japan. Encourage students to identify additional similarities and differences.

DIALOGUE—As students report differences between Great Britain and Japan, discuss those differences by naming the quality that is different. Establish this pattern: "**With regard to** (quality), (item one and its distinction), **but** (item two and its distinction)."

"With regard to **industrialization, Great Britain began industrialization two centuries ago, but Japan only became industrialized in the twentieth century**."

"Population density" refers to the average number of people who live within a unit of area. The population density of your classroom is arrived at by dividing the number of students by the area of your classroom in square feet. It is expressed as "students per square foot" and is usually reported as a decimal value. The population density of a class of 30 students in a classroom 20 feet by 30 feet is 0.05 students per square foot. The concept of a "part" of a person per square foot is not concrete enough to be understood easily by elementary students.

You may also demonstrate the effect of population density by dividing the square footage by the number of students in the class, giving you a sense of how many square feet is available for each student. Example: If your classroom is 20 feet by 30 feet, it contains 600 square feet. If you have 30 students, then every student theoretically has 20 square feet, a space 4 feet by 5 feet. That average, however, includes all the common space for aisles, storage, mobility, and the teacher's desk. Ask students to identify the kinds of activities that go on in the space that you have.

To illustrate the concepts of common space and individual space, measure your classroom and compute the area available to each student as square feet per student. Compute the perimeter of a rectangle that has this area. Use pieces of wood or cardboard to construct a rectangle with these dimensions. Ask a few students to lift the rectangle and place it surrounding one student. The area will seem large compared to the actual space occupied by the student's desk.

If a space ____ feet by ____ feet is available for (student's name), where is it? (Clarify that each student, in effect, gives up a portion of his or her space for common aisles, storage, mobility, furniture, and equipment.) **Why is common space important? How is common space in a classroom similar to the common space in cities?** (Examples include: streets, parks, warehouses, public buildings, shopping centers, entertainment facilities, etc.)

If 40 students occupied the same 20 by 30 foot space, then each student would have 15 square feet, or a space 3 feet by 5 feet.

What would be the effect of greater population density on the kinds of activities you can do in the classroom? What changes would you expect in movement, noise, privacy, storage, and habits? (More limited movement, limitations on the volume of students' belongings and classroom materials, rules to limit noise and movement, etc.)

Suppose that your 600 square feet of space were reduced by one-third to a space of 400 square feet, 20 feet by 20 feet. Mark off a space 20 feet by 20 feet. Ask students to imagine what a day would be like if all your activity was confined to a more limited space.

In this case, what would be the effect on the class with regard to movement, noise, privacy, storage, and the kinds of activities you can do in the class? What rules or habits would students have to develop to get along comfortably in a more densely populated space? What values and priorities would be different in that environment?

Relate the effect of not being able to use a large portion of your space to the limited land area available for cities in Japan.

Which of the factors we have discussed about our class are likely to be true of a nation whose cities are proportionately more population-dense? What is the effect on industry, basic needs, government services, laws, and people's habits and values?

Use information from your social studies text or a research assignment on Japan to identify values, habits, traditions, and conditions which illustrate the influence of population density. Examine the effect of both nations' reliance on trade in order to secure raw materials. From American history lessons about the American Revolution, students identify Britain as a colonial power which needed raw materials from America.

Although Britain was the cradle of the Industrial Revolution, the general public no longer views Britain as a technological innovator. Japan, on the other hand, illustrates significant current industrial and technological development.

RESULT—Although Japan and Great Britain are located across the globe from each other, their geographic features and resources are amazingly similar. Their economic, political, and technological influences have been significant.

WRITING EXTENSION
- **Describe how Great Britain and Japan are alike and how they are different.**
- **What is population density? What is its effect on people's habits and values?**

THINKING ABOUT THINKING
- **How did using the graph help you understand and remember the similarities and differences between Japan and Great Britain? How does this differ from the way you understood the written passage?**
- **Suggest another lesson in which comparing and contrasting would help you understand what you are learning.**
- **Design another diagram that would help you organize information that compares two countries.** (Students may find that the class relationships diagram can be used to depict similarities and differences between two countries.)

SIMILAR SOCIAL STUDIES LESSONS
- To compare any two cultures, forms of government, the structure or function of two levels or divisions of government, economic systems, historical trends, migrations of people, sociological or anthropological aspects of any two cultures, historical figures, two discoveries of previously unknown land or technological change, two historical events, effects of geographical features or natural resources on cultural development.

GREAT BRITAIN AND JAPAN

DIRECTIONS: Read the passage carefully to determine how Great Britain and Japan are alike and how they are different. Use the graphic organizer to record their similarities and differences.

Both Great Britain and Japan are densely populated island nations. Great Britain has 56,000,000 people living on 94,000 square miles with an average population density of about 600 people per square mile. It is possible to live anywhere on the island.

Japan has 121,000,000 people living on 146,000 square miles with an average population density of about 830 people per square mile. Inland mountain ranges in Japan limit the area available for people to live on.

Both countries are located near densely populated continents. Both are well located for shipping and rely on trade to support their large populations. Great Britain started the Industrial Revolution in the eighteenth and nineteenth centuries. Japan became an industrial nation in the twentieth century, and in the last ten years it has become a major exporter of automobiles, electronic equipment, and appliances.

Both nations have a monarch, but in each country the prime minister is the head of the government, with the real decision-making power held by an elected legislature. Great Britain developed representative government in the seventeenth and eighteenth centuries, while Japan has only enjoyed democratic government for the last forty years.

GREAT BRITAIN AND JAPAN

GREAT BRITAIN	JAPAN

HOW ALIKE?

Both densely populated island nations

Both near densely populated continents and rely on trade

Both industrialized

Both have democratic government and a monarch

Both have a prime minister as head of government and an elected legislature.

 ## HOW DIFFERENT?

WITH REGARD TO

GREAT BRITAIN		JAPAN
Became industrialized two centuries ago	**WHEN INDUSTRIALIZED**	*Became industrialized in the twentieth century*
Has had democratic government for two centuries	**DEMOCRATIC GOVERNMENT**	*Has had democratic government for forty years*
Entire island	**POPULATED AREA**	*Mountainous inland limits places people can live*
About 600 people per square mile	**POPULATION DENSITY**	*About 830 people per square mile*

LAND FORMS AND BODIES OF WATER

THINKING SKILL: Verbal classification

CONTENT OBJECTIVE: Students will use the branching diagram to identify types of land and water forms.

DISCUSSION: TECHNIQUE—Use a transparency of the branching diagram to record student responses about land and water forms as they compare labeled terms on a map to descriptions of a variety of land and water forms. Use the cut-out terms and definitions as "paper manipulatives" to allow students to match descriptions with map locations.

DIALOGUE—State the category to which each term belongs and the characteristics that make it different from others in that category. For example,

A gulf is a large body of water that is partly surrounded by land. A bay is a small body of water that is partly surrounded by land. (Size is the distinguishing characteristic that differentiates a gulf from a bay. Both bay and gulf are portions of an ocean and are therefore coastal bodies of water.) **A lake is a body of water that is completely surrounded by land.** (A lake is different from a gulf or bay because it is completely surrounded by land.)

In discussing land forms and bodies of water, emphasize the importance of sufficient qualifiers to distinguish the given term from similar ones and encourage students to select the most precise category which fits the term. Generalize the characteristics used to describe land and water forms: location, elevation, surrounding areas, shape, size, purpose, and whether it is natural or man-made. This graphic makes an interesting bulletin board design.

RESULT—One may clarify geographic terms by defining them carefully and by identifying the categories and characteristics clearly.

WRITING EXTENSION
- **What characteristics are used to distinguish among various types of land forms and bodies of water?**

THINKING ABOUT THINKING
- **How did using the diagram help you understand and remember the types of land forms and bodies of water?**
- **How does using the graph to classify land forms and bodies of water help you understand them more clearly? How does this differ from the way you understood the information from the map?**
- **Design another diagram that would help you distinguish land forms and bodies of water.** (Students may find that the class relationships diagram or the compare and contrast diagram can be used to distinguish geography terms.)

SIMILAR SOCIAL STUDIES LESSONS
- To depict branches or divisions of governments or institutions.
- To describe dwellings, weapons, artifacts, household articles, or tools belonging to various eras, cultures, people, events, or groups.
- To describe the functions of buildings, governmental divisions, or community institutions.

LAND FORMS AND BODIES OF WATER

DIRECTIONS: Examine the map carefully to determine the significant characteristics of the land formations and bodies of water which are labeled on the map. Cut apart the definitions and match each term to its definition. Record the information on the branching diagram.

LAND FORMS AND BODIES OF WATER

BASIN	a broad, flat area surrounded by hills or mountains	**LAKE**	a large body of water completely surrounded by land
BAY	a small area of ocean partly surrounded by land	**MARSH**	low, wet land
CANAL	a manmade waterway for transportation or irrigation	**MESA**	a flat-topped hill with steep sides; common in deserts
CANYON	a narrow valley with high, steep sides	**PEAK**	the pointed top of a mountain
CHANNEL	a narrow waterway connecting two bodies of water	**PENINSULA**	land surrounded by water on three sides
DELTA	a land deposit at a river's mouth	**PLAIN**	a large area of flat or gently rolling land
GULF	a large body of water partly surrounded by land	**PLATEAU**	an area of high, flat land
HARBOR	a sheltered area along a seacoast where ships can anchor	**RESERVOIR**	a manmade lake for storing water
ISLAND	land completely surrounded by water	**STREAM**	a small body of flowing water
ISTHMUS	a narrow strip of land connecting two larger land areas	**TRIBUTARY**	a stream that flows into a larger river

DEFINITIONS FOR LAND FORMS AND BODIES OF WATER

an area of high flat land	a man-made lake for storing water
a broad, flat area surrounded by hills or mountains	a man-made waterway for transportation or irrigation
a flat-topped hill with steep sides; common in deserts	a narrow strip of land connecting two larger land areas
a land deposit at a river's mouth	a narrow valley with high, steep sides
land completely surrounded by water	a narrow waterway connecting two bodies of water
land surrounded by water on three sides	the pointed top of a mountain
a large area of flat or gently rolling land	a sheltered area along a seacoast where ships can anchor
a large body of water completely surrounded by land	a small area of ocean partly surrounded by land
a large body of water partly surrounded by land	a small body of flowing water
low, wet land	a stream that flows into a larger river

LAND FORMS AND BODIES OF WATER

DIRECTIONS: Write each term for land forms or bodies of water in the box that best describes it.

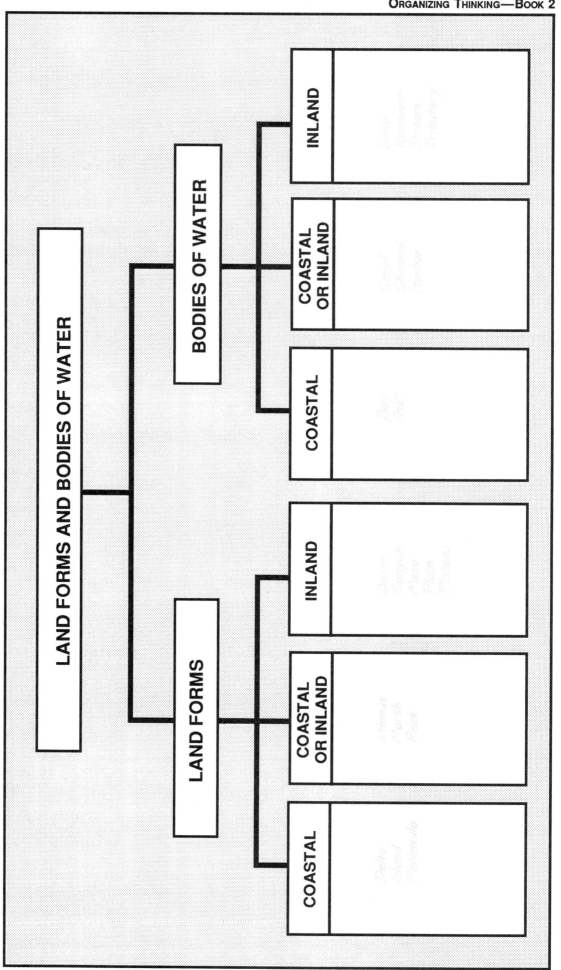

COLONIAL STOCK COMPANIES

THINKING SKILL: Verbal sequences, inferences

CONTENT OBJECTIVE: Students will use a cycle graph to depict the process of investment by which British stock companies colonized the United States in the seventeenth and eighteenth centuries.

DISCUSSION: TECHNIQUE—Use a transparency of the cycle graph to record responses as students discuss the investment cycle of British stock companies.
    DIALOGUE—Examine the implications of colonizing for profit.

If the purpose of the colony was to produce profit for the stockholders, what restrictions might the companies have placed on the colonists? What is likely to have been the stockholders' attitude toward the colonists? How might wealthy stockholders in the British companies have influenced the colonial policies of the British Parliament? Find examples of policies which might have been unacceptable to the colonists. (Stamp Act, Townshend Acts) **Explain your choices.**
    How does understanding the role of the colonial stock companies add to or change your understanding of the colonists' decisions to come to this country? How might their obligations to the British stock companies influence their view of themselves as citizens of the British Crown? How might these obligations influence their view of themselves as free men empowered to make their own political decisions?
    How did the cycle of trade and investment affect the dependence of the American colonies and the British investors on each other? How long was it from the time colonists settled in the eastern United States until they separated themselves from Britain?(About 150 years—from the earliest colonies in the seventeenth century until the Declaration of Independence in 1776.)

    Examine the implications of a cycle of investment. Help students trace the steps in the cycle. Discuss with students the nature of cycles, using the example of British stock companies to describe the key features of a cycle.

What makes a cycle different from other patterns? What makes a cycle work? (A cycle describes a repeating process that flows in one direction and requires each step to maintain its action. Cycles can remain constant, can slow down or stop, or can expand.)
    How might the cycle become an upward spiral of profit or a downward spiral of poor investment for the stockholders? What would happen if there were a break in the cycle? What might cause a break in the cycle? Is there a point in the cycle at which a break might be more likely to occur? Identify other examples of economic cycles. Why do you think cycle patterns are common in economics?

    RESULT—British investment in the American colonies involved a cycle of profit and reinvestment. Understanding British colonization as an economic cycle clarifies our understanding of American ties to British interests. The cycle illustrates the interdependence of British business interests and American colonists.

WRITING EXTENSION
- **Describe the trade cycle that funded the development of the American colonies.**
- **Choose one part of the cycle and predict how a change in that action would affect the other parts of the cycle. Give some examples of what might happen.**

THINKING ABOUT THINKING
- **How does a cycle demonstrate the interdependence among the people or organisms in the process? Identify other cycles that demonstrate interdependence.**
- **How does using the graph to picture the cycle help you understand the relationship between British business interests and the American colonies? How does this differ from the way you understood it from the written passage?**
- **Suggest another lesson in which using a cycle graph might help you understand or clarify what you are learning?**

SIMILAR SOCIAL STUDIES LESSONS
- To depict trade cycles (e.g., slave trade, raw material trade, etc.).
- To depict cycles in governmental actions (e.g., legislative processes, election processes, judicial review processes, etc.).
- To depict economic cycles (flow of personal income; taxes; etc.).

COLONIAL STOCK COMPANIES

DIRECTIONS: Read the passage carefully. Determine the cycle of British stock company investment in colonial America. Record the information on the cycle graph.

Stock companies were formed by investors who contributed money to the company. They expected to share in the profits of the colony.

Stock companies were chartered by the king, who set aside land from royal holdings for the company. These charters gave the company the power to make laws in the colony. The companies recruited colonists, explorers, and traders and used the money from the investors to purchase ships and supplies.

In the New World lumber, fish, and fur were exported to England. These goods were sold to make profits for the companies. As the companies made money, more ships were bought and more colonists and traders were sent out.

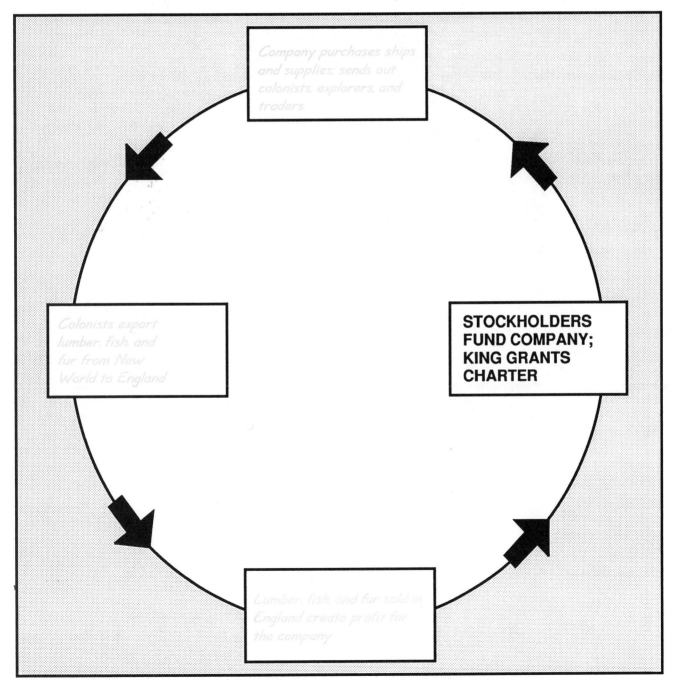

Company purchases ships and supplies; sends out colonists, explorers, and traders

Colonists export lumber, fish, and fur from New World to England

STOCKHOLDERS FUND COMPANY; KING GRANTS CHARTER

Lumber, fish, and fur sold in England create profit for the company

EARLY PRESIDENTS

THINKING SKILL: Verbal sequences, identifying chronological order

CONTENT OBJECTIVE: Students will use the transitive order graph to show the order in which the first seven presidents held office.

DISCUSSION: TECHNIQUE—Use a transparency of the transitive order graph to record responses as the class discusses the order in which our early presidents served.

DIALOGUE—Identify the "signal words" which served as clues to the order in which the presidents served. Encourage students to "think out loud" about how they determined and changed the order as new information was given.

RESULT—Information is not always given to us in the order in which events occur. Signal words and diagrams may help us determine the correct order.

WRITING EXTENSION
- Identify the order in which the first seven presidents served.

THINKING ABOUT THINKING
- Why is knowing the order of occurrence important?
- How did using the diagram help you list the presidents in order? How did using it help you remember the order in which they served?
- Suggest another lesson in which using a transitive order graph might help you organize or understand what you are learning.

SIMILAR SOCIAL STUDIES LESSONS:
- To organize the chronological order of events, eras, artifacts, cultures, and individuals.
- To depict sequential changes in technology, institutions, and ideas.
- To depict levels or divisions of organizational structures.

EARLY PRESIDENTS

DIRECTIONS: Read the passage carefully to determine the order in which early presidents served. Record each president on the transitive order graph.

John Adams became president of the United States after serving as vice president during the term of George Washington. Adams was the father of the sixth president, John Quincy Adams. John Quincy Adams became president after the term of James Monroe and before the presidency of his political rival, Andrew Jackson.

Thomas Jefferson, the author of the Declaration of Independence, was the third president. Jefferson was followed by his Virginia neighbor James Madison.

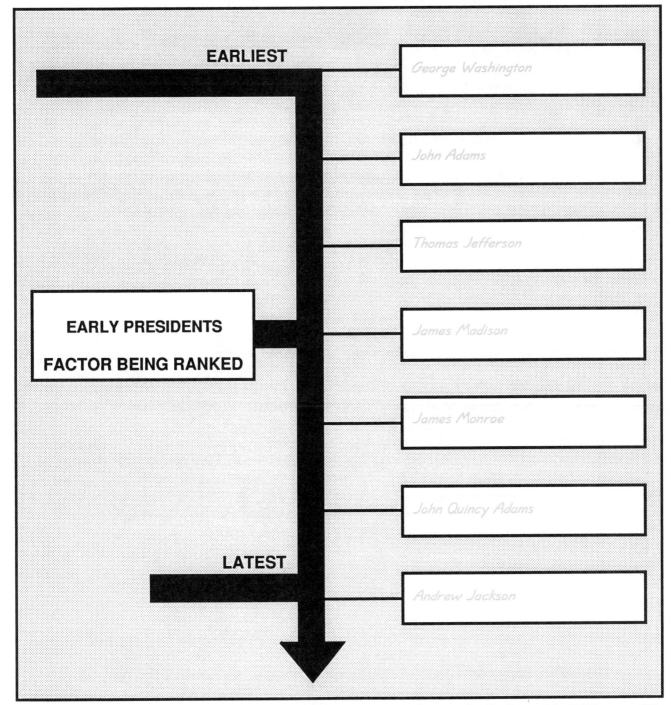

EARLIEST

George Washington

John Adams

Thomas Jefferson

James Madison

EARLY PRESIDENTS

FACTOR BEING RANKED

James Monroe

John Quincy Adams

LATEST

Andrew Jackson

ABRAHAM LINCOLN AND FREDERICK DOUGLASS: TWO BIOGRAPHIES

THINKING SKILL: Identifying chronological order, prediction

CONTENT OBJECTIVE: Students will use the interval graph to correlate events in the lives of Abraham Lincoln and Frederick Douglass. *NOTE: This is the first of three lessons based on the same text. These lessons compare the lives and contributions of Abraham Lincoln and Frederick Douglass. To allow sufficient time for discussion, schedule these lessons in three different time periods. The lessons on essay writing and the characteristics of leaders extend these three lessons.*

DISCUSSION: TECHNIQUE —Use a transparency of the interval graph to record student responses as the class discusses events in the lives of Abraham Lincoln and Frederick Douglass. Encourage students to identify additional events in American history during the lives of these two leaders which might effect their values and priorities.

DIALOGUE—The purpose of a parallel time line is to demonstrate how two sets of events occur in relation to each other and to place those events in the larger context of what was going on in history during the same time period.

Although the two men lived at the same time, how was Douglass's life different from Lincoln's? What was happening in American history during their childhood and youth that might have affected their values and opportunities? What events and policies regarding slavery and free black Americans occurred during this time period? What influence might these events have had on the later decisions and policies of these two men?

Depicting events on an interval graph allows students to distinguish the relative importance of various types of information about the two men. Some will tend to regard all information, trivial or significant, with the same weight. This lesson may be used to help students understand that one may select different events in describing an individual's contributions to history, in understanding his character and values, in explaining significant changes in his conditions or beliefs, or in shedding light on his personal habits and daily experiences. For example, one does not use the same events to discuss Lincoln's contribution to history as one uses to describe his personality and daily life.

The goal of this instruction is to help students learn the suitability of examples to support inferences that one might draw about the two leaders. Although when they were born, when they married, or how many children they had may be interesting biographical information, it may not be relevant to more abstract judgments about the individual's contribution to history.

To demonstrate this principle, ask students to circle those events that seem significant to describing the leaders' contribution to history. Then, ask them to explain why those choices relate to Lincoln's and Douglass's influence on policies, opportunities, and attitudes toward black Americans. Ask them to put a star by those events that refer to the leader's personal life and character.

Count the number of starred items that are also circled. Why do you think that the events you chose to describe Douglass's or Lincoln's backgrounds are different from the one's you chose to describe their achievements? (The biographical information must fit the type of conclusion that one is trying to draw about a person.)

Interval graphs can also be used for a chronological framework for making predictions:

Historians often wonder how conditions after the Civil War might have been different if Abraham Lincoln had not been assassinated. They base their ideas on examples of what Abraham Lincoln said or did in similar circumstances. Identify events in American history that occurred in the period between Lincoln's death and Douglass's death. What might Lincoln have thought or done about those events? How might he have affected policies and attitudes toward black Americans after the Civil War? Explain your reasoning.

Interval graphs may also be used to direct students' comparison and contrast of two individuals:

Look at the events in the lives of these two men, listed side by side. Pick a year and compare what each man was doing at that time. What interesting similarities do you see? What significant differences do you see? Note the years of his life that Douglass spent in slavery. Discuss how being a slave or a free citizen makes a difference in a person's perceptions of himself and his ability to make independent choices.

RESULT—Events and conditions in which we grow up influence, but do not determine what we believe about ourselves and our ability to change conditions. To describe significant contributions or judgments about the effectiveness of a leader, one must select examples of events that apply to that judgment. Examining events which occurred during Douglass's lifetime, after the death of Lincoln, provides a framework for our predictions regarding how these two leaders might have viewed and affected conditions for black Americans, based on what they said and did in similar situations.

WRITING EXTENSION

- Describe how the lives of Abraham Lincoln and Frederick Douglass are alike and how they are different.
- Choose one condition or policy that either Frederick Douglass or Abraham Lincoln influenced. Write a fictional diary that shows what he believed about that issue and the action that he might have selected to change the condition or policy.

THINKING ABOUT THINKING

- What was significant about the events that you circled which help explain the effectiveness of these leaders? How were these events different from those which explain each man's personal development and character.
- How did using the diagram help you understand and remember the similarities and differences between Abraham Lincoln and Frederick Douglass? How does this differ from the way you understood the information from the written passage.
- Suggest another lesson in which comparing and contrasting would help you understand what you are learning.
- Design another diagram that would help you organize information that compares two leaders.

SIMILAR SOCIAL STUDIES LESSONS

- To compare significant events in the lives of famous leaders.
- To relate historical events to sequential changes in technology, institutions, and theories.
- To correlate historical, sociological, economic, or political events from different cultures or countries during a specific time period.

ABRAHAM LINCOLN AND FREDERICK DOUGLASS: TWO BIOGRAPHIES

ABRAHAM LINCOLN

Abraham Lincoln was born in Hardin County, Kentucky in 1809. When he was eight, the family moved to Spencer County, Indiana, where he grew up. His mother died when he was ten years old. Since his family was very poor, Lincoln began working at an early age.

Although there were some schools in the Indiana territory, he had little schooling and was largely self-taught. He worked on a farm until he was twenty-two years old. Then in 1831 moved to Menard County, Illinois, where he worked as a clerk in a store. From 1834 to 1840 Lincoln served in the Illinois legislature, studied to become a lawyer, and moved to Springfield, Illinois, to practice law. He served one term in the U.S. House of Representatives from 1847 to 1849 and then returned to his law practice.

In 1860 Abraham Lincoln was elected president of the United States. He immediately was faced with the secession of southern states from the Union and the beginning of the Civil War. Although he disapproved of slavery, Lincoln was not an abolitionist (one who believed that slavery should be done away with). He recognized that slave owners had paid for their slaves. Since slaves were considered to be property, it was believed to be unlawful to take someone's property away.

Once the southern states had become enemies of the Union, President Lincoln had the authority to use his war powers as Commander-in-chief of the Army to abolish slavery in the southern states. In September, 1862, Lincoln proclaimed that, unless the southern states rejoined the Union by January 1, 1863, their slave property would be considered legally confiscated. Thus Lincoln acquired the legal right to free the slaves.

Abraham Lincoln was elected to a second term as president of the United States in 1864, but was assassinated shortly thereafter.

FREDERICK DOUGLASS

Frederick Douglass was born a slave in Tuckahoe, Maryland. Since slaves were seldom told their ages, Douglass could only estimate that he was born about 1818. His mother, Harriet Bailey, was hired out to a distant farmer shortly after his birth and died when Douglass was about eight years old. Like many slaves, Douglass never knew who his father was.

Frederick Douglass was taught the alphabet by Mrs. Thomas Auld, until his master, Mr. Auld, discovered that she was teaching Frederick to read. It was unlawful to teach a slave to read. Frederick realized that reading was an important distinction between slaves and free men. He overheard Mr. Auld say that reading "made a slave of little use to his master." Frederick began to bribe young boys to teach him how to read. He taught himself to write by copying words in the spaces of his young master's writing book.

In 1838 Douglass bluffed his way onto a train to Delaware, a slave state, then went by boat to Philadelphia and freedom. In September of that year he married Anna Murray, moved to Massachusetts, and selected the name Douglass to replace his slave name.

In 1847 Douglass, who had bought his freedom from his old master, started a newspaper in Rochester, New York. The newspaper advocated both the abolition of slavery and voting rights for women.

Douglass encouraged Lincoln to include black troops in the Union Army and used the power of his newspaper to encourage blacks to enlist. The first black regiment was formed in 1863, with Douglass' own sons among the first to enlist. In 1864 Mr. Douglass met with President Lincoln to secure the same wages, protection, and awards for black soldiers as for white soldiers. Frederick Douglass died in 1895 of a heart attack.

ABRAHAM LINCOLN AND FREDERICK DOUGLASS: TWO BIOGRAPHIES

DIRECTIONS: Read the passage carefully to identify events in the lives of Abraham Lincoln and Frederick Douglass. Use the interval graph to record the events in chronological order.

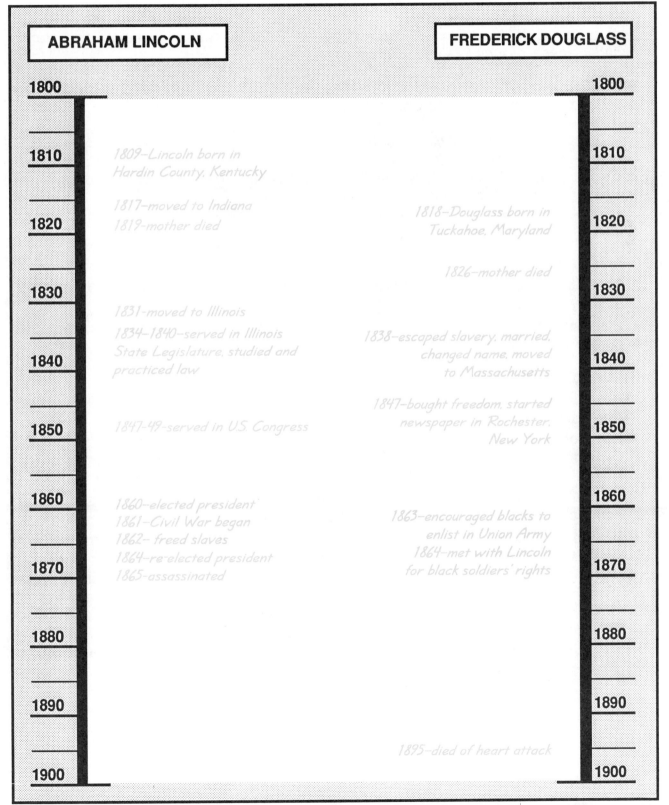

ABRAHAM LINCOLN

FREDERICK DOUGLASS

1800

1810

1809–Lincoln born in
Hardin County, Kentucky

1817–moved to Indiana
1819–mother died

1818–Douglass born in
Tuckahoe, Maryland

1820

1826–mother died

1830

1831–moved to Illinois
1834–1840–served in Illinois
State Legislature, studied and
practiced law

1838–escaped slavery, married,
changed name, moved
to Massachusetts

1840

1847–bought freedom, started
newspaper in Rochester,
New York

1847–49–served in U.S. Congress

1850

1860

1860–elected president
1861–Civil War began
1862– freed slaves
1864–re-elected president
1865–assassinated

1863–encouraged blacks to
enlist in Union Army
1864–met with Lincoln
for black soldiers' rights

1870

1880

1890

1895–died of heart attack

1900

ABRAHAM LINCOLN AND FREDERICK DOUGLASS: COMPARING LEADERS

THINKING SKILL: Compare and contrast

CONTENT OBJECTIVE: Students will use the flowchart to compare similar situations, circumstances, and outcomes in the lives of Abraham Lincoln and Frederick Douglass. *NOTE: This is the second of three lessons, using the same text, comparing the lives and contributions of Abraham Lincoln and Frederick Douglass. To allow sufficient time for discussion, schedule these lessons for three different time periods.*

DISCUSSION: TECHNIQUE—Use a transparency of the flowchart to record student responses about similar situations, circumstances, and outcomes in the lives of Abraham Lincoln and Frederick Douglass.

DIALOGUE—Examine with students the similar issues, actions, and outcomes in the lives of these two leaders. One may take this opportunity to examine other leaders and decisions by parallel comparisons. Use the same technique to examine parallel plots, as in the *Aesop's Fables* lesson in the language arts chapter.

RESULT—To describe the contributions of an individual, one discusses specific issues, situations, actions, and outcomes.

WRITING EXTENSION
- **Describe the contribution of Abraham Lincoln and Frederick Douglass to ending slavery in America.**
- **Discuss the similarities and differences in the situations, circumstances, and outcomes in the lives of the two men.**

THINKING ABOUT THINKING
- **How did using the diagram help you understand and remember the contributions of Abraham Lincoln and Frederick Douglass?**
- **How does using the flowchart to compare Lincoln's and Douglass's leadership help you understand their similarities and differences more clearly? How does this differ from the way you understood the information from the written passage?**
- **Suggest another lesson in which examining the decisions made by a historical or fictional person would help you understand that person's character.**
- **Design another diagram that would help you organize information to compare two leaders or characters.**

SIMILAR SOCIAL STUDIES LESSONS
- To compare significant decisions in the lives of famous leaders.
- To understand sequential changes in technology, institutions, or ideas.
- To correlate historical, sociological, economic, or political developments from different cultures or countries during the same time period.

ABRAHAM LINCOLN AND FREDERICK DOUGLASS: COMPARING LEADERS

DIRECTIONS: Read the passage carefully to identify similar situations, circumstances, and outcomes in the lives of Abraham Lincoln and Frederick Douglass. Use the flowchart to record the decisions of these two leaders.

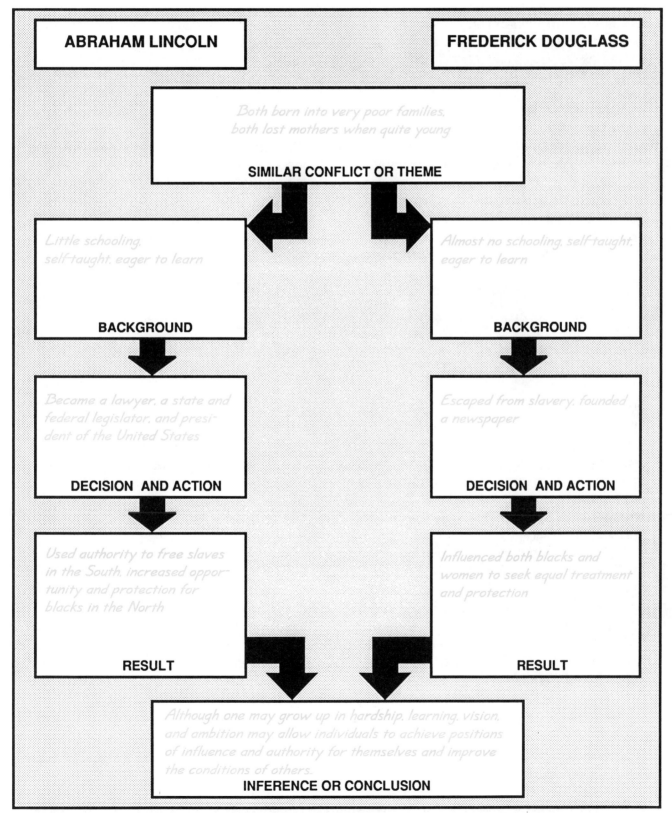

ABRAHAM LINCOLN

FREDERICK DOUGLASS

Both born into very poor families, both lost mothers when quite young

SIMILAR CONFLICT OR THEME

Little schooling, self-taught, eager to learn

BACKGROUND

Almost no schooling, self-taught, eager to learn

BACKGROUND

Became a lawyer, a state and federal legislator, and president of the United States

DECISION AND ACTION

Escaped from slavery, founded a newspaper

DECISION AND ACTION

Used authority to free slaves in the South, increased opportunity and protection for blacks in the North

RESULT

Influenced both blacks and women to seek equal treatment and protection

RESULT

Although one may grow up in hardship, learning, vision, and ambition may allow individuals to achieve positions of influence and authority for themselves and improve the conditions of others.

INFERENCE OR CONCLUSION

ABRAHAM LINCOLN AND FREDERICK DOUGLASS: CONDITIONS AND CONTRIBUTIONS

THINKING SKILL: Compare and contrast

CONTENT OBJECTIVES: Students will use the compare and contrast graph to chart conditions in the lives of Abraham Lincoln and Frederick Douglass and the contributions of these two leaders in influencing public opinion about slavery. *NOTE: This is the third of three lessons, using the same text, comparing the lives and contributions of Abraham Lincoln and Frederick Douglass. To allow time for sufficient discussion, schedule these lessons for three different time periods.*

DISCUSSION: TECHNIQUE—Use a transparency of the compare and contrast graph to record student responses about similarities and differences in the lives of Abraham Lincoln and Frederick Douglass. Direct students to review the passage, reading for similarities and differences in the conditions in the early lives of these two leaders and in the contributions each made in ending slavery in America. Encourage students to list the similarities and differences as they read. Ask students to identify additional similarities and differences from text information and independent reading.

DIALOGUE—As students report differences between Lincoln and Douglass, discuss those differences by naming the quality that is different. Establish this pattern:

"**With regard to** (quality), (item one and its distinction), **but** (item two and its distinction)." For example, "**With regard to civil rights, Lincoln was born a free citizen with all the protection of the Constitution, but Douglass was born a slave with no rights as a citizen.**"

To understand the nature of the obstacles Douglass faced, students must have basic background information about the institution of slavery.

Although the two men were living at the same time, how were the conditions of Douglass's life different from those of Lincoln's?

Students will also need some background on the limitations imposed on slaves. Since slaves were treated as property, they were usually not allowed to marry, to have a last name, to have any record of their past, or to maintain any family relationships, since a mother or a brother might be sold or hired out. Douglass mentioned in his autobiography that slaves had no more knowledge of their age than a horse, and he resented being deprived of such basic human information as the date and circumstances of his birth.

Students may obtain more information from biographies of Lincoln and Douglass, such as *Two Roads To Greatness* (Macmillan Company, New York, 1967). Other characteristics of the two leaders might be discussed, such as their persuasive use of language or how each was regarded by the public opinion of the times.

Many works of literature have been written about each man. Lincoln poems include "When Lilacs Last in the Dooryard Bloomed" and "Oh Captain, My Captain" by Walt Whitman, "What Is God's Will?" and "Abraham Lincoln" by Stephen Vincent Benet, and "Lincoln" by John Gould Fletcher. Douglass poems include "I Was Frederick Douglass" by Hildegard Smith and "Frederick Douglass" by Paul Laurence Dunbar.

Ask students to compare other leaders using the same process or to apply the compare and contrast process to other black leaders, such as comparing Frederick Douglass to Dr. Martin Luther King. Encourage your students to use the compare and contrast diagram as a memory tool when reviewing for a test. It can also be used as a design format for a poster or bulletin board.

RESULT—Although an individual may experience hardships and social limitations in his/her life, this does not curtail lifetime accomplishments. Frederick Douglass and Abraham Lincoln are two examples of such individuals, but they were able to change conditions for large numbers of people in their own lifetimes and for generations to come. They accomplished great things because they were highly motivated and they knew how to use language in a powerful way. Although Lincoln and Douglass differed regarding their assumptions about slavery, both men influenced public opinion and contributed to the end of slavery in America.

WRITING EXTENSION
A writing assignment for this lesson is featured in the "Essay Writing: Compare and Contrast" lesson in the writing chapter.

THINKING ABOUT THINKING
- How did you select what to list in comparing the two men? Why did you pick those characteristics rather than more general similarities, such as that both were men or that both could read?
- How did using the graph help you understand the similarities and differences between the two leaders' conditions and contributions? How does this differ from the way you understood the information from the written passage?
- Suggest another lesson in which comparing and contrasting would help you understand what you are learning.
- Use the same process to compare and contrast two people that you know. How does thinking about the two people using compare and contrast help you understand and appreciate things about their personalities in ways you may not have thought about before?
- Design another diagram that would help you organize information that compares two leaders.

SIMILAR SOCIAL STUDIES LESSONS
- To compare significant conditions in the lives of famous leaders.
- To compare changes in technology, social or political institutions, or ideas.
- To correlate historical, sociological, economic, or political developments from different cultures or countries.

ABRAHAM LINCOLN AND FREDERICK DOUGLASS: CONDITIONS AND CONTRIBUTIONS

DIRECTIONS: Read the passage carefully to determine how Abraham Lincoln and Frederick Douglass were alike and how they were different. Use the diagram to record their similarities and differences.

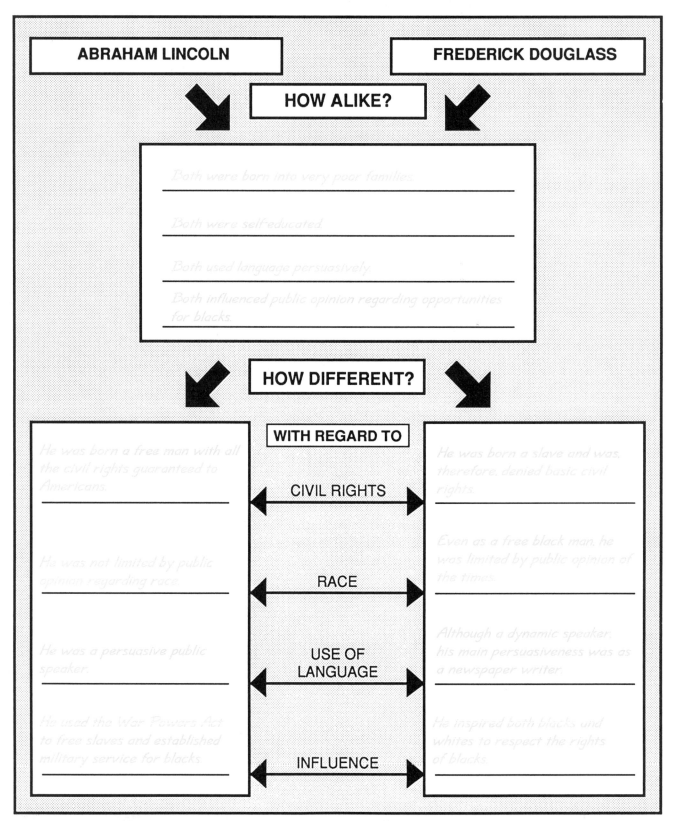

ABRAHAM LINCOLN

FREDERICK DOUGLASS

HOW ALIKE?

Both were born into very poor families.

Both were self-educated.

Both used language persuasively.

Both influenced public opinion regarding opportunities for blacks.

HOW DIFFERENT?

WITH REGARD TO

He was born a free man with all the civil rights guaranteed to Americans.

CIVIL RIGHTS

He was born a slave and was, therefore, denied basic civil rights.

He was not limited by public opinion regarding race.

RACE

Even as a free black man, he was limited by public opinion of the times.

He was a persuasive public speaker.

USE OF LANGUAGE

Although a dynamic speaker, his main persuasiveness was as a newspaper writer.

He used the War Powers Act to free slaves and established military service for blacks.

INFLUENCE

He inspired both blacks and whites to respect the rights of blacks.

PETROCHEMICAL PRODUCTS

THINKING SKILL: Verbal classification

CONTENT OBJECTIVE: Students will use the branching diagram to identify products and materials our families use which are made from petrochemicals. *NOTE: This lesson may be used alone or extended by the series of lessons on the Indian's use of the buffalo.*

DISCUSSION: TECHNIQUE—Use a transparency of the branching diagram to record students' identification of needed products which are produced from petrochemicals.

DIALOGUE— Ask students to identify many objects in the classroom that are made from petroleum products. Include items such as clothing, solvents, or plastics. Identify a natural material from which these objects could be made, such as an acrylic sweater and a wool sweater. Compare the prices of the two objects.

Why are petrochemical products cheaper than natural materials? (Natural products require more expensive processing; the source of wool is more limited than the source of petroleum.) **What makes petrochemical products (acrylic, nylon, rayon, polyurethane, polyethylene, polyester) so easy to find and to use?** (Many compounds can be made from petroleum. Synthetic products can be produced with special characteristics—washability, strength, imitation of natural materials, endurance, colorfastness, ease of storage, and ease of manufacture). **How does the abundance of petrochemical products affect our jobs and personal habits?** (Petrochemical products are used to manufacture computers, automobiles, television sets, appliances, food packaging, etc. Because petroleum products are less expensive, they are often thrown away.)

Petroleum products are usually less biodegradable than natural materials. How does that affect their disposal? Although petrochemical products seem plentiful and cheap, why should we use this resource efficiently? (Petrochemicals are a nonrenewable resource and may ultimately be used up or limited. Petrochemical producing nations may not always choose the United States as a market.) **What might happen if our source of petrochemicals became limited?** (Our technology would have to develop synthetic fibers and fuels from other materials; people would have to change their habits to accommodate the scarcity; recycling would become more important and cost effective.)

RESULT—By understanding the source of materials for the products we use, we can understand its significance to our habits, the costs of goods, and the effect on us if that source should be changed. Petrochemical products are versatile, cheap, and plentiful.

WRITING EXTENSION
- Describe the importance of petrochemicals in the products we use.

THINKING ABOUT THINKING
- How does seeing the many types of petrochemical products that we use pictured in this way help us understand how important petrochemicals are to us?
- How does understanding the significance of a resource affect the way we use it?

SIMILAR SOCIAL STUDIES LESSONS
- To depict branches or divisions of governments, institutions, or social science disciplines.
- To classify dwellings, weapons, household articles, tools, architectural structures.
- To describe people, events, artifacts, groups, or eras.

PETROCHEMICAL PRODUCTS

DIRECTIONS: Identify products we use that are made from petrochemical compounds. Use the branching diagram to record products by their uses.

Petrochemicals are chemicals made wholly or partially from petroleum or natural gas. They are used in a variety of industries and to manufacture products that our families use to meet our basic needs. Petrochemical products can be found in clothing, housing, food production and storage, transportation, recreation, and defense. Because there are so many forms of petrochemicals, and because they are part of, or used to make, other products, it is hard to estimate how much of what we use is made from petroleum.

Many of our clothes are made from synthetic fibers. Nylon, Orlon, Dacron, polyester, vinyl, and acrylic may look like natural fibers (cotton, wool, silk, leather, or linen), but they are made from petroleum. Space-age fibers are used to make lightweight, strong, long-lasting sports equipment and clothing. Because plastics are often made from petrochemical compounds, our buttons, zippers, and Velcro fasteners, even the detergents we use to clean our clothes, are produced to some extent from petroleum.

Many materials in our houses are made from petrochemical materials. Polyurethane varnishes, plastic pipes, acrylic carpets, electrical equipment, tiles and fixtures, insulation, flooring and roofing materials, and upholstery fabrics are manufactured from petrochemical compounds.

The most significant use of petrochemicals in our homes cannot be seen directly. Petrochemicals are the major fuel source in the United States and include heating oil, kerosene, natural gas, propane, and electricity produced by plants powered by fuel oil.

Our food is fertilized and protected by petrochemical compounds, and stored in plastic produced from petrochemical materials.

Petrochemicals are used in pesticides and weed killers and in the production of fertilizer. Saran and polyethylene plastics are used to wrap food from the farm to the fast-food restaurant. Even medicines are processed with petrochemical compounds.

We use petrochemicals for fuels used for transportation. From the neighborhood gas station to jet fuels for airliners, vehicles run on petroleum products. The cost of petroleum affects the price of almost anything we buy, since it takes fuel to transport goods to local stores. Petrochemicals are also used to make synthetic rubber, vinyl upholstery, and the interior surfaces in automobiles. Oils and greases used to reduce friction in cars, boats, and trains are made from petroleum.

Petrochemical plastics are used in boats, luggage, safety helmets, and a variety of recreation and sports equipment. Television sets, VCRs, tape decks, and radios contain plastic parts made from petrochemicals. Audio and video tapes, even credit cards, contain plastics.

Synthetic materials made from petrochemicals became plentiful during World War II. The war effort required aviation fuel, rubber, plastics, explosives, oils, and greases. Space-age technology, so vital to national defense today, relies on petrochemicals for plastic components or synthetic fibers for computers, insulation material, and structural material for airplanes, boats, and military vehicles.

In addition to using petrochemicals to produce goods, petroleum is burned to produce energy. The United States has 6% of the world's population, but uses 35% of the world's energy, two-thirds of which comes directly or indirectly from petroleum. We need to under-stand and manage this vital natural resource well.

PETROCHEMICAL PRODUCTS

DIRECTIONS: Read the passage carefully to determine what products we use that are made from petrochemicals. Use the branching diagram to record products by their uses.

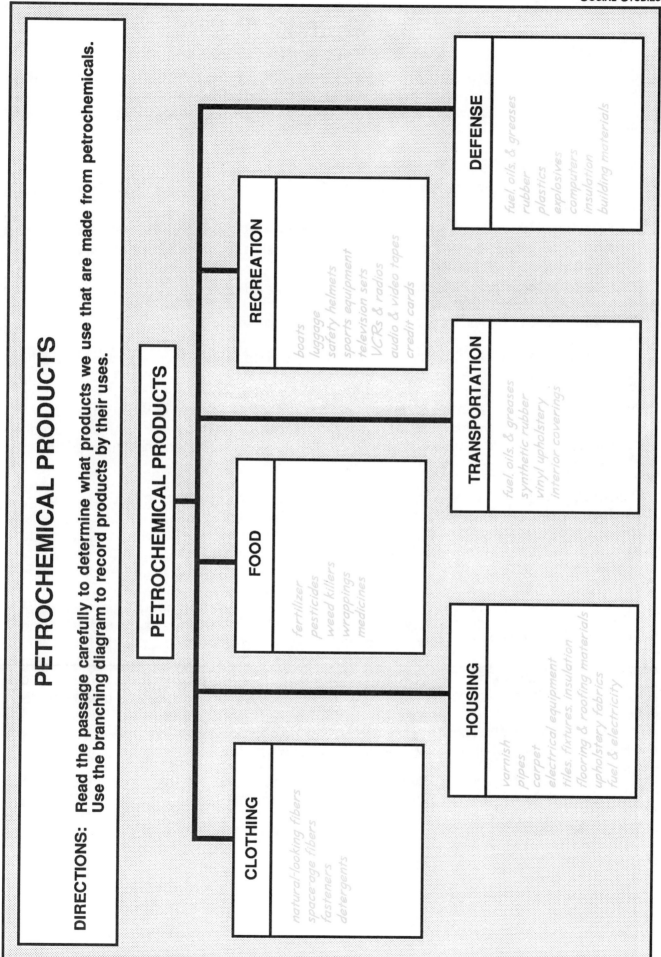

PETROCHEMICAL PRODUCTS

RECREATION
boats
luggage
safety helmets
sports equipment
television sets
VCRs & radios
audio & video tapes
credit cards

DEFENSE
fuel, oils, & greases
rubber
plastics
explosives
computers
insulation
building materials

FOOD
fertilizer
pesticides
weed killers
wrappings
medicines

TRANSPORTATION
fuel, oils, & greases
synthetic rubber
vinyl upholstery
interior coverings

CLOTHING
natural-looking fibers
space-age fibers
fasteners
detergents

HOUSING
varnish
pipes
carpet
electrical equipment
tiles, fixtures, insulation
flooring & roofing materials
upholstery fabrics
fuel & electricity

NEEDS AND RESOURCES:
SURVIVAL AND QUALITY-OF-LIFE NEEDS IN TWO CULTURES

NOTE: This is the first in a series of three lessons comparing the needs and sources of goods of today's families with the needs and sources of goods of Plains Indian families one hundred years ago.

SERIES CONTENT OBJECTIVES:
• Students will recognize that all people have the same basic needs but use different goods to fill those needs.
• Students will recognize that people secure needed goods from available sources.
• Students will recognize that, if a culture secures most of its needs from a single source, it will become significantly dependent on that supply.
• Students will recognize that any culture should make efficient use of available resources.

THINKING SKILL: Verbal classification, compare and contrast

CONTENT OBJECTIVE: Students will identify basic needs in our society and in the Plains Indian culture one hundred years ago. *NOTE: This lesson applies key concepts regarding basic needs and sources of supply commonly featured in elementary social studies textbooks. Because petroleum is a significant source of plastics and fuel in our culture, use the petroleum lesson before teaching this one. Allow adequate time to review students' understanding of needs and sources of supply, as well as their understanding of the culture of Plains Indians.*

DISCUSSION: TECHNIQUE—Use a transparency of the web diagram to record responses as students identify needs of families today and products which we use to fill those needs. Ask students to identify types of needs and write them in the large boxes. Ask students to identify products that we use to fill those needs and write those products on the arms. Discuss whether each product fills a basic need or improves the quality of life. As the chart is being filled, circle survival needs in red and quality of life needs in green.

Repeat this process to review students' understanding of the needs and sources of supply for Plains Indians one hundred years ago. Determine whether each product is an example of one that is necessary for survival or one that improves the quality of life.

DIALOGUE—As you discuss the products used to fill needs, ask each student who suggests a product to identify what it is made from and how we get the product. The source and materials for needed goods is featured in all three lessons and should be clearly identified.

As you discuss each product, examine whether that product is an example of one that is necessary for survival or one that improves the quality of life.

How do we decide whether something is a survival need or a quality of life need? What criteria do we use to decide what "survival" means?

List criteria for survival needs on the board. There will be some products that students will clearly identify as necessary for survival and some products that are clearly related to the quality of life. The key point of this lesson lies in what constitutes survival: survival needs commonly refer to air, food, water, shelter, clothing, safety, and transportation to secure needed products. Students may relate these needs to the conditions of the homeless in our society, the daily difficulties the homeless face to secure their basic needs, and the long term consequences of lack of basic survival needs.

As the class examines the two web diagrams, one sees that Plains Indians had more goods related to survival needs and fewer goods related to the quality of life compared to families today. Students should also recognize that families who lived in American cities one hundred years ago also had fewer goods related to the quality of life when compared to families today.

Students should recognize that most of today's goods are processed or manufactured and may come from countries across the globe. Plains Indian families secured needed goods from sources around them. It may be helpful to remind students that families in American cities a hundred years ago also had some goods that were manufactured and brought from other areas, but more goods were produced locally or made by the family itself than is commonly practiced today.

It may be useful to point out that Plains Indian families today no longer use the same goods and sources that they did one hundred years ago. When Plains Indian people today create the same products or enact the same ceremonies and activities, they do so to keep their ethnic skills and heritage alive and for their personal satisfaction.

RESULT—Students shall recognize that basic needs are the same across cultures. Some quality-of-life needs are more significant than others in the two cultures and the sources of goods may be different.

WRITING EXTENSION

• **Describe basic human needs and the sources of goods our families use to fill those needs. Describe the sources of goods used by Plains Indian families to fill those same needs.**

THINKING ABOUT THINKING

• **How did using the diagrams help you identify similarities and differences between the sources of goods needed by today's families and those used by Plains Indians one hundred years ago?**

• **How does using the diagram help you understand the information differently from the way you might understand the same information in a written passage?**

• **Suggest another lesson in which using this diagram would help you understand what you are learning.**

• **Design another diagram that would help you compare two cultures.** Students may find the compare and contrast diagram helpful to depict similarities and differences.

SIMILAR SOCIAL STUDIES LESSONS

• To depict branches or divisions of governments, institutions, or social sciences.

• To compare types of dwellings, weapons, household articles, tools, artifacts, costumes, communities, governments, and social systems belonging to various eras or cultures.

• To describe the functions of architectural structures, governmental divisions, or community institutions.

• To describe people, events, artifacts, groups, or eras.

NEEDS AND RESOURCES OF MODERN FAMILIES

DIRECTIONS: Identify the needs of families today. Record the types of needs in the larger boxes and the products that fill those needs in the smaller boxes on the arms of the diagram. Determine whether each product is necessary for survival or adds to the quality of life. Circle survival needs in red and quality-of-life needs in green.

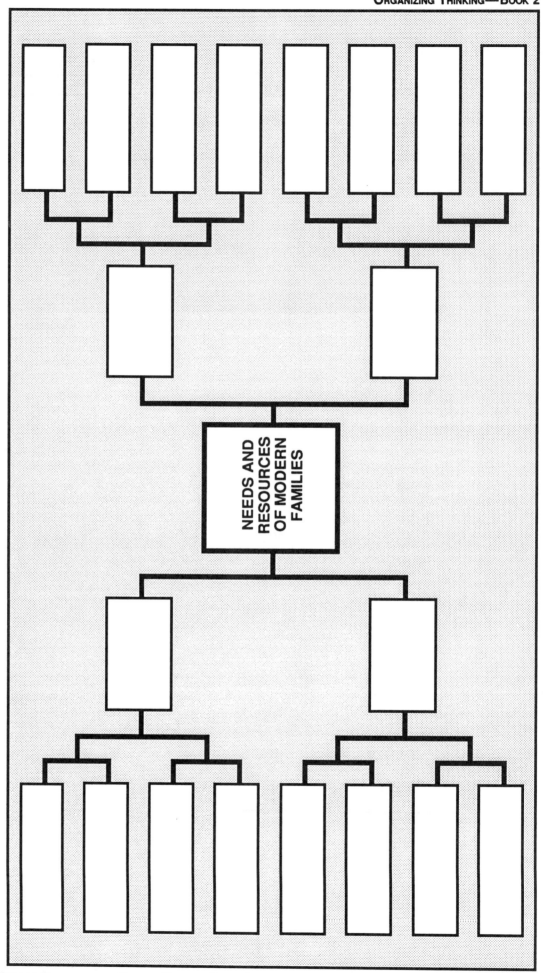

NEEDS AND RESOURCES OF MODERN FAMILIES

NEEDS AND RESOURCES OF PLAINS INDIAN FAMILIES

DIRECTIONS: Identify the needs of Plains Indian families of one hundred years ago. Record the types of needs in the larger boxes and the products that fill those needs in the smaller boxes on the arms of the diagram. Determine whether each product is necessary for survival or adds to the quality of life. Circle survival needs in red and quality-of-life needs in green.

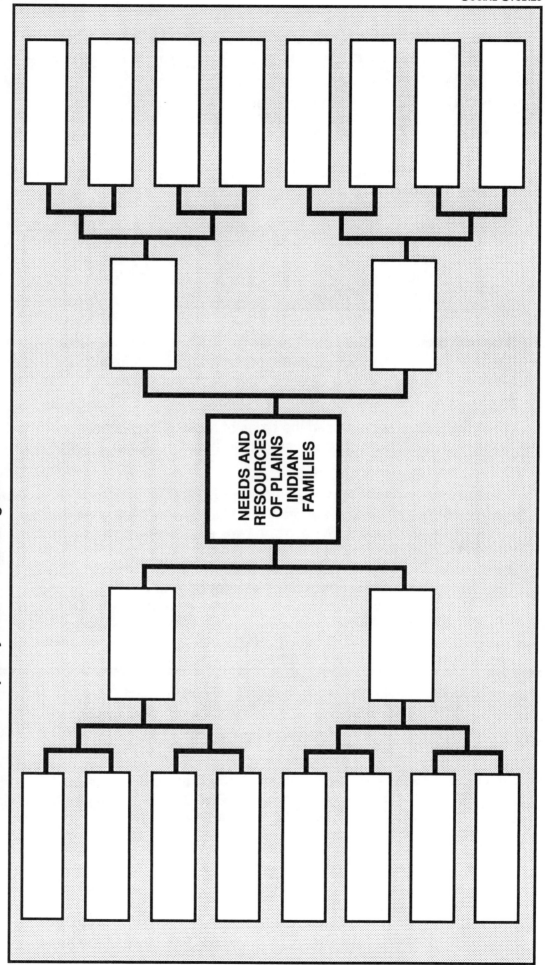

NEEDS AND RESOURCES OF PLAINS INDIAN FAMILIES

NEEDS AND RESOURCES:
THE BUFFALO AS A SOURCE OF SUPPLY

THINKING SKILL: Verbal classifications

OBJECTIVE: Students will use a branching diagram to identify products which Plains Indians obtained from the buffalo. *NOTE: This is the second in a series of three lessons comparing the needs and sources of goods of today's families with the needs and sources of goods of Plains Indian families one hundred years ago.*

DISCUSSION: TECHNIQUE—Use a transparency of the branching diagram to record responses as students read the passage and discuss products which Plains Indians obtained from the buffalo.

DIALOGUE—Examine the variety of products that Plains Indians made from the buffalo and the economy of using every part of the animal. As you discuss each item, ask the student who suggested the item to identify the key characteristic required for that product.

What characteristic does this buffalo product offer? (The buffalo material may be warm, tough, waterproof, sticky, or lightweight; separated into strings; carved or drilled; folded and easily transported; cooked or dried; burned or melted for tallow; softened for leather; or capable of producing a sound when vibrated.)

When the class has discussed the types of needs and products available from the buffalo, compare the information on the branching diagram with that from the Plains Indians web diagram in the last lesson.

To what extent were Plains Indians dependent on the buffalo for basic needs? (Identify the number and significance of products which Plains Indians needed for which the buffalo was the source of supply.) **What goods were not secured from the buffalo? What other sources of goods were available to them?** (Students should recognize that a culture which secures most of its needs from a single source becomes significantly dependent on that source.) **As natural and man-made conditions reduced or eliminated the number of buffalo, what effect did that have on the survival and/or life style of the Plains Indians? What conditions reduced the buffalo herds of the nineteenth century?** (Students may discuss the exploitative hunting of the buffalo and the encroachment by American settlers on their grazing and migration lands.)

Students should also recognize that any culture must strive to make efficient use of its available resources, whether those resources are petrochemicals in contemporary society or the buffalo one hundred years ago. This lesson demonstrates that the Plains Indians used all the body materials of the buffalo for some needed product.

Why was it necessary to use all the body materials of the buffalo for some needed product? How did the life style of the Plains Indians limit the processing of most goods to the site of the slaughter of the animal? How might they have learned to use all the materials so cleverly?

Students should recognize that, since many products made from the buffalo were necessary for the survival of Plains Indian people, the buffalo became significant in their religion, customs, and art.

Discussion may also extend to efficient use of the entire whale in the nineteenth century or cows in modern stockyards. Although these comparisons are not quite so strong as the diversity and prevalence of today's petrochemical by-products they emphasize the significance of animal products in the past and in present times.

Help students identify contemporary situations which cause families to travel in search of sources of economic support. The life style of migrant families who follow the harvests is not unlike that of the Plains Indian families of a century ago. Each must be unusually knowledgeable about the source of their livelihood, whether vegetables or buffaloes. Each must travel to find available sources. Each is at the mercy of natural and man-made conditions which may affect the supply of their needed goods.

RESULT— A culture must make efficient use of the resources available to it. Plains Indians were resourceful in using all the body materials of the buffalo for some needed product. Since products made from the buffalo were necessary for the survival of Plains Indian people, the buffalo became significant in their religion, their customs, and their art. If a culture is dependent on a source of supply, people become knowledgeable about the source, able to secure the goods, and, to some extent, dependent on natural and man-made conditions which may affect their supply.

WRITING EXTENSION

• Describe how Plains Indians used the buffalo to meet their survival needs.

• Discuss the significance of the efficient use of materials to produce needed goods.

THINKING ABOUT THINKING

• What does their efficient use of buffalo materials suggest about the values and ingenuity of Plains Indian people?

• What kinds of thinking do you expect they would value? Why?

• How does knowing about their creativity and economy change your understanding of their culture?

• How did using the diagram help you understand and remember the needs and sources of supply of Plains Indians?

• Suggest another lesson in which using this diagram would help you understand what you are learning.

• Design another diagram that would help you organize information to describe needs and sources of supply.

SIMILAR SOCIAL STUDIES LESSONS

• To depict branches or divisions of governments, institutions, or social science disciplines.

• To depict classes/subclasses of dwellings, weapons, household articles, or tools belonging to various eras or cultures.

• To depict part/whole relationships of dwellings, artifacts, costumes, communities, governments, and social systems.

• To describe the functions of architectural structures, governmental divisions, or community institutions.

• To describe people, events, artifacts, groups, or eras.

NEEDS AND RESOURCES:
THE BUFFALO AS A SOURCE OF SUPPLY

DIRECTIONS: Read the passage carefully to determine how the Plains Indians used the buffalo. Use the branching diagram to record the uses of items which the Plains Indians made from the buffalo.

The Plains Indian tribes of the nineteenth century followed herds of buffalo for food. These tribes used every bit of the buffalo's body to make products which they needed.

The buffalo's hide was a source of clothing material for Plains Indian people. The strong hide provided belts and waterproof moccasins. The soft, warm skin provided ear flaps, shirts, and winter robes. Thin strands of stringy muscle tissue from the legs and thighs of the buffalo served as thread to hold garments together. The bone of the buffalo was fashioned into headdress ornaments.

The Plains Indians used buffalo products to build shelters and to keep warm. The warm, strong, waterproof buffalo hides were used as tent covers and doors to keep out the bitter winter cold in the northern plains. Hides were used for bed covers and rugs. Other buffalo by-products were used as sources of heat and light. The dried waste droppings of the buffalo were burned for fuel. Bones were fashioned into tent ornaments. Buffalo fat was melted and used as tallow for lamps.

The Plains Indians used buffalo products to defend themselves against attackers. The muscle tissue was used for bow strings and for fastening an arrowhead to the shaft of the arrow. The strong, lightweight hide was shrunk to give it extra strength, then stretched across a frame to produce a shield.

Buffalo hide was used for travel equipment. The hides were used as saddle blankets for the comfort and health of horses. The strong, lightweight hides, stretched across a light wooden frame, formed a dragged sled called a *travois*. An envelope made of buffalo skin—called a *parflech*—was used by Indians to store dried buffalo meat.

The Plains Indians used buffalo products as tools or utensils within the home. They made cups and spoons from horns. They created paint brushes by chewing a small bone until it was soft. Knife sheaths, lariats for catching animals, ropes for houses and animals, and tie-strings for the doors of tents were all made from buffalo hide. Plains Indians made glue by boiling the buffalo hoofs. They used the stomach of the buffalo for a cooking pot or as a bucket for carrying drinking water long distances.

The buffalo was both the subject of and the material for religious objects. Plains Indians fashioned rattles from buffalo hide and made religious objects from buffalo bone and teeth. Drum heads and altar covers for the Sun Dance were made from buffalo hides.

PRODUCTS WHICH PLAINS INDIANS OBTAINED FROM THE BUFFALO

DIRECTIONS: Read the passage carefully to determine how the Plains Indians used the buffalo. Write each item in the box which best describes its use.

arrowhead wrappings, bed covers, belts, bow strings, cooking pots, cups, doors for tents, drum heads, ear flaps, fuel, glue, headdress ornaments, knife sheaths, lariats, moccasins, ornaments for tents, paint brushes, parfleches, rattles, ropes, rugs, saddle blankets, shields, shirts, spoons, Sun Dance altar covers, tallow, tent covers, tie strings, thread, travois, water buckets, winter robes.

PRODUCTS PLAINS INDIANS OBTAINED FROM THE BUFFALO

CLOTHING
Belts
Ear Flaps
Headdress
   Ornaments
Moccasins
Shirts
Thread
Winter Robes

HOUSING
Bed Covers
Tent Doors
Fuel
Tent Ornaments
Rugs
Tallow
Tent Covers

DEFENSE
Arrowhead
   Wrappings
Bow Strings
Shields

TRANSPORTATION
Parfleches
Saddle Blankets
Travois

TOOLS/UTENSILS
Cooking Pots
Cups
Glue
Knife Sheaths
Lariats
Paint Brushes
Ropes
Spoons
Tie Strings
Water Buckets

RELIGIOUS OBJECTS
Drum Heads
Rattles
Sun Dance altar
   covers

NEEDS AND RESOURCES: COMPARING GOODS

THINKING SKILL: Verbal classification, analogy, compare and contrast

CONTENT OBJECTIVE: Students will use the branching diagram, the class relationships diagram and the compare and contrast diagram to relate the needs and sources of supply of Plains Indian families with those of families today. *NOTE: This is the third in a series of three lessons comparing the needs and sources of goods of today's families with the needs and sources of goods of Plains Indian families one hundred years ago.*

DISCUSSION: TECHNIQUE—Use a transparency of the branching diagram to record products that today's families use to fill the same types of needs as were identified in the last lesson about the Plains Indians. Use a transparency of the class relationships diagram to record products that were used only by Plains Indian families, only by today's families, or used in some form by both.

In the first lesson in this series, the purpose of the activity was to distinguish between basic needs and quality-of-life needs. In this lesson, students again examine the needs and resources of today's families and Plains Indian families, but the emphasis of the lesson is on the source of materials and products.

DIALOGUE—Examine the variety of products that today's families use to fill basic needs. As each student reports, ask the student to identify the type of material that goes into the product and its source. Make two lists on the chalkboard, one column for materials and one for the source (in this case including the geographic area). Make an additional check mark each time a type of material or source is mentioned.

The second part of this lesson asks students to draw analogies between the needs and goods of the Plains Indians families of a century ago with those of today's families. These analogies focus on similar needs and the various sources of materials available to fill those needs. Students may suggest analogies such as "Indians had buffalo hide coats and today's people have cloth coats." The point is not that both groups wear coats, but that the Indians obtained the material from a single source, while today's families buy coats made from a variety of materials, originating in many geographical areas and processed in many ways. The key analogy is the reliance of both cultures on a major source of materials.

Which types of material and sources are often used in products for today's families? (Since petroleum is used as fuel and in the production of fabrics, plastics, electricity, fertilizers, medicines, and a variety of building materials, it is likely to be cited as the most common source of materials and products.)

What natural or man-made conditions might affect the supply of those materials? Are today's families dependent on any source to the extent that the Plains Indians were dependent on the buffalo for basic needs? What alternative sources of goods are available to us?

Suppose that our culture depended on petroleum to the same degree that the Indians relied on the buffalo. What kinds of advertisements or rules might the society develop? What clothing ornaments or habits might people have? (Students should realize that the buffalo became significant in the religion, customs, and art of Plains Indian people.)

As you discuss the class relationships diagram, identify why many of the products that today's family needs would not be desirable, appropriate, or possible for the Plains Indian family of one hundred years ago. Students may also wish to use a compare and contrast diagram to summarize the similarities and differences between the needs and goods of the two cultures and to examine the conclusions that they draw from the comparison.

RESULT—Today's families use products which are made from a variety of materials, come from a variety of sources, and are processed in a variety of ways. Today's families obtain goods from global, rather than local or regional, sources. Modern life generates needs that require more complex products than the society of the Plains Indians. Today's families are not as directly involved as the Plains Indians were in securing and processing the items that they use.

WRITING EXTENSION

- Describe the similarities and differences between how the Plains Indian families met and today's families meet their basic needs.
- Discuss why it is more difficult for people today to be knowledgeable about the sources of goods that they need.

THINKING ABOUT THINKING

- In this lesson we drew some analogies between modern and Plains Indian families. An analogy is a way of describing or explaining something by its similarity to something else. How does using an analogy help us understand both things differently than if we had examined them individually?
- Are there some limitations in using analogies to describe or explain things? How do you decide whether an analogy is good enough to use?
- How might people who do not think with analogies very much learn to use analogies more effectively?
- How did using the diagram help you understand the needs and supply sources for today's families?
- Suggest another lesson in which using this diagram would help you understand what you are learning.
- Design another diagram that would help you organize information to describe needs and sources of supply.

SIMILAR SOCIAL STUDIES LESSONS

- To depict branches or divisions of governments, institutions, or social science disciplines.
- To depict classes/subclasses of dwellings, weapons, household articles, or tools belonging to various eras or cultures.
- To describe the types of symbols in a map legend (type of road, size of cities, elevation, points of interest, mileage, etc.).
- To depict part/whole relationships of dwellings, artifacts, costumes, communities, governments, and social systems.
- To describe the functions of architectural structures, governmental divisions, or community institutions.
- To describe people, events, artifacts, groups, or eras.

PRODUCTS TODAY'S FAMILIES NEED

DIRECTIONS: In the previous lesson, you classified items which Plains Indians made from the buffalo according to the type of need. Use this branching diagram to list common objects that today's families use for the same purposes. In parentheses after each item, write the primary material from which that item is made.

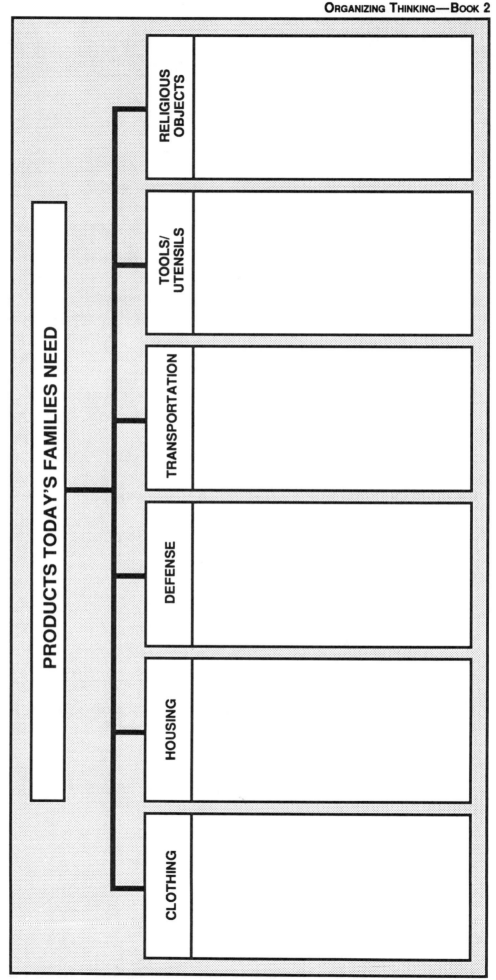

PRODUCTS USED BY THE PLAINS INDIAN AND/OR TODAY'S FAMILIES

DIRECTIONS: Use the class relationships diagram to record whether each of the items listed below was used by Plains Indian families, modern families, or both. In the circle on the left, write each item which only Plains Indian families used. In the intersection of the two circles, write each item which both Plains Indian families used and modern families use. In the circle on the right, write items which only today's families use.

arrowhead wrappings, bed covers, belts, bow strings, cooking pots, cups, drum heads, fuel, glue, knife sheaths, lariats, paint brushes, parfleches, rattles, ropes, rugs, saddle blankets, shields, shirts, spoons, strings, Sun Dance altar covers, tallow, tent covers, tent ornaments, thread, travois, water buckets, winter clothes.

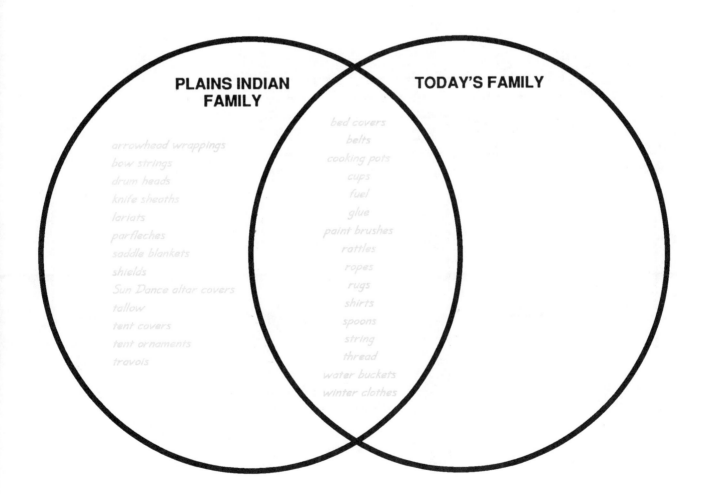

PLAINS INDIAN FAMILY

arrowhead wrappings
bow strings
drum heads
knife sheaths
lariats
parfleches
saddle blankets
shields
Sun Dance altar covers
tallow
tent covers
tent ornaments
travois

TODAY'S FAMILY

bed covers
belts
cooking pots
cups
fuel
glue
paint brushes
rattles
ropes
rugs
shirts
spoons
string
thread
water buckets
winter clothes

NEEDS AND RESOURCES:
PLAINS INDIAN FAMILIES OF THE 1800s AND FAMILIES OF TODAY

DIRECTIONS: Use the compare and contrast graph to record how the needs and resources of Plains Indian families of the 1800s and those of today's families are alike and how they are different.

PLAINS INDIAN FAMILY		TODAY'S FAMILY

HOW ALIKE?

Both have similar basic needs: food, clothing, housing, and transportation.

Both must use available products to fill needs.

Both must make efficient use of available resources.

HOW DIFFERENT?

WITH REGARD TO

PLAINS INDIAN FAMILY		TODAY'S FAMILY
Limited to local resources, primarily the buffalo	VARIETY OF SOURCES	World-wide resources
Indian families processed the goods themselves	DEGREE OF PROCESSING	Buy processed goods
Spent more time meeting survival needs	SIMPLICITY OF NEEDS	Spend more time on quality-of-life needs
Individuals contributed directly to group's defense	DEFENSE	Contribute to defense by paying taxes
Used simple tools	TECHNOLOGY	Rely on electric and mechanical devices

 © 1990 MIDWEST PUBLICATIONS • CRITICAL THINKING PRESS & SOFTWARE • P. O. Box 448, Pacific Grove, CA 93950

STATE AND FEDERAL GOVERNMENT

THINKING SKILL: Verbal differences

CONTENT OBJECTIVE: Students will use the contrast graph to differentiate between the types of laws which the federal government can make and those which state governments can make.

DISCUSSION: TECHNIQUE—Use a transparency of the contrast graph to record responses as students examine the differences between federal and state laws and services. Encourage students to research additional differences in powers and responsibilities of federal and state governments.

DIALOGUE—Some elementary students do not realize that in the United States "federal" and "national" mean the same thing. Some students believe that federal refers to a branch of government, another level of government, or relates only to Washington, D.C. Take time to confirm that students understand these terms correctly.

Help students understand the purposes of distinguishing between the powers and responsibilities of state and federal agencies. Encourage them to give examples of current events, such as the enforcement of drug laws, which illustrate the cooperation between agencies and the differentiation in their areas of responsibility.

As students report differences between federal and state government, discuss those differences by **naming** the quality that is different. Establish this pattern:

With regard to (quality), (item one and its distinction), **but** (item two and its distinction). For example, **With regard to producing currency, the federal government may coin and print money, but states may not.**

RESULT—To understand the effectiveness of public services and policies, one must determine which type of government is responsible.

WRITING EXTENSION

* **Why is it helpful to know which laws and services are the responsibility of federal or state government?** (Understanding the effect of changes in government spending; obtaining appropriate services from government agencies; assessing the qualifications of candidates for public office)
* **Describe the differences in services and responsibilities between state and federal agencies.**

THINKING ABOUT THINKING

* **How did using the graph to compare government responsibility help you understand the laws and services of different governmental levels? How does this differ from the way you understood the written passage?**
* **Suggest another lesson in which using this graph to compare and contrast would help you understand what you are learning.**
* **Design another diagram that would help you organize information to compare two institutions.**

SIMILAR SOCIAL STUDIES LESSONS

* To contrast any two cultures, e.g., Soviet with American cultures or the development of Mesopotamian civilization with that of ancient Egypt.
* To contrast any two forms of government, e.g., democracy with dictatorship.

- To contrast two economic systems, e.g., capitalism with communism; socialism with capitalism or communism; indentured servitude with slavery; economics of New England with those of colonial Virginia; industrial development of northern states with agricultural development of southern states before the Civil War.

- To contrast historical trends, e.g., development of human-rights policies in different historical eras and different countries; changes in the roles of or attitudes toward women or minorities in different historical eras and different countries; migrations of people in different historical eras.

- To contrast sociological or anthropological aspects of any two cultures, e.g., various groups of American Indians, European ethnic groups, African tribes, Middle Eastern ethnic groups, cultures of southeast Asia and Australia.

- To contrast events involving historical figures, e.g., Alexander the Great and Julius Caesar; military campaigns of Napoleon and Hitler; travels of Marco Polo and Christopher Columbus.

- To contrast any two historical events, e.g., battles, revolutions, invasions, cultural blendings, formation of institutions, publications, trade developments, discoveries of unknown land, technological change.

- To contrast the effect of geographical features or natural resources on the development of cultures in various parts of the world.

© 1990 MIDWEST PUBLICATIONS • CRITICAL THINKING PRESS & SOFTWARE • P. O. Box 448, Pacific Grove, CA 93950

STATE AND FEDERAL GOVERNMENT

DIRECTIONS: Read the passage carefully to determine what kinds of actions federal and state governments may and may not take. Use the graphic organizer to record the following areas of responsibility: production of currency, conduct of foreign relations, taxation of goods and income, regulation of transportation, regulation of commerce, maintenance of military services, and education.

There are clear differences between the types of laws that the federal government and the various state governments can make. Some rights and powers are reserved for the federal government alone. For example, only the federal government may coin and print money or declare war and make treaties with foreign governments.

Other rights and powers belong to both federal and state governments. For example, both the federal and state governments may set and collect taxes. The federal government taxes imports and certain specialty products (excise taxes). States may tax general retail sales (sales tax). Both governments may tax corporate and individual income, although not all states choose to do so.

The federal government funds interstate highways and regulates airline routes. State governments fund state highways and bridges and operate the highway patrol. The federal government controls the transportation of goods (commerce) between states; state governments control commerce within state borders.

The federal government maintains the armed services. The president of the United States is the commander in chief of the armed services. State governments maintain state militia (also called the National Guard). The governor of each state is the commanding officer of the state militia, although the president of the United States may assume command in a period of emergency.

In education the federal government may provide money for research that can be used in schools across the country. It also administers national educational-aid programs (student loans, scholarships, and aid to school districts serving military bases). State governments provide some funding to local school districts, recommend or adopt textbooks, certify teachers, and operate state universities, colleges, community or junior colleges, and technical schools.

STATE AND FEDERAL GOVERNMENT

FEDERAL

STATE

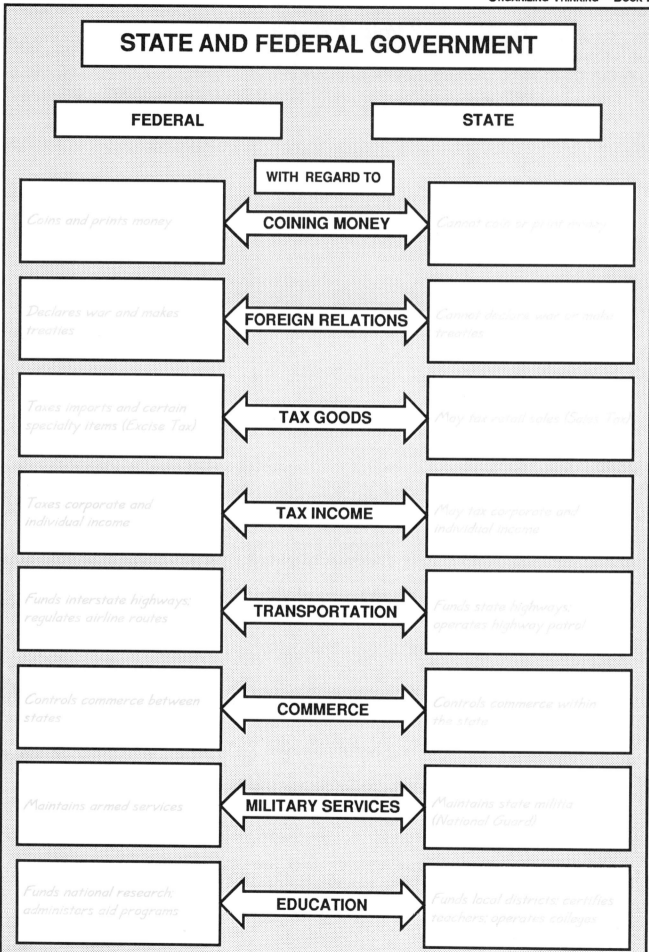

WITH REGARD TO

FEDERAL	WITH REGARD TO	STATE
Coins and prints money	COINING MONEY	Cannot coin or print money
Declares war and makes treaties	FOREIGN RELATIONS	Cannot declare war or make treaties
Taxes imports and certain specialty items (Excise Tax)	TAX GOODS	May tax retail sales (Sales Tax)
Taxes corporate and individual income	TAX INCOME	May tax corporate and individual income
Funds interstate highways; regulates airline routes	TRANSPORTATION	Funds state highways; operates highway patrol
Controls commerce between states	COMMERCE	Controls commerce within the state
Maintains armed services	MILITARY SERVICES	Maintains state militia (National Guard)
Funds national research; administers aid programs	EDUCATION	Funds local districts; certifies teachers; operates colleges

LOCAL, STATE, AND FEDERAL GOVERNMENT

THINKING SKILL: Verbal classifications

CONTENT OBJECTIVE: Students will use a matrix chart to differentiate among local, state, and federal governments.

DISCUSSION: TECHNIQUE—Use a transparency of the matrix diagram to record responses as students discuss the leaders, locations, and law enforcement agencies of local, state, and federal governments. It is often taken for granted that students know these terms and can distinguish among levels of government. Use this opportunity to list the names of local elected officials and to discuss your community's terms and titles for agencies and elected officials.

DIALOGUE—Some elementary students do not realize that in the United States "federal" and "national" mean the same thing. Others may believe that federal refers to a branch of the government, another level of government, or only to Washington, D.C. Take the time to confirm that students understand these terms correctly.

Help students understand the purposes of distinguishing among the elected officials, locations, and law enforcement responsibilities of local, state, and federal agencies. Encourage them to give examples of current events, such as the enforcement of drug laws, which illustrate the cooperation between law enforcement agencies, and differentiate among their areas of responsibility. Encourage students to identify individuals who serve in local, state, and federal positions. Bulletin boards or picture displays of individuals, buildings, vehicles, or symbols may help students identify the various levels of government responsibility.

Confirm that the chief official is an administrator, not a legislator. Some elementary students believe that the president makes the laws and runs the Congress. Some also believe that the governor runs the state legislature.

In some city governments the mayor is elected as an administrator who runs the city. In others the mayor is a city council member who presides over meetings and has ceremonial responsibilities, but does not directly supervise the city's business dealings. In the New England town meeting form of government, citizens make laws directly and the elected officials (selectmen) have administrative assignments. Confirm your city's form of municipal government.

Why is it helpful to know which individuals, locations, and law enforcement agencies are associated with local, state, or federal government? (Identifying proper agencies or administrators when seeking to remedy a problem; addressing questions to elected officials with responsibility over participating agencies; assessing the qualifications of candidates for public office and their views on policies related to that agency.) **News broadcasts sometimes show pictures or symbols to remind us that an issue being reported is local, state, or federal. Why do broadcasters find it helpful to cue the viewer by using symbols when reporting the news?** (Using a picture of a recognized elected official, such as the governor or the president, allows the viewer to understand immediately the level of government that the story concerns.)

RESULT—To understand the effectiveness of public services and policies, one must differentiate which type of government is providing it.

WRITING EXTENSION

• **Describe the differences in chief officials, locations, and law enforcement responsibilities of local, state, and federal governments.**

THINKING ABOUT THINKING

* **How did using the diagram help you understand significant differences in local, state, and federal governments?**
* **How does comparing government responsibility this way allow us to understand laws and services more quickly than we would perceive them from reading isolated passages?**
* **Suggest another lesson in which you think that recording information this way would help you understand what you are learning.**
* **Design another diagram that would help you organize information about the three levels of government.**
* **Suggest another lesson in which you think that using this graph would help you understand what you are learning.**

SIMILAR SOCIAL STUDIES LESSONS

* To describe cultures, governments, economic systems, historical trends, or sociological or anthropological aspects of any two cultures, historical figures, discoveries of unknown land, technological change, historical events, geographical features or natural resources.
* To depict statistics and survey results
* To record characteristics of people, places, events, nations, institutions, or concepts by two variables.

LOCAL, STATE, AND FEDERAL GOVERNMENT

DIRECTIONS: Use the matrix chart to identify the chief official, the building where law-makers meet, and the law enforcement agency of local, state, and national governments.

There are three major levels of government in the United States. These different levels are easy to identify by the title of the chief official, the name of the place the lawmakers meet, and the name of the department that enforces the laws.

The chief official of a local government is called the **mayor.** Mayors are usually elected to that position, although in some cities the mayor may be appointed by the city council. The mayor and the city council make laws for the city in public meetings held at the **city hall.** These laws are enforced by the local **police department**.

The **governor** is the chief official of a state. The governor sees that the laws made by the state legislature are carried out. The state legislature meets in the **state capitol building**.

State laws are enforced by the **state highway patrol** or the **state police**. In a state emergency, the governor can also call out the **state militia (national guard)** to enforce state laws.

The chief official of our national government is the **President** of the United States, who carries out laws passed by Congress. Congress meets in the **Capitol Building** in Washington, D.C. The **Federal Bureau of Investigation (FBI)** is the main national law-enforcement agency. They investigate and make arrests in crimes concerning federal or Constitutional laws. **Treasury Agents**, who also work for the federal government, enforce alcohol, tobacco, and firearms laws and investigate fraud, forgery, and counterfeiting cases. Federal drug laws are enforced by the **Drug Enforcement Agency (DEA)**.

	LOCAL	STATE	NATIONAL
CHIEF OFFICIAL	Mayor	Governor	President
BUILDING WHERE LAWMAKERS MEET	City Hall	State Capitol Building	Capitol Building (Washington, D.C.)
LAW ENFORCEMENT AGENCY	Police Department	State Police Highway Patrol State Militia	Federal Bureau of Investigation (FBI) Treasury Agents Drug Enforcement Agency (DEA)

THE UNITED NATIONS

THINKING SKILL: Verbal classification

CONTENT OBJECTIVE: Students will use a central idea graph to depict the organization of the United Nations by illustrating its branches.

DISCUSSION: TECHNIQUE—Use a transparency of the central idea graph to record responses as students discuss the organizational structure of the United Nations.

DIALOGUE—As students identify branches of the United Nations, ask them to identify the purpose of each division. Encourage students to research current issues and projects of United Nations agencies.

RESULT—To understand the organization of the United Nations, one must identify its branches and the purposes of each.

WRITING EXTENSION

• Describe the divisions of the United Nations and their purposes.

THINKING ABOUT THINKING

• Why is knowing all the divisions important to understanding the activities and purposes of the United Nations?

• How did using the diagram help you understand and remember the divisions of the United Nations? How did this differ from the way you understood and remembered information in the written passage?

• Suggest another lesson in which using this graph would help you understand what you are learning.

• Design another diagram that would help you picture the organization of the United Nations.

SIMILAR SOCIAL STUDIES LESSONS

• To depict branches or divisions of governments, institutions, or social science disciplines.

• To depict classes/subclasses of dwellings, weapons, household articles, or tools belonging to various eras or cultures.

• To describe types of symbols in a map legend (type of road, size of cities, elevation, points of interest, mileage, etc.)

• To depict part/whole relationships for dwellings, artifacts, costumes, communities, governments, and social systems.

• To describe the functions of architectural structures, governmental divisions, or community institutions.

• To describe people, events, artifacts, groups, or eras.

• To depict main idea and supporting details.

THE UNITED NATIONS

DIRECTIONS: Read the following passage carefully to determine how to record the divisions of the United Nations on the central idea graph.

The United Nations is an organization of representatives of the world's nations. It tries to settle disputes among nations in a peaceful way. The United Nations has six branches, which are listed and described below.

The **General Assembly** is the meeting of nations. Each nation has one vote, and most decisions are made by majority rule. The General Assembly can discuss any subject covered by the charter. It also admits new members.

The **Security Council** tries to settle disputes among nations and may send in U.N. peace-keeping troops to try to prevent armed conflict. It has five permanent members and six members elected for two-year terms.

The **Secretariat** is the executive branch, including clerks, translators, and administrators. It is the record keeping and program branch of the U.N.

The **Economic and Social Council** works to improve education and health and reduce unemployment throughout the world.

The **International Court of Justice**, which is made up of fifteen judges from different nations, settles treaty disputes.

The **Trusteeship Council** supervises colonies that do not yet have independence.

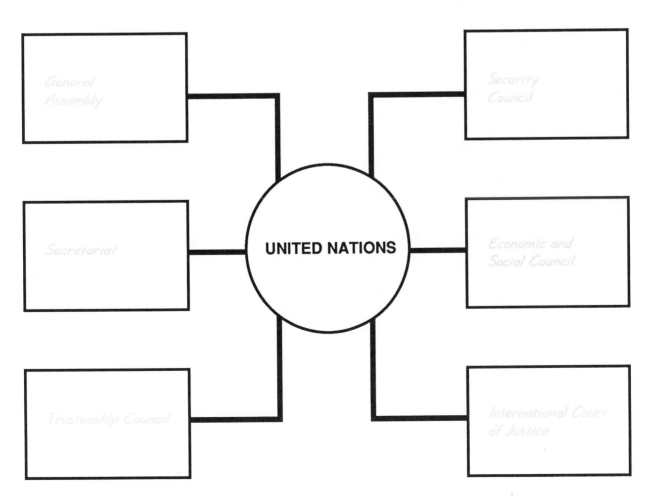

THE DEVELOPMENT OF CIVILIZATION

THINKING SKILL: Verbal sequences

CONTENT OBJECTIVE: Students will use a flowchart to trace the development of money as a medium of exchange.

DISCUSSION: TECHNIQUE—Use a transparency of the flowchart to record responses as students read the passage and answer the question that appears in each diamond. Students will find that the flowchart format helps clarify basic economic information concerning the effect of supply and demand, the division of labor, the flow of trade, the abundance of food, and the development of money in ancient civilizations.

This lesson describes the evolution of money as a means of exchange in Sumer. Encourage students to draw parallels between Sumer and other ancient cultures. Identify cultures today which function at each level of economic development described in the diamonds. Confirm that the development process described in this lesson occurred over many centuries. It was not intentionally planned by any leader or legislature.

How would a lack of surplus food affect the development of art, music, artifacts, or literature in a culture? (Individuals in such a culture must obtain food to survive and therefore would have little time to develop artistic expressions. Identify examples of sustenance cultures.) **What effect did a division of labor have on the food supply?** (As some individuals grew food and others hunted, herded, or processed food, a greater variety of food became available. This diversity lessens the threat of a famine wiping out the sole source of food. Identify examples of contemporary cultures that are just able to produce a surplus of food or other trade commodities. It is helpful to remember that although the rise of civilization in Sumer involved food as a trade commodity, food is not the only thing which cultures may exchange.) **How is the surplus of food distributed among the people who need it?** (People who do not grow or gather food must buy or barter their goods or services for food. Help students identify examples of contemporary cultures in which food is not efficiently distributed to those who need it. Identify the conditions which keep people who need food from getting it.)

In what way do cities contribute to the efficient exchange of goods within a culture? (Since food is needed daily and may spoil, people must buy or barter food on a regular basis. Groups of people living together can produce and exchange goods and services for the food that they need. Identify examples of cultures which do exchange goods without living in cities. Identify how the exchange occurs.) **What effect did exchanging the food surplus have on the Sumerians' ability to get other goods and materials?** (Since all people need food, it is a desirable commodity to exchange for resources and products. The Sumerians specialized in producing food efficiently and effectively. They acquired materials and goods not readily available in their region because of the demand for the food they produced by groups with which they traded. Identify contemporary examples of nations that are food producers and nations that exchange manufactured goods for food. Compared to manufactured goods, examine whether food is considered as valuable as its significance suggests.) **Why is food itself a poor medium of exchange?** (Limitations of weight, spillage, spoilage, and the match between the type and quantity of food offered for sale with the type and value of desired resources or goods. Identify mediums of exchange other than money that are used among people and cultures.)

RESULT —Three criteria for the development of a civilization include a surplus of food, a division of labor, and the growth of cities. Each is necessary to give people within the culture security from famine and the opportunity to develop specialization and a means of livelihood. Developing a medium of exchange allows a culture to improve the quality of life and opportunities to secure and export goods and materials.

WRITING EXTENSION

- **Describe the development of money in Sumer.**
- **How does a medium of exchange allow a culture to improve the quality of life and opportunities to secure and export goods and materials.**

THINKING ABOUT THINKING

- **How does a flowchart illustrate the steps in an evolutionary process?**
- **How does depicting the consequences of the lack of a condition or resource help you understand its significance?**
- **How is explaining a process with a flowchart like making individual choices?**
- **Why is knowing the order of occurrence important in understanding a development?**
- **Suggest another lesson in which using this graph would help you understand what you are learning.**
- **Design another diagram that would help you picture the development of civilization in Sumer.**

SIMILAR SOCIAL STUDIES LESSONS

- To illustrate the evolution of institutions, products, inventions, laws, or ideas.
- To depict contrary-to-fact consequences of historic events; e.g., "If the South had won the Civil War…"
- To predict the consequences of economic, social, or political changes.

THE DEVELOPMENT OF CIVILIZATION

DIRECTIONS: Read the passage on the development of civilization. Use the flowchart on the following page to depict the development of civilization in ancient Sumer.

The development of civilization in ancient Sumer involved the change from a food-gathering culture to one that traded food for goods. The land in Sumer had rich soil, water from the flooding of two rivers, and a long growing season. Until people could depend on the food supply, each individual or family had to hunt, trap, or gather food to survive.

Over many centuries people in Sumer had observed that grains and grasses which had been gathered wild could be planted and harvested at predictable times. The animals they tamed were used for milk and meat. The food supply increased and became steady.

As the Sumerians learned to grow predictable harvests and a variety of food, not every Sumerian had to be a farmer. Some of them were able to grow enough food for all of the people. A few Sumerians became craftsmen, raised animals, or managed the storage and distribution of food. Some craftsmen learned to turn fiber-producing plants into cotton and linen cloth. All of these people were able to eat by exchanging their goods or services for food. In this way the culture distributed adequate food among its own people.

The development of agriculture and irrigation allowed the Sumerians to grow much more food than they needed for their own survival. As a surplus of food accumulated and the Sumerians became less likely to face famine, they began to store the surplus. Then they had to guard against its spoilage.

They began trading their surplus food for things they didn't have. They developed a surplus of barley, other grains, and cotton, but they had no timber, stone, or metals. For centuries the Sumerians bartered barley and other grains for needed goods. Because the barley was heavy, could spoil or spill, and was hard to transport over long distances, the Sumerians were limited to trading with nearby groups and with people who wanted barley for their goods.

The amount of barley the Sumerians wanted to sell, however, did not always match the value of the goods that they wanted to buy. Sumerian merchants found that silver was accepted almost everywhere and could be used to purchase a great variety of goods. A small amount of silver could be traded for a large quantity of barley or other goods, so silver money could be easily transported to solve the problems of trading with distant merchants. The Sumerians developed small bars of silver, stamped to show its weight. This became the world's first metal money.

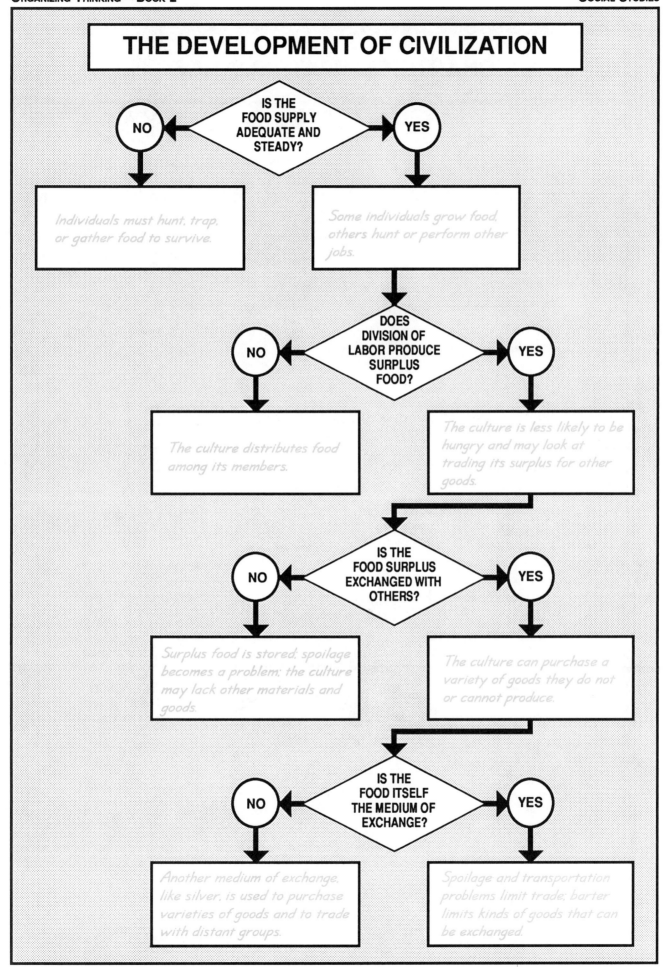

THE DEVELOPMENT OF CIVILIZATION

IS THE FOOD SUPPLY ADEQUATE AND STEADY?

NO → *Individuals must hunt, trap, or gather food to survive.*

YES → *Some individuals grow food, others hunt or perform other jobs.*

DOES DIVISION OF LABOR PRODUCE SURPLUS FOOD?

NO → *The culture distributes food among its members.*

YES → *The culture is less likely to be hungry and may look at trading its surplus for other goods.*

IS THE FOOD SURPLUS EXCHANGED WITH OTHERS?

NO → *Surplus food is stored; spoilage becomes a problem; the culture may lack other materials and goods.*

YES → *The culture can purchase a variety of goods they do not or cannot produce.*

IS THE FOOD ITSELF THE MEDIUM OF EXCHANGE?

NO → *Another medium of exchange, like silver, is used to purchase varieties of goods and to trade with distant groups.*

YES → *Spoilage and transportation problems limit trade; barter limits kinds of goods that can be exchanged.*

CHAPTER 5 – MATHEMATICS

COMMON FACTORS (Class Relationships Diagram)		FACTOR TREE (Branching Diagram)
	COMMON MULTIPLES AND PRIME NUMBERS (Class Relationships Diagram)	
FINDING A MATHEMATICAL RULE (Matrix Chart)		VALUE OF FRACTIONS (Transitive Order Graph)
	HOW TO ADD FRACTIONS (Flowchart)	
ADDING AND MULTIPLYING FRACTIONS (Matrix Chart)		FRACTIONS AND DECIMALS (Compare and Contrast Graph)
	DESCRIBING TRIANGLES (Central Idea Graph)	
QUADRILATERAL SERIES: CLASSIFYING POLYGONS (Branching Diagram)		DESCRIBING QUADRILATERALS (Matrix Chart)
	CLASSIFYING QUADRILATERALS (Various Organizers)	
WORLD POPULATION GROWTH (Grid Diagram)		EFFECT OF INFLATION ON YOUR BUYING POWER (Interval Graph)

COMMON FACTORS

THINKING SKILL: Symbol classification

CONTENT OBJECTIVE: Students will use a class relationships diagram to find common factors of two numbers.

DISCUSSION: TECHNIQUE—The diagram shows that two numbers may have several factors in common and leads students to identify the greatest common factor that two numbers share. Finding the greatest common factor is helpful in reducing fractions to the simplest form.

DIALOGUE—To explain the example, ask students to list all combinations of factors that will produce 6 and 8. The class relationships diagram has been produced by merging the factors of the two numbers together. The numbers in the intersection are common factors of both 6 and 8. Repeat this process to find the common factors of other numbers.

Reduce the fraction 6/8 to its simplest form. Since 2 is the greatest common factor of 6 and 8, divide both 6 and 8 by 2 to reduce the fraction to its simplest form.

$$\frac{6}{8} \div \frac{2}{2} = \frac{6 \div 2}{8 \div 2} = \frac{3}{4}$$

Students often confuse the greatest common factor (GCF) and the least common multiple (LCM). The class relationships diagram is one way of showing GCF. The branching diagram is a way of showing the LCM factors. (See the "Factor Tree" lesson.) Students may use the diagrams as visual reminders of what the two terms mean and how to calculate them.

RESULT—The class relationships diagram helps identify the greatest common factor and reminds students how to calculate it.

WRITING EXTENSION
- **How does finding the GCF help you reduce a fraction to its simplest form?**

THINKING ABOUT THINKING
- **How does using the class relationships diagram help you "see" common factors of two numbers?**
- **How does using the class relationships diagram help you "see" the least common factor? How can you use the least common factor in fraction problems?**
- **Suggest another lesson in which showing information on a class relationships diagram would help you understand what you are learning.**

  Use the following question when both the "Common Factors" and "Factor Tree" lessons have been taught.
- **How does using the diagrams help you "see" the difference between the greatest common factor and the least common multiple?**

SIMILAR MATHEMATICS LESSONS
- To illustrate or explain sets or set theory.
- To illustrate multiples or factors of numbers, geometry terms, polygons, or polyhedra.

COMMON FACTORS

DIRECTIONS: Write all the combinations of factors of 6 in the left circle and factors of 8 in the right circle. Next, identify those that are factors of both 6 and 8. Write the common factors of both 6 and 8 in the intersection. Repeat this pattern to find common factors of other number pairs.

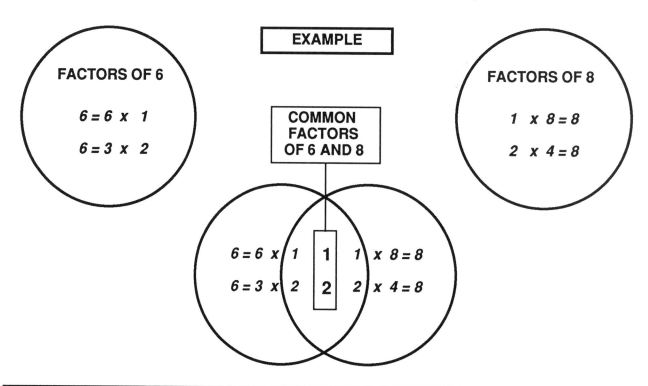

EXAMPLE

FACTORS OF 6

6 = 6 x 1

6 = 3 x 2

COMMON FACTORS OF 6 AND 8

FACTORS OF 8

1 x 8 = 8

2 x 4 = 8

6 = 6 x 1 **1** 1 *x 8 = 8*

6 = 3 x 2 **2** 2 *x 4 = 8*

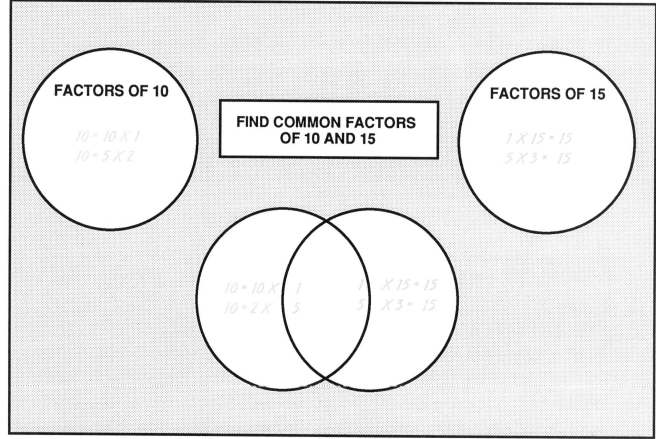

FACTORS OF 10

10 = 10 X 1
10 = 5 X 2

FIND COMMON FACTORS OF 10 AND 15

FACTORS OF 15

1 X 15 = 15
5 X 3 = 15

10 = 10 X 1   1 *X 15 = 15*
10 = 2 X 5   5 *X 3 = 15*

COMMON FACTORS

FACTORS OF 9

$9 = 9 X 1$
$9 = 3 X 3$

FIND COMMON FACTORS OF 9 AND 12

FACTORS OF 12

$1 X 12 = 12$
$2 X 6 = 12$
$3 X 4 = 12$

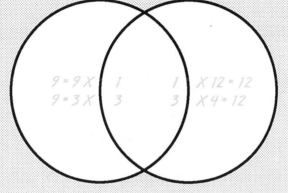

$9 = 9 X$ 1 1 $X 12 = 12$
$9 = 3 X$ 3 3 $X 4 = 12$

FACTORS OF 12

$12 = 12 X 1$
$12 = 6 X 2$
$12 = 4 X 3$

FIND COMMON FACTORS OF 12 AND 15

FACTORS OF 15

$1 X 15 = 15$
$3 X 5 = 15$

$12 = 12 X$ 1 1 $X 15 = 15$
$12 = 4 X$ 3 3 $X 5 = 15$

FACTOR TREE

THINKING SKILL: Attributes of numbers

CONTENT OBJECTIVE: Students will use a branching diagram to represent a number as a product. This lesson reviews factors and distinguishes between the greatest common factor and the least common multiple.

DISCUSSION: TECHNIQUE—Use a copy of the branching diagram to record answers as students identify factors of each complex number.

    DIALOGUE—Encourage students to describe how using the diagram helps them "see" the factoring process. Use two branching diagrams side-by-side to factor the numbers in the denominators of two fractions and to compute the least common multiple.

Example: 1/6 + 3/8 = _____

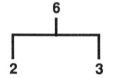

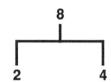

Pretend that you want to drop only one of each factor "into a bowl." By multiplying all the factors "in the bowl" together, you find the lowest number that is a multiple of both 6 and 8. (2 x 3 x 4= 24) The answer, 24, is the smallest number that can be the new denominator for both 1/6 and 3/8.

What do you have to do to 6 to make 24? (Multiply by 4.) Now multiply the numerator by the same number. (1 x 4 = 4) The fraction 4/24 equals 1/6.

Now, what do you have to do to 8 to make 24? (Multiply by 3.) Multiply the numerator by the same number. (3 x 3 = 9) The fraction 9/24 equals 3/8. Therefore, 4/24 + 9/24 = 13/24.

    Students often confuse the greatest common factor (GCF) and the least common multiple (LCM). Using the class relationships diagram is a way of showing GCF. (See the "Common Factors" lesson).

    RESULT—The diagram shows what the Lowest Common Multiple means and how to calculate it.

WRITING EXTENSION

- **What are factors? When is it helpful to be able to identify them?**
- **What is the least common multiple? Why is it helpful?**

THINKING ABOUT THINKING

- **How does the branching diagram help you "see" factors?**
- **What other mathematics operations could you see more easily if you drew them?**
- **Suggest another lesson in which using the branching diagram would help you understand what you are learning.**

Use after both the "Common Factors" and "Factor Tree" lessons have been taught.

- **How does using the diagrams help you "see" the difference between the greatest common factor and the least common multiple?**

SIMILAR MATHEMATICS LESSONS

- To classify polygons.
- To describe set/subset relationships, geometric and number properties.

FACTOR TREES

DIRECTIONS: Fill in the missing factors for the factor trees below.

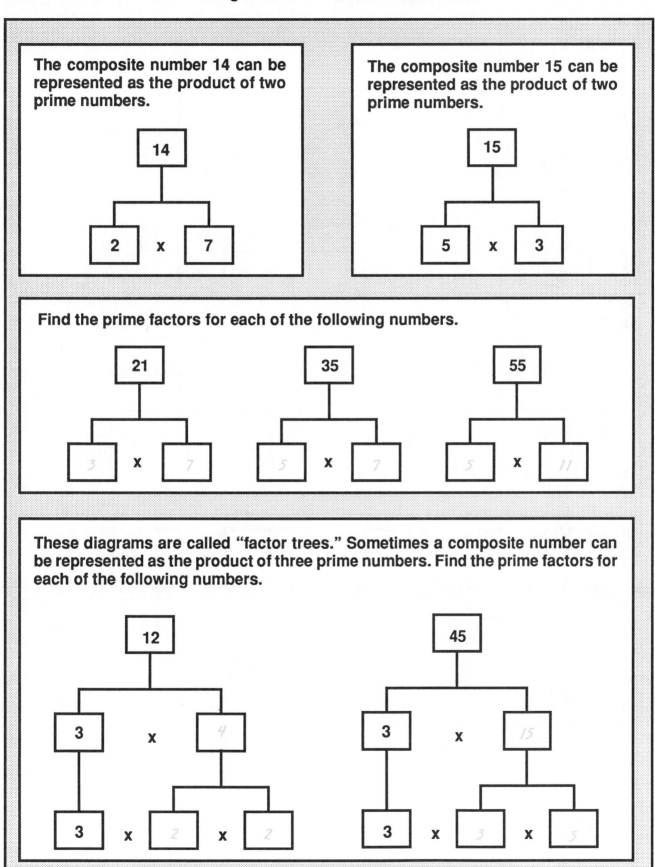

The composite number 14 can be represented as the product of two prime numbers.

14

2 x 7

The composite number 15 can be represented as the product of two prime numbers.

15

5 x 3

Find the prime factors for each of the following numbers.

21

3 x 7

35

5 x 7

55

5 x 11

These diagrams are called "factor trees." Sometimes a composite number can be represented as the product of three prime numbers. Find the prime factors for each of the following numbers.

12

3 x 4

3 x 2 x 2

45

3 x 15

3 x 3 x 5

FACTOR TREES

DIRECTIONS: Fill in the missing factors for the factor trees below.

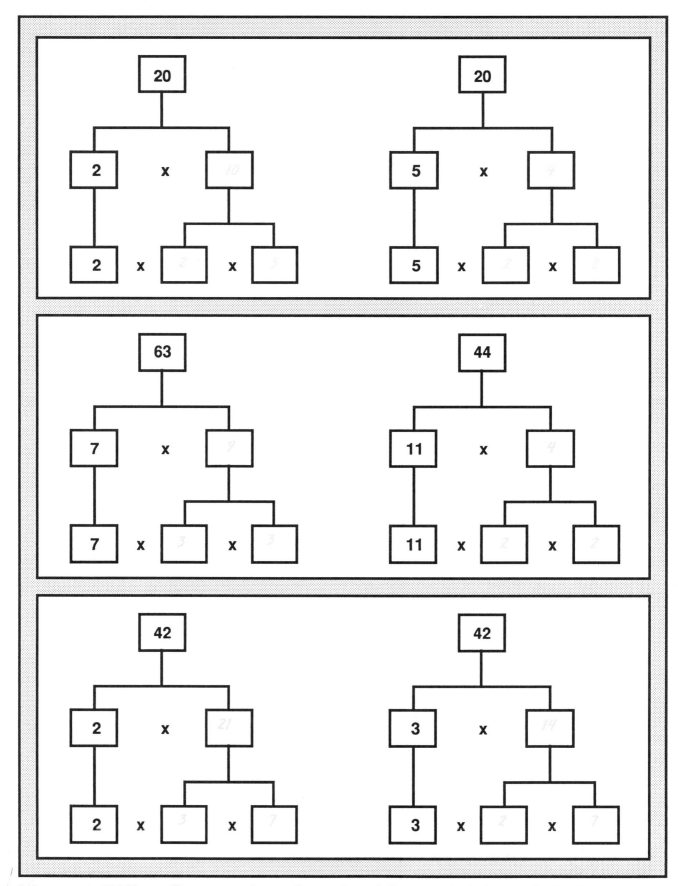

COMMON MULTIPLES AND PRIME NUMBERS

THINKING SKILL: Symbol classification

CONTENT OBJECTIVE: Students will use a class relationships diagram to identify common multiples and prime numbers. N*OTE: Use this lesson after the "Common Factors" and "Factor Tree" lessons.*

DISCUSSION: TECHNIQUE—Use a transparency or chalkboard drawing of the class relationships diagram to illustrate multiples of 2 or 3 and prime numbers less than 18. The lesson may be taught directly or by inductive thinking. For a direct instruction lesson, explain what a prime number is and that all numbers less than 18 that are not multiples of 2 or 3 must be prime. Students may learn the principle of prime numbers inductively by putting all the numbers that are not multiples of 2 or 3 in the box and determining what is true of all those numbers. This exercise is more effective as a class participation or Think/Pair/Share activity than as an individual assignment.

DIALOGUE—Ask students where each number from 4–18 should be placed on the diagram: in the left or right circle, in the intersection, or in the box outside the diagram. Encourage students to explain that since 1, 2, and 3 are the smallest numbers, any number between 4 and 18 that is not a multiple of 2 or 3 must be prime.

The second activity illustrates the factors of whole numbers from 2 to 30, identifying additional prime numbers, as well as the most frequently used common denominators.

RESULT—By examining numbers that are not multiples of 2 or 3, we can generate prime numbers and illustrate the concept of "prime." (See the "Common Factors" Lesson.)

WRITING EXTENSION
- **What is a prime number?**
- **When is it helpful to recognize whether a number is prime or not?**

THINKING ABOUT THINKING
- **How does using the class relationships diagram help you "see" the common factors of two numbers?**
- **How does using the class relationships diagram help you "see" which numbers are prime?**
- **Suggest another lesson in which you think that using the class relationships diagram would help you understand what you are learning.**

SIMILAR MATHEMATICS LESSONS
- To illustrate or explain sets or set theory.
- To illustrate multiples or factors of numbers.
- To illustrate geometry terms which define types of polygons or polyhedra.

MULTIPLES OF 2 AND 3 AND PRIME NUMBERS

DIRECTIONS: A prime number is a number which is divisible only by itself and 1. Thus, 2 and 3 are prime numbers. Using the numbers from 4 to 18, in the intersecting circles diagram write only multiples of 2 in the left circle. Write multiples of 3 in the right circle. If a number is a multiple of 2 <u>and</u> a multiple of 3, write it in the intersection. The numbers that don't fit inside the diagram are prime. Write the prime numbers in the box on the left.

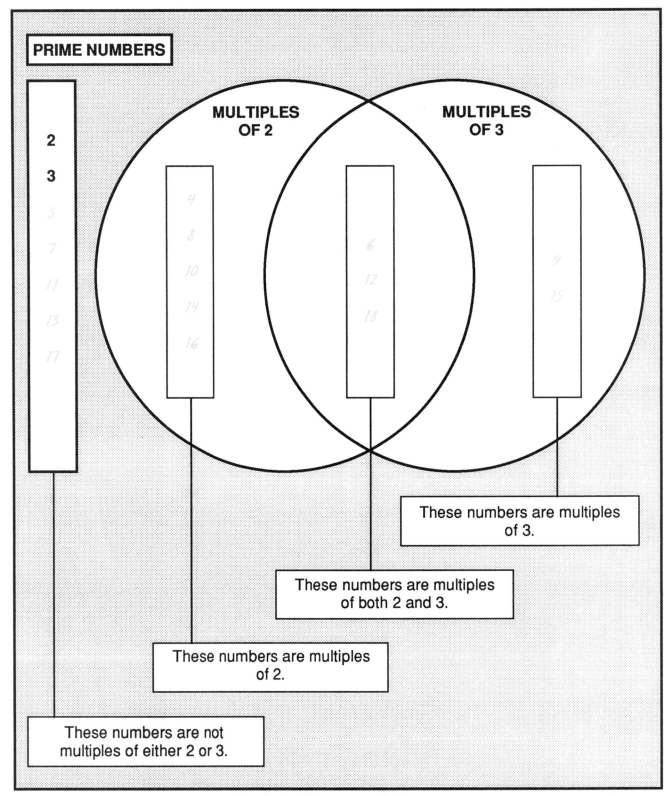

PRIME NUMBERS

2
3
5
7
11
13
17

MULTIPLES OF 2

4
8
10
14
16

MULTIPLES OF 3

6
12
18

9
15

These numbers are multiples of 3.

These numbers are multiples of both 2 and 3.

These numbers are multiples of 2.

These numbers are not multiples of either 2 or 3.

MULTIPLES OF 2, 3, AND 5

DIRECTIONS: A prime number is a number which is divisible only by itself and 1. Thus, 2, 3, and 5 are prime numbers. Write the numbers from 6 to 30 in the diagram showing multiples of 2, 3, or 5. The number 4 has already been placed for you. The numbers that don't fit inside the diagram are prime numbers. Write the prime numbers in the box on the left.

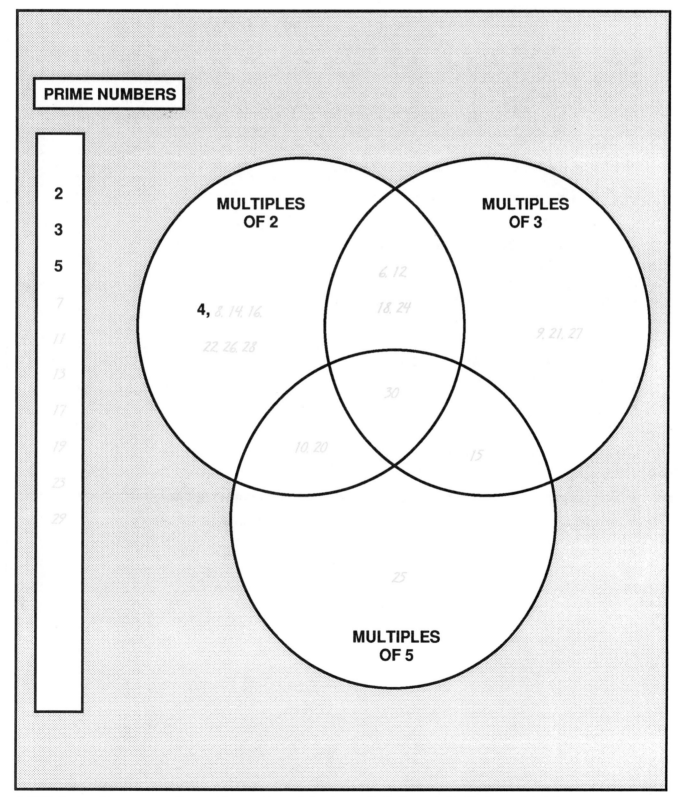

FINDING A MATHEMATICAL RULE

THINKING SKILL: Symbol sequences, inferring rules or patterns

CONTENT OBJECTIVE: Students will use a matrix chart to discover a mathematical rule.

DISCUSSION: TECHNIQUE—Encourage students to identify the clues to find the rule and to prepare their own "rules" for other students. Use subtraction, division, or combinations of any two operations.

DIALOGUE—Encourage students to explain how they discovered the rule.

Look at the matrix. Along the top and along the side you see the numbers 2, 3, 4, and 5. How are these numbers related to the four numbers shown in the small squares? For example, how are 2 and 2 related to 4? (2 + 2 = 4 or 2 x 2 = 4). **How are 2 and 3 related to 6?** (2 x 3 = 6) **Does this rule also work for 3, 3, and 9?** (Yes, 3 x 3 = 9)

RESULT—Students can discover number patterns and create mathematical puzzles to challenge their classmates' ability to find a rule.

WRITING EXTENSION
- **Why is it important to figure out rules or number patterns?**
- **When might it be useful to recognize number rules or patterns?**

THINKING ABOUT THINKING
- **How did using the matrix help you figure out the rule?**
- **What was your first clue about the rule in each matrix?**
- **How did the difference between the numbers in the two matrices suggest that addition is the operation in the second matrix?**
- **In what way did making your own rule help you understand number patterns?**
- **Suggest another lesson in which using a matrix might help you understand what you are learning.**

SIMILAR MATHEMATICS LESSONS
- To set up problems which allow students to discover a number rule.
- To classify numbers, polygons, or polyhedra by more than one variable.
- To use or construct probability, statistical, or arithmetic charts.

 © 1990 MIDWEST PUBLICATIONS • CRITICAL THINKING PRESS & SOFTWARE • P. O. Box 448, Pacific Grove, CA 93950

FINDING A MATHEMATICAL RULE

DIRECTIONS: Four numbers are filled in on each matrix below. Determine how those numbers were obtained and fill in the rest of each matrix.

	2	3	4	5
2	4	6	8	10
3	6	9	12	15
4	8	12	16	20
5	10	15	20	25

	2	3	4	5
2	4	5	6	7
3	5	6	7	8
4	6	7	8	9
5	7	8	9	10

CREATE A RULE

DIRECTIONS: Use the top matrix to create your own number puzzle. In the bottom matrix, write in just enough clues for another student to figure out your number rule. Leave as many boxes blank as possible. Ask another student to identify your number rule and fill in the rest of the matrix.

Your completed puzzle

Your challenge puzzle

VALUE OF FRACTIONS

THINKING SKILL: Number sequences

CONTENT OBJECTIVE: Students will use the transitive order graph to arrange fractions in order from smallest to largest. *NOTE: This lesson reviews and clarifies fraction conversion and is not recommended to introduce the concept.*

DISCUSSION: TECHNIQUE—Use a transparency of the transitive order graph to illustrate the relative value of fractions. The lesson is designed to clarify students' misconceptions about the relative value of common fractions. It demonstrates that if the numerator remains the same, the value of the fraction gets smaller as the denominator gets larger.
     DIALOGUE—Encourage students to use their own words to describe the pattern that emerges as the numerator of a fraction increases.

What relationship did you see between the value of the fraction and the value of the numerator? How did using a common denominator help you check the relative value of the fractions? Why was 18 an easy denominator to use? Why is it helpful to convert the fractions to a common denominator and then back to the original form to list them in order?

If students are still uncertain about the relationship between the value of a fraction and the size of the denominator, encourage them to use the graph to confirm the relative value of other fractions.
     RESULT—Picturing various fractions confirms the principle that when the numerator stays the same, the larger the value of the denominator, the smaller the value of the fraction.

WRITING EXTENSION
• **Why does the value of the fraction decrease as the denominator increases?**

THINKING ABOUT THINKING
• **What clues did you find to help you see the relationship between the value of the fraction and the size of the denominator?**
• **How did using the graph help you understand the relative value of fractions?**
• **Suggest another lesson in which using a transitive order graph would help you understand what you are learning.**
• **Why do people sometimes believe that 3/4 is smaller than 3/8? How does using the graph prevent that mistake?**

SIMILAR MATHEMATICS LESSONS
• To depict transitive order in inequality statements or in the value of decimals.
• To depict order of occurrence in preparing flow charts of computer operations.
• To solve word problems involving transitive order.
• To describe geometric proportions in angle, length, area, or volume.

VALUE OF FRACTIONS

DIRECTIONS: Use the transitive order graph to record the following fractions in order of value from lowest to highest. If necessary, use the table to convert the fractions to equivalent fractions with a common denominator.

FRACTIONS: 1/2, 1/3, 1/6, 2/3, 2/9, 5/18, 7/9, 8/9, 11/18

Given Fractions	Equivalent fraction expressed with a common denominator
1/2	$1/2 \times 9/9 = 9/18$
1/3	$1/3 \times 6/6 = 6/18$
1/6	$1/6 \times 3/3 = 3/18$
2/3	$2/3 \times 6/6 = 12/18$
2/9	$2/9 \times 2/2 = 4/18$
5/18	$5/18 \times 1/1 = 5/18$
7/9	$7/9 \times 2/2 = 14/18$
8/9	$8/9 \times 2/2 = 16/18$
11/18	$11/18 \times 1/1 = 11/18$

Values of fractions with the same denominator:

Lowest ← → Highest

3/18   5/18   9/18   12/18   16/18

4/18   6/18   11/18   14/18

Values of fractions in lowest terms:

Lowest ← → Highest

1/6   5/18   1/2   2/3   8/9

2/9   1/3   11/18   7/9

HOW TO ADD FRACTIONS

THINKING SKILL: Operation analysis

CONTENT OBJECTIVE: Students will use a flowchart to show how to add fractions. *NOTE: This lesson is intended to review and clarify fraction conversion and addition and is not recommended to introduce the operation.*

DISCUSSION: TECHNIQUE—Use a transparency of the flowchart to record responses as students describe the operation that results from each YES or NO question. Identify other multi-step mathematics operations which can be clarified by a flowchart.

    DIALOGUE—Relate the symbols and sequential steps of this exercise to flowcharting activities in the computer literacy exercises in your mathematics texts. Review flowchart symbols with your students.

    RESULT—Upon completion of the flowchart, students have a graphic reminder of the steps that must be followed when adding fractions.

WRITING EXTENSION
- **Identify the steps in adding fractions.**
- **What might happen if the sequence of steps in adding fractions were not correctly followed?**

THINKING ABOUT THINKING
- **How did using the flowchart help you remember the steps in adding fractions?**
- **What other mathematics operations can be pictured by using a flowchart?**
- **Suggest another lesson in which using a flowchart would help you understand what you are learning.**

SIMILAR MATHEMATICS LESSONS
- To illustrate steps in solving multi-step mathematics problems.
- To depict the steps in classifying polyhedra or types of numbers.
- To illustrate steps in troubleshooting procedures for computer operations.
- To map out operational steps in programming a computer.
- To check computations by determining whether correct procedures were followed.

ADDING FRACTIONS

DIRECTIONS: Complete the flowchart to show the steps in adding fractions.

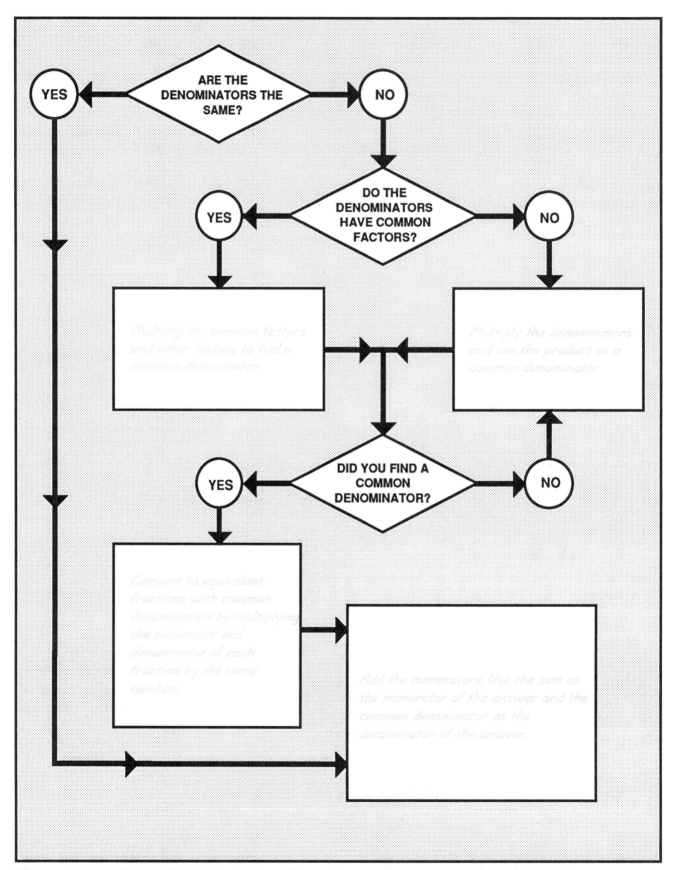

ADDING AND MULTIPLYING FRACTIONS

THINKING SKILL: Symbol classification

CONTENT OBJECTIVE: Students will use a matrix chart to identify patterns in multiplying and adding fractions.

DISCUSSION: TECHNIQUE—Encourage students to recognize that the product of two fractions is much smaller than the sum of the same fractions.

DIALOGUE—Since the numbers are the same, encourage students to describe the difference in the number patterns of the answers resulting from the two operations. So that students may recognize this difference, use the transitive order graph to show the relative value of the fractions in the answers. Point out that the answers to the multiplication problems become smaller much more rapidly than the answers to the addition problems.

In the first matrix, are the answers getting larger or smaller as you multiply by fractions with a larger denominator? What number patterns do you see in the rows and the columns? How does seeing the pattern help you understand the difference between adding and multiplying fractions?

What patterns do you see in the second matrix? Since we usually think of multiplication as more advanced than addition, why do many people think that adding fractions is more complex than multiplying them?

RESULT—When fractions are multiplied, the product becomes increasingly smaller compared to the sum of fractions, which becomes increasing larger when fractions are added.

WRITING EXTENSION
- Explain why the product of 1/5 x 1/5 is so much smaller that the sum of those two fractions.

THINKING ABOUT THINKING
- Suggest another lesson in which using the transitive order graph would help you understand what you are learning.

SIMILAR MATHEMATICS LESSONS
- To set up problems which allow students to discover a number rule.
- To describe numbers, polygons, or polyhedra by more than one variable.
- To interpret or construct probability, statistical, or arithmetic charts.

ADDING AND MULTIPLYING FRACTIONS

DIRECTIONS: In the first matrix, multiply the fraction in each row by the fraction in each column and complete the matrix diagram. In the second matrix, add the fraction in each row to the fraction in each column and complete the matrix diagram. Keep this completed page to use in the next activity.

MULTIPLYING FRACTIONS

		Column 1	Column 2	Column 3	Column 4
	X	1/2	1/3	1/4	1/5
Row 1	1/2	1/4	1/6	1/8	1/10
Row 2	1/3	1/6	1/9	1/12	1/15
Row 3	1/4	1/8	1/12	1/16	1/20
Row 4	1/5	1/10	1/15	1/20	1/25

ADDING FRACTIONS

		Column 1	Column 2	Column 3	Column 4
	+	1/2	1/3	1/4	1/5
Row 1	1/2	1	5/6	3/4	7/10
Row 2	1/3	5/6	2/3	7/12	8/15
Row 3	1/4	3/4	7/12	1/2	9/20
Row 4	1/5	7/10	8/15	9/20	2/5

ADDING AND MULTIPLYING FRACTIONS

DIRECTIONS: Using your answers in the matrices from the previous activity, arrange the fractions from largest to smallest on the graph below. An easy way to determine which fractions are larger or smaller is to convert the fractions to decimal form. For example:

$$1/4 = 1 \div 4 = 0.25$$

Do your conversion calculations with pencil and paper first and then check your answers on a calculator. Arrange your fractions and their decimal equivalents in order from largest to smallest. Then write both kinds of answers in the boxes on the transitive order graph below, using the top graph for multiplication answers and the bottom one for additon answers.

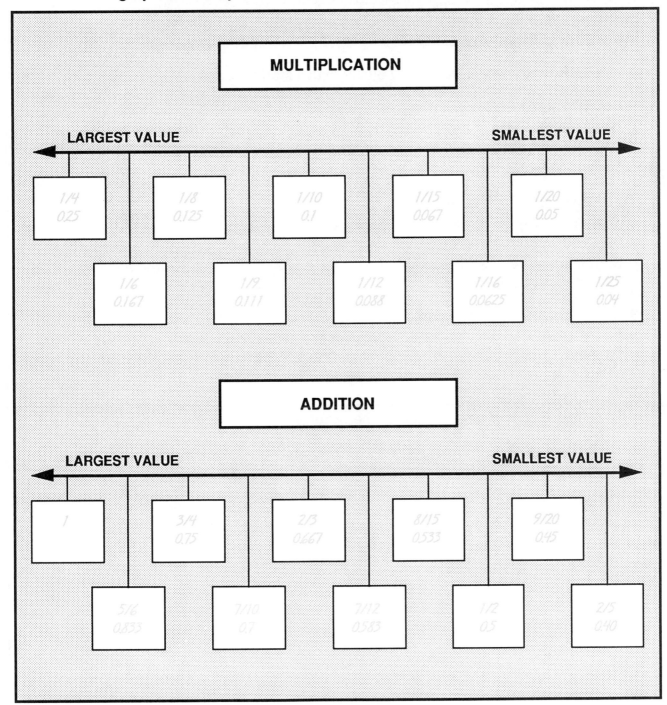

FRACTIONS AND DECIMALS

THINKING SKILL: Compare and contrast

CONTENT OBJECTIVE: Students will use the compare and contrast graph to differentiate between fractions and decimals.

DISCUSSION: TECHNIQUE—Use the compare and contrast graph to record students' discussion of fractions and decimals. Record each idea as it is discussed.

DIALOGUE—Encourage students to identify additional similarities or differences between fractions and decimals. As they state differences between fractions and decimals, discuss those differences by naming the quality that is different. Establish this pattern:

"With regard to (quality), (item one and its distinction), but (item two and its distinction)." For example, "With regard to the denominator, fractions may have any number in the denominator, but decimals are always expressed as tenths or products of tenths."

RESULT—Decimals are usually easier to use than fractions.

WRITING EXTENSION
- Describe the difference between fractions and decimals.
- In what types of problems would you find it easier to work in decimals? In fractions? Explain your reasons.

THINKING ABOUT THINKING
- How did using the compare and contrast graph help you understand the difference between fractions and decimals?
- Suggest another lesson in which comparing and contrasting would help you understand what you are learning.

SIMILAR MATHEMATICS LESSONS
- To compare ratios and fractions, or ratios and decimals.
- To compare the usefulness of various statistical representations in depicting the same data: charts, graphs, pictograms, pie diagrams, etc.
- To clarify mathematics terms for operations and geometric figures.
- To compare units of time, money, or measurement.

FRACTIONS AND DECIMALS

DIRECTIONS: Read the passage carefully to determine how fractions and decimals are alike and how they are different. Use the compare and contrast graph to record their similarities and differences.

Both fractions and decimals express a "part," a value between 0 and 1. Each can be expressed alone (1/2 or 0.5) or with whole numbers (1 1/2 or 1.5). Both can be added, subtracted, multiplied, or divided.

Fractions may contain any number as the denominator and must usually be converted into a common denominator to be added or subtracted. To express a fraction as a percen-

tage, divide the numerator by the denominator and convert the resulting decimal to a percentage by multiplying by one hundred.

Decimals are always expressed as tenths (0.1) or as products of tenths (0.1 × 0.1 = 0.01; 0.1 × 0.01 = 0.001, etc.). Decimals can be added or subtracted as given and can be easily expressed as a percentage by multiplying by one hundred.

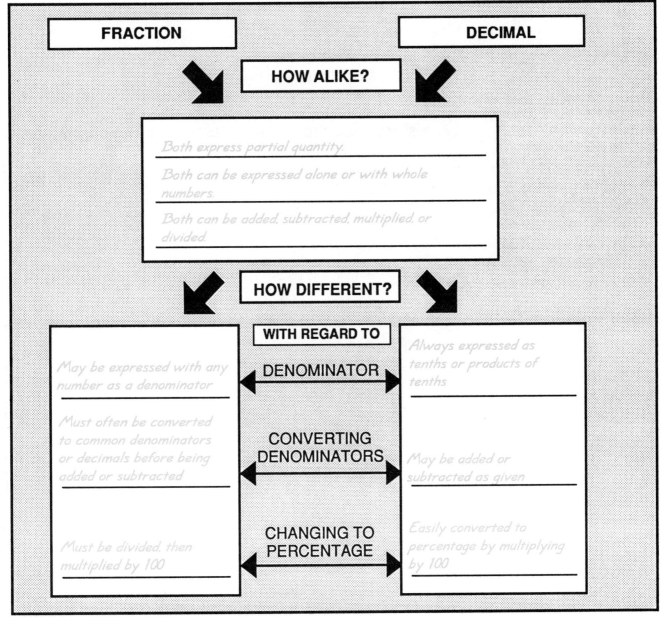

FRACTION   **DECIMAL**

HOW ALIKE?

Both express partial quantity.

Both can be expressed alone or with whole numbers.

Both can be added, subtracted, multiplied, or divided.

HOW DIFFERENT?

WITH REGARD TO

DENOMINATOR

May be expressed with any number as a denominator

Always expressed as tenths or products of tenths

CONVERTING DENOMINATORS

Must often be converted to common denominators or decimals before being added or subtracted

May be added or subtracted as given

CHANGING TO PERCENTAGE

Must be divided, then multiplied by 100

Easily converted to percentage by multiplying by 100

DESCRIBING TRIANGLES

THINKING SKILL: Figural similarities and differences, verbal similarities and differences, figural classification

CONTENT OBJECTIVE: Students will use the central idea graph to identify triangles according to the size of the angles and length of the sides.

DISCUSSION: TECHNIQUE—Use a transparency of the central idea graph to record responses as students discuss the terms to describe triangles.

DIALOGUE—Encourage students to recognize that each triangle can be described by BOTH characteristics. Stress the use of both types of terms (angles and sides), as each triangle is discussed. To illustrate both characteristics another way, use the class relationships diagram to illustrate which triangles are acute, scalene, or both and to verify student understanding.

RESULT—Any triangle can be described two ways: according to the size of the angles and according to the comparative length of the sides.

WRITING EXTENSION
- Define the terms which describe the angles of a triangle.
- Define the terms which describe the sides of a triangle.
- Explain the steps you would take to classify a triangle.

THINKING ABOUT THINKING
- Why do students sometimes get confused about the terms used to describe triangles?
- How did using the graph help you clarify the differences between terms describing angle measures and terms describing side measures?
- How did using the graph help you remember the differences between the terms?

SIMILAR MATHEMATICS LESSONS
- To describe geometric properties.
- To describe number properties.

DESCRIBING TRIANGLES

DIRECTIONS: Each of the five triangles below can be described two ways—by its angles and by its sides. Label each triangle with the term that describes its angles and the term that describes its sides.

There are two diagrams on the next page. On the central idea graph write the number of the triangle(s) which have the given characteristic. On the class relationships diagram write the number of the triangle(s) that belongs in each part of the diagram.

A triangle may be described by the size of its angles or by comparing the length of its sides. If all angles of a triangle measure less than 90 degrees, the triangle is **acute**. If the triangle has one 90 degree angle, then it is a **right** triangle. If the triangle has one angle greater than 90 degrees, then it is an **obtuse** triangle.

There are also special names which describe a triangle by comparing the lengths of its sides. If the triangle has only two sides of equal length, it is said to be an **isosceles** triangle. If all three sides are the same length, it is an **equilateral** triangle. If all three sides are different lengths, then the triangle is a **scalene** triangle.

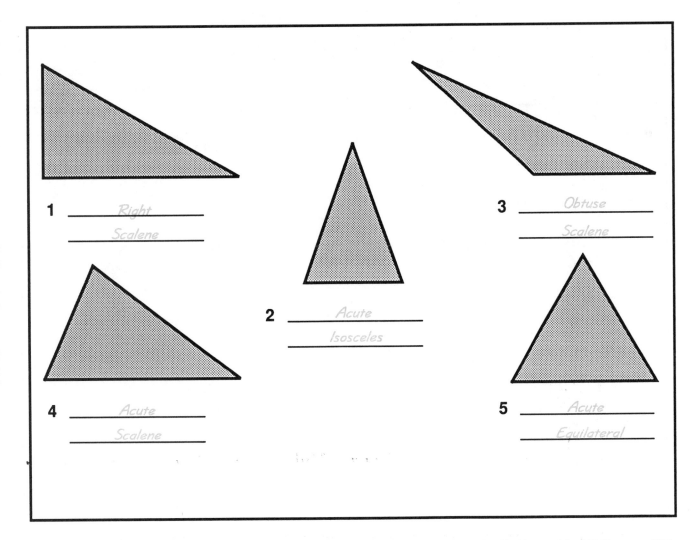

1 _____ Right _____
_____ Scalene _____

3 _____ Obtuse _____
_____ Scalene _____

2 _____ Acute _____
_____ Isosceles _____

4 _____ Acute _____
_____ Scalene _____

5 _____ Acute _____
_____ Equilateral _____

CENTRAL IDEA GRAPH

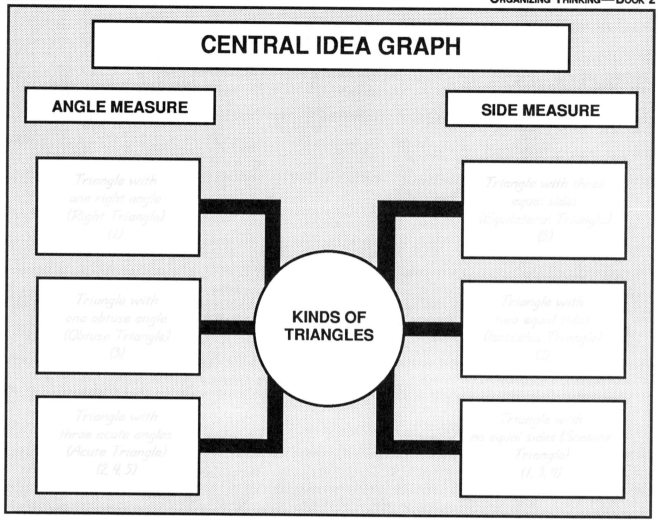

ANGLE MEASURE

SIDE MEASURE

Triangle with
one right angle
(Right Triangle)
(1)

Triangle with three
equal sides
(Equilateral Triangle)
(5)

Triangle with
one obtuse angle
(Obtuse Triangle)
(3)

Triangle with
two equal sides
(Isosceles Triangle)
(2)

KINDS OF
TRIANGLES

Triangle with
three acute angles
(Acute Triangle)
(2, 4, 5)

Triangle with
no equal sides (Scalene
Triangle)
(1, 3, 4)

CLASS RELATIONSHIPS DIAGRAM

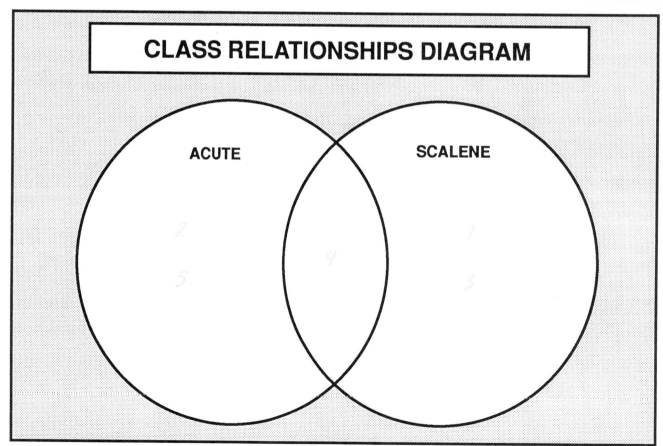

ACUTE

SCALENE

2

5

4

1

3

QUADRILATERIAL SERIES: CLASSIFYING POLYGONS

THINKING SKILL: Figural and verbal classification

CONTENT OBJECTIVE: Students will use a branching diagram to identify quadrilaterals in a collection of polygons. *NOTE: Students will need colored pens or crayons for this exercise.*

DISCUSSION: TECHNIQUE—This is the first in a series of lessons in which students will:

1. Identify quadrilaterals.
2. Confirm definitions of geometry terms describing quadrilaterals.
3. Determine that quadrilaterals are described by characteristics of sides or angles.
4. Recognize that many quadrilaterals can be described by more than one term.

The goal of this first lesson is to define polygons by the number of sides and to categorize shapes appropriately. Students tend to identify any shape that looks somewhat like a rectangle or a parallelogram as a quadrilateral. In this lesson, students must count the number of sides in each polygon, then draw that polygon in the appropriate category of the branching diagram. (Grids are provided to help students draw each polygon more accurately.) Make polygon shapes more apparent by using felt tip pens or crayons to color the sample polygon and the student's drawing of the same shape. This diagram is a visually attractive design for bulletin boards.

DIALOGUE—After students have drawn each shape in the appropriate category, ask them to label each shape with the given number. Class discussion of each category should include identifying and defining each type of polygon. Students should state why the term applies to a given shape. For example, to describe the first shape in the exercise, ask:

Is this figure a quadrilateral? What makes you think so? (Yes; a quadrilateral has four sides. This figure has four sides.) **Can any other terms apply to this shape?** (Yes, it is a rectangle because it has four right angles. It is also a parallelogram because it has two sets of parallel sides.)

RESULT—Polygons can be classified by counting the number of sides.

WRITING EXTENSION
* **Describe how polygons are alike and how they are different.**
* **Describe how quadrilaterals are alike and how they are different.**

THINKING ABOUT THINKING
* **Suggest another lesson in which using a branching diagram would help you understand what you are learning? How did drawing the polygons help you understand the difference between quadrilaterals and other polygons?**

SIMILAR MATHEMATICS LESSONS
* To compare ratios and fractions or ratios and decimals.
* To compare mathematics operations.
* To compare British measure and metric measure.
* To compare similarity and congruence or terms for angles, polygons, and polyhedra.

CLASSIFYING POLYGONS

DIRECTIONS: A polygon is a closed shape with straight sides. We describe a polygon according to the number of sides it has. Shapes with four sides are called quadrilaterals. Shapes with five sides are called pentagons. Shapes with six sides are called hexagons.

For each shape given below, count the number of sides and decide whether the shape is a quadrilateral, a pentagon, or a hexagon. On the branching diagram, draw each polygon in the appropriate box. Try to make your drawing the same size as the sample shape. Use the grid to help you copy the size of each side in the shape. Number each drawing with the same number as in the sample.

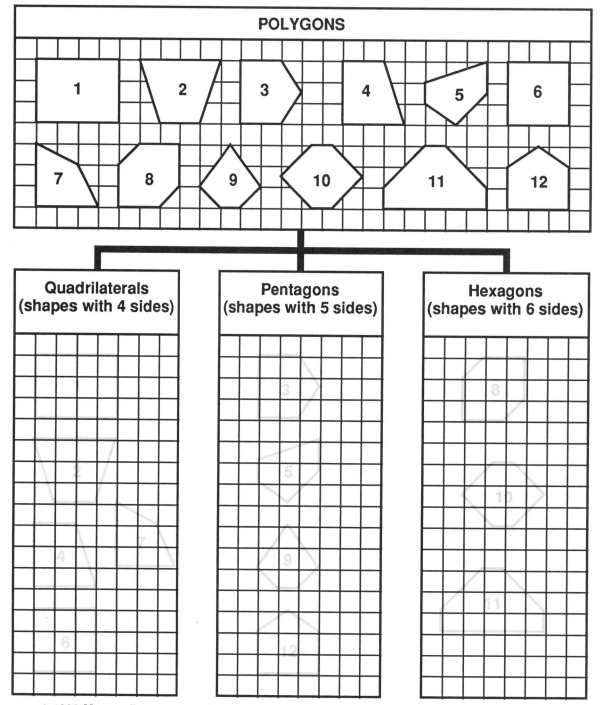

DESCRIBING QUADRILATERALS

THINKING SKILL: Figural and verbal classification

CONTENT OBJECTIVE: Students use a matrix chart and a class relationships diagram to define and categorize four-sided figures.

DISCUSSION: TECHNIQUE—This is the second in a series of lessons on analyzing types of quadrilaterals. The goal of this lesson is to define terms that accurately describe quadrilaterals and to recognize that many common quadrilaterals can be described by more than one term. Not realizing that several of these terms apply to broader categories, students tend to associate a term with one particular polygon. For example, students attach the term "parallelogram" to quadrilaterals with slanted sides. They sometimes do not recognize that rectangles and squares are also parallelograms, or that quadrilateral and polygon are also terms which apply to parallelograms.

Check the matrix through class discussion of each shape. Ask students to define the term each time and to state why each term does or does not apply to the given shape.

DIALOGUE—Discussion of each shape might proceed in the manner illustrated below for the first shape.

Is this shape a parallelogram? How do you know? (No, a parallelogram has two sets of parallel sides. This shape has no parallel sides.) **Is this shape a quadrilateral? Why do you think so?** (Yes, a quadrilateral is a polygon that has four sides. This shape has four sides.) **Is this shape a rectangle? How do you know?** (No, a rectangle has two sets of parallel sides and four right angles. This shape has no parallel sides and only one right angle.) **Is this shape a rhombus? Why do you think so?** (No, a rhombus has two sets of parallel sides and four equal sides. This shape doesn't have any parallel sides or equal sides.) **Is this shape a square? How do you know?** (No, a square has two sets of parallel, equal sides and four right angles. This shape has no parallel sides, no equal sides, and only one right angle.) **Is this shape a trapezoid? Why do you think so?** (No, a trapezoid has one set of parallel sides. This shape has no parallel sides.)

Check the "target" diagram by asking students to define the term each time and to confirm all the classes to which each shape belongs. For example, to describe the first shape in the exercise the teacher might use the following questioning strategy.

Into which ring should the shape "P" be drawn? (The ring marked "parallelogram.") **Why?** (Because it has two sets of parallel sides.) *Move outward in the diagram.* **Are all parallelograms quadrilaterals?** (Yes, both parallelograms and quadrilaterals have four sides.) **Is there any place on the diagram where things in the parallelogram ring are not also in the quadrilateral ring?** (No, because all parallelograms are inside the quadrilateral ring.) **How can we describe the relationship between parallelograms and quadrilaterals?** (All parallelograms are quadrilaterals, but not all quadrilaterals are parallelograms. Some quadrilaterals are not parallelograms.) **Show me a quadrilateral that is not a parallelogram.** (Shape "Q"). **Name all the classes that shape "P" belongs to.** (It is a parallelogram and a quadrilateral—and also a polygon.)

Follow this pattern as you discuss each shape. Because students describe the six quadrilaterals in this way, clarification and repetition clearly imprint the precise definitions and appearances of quadrilaterals.

1. Define the most specific term for the figure.
2. Locate the figure on the diagram.

3. Describe all terms that apply to the shape.

4. State the relationship between this shape and all the categories to which it belongs.

5. Summarize in a single sentence all the categories to which a shape belongs. (For example, a square is a rectangle and a parallelogram and a quadrilateral.)

We call a shape by the most specific term which applies to it. For example, the given rectangle is also a parallelogram, but there are some parallelograms that don't have right angles. Therefore, "parallelogram" is not specific enough to describe the rectangle. A square is also a rectangle, but it has the more specific characteristic of equal sides. "Square" doesn't apply to the rectangle in the lesson since the sides are unequal. Therefore, "rectangle" is the most specific term that applies to the given shape.

If you have mathematics manipulatives in the shapes given in the lesson, allow students to do this lesson in pairs, using a class relationships diagram drawn on large sheets of newsprint. This diagram can also be used as a colorful bulletin board reminder of the polygon lesson.

RESULT—More than one term can be used to describe quadrilaterals.

WRITING EXTENSION

• Explain why more than one geometric term can describe a rectangle.

THINKING ABOUT THINKING

• How did using the matrix help you understand that more than one term can describe a square?

• How did using the class relationships diagram help you understand that more than one term can describe a square?

• How did the way we described each quadrilateral in class help you understand and remember the difference in the terms?

• Can you recognize a pattern in the way we describe quadrilaterals?

• Suggest another lesson in which either a matrix or a class relationships diagram can help you understand what you are learning.

SIMILAR MATHEMATICS LESSONS

• To compare ratios and fractions or ratios and decimals.

• To compare addition and multiplication, subtraction and division, multiplication and exponentials, or division and calculation of square roots.

• To compare English measure with metric measure.

DESCRIBING QUADRILATERALS

DIRECTIONS: Put a check mark in the box of every geometry term that applies to each quadrilateral (four-sided shape).

DEFINITIONS:

Parallelogram—a closed, four-sided shape with two sets of parallel sides.
Quadrilateral—any closed, four-sided shape.
Rectangle—a parallelogram with four right angles.
Rhombus—a parallelogram with four equal sides.
Square—a rectangle with four equal sides.
Trapezoid—a quadrilateral with only one pair of parallel sides.

	PARALLELOGRAM	QUADRILATERAL	RECTANGLE	RHOMBUS	SQUARE	TRAPEZOID
(quadrilateral)		✓				
(trapezoid)		✓				✓
(rectangle)	✓	✓	✓			
(square)	✓	✓	✓	✓	✓	
(parallelogram)	✓	✓				
(rhombus)	✓	✓		✓		

DESCRIBING QUADRILATERALS

DIRECTIONS: Draw each shape in the ring of the diagram which best describes it.

DEFINITIONS:
> Parallelogram—a closed, four-sided shape with two sets of parallel sides.
> Quadrilateral—any closed, four-sided shape.
> Rectangle—a parallelogram with four right angles.
> Rhombus—a parallelogram with four equal sides.
> Square—a rectangle with four equal sides.
> Trapezoid—a quadrilateral with only one pair of parallel sides.

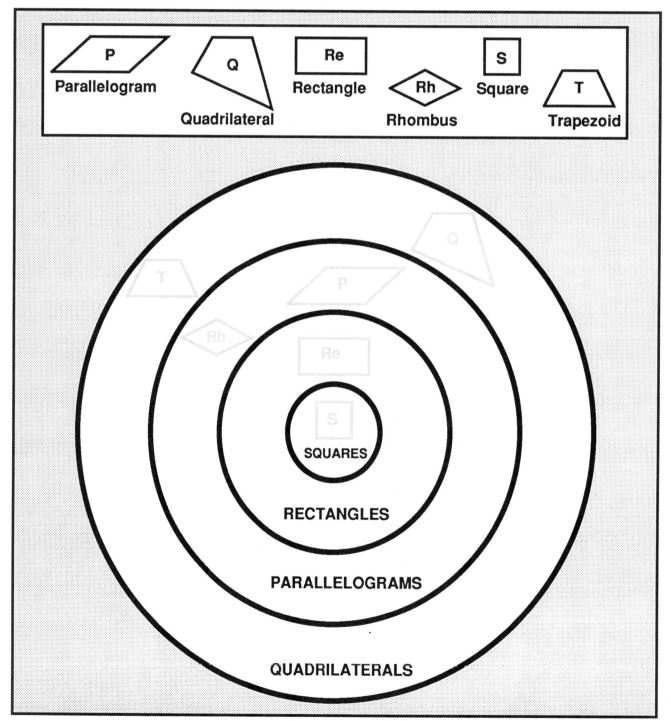

CLASSIFYING QUADRILATERALS

THINKING SKILL: Figural and verbal classification

CONTENT OBJECTIVE: Students will use one of several graphic organizers to analyze and describe quadrilaterals by type of angle or length of sides.

DISCUSSION: TECHNIQUE—This is the third in a series of lessons on analyzing types of quadrilaterals. The goal of this lesson is to identify significant characteristics of geometry terms used to describe quadrilaterals (characteristics of sides or characteristics of angles).

DIALOGUE—Students may understand terms more clearly if the teacher explains terms by discussing significant characteristics. In each of these graphics, the teacher and students should "talk out" the decision-making process to distinguish quadrilaterals by characteristics related to their sides or angles.

NOTE: Do not assign all four graphics of this lesson. Based on your previous experience in teaching geometry concepts, select the process that is most easily understood by your students. If necessary, select a second lesson to reteach quadrilateral terms.

RESULT—More than one term can be used to describe specialized quadrilaterals.

WRITING EXTENSION
- **Describe the significant characteristics of quadrilaterals and the geometry terms we use to describe them.**

THINKING ABOUT THINKING
- **How did using a diagram help you understand how more than one term can describe a quadrilateral?**
- **Can you recognize a pattern in the way we describe quadrilaterals?**
- **Suggest another lesson in which using a diagram would help you understand mathematics definitions.**

SIMILAR MATHEMATICS LESSONS
- To describe English measure and metric measure.
- To describe terms for types of angles, polygons, and polyhedra.

CLASSIFYING QUADRILATERALS BY SIDES

DIRECTIONS: Use the flowchart to name quadrilaterals by describing right angles, parallel sides, or equal sides. From the box below, select the shape which matches the answer to the question in each diamond. Draw and label the correct shape in each blank box.

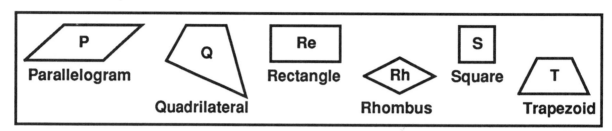

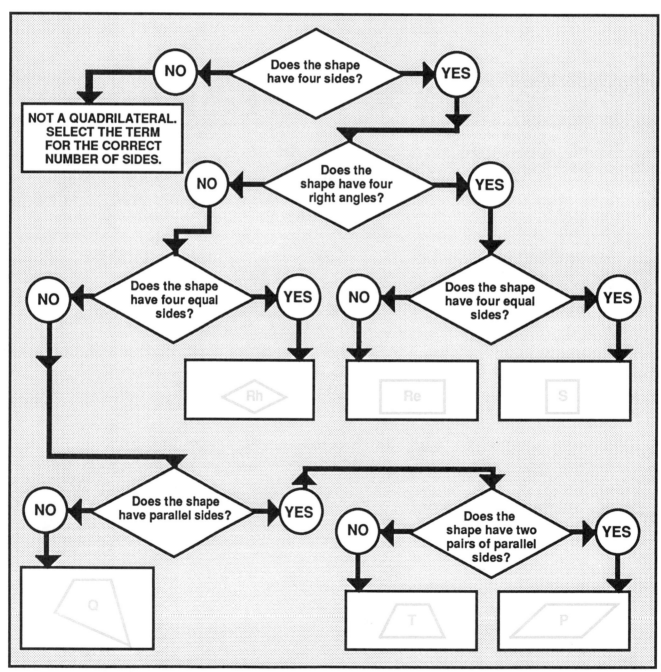

CLASSIFYING QUADRILATERALS BY ANGLES

DIRECTIONS: Use the branching diagram to name quadrilaterals described by right angles, parallel sides, or equal sides. Select the shape that fits the description in each box. Draw and label the correct shape in each blank box.

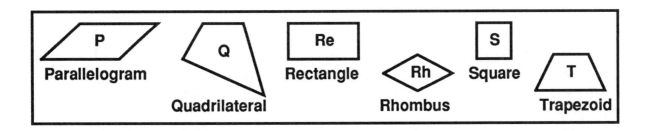

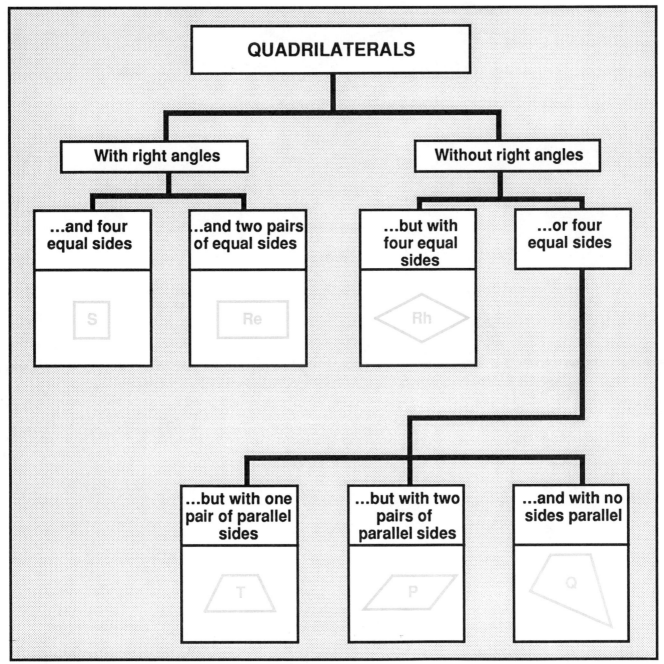

CLASSIFYING SHAPES–EQUAL ANGLES

DIRECTIONS: Use the class relationships diagram to identify terms which describe shapes by number of sides, size of angles, or parallel sides. Draw and label each shape from the box below in the region of the graph which best describes it.

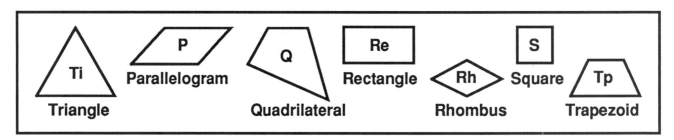

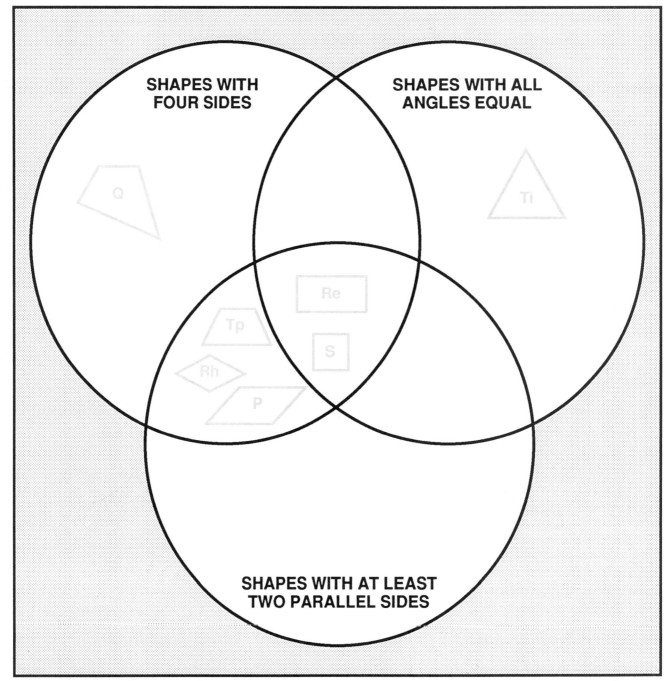

CLASSIFYING SHAPES–EQUAL SIDES

DIRECTIONS: Use the class relationships graph to identify terms which describe shapes by equal sides or parallel sides. Draw and label each shape in the region of the graph which best describes it.

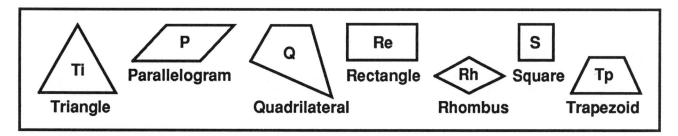

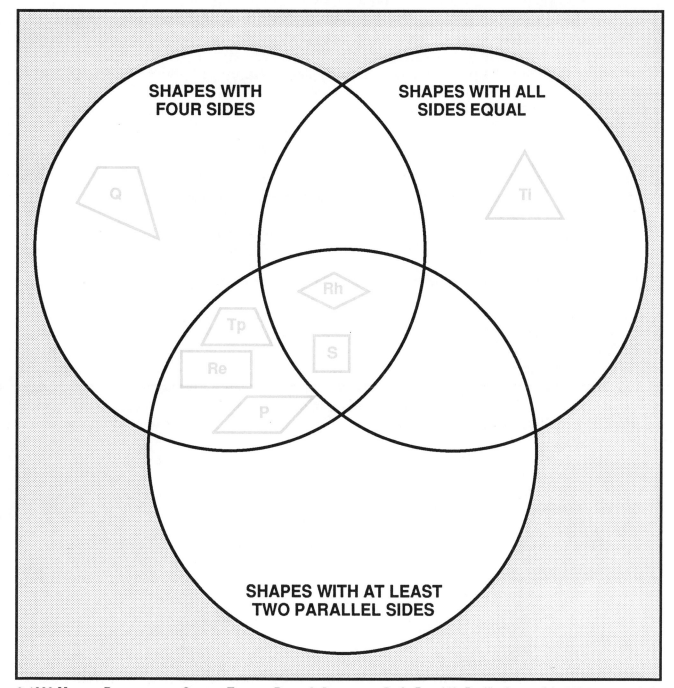

WORLD POPULATION GROWTH

THINKING SKILL: Constructing and interpreting graphs, extrapolation, prediction

CONTENT OBJECTIVE: Students will depict population data on a grid graph.

DISCUSSION: TECHNIQUE—Use a transparency of the grid graph to record population data from a written passage.

DIALOGUE—Encourage students to draw inferences from the completed graph. Sample inferences and questions might include the following.

World population is doubling more rapidly than it did earlier in history. (If necessary, guide students through the calculations.)

It took 1500 years, from 1 A.D. to 1500 A.D., for world population to double. It doubled again between 1500 and 1830, a period of 330 years. It doubled again between 1830 and 1930–100 years. In the following 45 years from 1930 to 1975, it doubled a fourth time. What predictions might you make from this information? What might affect this, either by speeding it up or slowing it down? Are there other "people statistics" that show as rapid an increase as population? Where might you find out? How many times more people were there in 1975 than in 1 A.D.? (250 million = 0.25 billion. 4 billion ÷ 0.25 billion = 16 times)

Factors affecting the length of life or the rate of birth must have changed since 1 A.D.

What do you think were some of the factors which have changed population growth?

If the rate of population doubling continues to increase, then the number of people on earth will continue to place demands on resources, food, space, water, and services.

What do you think some effects of population doubling will be on these factors?

(The following data may be helpful in discussing this question. For further information, refer to the *Guiness Book of Essential Facts,* Sterling Publishing: New York, 1979.) "If this trend continues, the world has only 15 generations left before the human race breeds itself to an overcrowded extinction. By 2600 A.D. there would be one person per square yard of habitable land surface....History's greatest war (World War II with 54,800,000 killed) made the merest dent in the inexorable advance in population between 1940–1950. Some demographers now maintain that the figure will (or must) stabilize at 10–15 billion in the 21st century."

Population is continuing to double more rapidly than it did earlier in history.

What reasons can you think of to explain this trend? Can you think of any ways to reverse the trend? Is reversing the trend desirable?

RESULT—The graph vividly shows that population of the world is increasing rapidly.

WRITING EXTENSION
- **Describe the trend of the doubling of world population.**
- **Describe some of the problems and benefits created by a rapidly increasing world population.**

- Describe some of the factors that have contributed to the decreased rate of death and the increased rate of birth.
- Describe life as you think it will be in the year 2005 A.D. What solutions do you think the world will have to come up with to deal with the increased population?

THINKING ABOUT THINKING

- How does the graph help you "see" how rapidly world population is doubling?
- Which conveys the idea more clearly, the graph or the written passage? Why do you think so? Can any written passage be clarified by using a graph?
- Suggest another lesson in which you think that using a graph would help you understand what you are learning.

SIMILAR MATHEMATICS LESSONS

- To record measurements of frequency or quantity.

WORLD POPULATION GROWTH

DIRECTIONS: Read the passage carefully. Determine how to record the data. Use this information to construct a graph of word population growth.

In 1500, the world population was 500 million, twice what it had been in 1 A.D. By 1960, world population was 3 billion. World population reached 4 billion people in 1975, twice what it had been in 1930, and four times the world population of 1830.

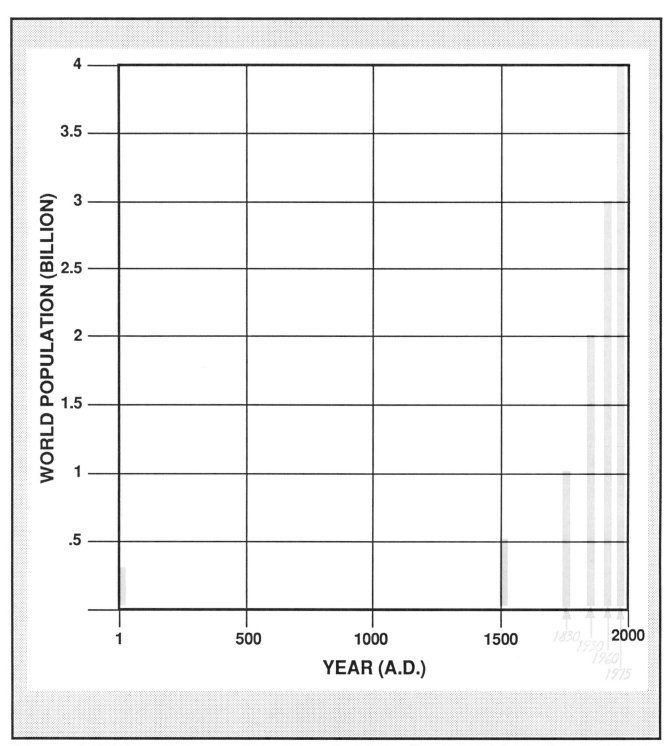

EFFECT OF INFLATION ON YOUR BUYING POWER

THINKING SKILL: Depicting number values

CONTENT OBJECTIVE: Students will recognize the effect of inflation on their purchases by using an interval graph to compare the prices of items they commonly purchase.

DISCUSSION: TECHNIQUE—Use a transparency of the blank graph to assist students in planning their graphs. Use three different colored markers to represent costs in 1975, 1980, and 1985. Model the procedure by graphing the cost of a fast-food lunch in each of the selected years.

    DIALOGUE—When students have completed their graphs, give them practice at computing averages (an easy application in this lesson since there are ten items).The average purchase price per item for 1975 is $0.34, for 1980 is $0.55, and for 1985 is $0.83. Encourage students to draw inferences from the graph.

How does the rate of increase in the totals for each of the five-year periods compare?
    1975–1980: $5.53 – $3.44 = $2.09; $2.09 ÷ $3.44 = 0.61 = 61%
    1980–1985: $8.31 – $5.53 = $2.78; $2.78 ÷ $5.53 = 0.51 = 51%

What trend in inflation is suggested by these calculations?
    Although prices have gone up over the ten-year period, the rate of inflation was lower during the second five-year period.

If inflation continues to slow down at this same rate, what would the inflation rate be from 1985 to 1990?
    61% – 51% = 10% decrease from 1980 to 1985
    51% – 10% = 41% if the 10% rate continues from 1985 to 1990

What would the total cost of these ten purchases be in 1990 if the rate of inflation continues to slow down at the same rate?
    $8.31 × 0.41 = $3.41 (amount of increase)
    $8.31 + $3.41 = $11.72 (projected total cost in 1990)

    RESULT—Bar graphs are an excellent tool for making and showing comparisons.

WRITING EXTENSION
- **Explain how "inflation" and the "rate of inflation" are different.**
- **What is the effect of increased prices on your buying power as the result of inflation?**
- **What can you, as students, do about the increasing prices of the given items to reduce the effect of inflation on your buying power?**

THINKING ABOUT THINKING
- **Suggest another lesson in which using a grid graph would help you understand what you are learning.**
- **How does using the graph help you "see" the price comparisons?**

SIMILAR MATHEMATICS LESSONS
- To show economic, demographic, geographic, political, or social statistics.

EFFECT OF INFLATION ON YOUR BUYING POWER

DIRECTIONS: To see what inflation (rising prices) is doing to your buying power, examine this list of things that students often buy. Record the price of each item for 1975, 1980, and 1985 on the first graph. Record the total purchases for each year on the second graph. Use a different color for each year and record the color for each year on the key.

ITEM	1975	1980	1985
Fast-food lunch (hamburger, small fries, small soft drink)	$0.80	$1.39	$1.97
Soft drink (vending machine)	.20	.40	.50
Chocolate bar	.15	.25	.40
Milk (at school)	.10	.10	.25
Postage stamp	.10	.15	.22
Crayons (8 pack)	.25	.45	.79
Glue (1.25 ounce)	.40	.50	.69
Comic Book	.25	.50	.75
45 rpm record	.79	1.29	1.79
Movie ticket (child's price)	1.50	2.00	2.50
TOTALS	**$4.54**	**$7.03**	**$9.86**

    © 1990 MIDWEST PUBLICATIONS • CRITICAL THINKING PRESS & SOFTWARE • P. O. Box 448, Pacific Grove, CA 93950

COMPARING THE EFFECTS OF INFLATION ON THE COST OF TEN ITEMS TYPICALLY PURCHASED BY STUDENTS

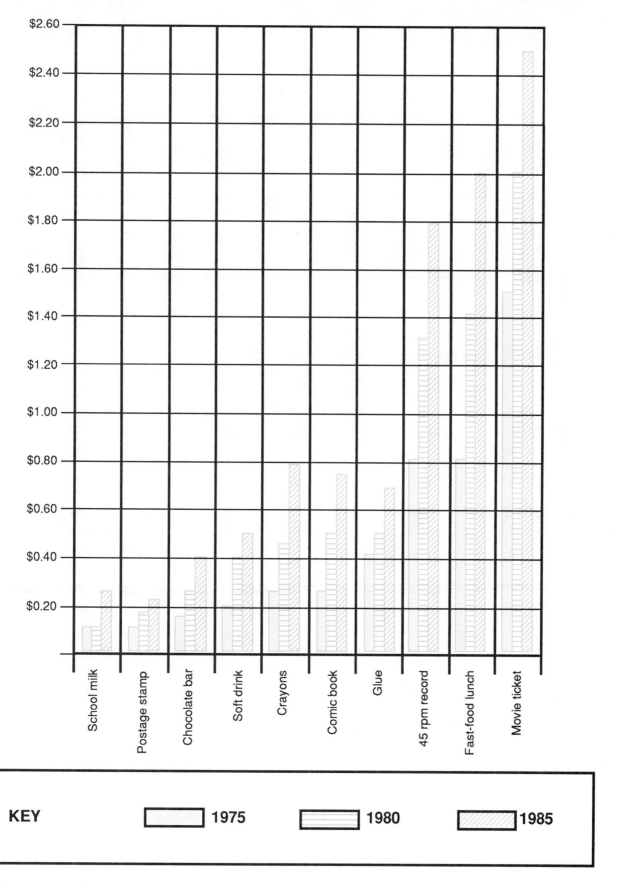

COMPARING THE TOTAL COST OF TEN ITEMS
IN 1975, 1980, AND 1985

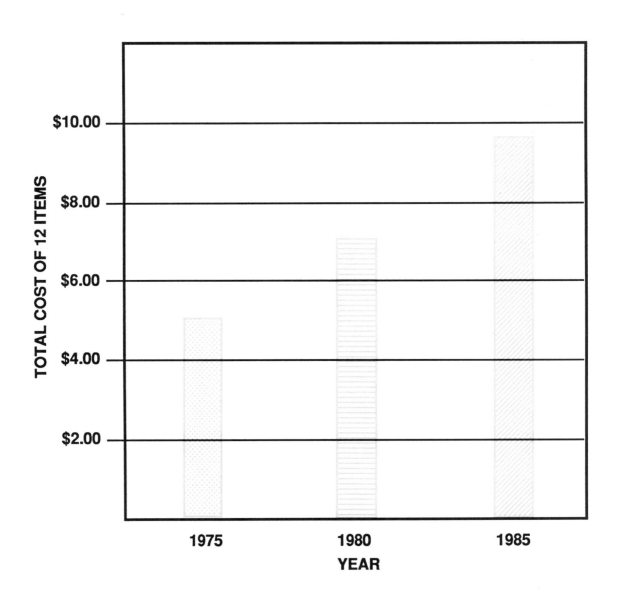

CHAPTER 6 – SCIENCE

LAND, WATER, AND FLYING ANIMALS (Class Relationships Diagram)		AMPHIBIANS AND REPTILES (Branching Diagram, Compare and Contrast Diagram)
	MAMMAL GESTATION PERIODS (Grid Diagram)	
FOOD CHAIN (Cycle Diagram)		MEANS OF CONTROLLING DISEASE (Branching Diagram)
	HANDEDNESS AND EYEDNESS (Matrix Chart)	
SIMPLE MACHINES (Central Idea Graph)		TESTING HARDNESS OF MINERALS (Transitive Order Graph)
	WEATHER OBSERVATIONS (Matrix Chart)	
THE TWIN PLANETS: EARTH AND VENUS (Compare and Contrast Diagram)		ENERGY TRANSFORMATIONS (Flowchart)

LAND, WATER, AND FLYING ANIMALS

THINKING SKILL: Verbal classification

CONTENT OBJECTIVE: Students will use the class relationships diagram to classify land, water, and/or flying animals.

DISCUSSION: TECHNIQUE—Use a transparency of the class relationships diagram to record responses as students discuss land, water, and flying animals.

DIALOGUE—To describe animals, discuss the type of animal it is, the habitat in which it lives, and its means of locomotion. Students recognize that some animals spend considerable periods of their lives both on land and in the water. (They may question why pelicans and sea gulls are listed as water animals, since they must obviously lay eggs on land. Their primary habitat, however, is the sea.) Encourage students to list as many additional animals as they can identify on the diagram. Examine differences in locomotion of animals in different habitats.

RESULT—Animals may be described in more than one way: by type, by habitat, and by means of locomotion.

WRITING EXTENSION

• **Identify the characteristics used to describe various types of animals.**

THINKING ABOUT THINKING

• **Why is knowledge about an animal's type, habitat, and means of locomotion important in understanding that animal?**
• **How did using the diagram help you understand and remember the animals' characteristics?**
• **Suggest another lesson in which using this graph would help you understand what you are learning.**
• **Design another diagram to help you describe animals.**

SIMILAR SCIENCE LESSONS

• To illustrate relationships within the plant or animal kingdoms.
• To illustrate relationships between elements in a compound or mixture.
• To illustrate similar concepts in various branches of science.

LAND, WATER, AND FLYING ANIMALS

DIRECTIONS: Use the class relationships diagram below to classify the following animals according to where they live. For example, if an animal lives primarily on land, classify it as a land animal. If an animal spends some time in several different habitats, classify it in the correct overlapping area.

> alligator, bat, deer, duck, eagle, frog, lizard, pelican, sea gull, swallow shrimp, whale

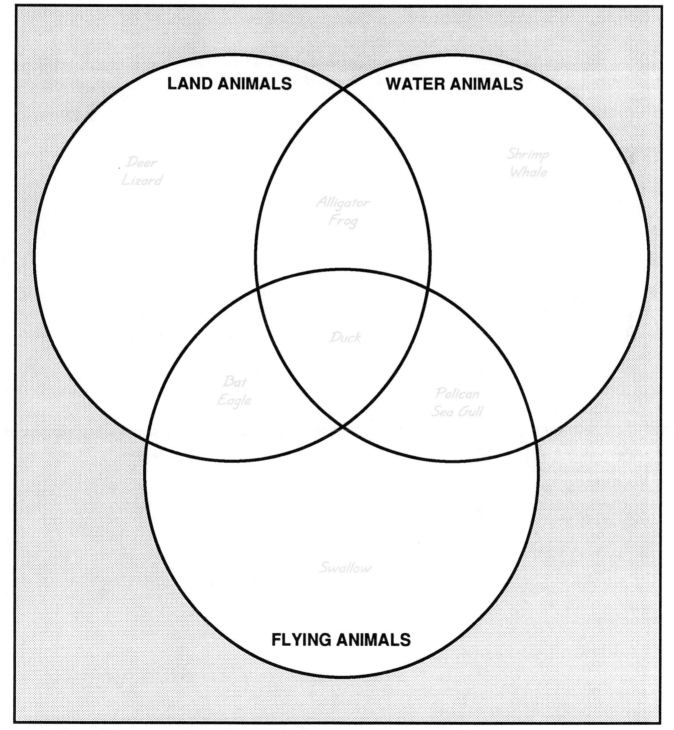

AMPHIBIANS AND REPTILES

THINKING SKILL: Verbal similarities and differences

CONTENT OBJECTIVE: Students will use the compare and contrast diagram to differentiate between amphibians and reptiles. *NOTE: Information from this lesson is used in the PERSONAL PROBLEM SOLVING lesson "How Do You Know That You Know?" and the WRITING lesson "Writing Definition."*

DISCUSSION: TECHNIQUE—Use a transparency of the branching diagram to record responses as students identify types of amphibians and reptiles. Encourage students to identify additional examples of amphibians and reptiles.

Use a transparency of the compare and contrast graph to record responses as students discuss the similarities and differences between amphibians and reptiles. Encourage them to identify additional similarities or differences.

DIALOGUE—The branching diagram illustrates the traditional hierarchical classification system used to describe phyla, species, and families. Use a branching diagram to design a large bulletin board display of the animal classes discussed in your textbooks.

Discuss the differences between amphibians and reptiles by naming the quality that is different. Establish the following pattern.

"With regard to (quality), (item one and its distinction), **but** (item two and its distinction)." For example, **"With regard to gills, baby amphibians have gills, but baby reptiles never have gills."**

Encourage students to discuss why amphibians are sometimes mistaken for reptiles. Clarify how understanding the significant differences between these animals prevents that confusion.

Why might people sometimes confuse amphibians with reptiles? (The shiny scales suggest that snakes are wet or slimy like amphibians. The shape of a salamander is similar to the shape of a lizard. Since both are cold-blooded vertebrates that lay eggs, students tend to believe that they are basically the same.) **How might you prevent confusing amphibians for reptiles?** (By remembering that amphibians change form, but reptiles do not, and by remembering skin and respiratory characteristics of the two species.)

In listing examples of amphibians, encourage students to identify the differences in toads, frogs, and salamanders and to think of additional examples. In listing examples of reptiles, encourage students to identify the differences in snakes, alligators, and lizards and to think of additional examples.

RESULT—Identifying significant similarities and differences between amphibians and reptiles and recognizing examples of each promotes the clearer understanding of the body structure and development of the two types of animals.

WRITING EXTENSION
· **Describe how amphibians and reptiles are alike and how they are different.**

THINKING ABOUT THINKING
· **How does identifying characteristics help you understand significant differences between amphibians and reptiles?**
· **How does understanding their significant differences prevent you from mistaking amphibians for reptiles?**

- **How did using the diagram help you understand and remember the characteristics of the animals?**
- **Suggest another lesson in which using this diagram would help you understand what you are learning.**
- **Design another diagram that would help you describe animals.**

SIMILAR SCIENCE LESSONS

- To compare phyla of plants, animals, and microorganisms.
- To compare systems within the human body with those in less complex life forms; types of tissue; illnesses or trauma; bone formation or location.
- To compare living and nonliving things; predators and prey; ecologically supportive and ecologically destructive conditions; ecosystems and habitats.
- To distinguish between plants and animals.
- To compare land formations or types of rocks.
- To compare weather phenomena.
- To compare physical science phenomena: types of energy, types of machines, types of instruments; energy, work, and power; electrical measuring units.
- To compare relative distances of planets from the sun.

AMPHIBIANS AND REPTILES

DIRECTIONS: Read the passage carefully to determine how amphibians and reptiles are alike and how they are different. Use the branching diagram below to list examples of amphibians and reptiles. Use the compare and contrast diagram to record their similarities and differences.

Amphibians are vertebrates that spend their early lives in water and their adult lives on land. Almost all amphibians hatch from eggs and have an immature form, such as a tadpole. The immature form of an amphibian has gills, which are replaced by lungs as it develops. As the tadpole grows lungs and legs, it is ready to leave the water and live on land.

Amphibians are cold-blooded and must hibernate in cold climates to survive the winter. They must also live near water or their soft skins will soon dry out. Some adult amphibians get oxygen through their skin, as well as through their lungs. Common amphibians include toads, frogs, and salamanders.

Reptiles are vertebrates that have lungs. Most reptiles spend their entire life on land. However, some reptiles live in the water and must come to the surface to breathe. Like amphibians, most reptiles are hatched from eggs. The young look almost exactly like their parents and do not change form as amphibians do. Reptiles are cold-blooded. Their dry, scaly, or leathery skin protects their bodies from attack and loss of moisture. Common reptiles include snakes, alligators, and lizards.

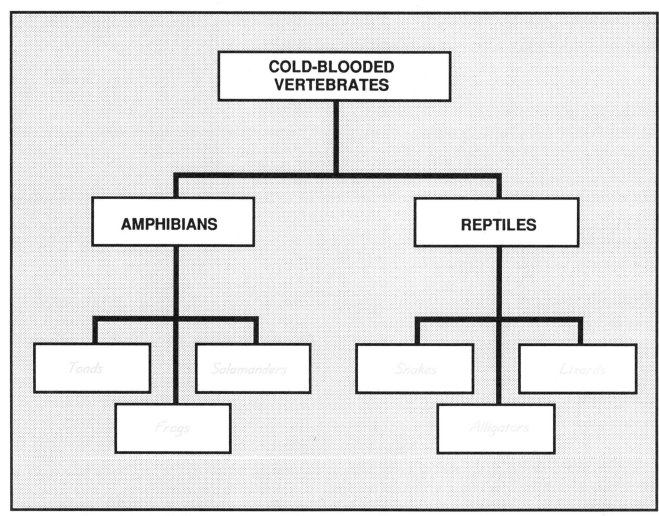

AMPHIBIANS AND REPTILES

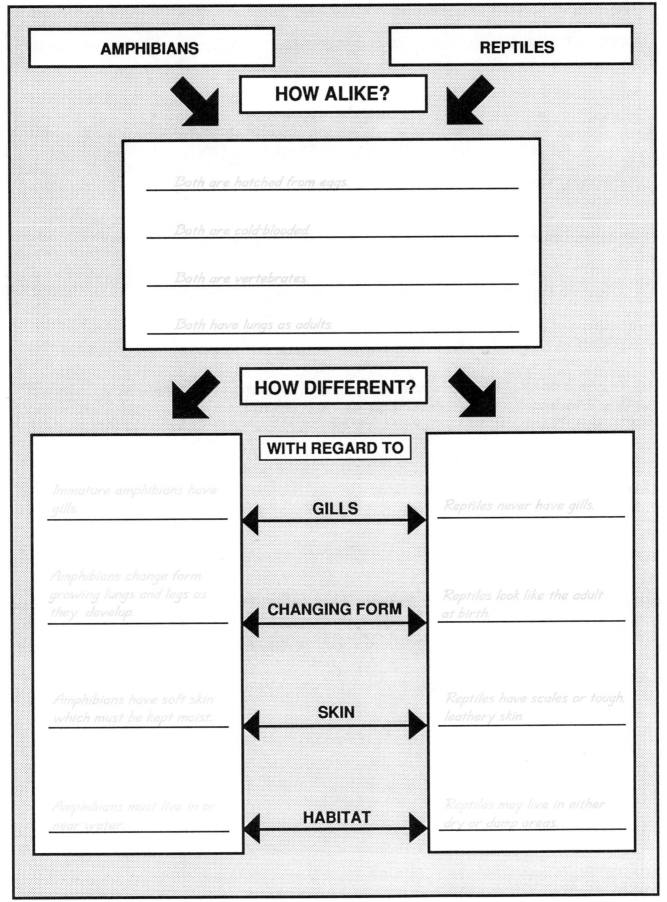

AMPHIBIANS		REPTILES

HOW ALIKE?

Both are hatched from eggs.

Both are cold-blooded.

Both are vertebrates.

Both have lungs as adults.

HOW DIFFERENT?

WITH REGARD TO

	GILLS	
Immature amphibians have gills.		Reptiles never have gills.
Amphibians change form, growing lungs and legs as they develop.	CHANGING FORM	Reptiles look like the adult at birth.
Amphibians have soft skin which must be kept moist.	SKIN	Reptiles have scales or tough, leathery skin.
Amphibians must live in or near water.	HABITAT	Reptiles may live in either dry or damp areas.

MAMMAL GESTATION PERIODS

THINKING SKILL: Depicting intervals, interpreting graphs

CONTENT OBJECTIVE: Students will use a grid diagram to depict and compare the gestation periods of several animals.

DISCUSSION: TECHNIQUE—Use a transparency of the grid diagram to record responses as students report information on the gestation periods of mammals.

DIALOGUE—Students should infer that the larger the mammal, the longer the gestation period. Discuss the clues that lead students to reach that conclusion. *NOTE: The generalization illustrated by the grid diagram refers to placentals. Larger marsupials, such as kangaroos, have a shorter gestation period. Their offspring are born in an underdeveloped state and must be carried in the mother's pouch until adequately developed.*

RESULT—Recording information on a grid diagram makes trends or relationships more apparent. Larger mammals require a longer gestation period than smaller ones.

WRITING EXTENSION
- **Describe the differences in the gestation period in mammals.**

THINKING ABOUT THINKING
- **How did using the diagram help you understand and remember the gestation characteristics of mammals?**
- **Suggest another lesson in which depicting information on a graph would help you understand what you are learning.**
- **Design another diagram that would help you describe animals.**

SIMILAR SCIENCE LESSONS

Interval graphs
- To record the chronological order of scientific discoveries.
- To depict the speed, number, weight, and lifespan of different organisms.
- To depict frequency or quantity in physical science.
- To depict geologic ages or hardness of minerals in earth sciences.
- To describe physical or biological processes chronologically.

Parallel interval graphs
- To relate any two measures of the same data on different scales, such as depicting temperature on the Fahrenheit and Celsius scales.
- To relate the history of science to other historical developments.

Grid graphs
- Bar graphs, line graphs, and records of measurement of frequency or quantity.

MAMMAL GESTATION PERIODS

DIRECTIONS: Read the passage carefully to determine how to record the information on the graphic organizer.

The length of time that a mother animal carries her baby before it is born is called the **gestation period**. Mammals are animals which carry their young within their bodies until the young can survive outside the warmth and protection of the mother. The following list illustrates the length of time that various mammals carry their babies before birth. Change the number of days into months (30 days = 1 month).

Cat – 63 days   Mouse – 20 days
Elephant – 21 months   Pig – 115 days
Horse – 11 months   Rabbit – 31 days
Human – 9 months   Whale – 12 months

LENGTH OF TIME MAMMALS CARRY THEIR BABIES BEFORE BIRTH

ANIMAL	TIME IN MONTHS
	0 4 8 12 16 20 24
Mouse	
Rabbit	
Cat	
Pig	
Human	
Horse	
Whale	
Elephant	

FOOD CHAIN

THINKING SKILL: Transitive order

CONTENT OBJECTIVE: Students will use a cycle diagram to depict the steps in the food chain.

DISCUSSION: TECHNIQUE—Use a transparency of the cycle diagram to record responses as students discuss the steps in the food chain.

DIALOGUE—Ask students to trace the steps in the food chain cycle and explain why each step is necessary. Identify what each organism contributes. Discuss the nature of cycles.

What makes a cycle different from other patterns? (A cycle is a repeating process that flows in one direction and requires each step to maintain its action. Cycles can remain constant, slow down or stop, or expand.) **What makes a cycle work? What would happen if there were a break in the cycle? What could cause a break in the cycle? Is there a point in the cycle in which a break might be more likely to occur? What other examples of cycles can you think of?** (water cycle, photosynthesis/respiration cycle, seasonal cycle) **Why is a cycle a frequent pattern in nature?**

RESULT—Each organism provides food for another in an efficient cycle that supports life and decomposes waste. The cycle shows the interdependence of plants and organisms.

WRITING EXTENSION
- **Describe the food chain cycle. Give examples of each part of the cycle.**

THINKING ABOUT THINKING
- **How does this cycle demonstrate the interdependence among the organisms in the process? Identify other cycles that demonstrate interdependence.**
- **Suggest another lesson in which using this graph would help you understand what you are learning.**

SIMILAR SCIENCE LESSONS
- To depict natural cycles (e.g., water cycle, photosynthesis/respiration cycle, seasonal cycle, raw material trade, electrical current cycle, gasoline engine cycle).

FOOD CHAIN

DIRECTIONS: Read the passage carefully, then use the information to complete the food chain cycle diagram.

In the food chain, plants produce food for herbivores (animals who eat plants). A corn plant, for example, uses sunlight and nutrients from the soil to make food. Corn is a food source for many herbivores, including worms.

Meat-eating animals (carnivores) feed on plant-eating animals or other meat-eaters. Each food chain leads to an animal that is not eaten by other animals. Worms are eaten by sparrows which are eaten by hawks. Hawks have no natural non-human enemies.

When members of a food chain die, they become food for decomposers (yeast, mold, or bacteria). These decomposers break down waste and dead organisms all along the chain. The decomposed materials go back into the soil or water and provide fertilizer for the production of plants.

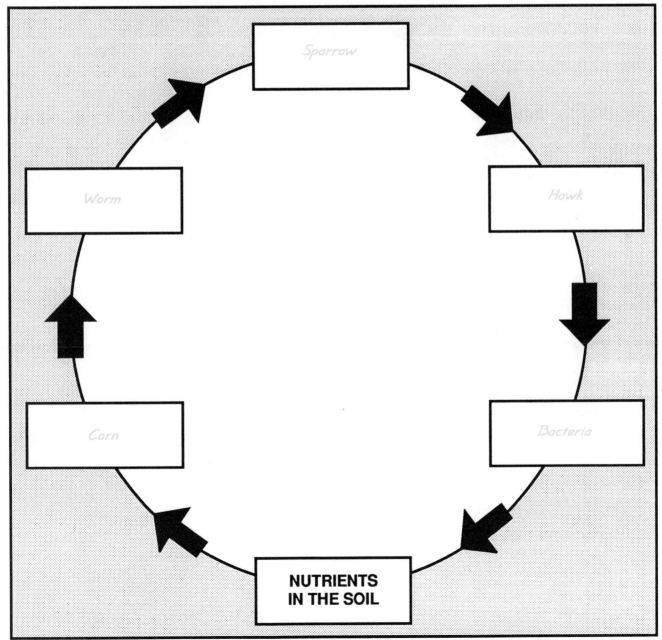

MEANS OF CONTROLLING DISEASE

THINKING SKILL: Verbal classification

CONTENT OBJECTIVE: Students will use a branching diagram to depict the various means of controlling disease.

DISCUSSION: TECHNIQUE—Use a transparency of the branching diagram to record responses as students report means of controlling diseases.

DIALOGUE—As students discuss various means of controlling diseases, prompt them to identify the source of the disease and the means that might be necessary to eliminate the source. Clarify the term "immunization" (the action of antibodies to kill germs). Emphasize the difference between inoculation and vaccination. An inoculation is an injection of a serum, usually produced by an animal, which contains antibodies that provide immunity against disease-causing bacteria. A vaccination is an injection of a weakened bacteria or virus to produce immunity against stronger organisms.

Which is likely to create greater discomfort or illness in the patient—inoculation or vaccination? What other illnesses can you think of that are controlled by vaccination or inoculation? What illnesses can you think of that were spread in epidemics but have now been virtually eliminated? How is the spread of disease reduced: by controlling the source or by vaccination or inoculation? Why is it easier to control the source than to kill infection?

Encourage students to identify other means of controlling diseases. Identify local, county, state, national, and international agencies responsible for the control of disease. Encourage students to use a matrix to depict their research about epidemics, including the time period, location, casualty statistics, consequences of the epidemic, and discovery of the means of controlling it.

RESULT—Understanding how serious illnesses are controlled helps us understand the significance of health organizations and the value of immunization.

WRITING EXTENSION

- Describe how serious illnesses are controlled.
- Why is controlling the source of disease more effective than treating or immunizing against it?

THINKING ABOUT THINKING

- How did using the diagram help you understand and remember the different means of disease control?
- Suggest another lesson in which depicting information on a graph would help you understand what you are learning.
- Design another diagram that would help you describe means of disease control.

SIMILAR SCIENCE LESSONS

- To depict technological or industrial developments.
- To classify plants, animals, or elements according to predetermined characteristics.
- To depict a balanced diet.
- To depict solar system organization.

MEANS OF CONTROLLING DISEASE

DIRECTIONS: Read the passage carefully to determine how to record the data on the branching diagram.

The easiest way to control a disease is to eliminate or control its source. Bubonic plague is a microorganism that killed millions in Europe and Asia in the 1300s and is spread by fleas from infected rats. Yellow fever and malaria are caused by microorganisms which are carried by mosquitoes. Controlling rats and mosquitoes helps reduce the spread of these diseases.

Typhoid and cholera are caused by microorganisms which grow in human and animal waste. If sewage and animal waste are properly treated and disposed of, these microorganisms have no environment in which to grow.

Our bodies use antibodies to kill germs. Antibodies are a protein in blood that breaks down harmful substances and makes our bodies immune to them. Two procedures give us antibodies to help us fight serious diseases. The first is vaccination with disease microorganisms that are too weak to make us sick. Our bodies produce antibodies against this weakened form, which keeps us from getting sick if we are exposed to a stronger form of the disease. Smallpox and polio are examples of diseases prevented by vaccination.

A second procedure is injection with a serum which contains antibodies. This serum is obtained from animals or people who have already had a disease. Whooping cough, diphtheria, and tetanus are examples of diseases that can be treated with this kind of injection.

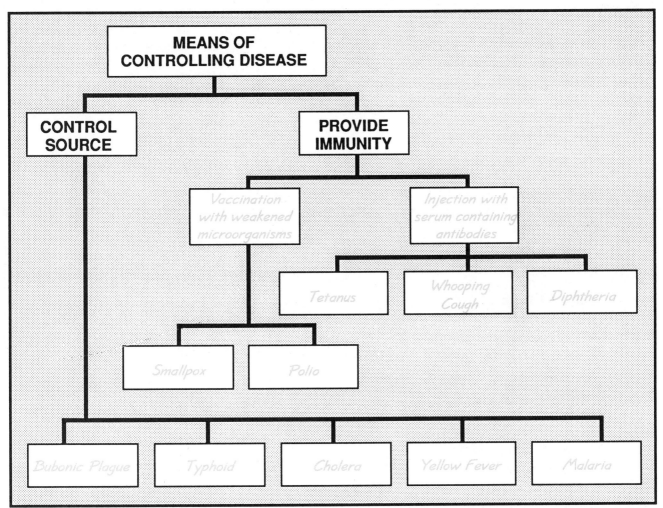

HANDEDNESS AND EYEDNESS

THINKING SKILL: Verbal classification, generalizing

CONTENT OBJECTIVE: Students will use a matrix to identify handedness, eyedness, and mixed dominance among classmates.

DISCUSSION: TECHNIQUE—When students have recorded handedness and eyedness information in pairs, summarize the data by class discussion or by assigning "student researchers" to compile all the information on the class matrix graph. Compute the totals and record the data on a transparency of the second matrix graph. Encourage your students to draw inferences from the information on the graph.

DIALOGUE—Students identify handedness easily, although a few students may retain some degree of ambidextrous skill. Some students, for example, may write with one hand and throw or hit a baseball with the other. Even some upper-elementary students must consciously choose which hand will be used for different tasks. Ambidextrous skill is a mixed blessing. Students may wish to discuss the advantages and disadvantages of being ambidextrous.

Eyedness includes acuity, to a degree, and the ease or preference in using one eye rather than the other. (This exercise should not be used for any clinical interpretation, since lack of acuity can explain eye dominance preference. Cognitive development research offers mixed interpretations of the effect of mixed dominance. For classroom purposes, self-knowledge is the primary objective of this exercise. The number of students who are right-handed and right-eyed, who are left-handed and left-eyed, and who have mixed dominance will probably be similar to that of the general population.)

Do you think it makes any difference in the speed, accuracy, or ease of doing routine tasks to have one side dominant or to have mixed dominance? (For most individuals mixed dominance has no perceivable effect; for others it becomes a limitation on speed, dexterity, and balance. Students may be interested in exercises or activities which allow those with mixed dominance to function more easily. Consult your learning disabilities specialist for information on this topic.)

RESULT—Handedness and eyedness influence how easily people perform simple tasks.

WRITING EXTENSION
- **What is handedness? What is eyedness? What is mixed dominance?**

THINKING ABOUT THINKING
- **How did using the diagram help you understand dominance?**
- **How did using the diagram help you understand how many people in the general population have mixed dominance?**
- **How is this experiment similar to the way scientists gather information, interpret data, and form principles from statistical information?**
- **Suggest another lesson in which depicting information on a graph would help you understand what you are learning.**

SIMILAR SCIENCE LESSONS
- To construct or interpret probability charts.
- To report experiment results.

HANDEDNESS AND EYEDNESS

DIRECTIONS: Record the handedness and eyedness of your partner. Compile information for your class and compute the number of students who are right-handed and right-eyed, left-handed and left-eyed, or mixed dominant.

Most people are either right-handed or left-handed. A few can use either hand easily for certain tasks and are said to be "ambidextrous." Similarly, most people use either their right eye or their left eye more easily than the other. Some people also use either eye equally well. Choose a partner, then test each other to see if you are right-eyed or left-eyed. Record the results on the matrix chart below.

1. Punch a round hole about 1/4 inch in diameter in a piece of paper.
2. Hold the paper at arm's length. Look through the hole at some object with both eyes open.
3. Once the object is sighted, close the right eye. Can you see the same object without moving the paper?
4. Open the right eye and close the left one. Can you see the object again without moving the paper?

Most people will see the object more clearly and easily with one eye than with the other.

NAME	HANDEDNESS			EYEDNESS		
	Left	Right	Both	Left	Right	Both

HANDEDNESS AND EYEDNESS—CLASS DATA

NAME	HANDEDNESS			EYEDNESS		
	Left	Right	Both	Left	Right	Both

	LEFT-EYED	RIGHT-EYED	TOTALS
LEFT-HANDED			
RIGHT-HANDED			
TOTALS			
TOTAL WITH SAME SIDE DOMINANCE			
TOTAL WITH MIXED DOMINANCE			

SIMPLE MACHINES

THINKING SKILL: Verbal classification

CONTENT OBJECTIVE: Students will use the central idea graph to identify different types of simple machines.

DISCUSSION: TECHNIQUE—Use a transparency of the central idea graph to record classes and examples of simple machines.

DIALOGUE—Encourage students to identify how force changes with the use of each type of simple machine and think of other examples of each type.

Can you think of some objects or machinery which involve more than one simple machine? (In less-industrialized times, most complex machines were combinations of simple machines.) **Can you identify some mechanisms which use electronic or magnetic devices to do more complex tasks?**

RESULT—Knowing how simple machines put forces to work helps us do certain tasks more quickly and easily.

WRITING EXTENSION
* **Describe how simple machines use force efficiently to help us do tasks more easily and quickly.**
* **Describe and give examples of each type of simple machine.**

THINKING ABOUT THINKING
* **How did using the diagram help you understand and remember types of simple machines and examples?**
* **Suggest another lesson in which depicting information on this graph would help you understand what you are learning.**
* **Design another diagram that would help you describe simple machines.**

SIMILAR SCIENCE LESSONS
* To recognize main ideas and supporting details in critical reading activities from science texts.
* To illustrate classes and subclasses of organisms, minerals, weather phenomena, or chemical terms (elements, mixtures, or compounds).
* To illustrate part/whole relationships: parts of a microscope or other scientific equipment, parts of body systems, tissues, cells, organisms, atomic structure, structure of the earth, or the solar system.
* To illustrate the divisions and subdivisions of science disciplines.
* To illustrate multiple consequences of or developments leading to a scientific innovation.

SIMPLE MACHINES

DIRECTIONS: Read the passage carefully for information about simple machines. Record one type of simple machine in each box on the central idea graph. Add an example of each simple machine in parentheses.

Machines put forces to work which help us do things more easily and usually more quickly. Simple machines are not driven by motors. They take advantage of simple, but effective, forces to make work easier. Simple machines magnify a person's ability to move an object.

A **lever** is a bar used to pry up objects, like the claw of a hammer removes a nail. Levers include crow-bars, pliers, bottle openers, baseball bats, and seesaws.

A **wheel and axle**, like the pedals and chain of a bicycle, allows the small motion of the pedals to be changed into the larger motion of the bike wheel over the ground. A pencil sharpener is another example of a wheel and axle. It changes the smaller force on the handle into a larger force on the blades which sharpen the pencil.

A **pulley** is a set of wheels with a rope running over them. Pulleys can make it easier to lift heavy objects by fastening them to one

end of a rope and pulling on the other end. With a pulley, a person uses a small force through a long distance to lift a heavy load a short distance. The cords on Venetian blinds are wrapped around pulley wheels.

An **inclined plane** is a ramp that allows a person to slide an object too heavy to lift. The heavy object slides a long distance along the ramp and rises a short distance.

A **screw** is a coiled inclined plane that allows a small force on the big head to produce a large force on the small tip. For example, a hardware screw applies a great force to dig into wood. Likewise, a shop vise multiplies a small force on the handle to become a great force on the jaws which hold an object securely.

A **wedge** is a narrow triangular blade used to split or cut wood or metal. Its shape allows a small force applied to the broad end to produce a large force at the blade end. Chisels, knives, scissors, and door stops are all wedges.

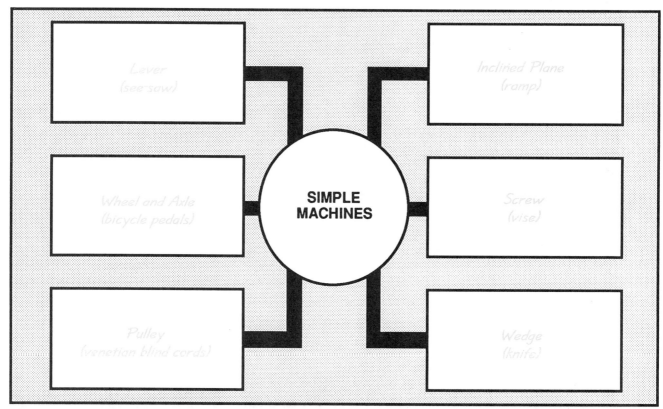

TESTING HARDNESS OF MINERALS

THINKING SKILL: Verbal sequence, transitive order

CONTENT OBJECTIVE: Students will use the transitive order graph to identify tests for mineral hardness.

DISCUSSION: TECHNIQUE—Use a transparency of the transitive order graph to record responses as students discuss the relative hardness of minerals. (An effective way to teach this lesson is to gather the minerals involved and demonstrate the testing described in the lesson.)

DIALOGUE—The key principle in testing for the hardness of minerals is whether a harder test material will make a mark on a softer mineral. A softer material will not scratch a harder mineral. Fingernails are obviously harder than fingers. Pennies are obviously harder than fingernails. The blade of a knife would make a mark more easily than the edge of a penny. A file with its numerous cutting edges and its hard metal composition would do more damage than the blade of a knife.

Students should also learn from this lesson that, although glass is fragile in thin sheets, it is actually very hard. A mineral that is so hard you need a file to scratch it may not be hard enough itself to scratch glass.

RESULT—The relative hardness of a given mineral can be demonstrated by what it can scratch and what can scratch its surface. Hardness and strength are not the same thing, as demonstrated by glass.

WRITING EXTENSION
* Describe how to test for the hardness of minerals.

THINKING ABOUT THINKING
* How did using the diagram help you understand and remember the relative hardness of minerals?
* Suggest another lesson in which depicting information on a transitive order graph would help you understand what you are learning.
* Design another graph to help you describe the relative hardness of minerals.

SIMILAR SCIENCE LESSONS
* To compare relative distances to planets.
* To compare relative weights of materials.
* To compare relative heights of clouds.
* To compare relative strengths of acids.
* To compare relative sizes of plants, seeds, fruits, or vegetables.
* To compare relative densities of materials.
* To compare relative brightness of stars.
* To compare relative speed, length of life, or size of animals.
* To compare relative height or position of land forms.
* To write organized reports of science processes, demonstrations, or experiments.
* To depict assembly order of equipment or models.

TESTING HARDNESS OF MINERALS

DIRECTIONS: Read the passage carefully to determine the tests for mineral hardness in order, from the softest to the hardest. Record the information on the transitive order graph below.

There are a number of simple ways to test the hardness of minerals. Some minerals are so soft they can be rubbed off with one's finger. The hardest minerals are so hard they will scratch glass. Some minerals are easily scratched with a knife. Some soft minerals can be scratched by a fingernail or, if they are slightly harder, by a penny. Some hard minerals can be scratched by a file but they are not hard enough to scratch glass.

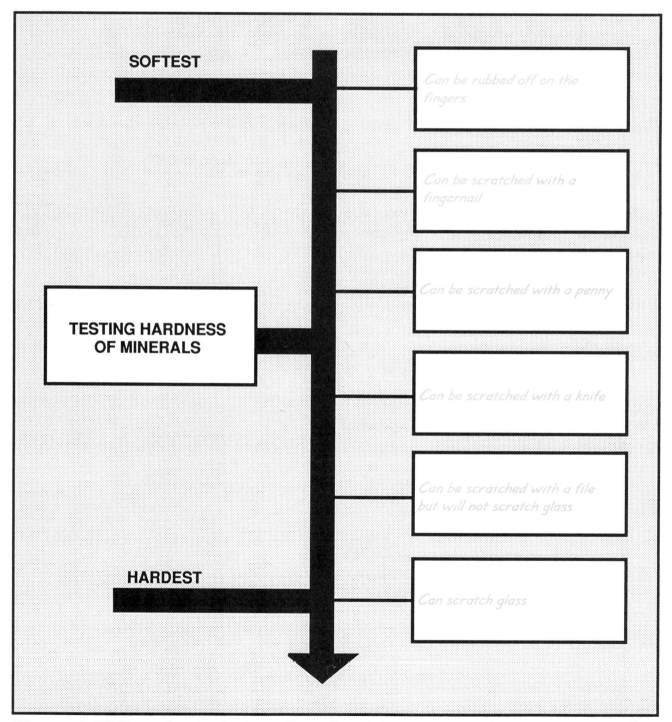

SOFTEST

Can be rubbed off on the fingers

Can be scratched with a fingernail

Can be scratched with a penny

TESTING HARDNESS OF MINERALS

Can be scratched with a knife

Can be scratched with a file but will not scratch glass

HARDEST

Can scratch glass

WEATHER OBSERVATIONS

THINKING SKILL: Verbal classification

CONTENT OBJECTIVE: Students will observe weather conditions and record their observations on a matrix graph.

DISCUSSION: TECHNIQUE—Use a transparency of the matrix graph to summarize weather observations for a two-week period. Encourage your students to draw inferences suggested by the information on the graph.

DIALOGUE—Examine each variable and describe its effect in producing weather conditions for your locale. Encourage students to identify control factors and variables in a science demonstration.

Why was it important to record the weather at the same time each day? What factors changed during the two-week period? How did weather conditions reflect that change? If those conditions are present again, are we likely to have similar weather?

RESULT—It is necessary to identify what remains constant and what changes in order to suggest a trend or principle when observing natural occurrences.

WRITING EXTENSION
- **Describe how one records and interprets weather information.**

THINKING ABOUT THINKING
- **How did using the diagram help you understand and suggest trends or principles about weather conditions?**
- **Suggest another lesson in which depicting information on a matrix graph would help you understand what you are learning.**
- **Design another graph that would help you describe weather conditions.**

SIMILAR SCIENCE LESSONS
- To record, summarize, and evaluate experimental or observational results or statistical data.
- To record probable and actual genetics data.
- To describe plants, animals, minerals, chemical elements, or physical phenomena by two characteristics.
- To interpret the periodic chart.

WEATHER OBSERVATIONS

DIRECTIONS: A good scientist learns to make careful observations and to keep records. Use a matrix graph like the one below to record weather conditions each day for a two-week period. Make sure all observations are made at the same time of day.

KEY			
CLOUD COVER:		**CLOUD TYPES**	
CLEAR	CL	CIRRUS	CI
SCATTERED CLOUDS	SC	CUMULUS	CU
PARTLY SUNNY	PS	STRATUS	ST
CLOUDY	CY		
OVERCAST	OC		

DATE							
CLOUD TYPE							
CLOUD COVER							
WIND DIRECTION							
WIND SPEED							
AIR PRESSURE							
TEMPERATURE							
PRECIPITATION							
GENERAL WEATHER CONDITIONS ·							

THE TWIN PLANETS: EARTH AND VENUS

THINKING SKILL: Verbal similarities and differences

CONTENT OBJECTIVE: Students will use the compare and contrast diagram to show similarities and differences between the Earth and Venus.

DISCUSSION: TECHNIQUE—Use a transparency of the compare and contrast diagram to record responses as students discuss the similarities of and differences between the twin planets, Earth and Venus.

DIALOGUE—Help the students use the passage to identify significant characteristics when describing a planet.

What characteristics might one discuss when describing a planet? (Size, weight, distance from the sun, temperature, presence of satellites, geographical features, chemical composition.) **Why is it important to know the conditions on other planets?**

Apply these characteristics in describing the other planets in our Solar System. Use a matrix diagram to record multiple characteristics for several planets, then use the design for a bulletin board display.

Encourage students to examine conditions related to supporting Earth's animal life.

What conditions are necessary for animal life on earth? (Moderate temperature, oxygen, water, and food.) **Which of these conditions are present on Venus? Which are absent? What conditions, if any, would make animal life impossible on Venus?**

Encourage students to do additional research about Venus's characteristics. Such research might also help prepare students for a meaningful creative writing assignment.

RESULT—Although the two planets are physically similar, Venus does not have the necessary conditions to support earth-type life.

WRITING EXTENSION

- **Identify the characteristics that one uses to describe planets.**
- **Create an animal-like life form that could live on Venus. Discuss its temperature, respiration, locomotion, food and fluid requirements, habits, and habitat. Draw a picture of it.**

THINKING ABOUT THINKING

- **How did using the diagram help you understand and remember the similarities and differences of the twin planets?**
- **Suggest another lesson in which using this graph would help you understand what you are learning.**
- **Design another graph that would help you describe planets.**

SIMILAR SCIENCE LESSONS

- To make comparisons within the plant or animal kingdoms.
- To make comparisons between chemical elements or compounds.

THE TWIN PLANETS: EARTH AND VENUS

DIRECTIONS: Use the compare and contrast diagram to illustrate the similarities and differences between the twin planets, Earth and Venus.

Earth and Venus are sister planets; their sizes and weights are about the same. They are close together and are about the same distance from the Sun. Venus is, however, closer to the sun than the Earth is.

Although Earth and Venus look alike, they are very different. The Earth has extensive plant and animal life, oceans, an atmosphere containing oxygen, and a reasonably mild climate.

Venus is a hot, lifeless planet with an atmosphere of carbon dioxide which traps the Sun's radiation causing the surface temperatures to remain far above the boiling point of water. There is very little water on Venus—and no sign of plant or animal life.

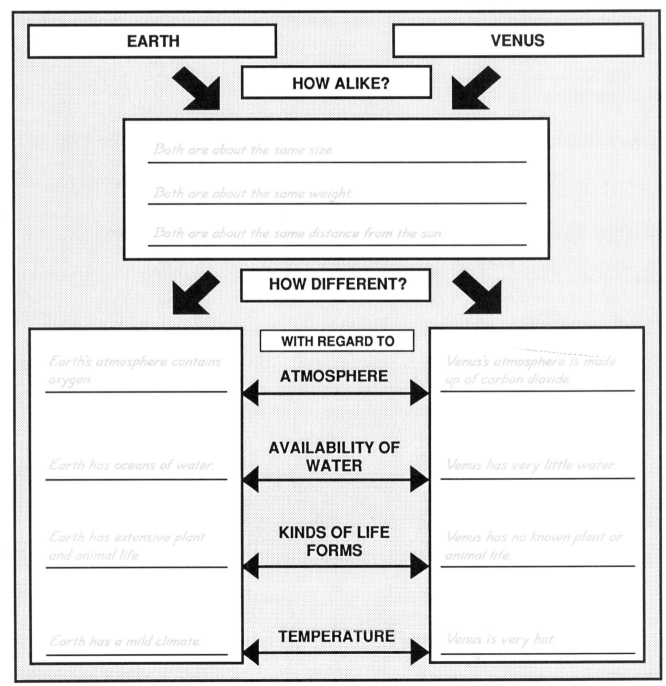

EARTH

VENUS

HOW ALIKE?

Both are about the same size.

Both are about the same weight.

Both are about the same distance from the sun.

HOW DIFFERENT?

WITH REGARD TO

Earth's atmosphere contains oxygen. — **ATMOSPHERE** — *Venus's atmosphere is made up of carbon dioxide.*

Earth has oceans of water. — **AVAILABILITY OF WATER** — *Venus has very little water.*

Earth has extensive plant and animal life. — **KINDS OF LIFE FORMS** — *Venus has no known plant or animal life.*

Earth has a mild climate. — **TEMPERATURE** — *Venus is very hot.*

ENERGY TRANSFORMATIONS

THINKING SKILL: Verbal sequences

CONTENT OBJECTIVE: Students will determine the order in which energy transformations occur and list them on a flowchart.

DISCUSSION: TECHNIQUE—Have the students cut apart the matrix of energy transformations and arrange the list in order of occurrence on the flowchart. Make a transparency of the flowchart and the energy transformations. Cut apart the energy transformations and, during the discussion, use these pieces to overlay the flowchart transparency.

DIALOGUE—Help students identify the clues that suggest order. They may recognize that the last word or phrase of an earlier step becomes the first word or phrase of the next step. Identify other sequences of energy changes. Clarify that energy must be stored or changed in form to be useful.

RESULT—There are many energy transformations in the production of artificial light.

WRITING EXTENSION
* **Identify the sequence of energy changes in making artificial light.**

THINKING ABOUT THINKING
* **Why is knowing about energy transformations important?**
* **How did using the diagram help you understand and remember the steps in producing light?**
* **Suggest another lesson in which using a flowchart would help you understand what you are learning.**
* **Design another diagram that would help you describe energy transformations.**

SIMILAR SCIENCE LESSONS
* To illustrate relationships within the plant or animal kingdoms.
* To illustrate relationships between elements in a compound or mixture.
* To illustrate similar concepts in various branches of science.

ENERGY TRANSFORMATIONS

DIRECTIONS: Six energy changes are listed on the left below. Decide which of the six changes must come first and which must come last. Cut them apart and arrange them in order of occurrence in the flowchart on the right.

COAL IS BURNED
TO PRODUCE
HEAT.

ELECTRICITY IS
CHANGED TO
LIGHT IN LAMPS.

HEAT BOILS WATER
TO MAKE STEAM.

STEAM RUNS
ELECTRIC
GENERATORS.

ENERGY FROM
PLANTS IS STORED
IN COAL.

THE SUN'S ENERGY
IS STORED IN LIVING
PLANTS.

THE SUN'S ENERGY IS
STORED IN LIVING
PLANTS.

ENERGY FROM PLANTS IS
STORED IN COAL.

COAL IS BURNED TO
PRODUCE HEAT.

HEAT BOILS WATER TO
MAKE STEAM.

STEAM RUNS ELECTRIC
GENERATORS.

ELECTRICITY IS CHANGED
TO LIGHT IN LAMPS.

CHAPTER 7 – ENRICHMENT

THE FLUTE AND
THE CLARINET
(Compare and Contrast Diagram)

DESCRIBING
A MUSICAL WORK
(Central Idea Graph)

ELEMENTS OF DESIGN
(Branching Diagram)

DESCRIBING A PICTURE
(Central Idea Graph)

COMPARING PICTURES
(Matrix Chart)

DESCRIBING PICTURES
AND MUSIC
(Class Relationships Diagram)

THE FLUTE AND THE CLARINET

THINKING SKILL: Verbal similarities and differences

OBJECTIVE: Students will use a compare and contrast diagram to differentiate between the flute and the clarinet. *NOTE: These lessons require no specialized knowledge of music or art. They may also be used as critical reading lessons and for writing-across-the-curriculum activities.*

DISCUSSION: TECHNIQUE—As students discuss the lesson, record each idea on a transparency of the compare and contrast diagram.

DIALOGUE—Encourage students to identify additional similarities or differences. After students have reported differences between the flute and the clarinet, discuss those differences by naming the quality that is different.

Establish this pattern: **"With regard to** (quality), (item one and its distinction), **but** (item two and its distinction)." For example, **"With regard to sound production, a flute produces sound by vibrating a column of air over the edge of the flute opening, but a clarinet produces sound by the vibration of a cane reed."**

RESULT—If one is clear about the differences between the structure and method of playing the flute and the clarinet, one will not get the two woodwinds confused.

WRITING EXTENSION
- **Describe how flutes and clarinets are alike and how they are different.**
- **Choose two other instruments in a band or orchestra and describe their similarities and differences.**

THINKING ABOUT THINKING
- **How did using the diagram help you understand woodwinds?**
- **Suggest another lesson in which depicting information on this graph would help you understand what you are learning.**
- **Design another diagram that would help you describe woodwinds.**

SIMILAR ENRICHMENT LESSONS
- To compare two art media or works, design principles, styles of art, or artists' biographies.
- To compare architectural terms and styles.
- To compare instruments, elements of musical composition, forms of music, types of music, the development of musical styles, composers' or performers' biographies, or dance styles.

THE FLUTE AND THE CLARINET

DIRECTIONS: Read the passage carefully to determine how the flute and clarinet are alike and how they are different. Use the compare and contrast diagram to record their similarities and differences.

The sound of a musical instrument is produced by vibrations. In woodwind instruments, these vibrations are made by blowing into or across the mouthpiece of the instrument. Flutes and clarinets are called woodwinds because they were originally made of wood. Today, however, woodwinds may be made of plastic, metal, or wood.

The flute is a tube-shaped woodwind which is usually held horizontally. Since the player forces air across an edge of the mouthpiece opening, flutes are known as "edge-vibrated" woodwinds. Flute players change the pitch by using their fingers to open and close holes along the "tube" of the flute.

The clarinet is also a tube-shaped woodwind, but it also has a small flair, or "bell," at one end. Unlike the flute, it is held nearly vertically in front of the player. A flat cane reed attached to the mouthpiece vibrates and produces a tone when the player blows into the mouthpiece. Instruments of this type are called "reed-vibrated" woodwinds. Clarinet players also change the instrument's pitch by using their fingers to open and close holes along the "tube" of the clarinet.

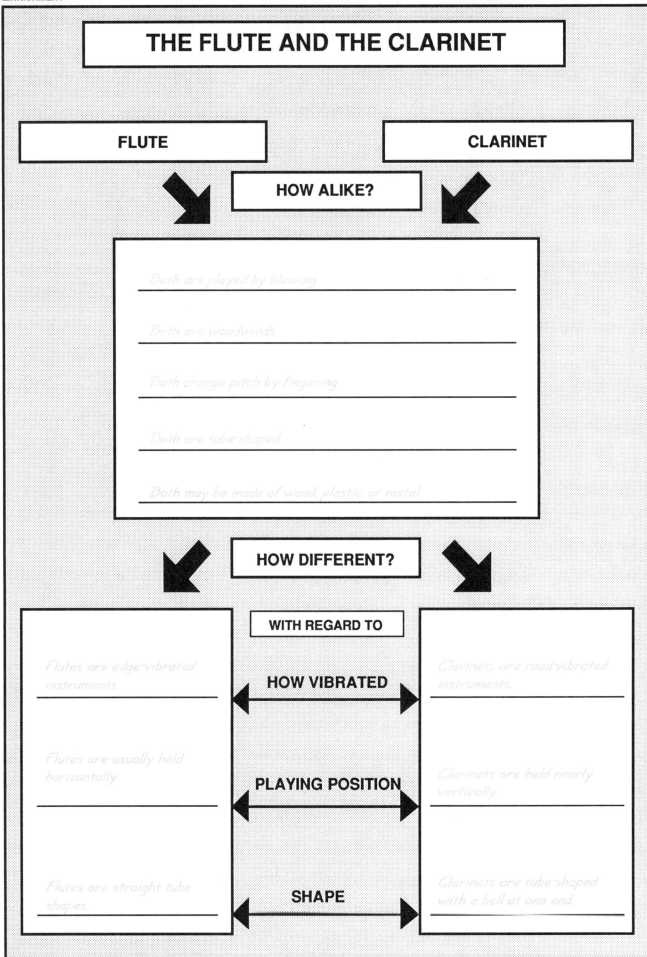

THE FLUTE AND THE CLARINET

FLUTE

CLARINET

HOW ALIKE?

Both are played by blowing

Both are woodwinds.

Both change pitch by fingering

Both are tube-shaped

Both may be made of wood, plastic, or metal.

HOW DIFFERENT?

WITH REGARD TO

Flutes are edge-vibrated instruments.

HOW VIBRATED

Clarinets are reed-vibrated instruments.

Flutes are usually held horizontally.

PLAYING POSITION

Clarinets are held nearly vertically.

Flutes are straight tube shapes.

SHAPE

Clarinets are tube-shaped with a bell at one end.

DESCRIBING A MUSICAL WORK

THINKING SKILL: Verbal classification

CONTENT OBJECTIVE: Students will use the central idea graph to describe elements of a musical work: melody, rhythm, harmony, tone color, form, and style. *NOTE: This lesson requires no specialized knowledge of music. It may be used to supplement music instruction or as a critical reading or writing-across-the-curriculum lesson.*

DISCUSSION: TECHNIQUE—Use a transparency of the central idea graph to record responses as students discuss the elements of a musical work.
　　　DIALOGUE—Encourage students to apply these concepts as they listen to music.

How does the information on the diagram help you understand what to listen for in a musical work? How does it help you understand the differences between different works of music? How does knowing what to listen for in music help you enjoy and understand music differently?

Use the same graphic organizer to describe a simple piece of music, such as "Row, Row, Row Your Boat," "On Top of Old Smoky," or "Frère Jacques." Students may prefer to describe contemporary music. For additional discussion information, consult the music section at your school library, the district's instructional materials center, or the following resource books:
　　　Invitation to Music, Elie Siegmeister (Irvington-on-Hudson, NY: Harvey House, 1961).
　　　The Voice of Music, Robina Wilson (Atheneum, NY: Margaret K. McElderry, 1977).
　　　What to Listen for in Music, Aaron Copeland (New York: McGraw-Hill, 1957).
　　　RESULT—Knowing what to listen for in a piece of music helps one appreciate and understand it differently.

WRITING EXTENSION
- **Describe the different things to listen for in a piece of music.**

THINKING ABOUT THINKING
- **What other items could you organize quickly with a central idea graph?**
- **How did using the graph help you understand the elements of a musical work?**
- **Suggest another lesson in which depicting information on a central idea graph would help you understand what you are learning.**
- **Design another graph that would help you describe or analyze a musical work.**

SIMILAR ENRICHMENT LESSONS
- To classify music, art, architecture, or dance according to era, culture, or type.
- To classify tools according to purpose, type, function, or storage needs.
- To select music, art, flowers, decorations, or fashions appropriate to an occasion.

DESCRIBING A MUSICAL WORK

DIRECTIONS: Read the passage carefully to determine how to record the elements of a musical work: melody, rhythm, harmony, tone color, form, and style.

Six elements make up the uniqueness of a musical piece. These are **melody, rhythm, harmony, tone color, form, and style.**

Melody is the series of tones, individual notes, and rhythms arranged into the pattern that you recognize and remember as a particular song. Melody has two characteristics: **scale** and **melodic curve.** Not all music follows the familiar *do-re-mi-fa-sol-la-ti-do* scale. Because we hear and use that scale so much, any other "family of tones" seems strange. Songs may be written in major scales, which we usually believe to be orderly or happy, or minor scales, which we consider to be sad or serious.

The **melodic curve** describes the rising and falling of tones in a line of music. Rising melodies, like "This Land Is Your Land," contain tones which move up the scale. Falling melodies, like "I Dream of Jeannie With the Light Brown Hair" or "We Are the World," contain tones which start high and move down the scale. Waving melodies, like "Yankee Doodle" and "Frère Jacques," repeat up-and-down phrases. Songs like "On Top of Old Smoky" or "Twinkle, Twinkle Little Star" have arching melodies that start low then move up the scale and down again. A bowl melody starts high, moves down the scale and moves back up again. "Joy To the World" is an example of a bowl melody.

Rhythm is the steady beat that carries the music along. In dance music, marching music, and rock music, rhythm gives pep to the music. In some classical music and popular ballads, regular, controlled rhythms give a sense of peace or dignity to the music.

The strongest beat in a series is called the **accent.** Where the accent falls in a series changes the rhythm of the musical piece. The accent in "On Top of Old Smoky" gives it a flowing sound; the regular accent in "Old Folks at Home" ("Way Down upon the Swanee River") gives it a swinging sound. When two rhythms appear in the same song, the **cross-rhythms** produce interesting and complicated melodies. African-inspired music, like Paul Simon's "Graceland," or Spanish-sounding music, like Ravel's "Bolero," contain cross-rhythms. Another African-inspired rhythm, **syncopation**, occurs when an offbeat is strongly accented, such as in "Michael Row Your Boat Ashore."

Tempo refers to the rate of speed at which music is played: a fast tempo, a slow tempo, a moderate tempo, or a changing tempo.

Harmony is the blending of tones sounded at the same time, called **chords**. Gospel music, African music, and barbershop quartets are familiar examples. **Counterpoint** is a harmony produced by more than one melody line, such as the piccolo solo at the end of the "Stars and Stripes Forever" or the effect of singing any round, such as "Row, Row, Row Your Boat" or "Frère Jacques."

Tone color is the effect the composer achieves by choosing a volume, pitch, or combination of instruments to produce a mood or feeling. **Dynamics** refers to how loudly a piece is played. "The Star Spangled Banner" played softly and delicately would sound sad instead of rousing. **Pitch** refers to whether a melody uses high notes for light, cheerful sounds or low notes for serious sounds. In *Peter and the Wolf* the high notes suggest the bird; the bass notes suggest the grandfather. Furthermore, the flute sounds like the bird, and the bassoon sounds like the grumbling old grandfather.

Form refers to the organization of a musical piece: repeating melodies, contrasting melodies, and melodies that are changed slightly to give them a sense of difference. It also refers to the length of the piece or the combination of instruments or voices required.

Instrumental music may have many different forms. A **suite** is a group of pieces in contrasting moods. The *Nutcracker Suite,* for example, is a collection of dances connected to the Christmas dreams of a young girl. A **sonata** is a long composition, usually made up of four different, but related, sections called "movements." Each movement may have a different tempo and basic melody, and may be further divided into sections. Beethoven's "Moonlight Sonata" is a well-known example of the sonata form.

A **concerto** is a long instrumental composition which features an individual soloist backed by a full orchestra. It emphasizes the solo instrument. **Symphonies** are the most complex and dramatic of musical forms. They require more instruments, longer movements, and more complex themes than sonatas. Beethoven's "Fifth Symphony" is one of the best-known examples.

Forms of **vocal music** include the **chorale** (a long form of religious music, like Handel's *Messiah*), the **opera** (such as *Carmen* by Bizet), the **chorus** (ensembles of singers, from short pieces for quartets to long pieces for full choirs), and **musical theater** (such as *Westside Story*).

Style refers to types of music: the period in which it was composed, the purpose, and the intended audience. **Classical** music commonly refers to music composed before the middle of the nineteenth century. **Modern** music refers to long, serious works by twentieth-century composers, such as Leonard Bernstein and Aaron Copeland. **Popular** music includes ragtime, jazz, blues, rock and roll, rhythm and blues, country and western, and salsa. **Folk** music is traditional music, such as "On Top of Old Smoky," which continues to be popular. **Religious** music includes hymns, gospel songs, and contemporary light-rock music with religious themes.

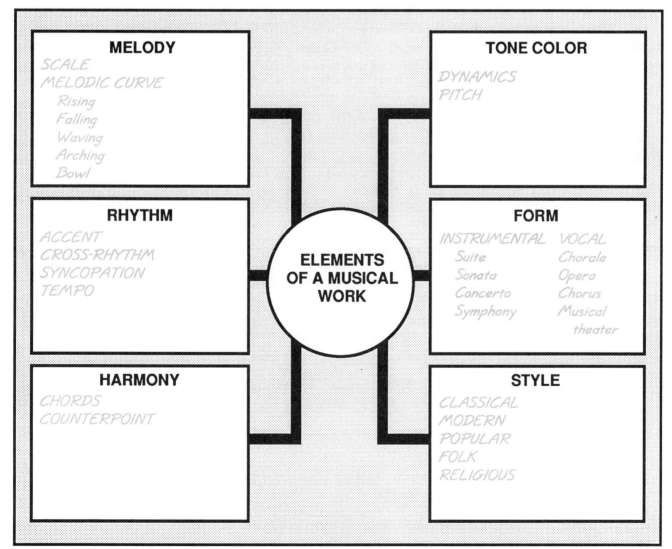

ELEMENTS OF DESIGN

THINKING SKILL: Verbal classification

CONTENT OBJECTIVE: Students will use a branching diagram to classify words which describe basic elements of design: color, shape, line, texture, and pattern. *NOTE: This lesson requires no specialized knowledge of art. It may also be used as a critical reading lesson and for a writing-across-the-curriculum activity. This is the first in a series of three lessons to develop students' abilities to describe works of art. This series helps students clarify common terms which are used to describe elements of design. It helps them use these terms when describing a given picture or comparing two or more pictures.*

DISCUSSION: TECHNIQUE—Use a transparency of the branching diagram to record students' responses as they discuss the elements of design. Review the five elements before assigning the student activity. Confirm that students understand the terms in the exercise before they sort them independently. It may be necessary to identify the terms that appear in more than one element. Discuss how the same term used to describe different elements has a similar effect; i.e., a soft color and a soft texture both suggest lightness or calm.
   DIALOGUE—Encourage students to apply the terms to specific pictures.

How does knowing terms that can apply to a picture help you understand what to look for in one? How does knowing what to look for change the way you appreciate art?

   Because we do not commonly discuss pictures with elementary school children, we expect that picture analysis is too difficult or too abstract for them. Young children, however, enjoy having words to describe what they see and sense. These terms can also be used to examine and describe buildings, furnishings, photographs, sculptures, magazine graphics, or bridges.
   RESULT—Knowing the words that people use to describe a picture helps one appreciate and understand it differently.

WRITING EXTENSION
- **Describe the elements that make up a picture. How do they contribute to the general effect of the picture? What would happen if one of the elements changed?**

THINKING ABOUT THINKING
- **How did using the diagram help you relate words you already knew to the elements of design? How did the diagram help you understand the differences between the various elements of design?**
- **Suggest another lesson in which classifying information on a graph would help you understand what you are learning.**
- **Design another diagram that would help you learn terms to describe pictures.**
- **What other things might you organize quickly with a branching diagram?**

SIMILAR ENRICHMENT LESSONS
- To classify music, art, architecture, or dance according to era, culture, purpose, or type.
- To select music, art, flowers, decorations, or fashions appropriate to an occasion.
- To classify instruments by type or location in the orchestra.
- To classify musical organizations, forms, or types of compositions.

ELEMENTS OF DESIGN

DIRECTIONS: Sort the following terms by the element of design which each describes. Terms may be used in more than one box.

bright, circle, coarse, curved, diagonal, dull, fine, hard, horizontal, hue, irregular, oval, rectangle, regular, slick, smooth, soft, straight, thick, thin, tint, triangle, vertical, wavy, zigzag

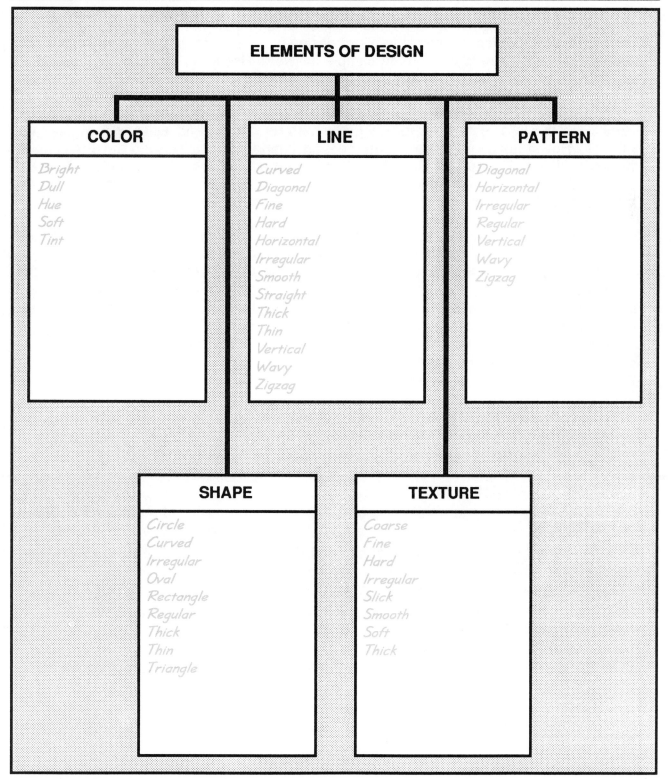

ELEMENTS OF DESIGN

COLOR
Bright
Dull
Hue
Soft
Tint

LINE
Curved
Diagonal
Fine
Hard
Horizontal
Irregular
Smooth
Straight
Thick
Thin
Vertical
Wavy
Zigzag

PATTERN
Diagonal
Horizontal
Irregular
Regular
Vertical
Wavy
Zigzag

SHAPE
Circle
Curved
Irregular
Oval
Rectangle
Regular
Thick
Thin
Triangle

TEXTURE
Coarse
Fine
Hard
Irregular
Slick
Smooth
Soft
Thick

DESCRIBING A PICTURE

THINKING SKILL: Verbal classification

CONTENT OBJECTIVE: Students will use a central idea graph to describe elements of a picture: color, line, shape, texture, pattern, and perspective. *NOTE: This is the second in a series of three lessons to develop students' abilities to describe works of art. This series helps students clarify common terms used to describe elements of design and use these terms when describing a given picture or comparing two or more pictures.*

DISCUSSION: TECHNIQUE—Students must be able to examine a large, high-quality reproduction as they discuss the elements of design in the picture. Vincent van Gogh's *The Starry Night* was used to provide the sample answers. Use a transparency of the central idea graph to record responses as students apply elements of design to describe a picture.
    DIALOGUE—Encourage students to apply the concepts as they examine pictures.

How does the information on the diagram help us understand what to look for in a picture? How does the information on the diagram help us understand the differences between different pictures? How does knowing what to look for in a picture help us appreciate it differently? How does the diagram help us describe the design of the picture, the effect of the picture, and the components of a picture?

Select a picture that students relate to or one, like *The Starry Night*, that demonstrates these elements clearly. Help the class discuss the painting, or ask students to write about it as an individual assignment. Discussing pictures is also an excellent Think/Pair/Share activity. Because we do not commonly discuss pictures with elementary school children, we expect that picture analysis is too difficult or abstract for them. In practice, however, children enjoy knowing words to describe what they see and sense. These terms can also be used to examine buildings, furnishings, photographs, sculptures, magazine graphics, or bridges.
    RESULT—Knowing the terms to use when describing the characteristics of a picture helps one describe it more clearly.

WRITING EXTENSION
- **Describe the elements of style that you look for in a picture.**
- **Use the elements of design to describe a picture of your choice.**

THINKING ABOUT THINKING
- **How did using the graph help you understand the elements of a picture? How did using it help you look at or understand a picture differently? Why?**
- **Suggest another lesson in which depicting information on a central idea graph would help you understand what you are learning.**
- **Design another graph that would help you describe pictures.**

SIMILAR ENRICHMENT LESSONS:
- To classify music, art, architecture, or dance according to era, culture, or type.
- To select music, art, flowers, decorations, or fashions appropriate to an occasion.

DESCRIBING A PICTURE

DIRECTIONS: Read the passage carefully. After each element is described, look for that characteristic in the picture you are looking at. For each element (color, line, shape, texture, pattern, and perspective), write details in each box on the diagram to describe that characteristic and its effect in the picture.

Six elements make up the uniqueness of a picture: **color, line, shape, texture, pattern,** and **perspective.** When we discuss a picture, we describe both the characteristic and the effect of the characteristic. For example, when discussing color we would describe the colors that appear in the picture and also the effect the colors have—how they make you feel or what they suggest.

To describe **color,** identify whether the colors are primary (red, yellow, blue) or secondary (orange, purple, green—colors made by mixing primary colors). If colors in a picture are next to each other on the color wheel (such as red, purple, blue), the effect is a blending of the colors that seems more calm and ordered. If colors are opposite each other on the color wheel (such as red and green), the colors contrast sharply with each other. The reds stand out from the greens. The effect is active, exciting, and dramatic.

Colors can also suggest objects, ideas, or attitudes. Red, yellow, and orange seem warm; blue, green, and purple seem cool. Blue and green give the appearance of water and plants and suggest woods, oceans, sky, quiet, and harmony. Red or orange suggest fire, speed, or energy.

We describe **line** in a picture by describing what the lines look like. Are they straight, curving, wavy, zigzag, or jagged? Each type of line has a different effect. Straight lines seem firm and strong; wavy or curving lines seem graceful or soothing; jagged or zigzag lines seem active or sharp.

The direction of the line also changes the effect. Vertical lines seem alert and alive; upright angles seems active and aggressive; horizontal lines seem quiet and stable. The thickness of the line has its effect too. Thin lines seem fragile and gentle; thick lines seem bold.

We also describe the placement of lines. If lines are arranged the same way on each side of a center, the design is said to be symmetrical. Symmetrical lines suggest order, stability, and regularity. Lines that, although arranged differently on each side of a center, still suggest balance, are said to be asymmetrical. Asymmetrical designs suggest variety, energy, and difference in weight. Lines arranged without balance have disturbing, disorganized, and unpleasant effects.

Shape is described by the type of geometric figure (circles, squares, trapezoids, triangles, spirals, or rectangles) used in the picture. Geometric shapes may be regular and stable or irregular (bulging or jagged). Irregular figures suggest energy or confusion. Shapes are also used to suggest or express meaning. For example, a heart or four-leaf clover suggests happy qualities. Religious symbols and traffic signs express meaning by shape alone, without using words.

Texture is the surface effect created by the lines or paint (how the surface would feel if we touched it): rough, scratchy, hard, smoky, smooth, soft, or wet. Texture can also suggest meaning: rough textures suggest strength and boldness; soft textures suggest gentleness and peace.

We describe **pattern** as the arrangement of shapes and lines in a picture. Repeating shapes create a rhythm in a picture the same way that repeating sounds create rhythm in music. Regular repetition suggests order, while irregular patterns suggest disorder or confusion.

Perspective is the appearance of three dimensions on a flat, two-dimensional surface.

The artist can trick our eyes by line, color, or shading. He or she can use these elements to give designs a solid appearance or a sense of distance. Perspective can be used to make a picture seem real to us or to make the objects in the picture seem related to each other in space. A picture that lacks perspective seems flat.

Select a picture and describe it on the central idea graph below. Use the elements identified in the reading. Isn't art more interesting when you know what to look for?

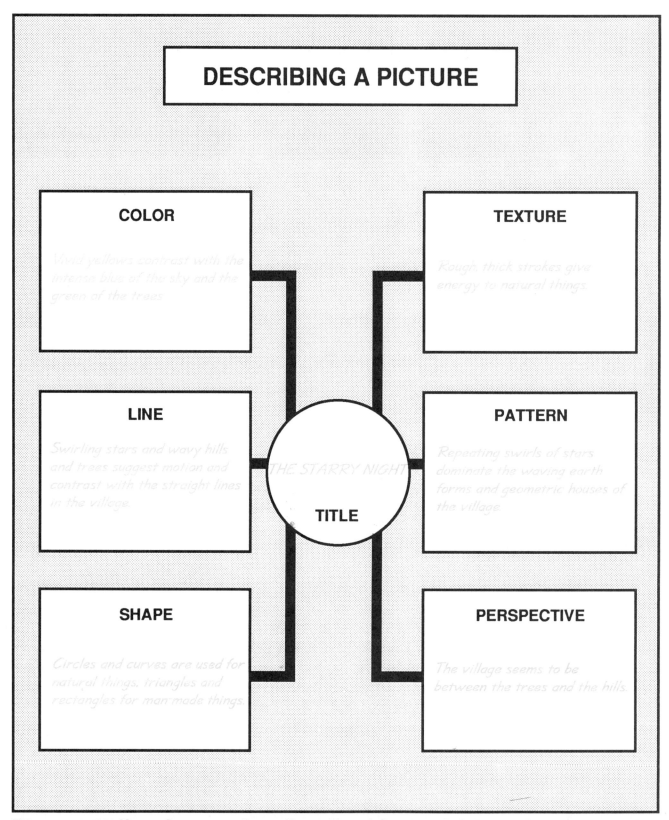

DESCRIBING A PICTURE

COLOR

Vivid yellows contrast with the intense blue of the sky and the green of the trees.

TEXTURE

Rough, thick strokes give energy to natural things.

LINE

Swirling stars and wavy hills and trees suggest motion and contrast with the straight lines in the village.

PATTERN

Repeating swirls of stars dominate the waving earth forms and geometric houses of the village.

THE STARRY NIGHT

TITLE

SHAPE

Circles and curves are used for natural things, triangles and rectangles for man-made things.

PERSPECTIVE

The village seems to be between the trees and the hills.

COMPARING PICTURES

THINKING SKILL: Verbal classification

CONTENT OBJECTIVE: Students will use the matrix chart to describe and compare the elements of design in three different works of art. *NOTE: This lesson requires no specialized knowledge of art. They may be used as a critical reading lesson and for writing-across-the-curriculum activities. This is the third in a series of three lessons to develop students' abilities to describe works of art. This series helps students clarify terms commonly used to describe elements of design and use these terms when describing a given picture or comparing two or more pictures.*

DISCUSSION: TECHNIQUE—Select any three pictures for this exercise or use the three examples if you prefer to follow the suggested answers. Students must be able to examine large, high-quality reproductions of the chosen pictures as they discuss the elements of design. Pictures used as examples in the lesson are commonly available from instructional resource centers, retail stores, or art books. Be certain that those chosen for the lesson illustrate dramatically different utilization of the elements of design.

Use a transparency of the matrix as students describe and compare the elements of design as they are used in the three pictures. If necessary, copies of page 249 may be distributed to students as a "memory jogger" for components of the design elements.

DIALOGUE—Discuss the various elements of design and encourage students to apply correct terminology as they examine the works of art. Because of their background from art education classes and the practice they have had in the two previous lessons, elementary students should experience growing confidence in their ability to describe what they see and sense. In subsequent lessons, you may ask students to select a picture that was not featured in this lesson, discuss it with a partner or in a cooperative group, and report the results to the class. These same terms may be used as students compare other works, such as buildings, furnishings, photographs, sculptures, magazine graphics, bridges, etc.

RESULT—Knowing what to look for in a picture helps one appreciate and express differences in design, effect, and elements among two or more works of art.

WRITING EXTENSION

- Use the elements of design to compare two pictures or other artistic works.
- Choose one of the pictures studied in this lesson and write about it.

THINKING ABOUT THINKING

- How did recording the information on the diagram help you understand the differences among pictures? Did using it help you feel more confident about describing pictures? Explain.
- How did knowing what to look for change the way you look at or talk about art?
- Suggest another lesson in which you think that organizing information on a matrix would help you understand what you are learning.
- What other items can we organize quickly with a matrix?
- Design another diagram that would help you compare pictures.

SIMILAR ENRICHMENT LESSONS

- To compare music, art, architecture, or dance according to era, culture, or type.
- To select music, art, flowers, decorations, or fashions appropriate for different occasions.

COMPARING PICTURES

DIRECTIONS: In each box write a few words to describe how each of the elements of design affects each picture.

	PICTURE 1	PICTURE 2	PICTURE 3
TITLE	THE STARRY NIGHT	BREEZING UP	THE NIGHT OF THE POOR
ARTIST	VINCENT VAN GOGH	WINSLOW HOMER	DIEGO RIVERA
NATIONALITY	DUTCH	AMERICAN	MEXICAN
COLOR	Vivid yellows contrast with intense blues and greens.	Light, golden reds and browns contrast with the dark green and blue of the sea.	Subdued, dark colors suggest weariness and despair.
LINE	Swirling stars and wavy hills and trees suggest motion; straight lines of the village suggest stability.	Curves of the waves suggest energy; diagonal lines of the boat suggest movement.	Clear outlines and repeating curves suggest slumber and simplicity.
SHAPE	Circles and curves are used for natural things; geometric forms for man-made things.	Triangles give the boat direction; curves of hats and clothing make people seem calm.	Ovals and waves suggest solidness and peace.
TEXTURE	Rough, thick strokes give energy to natural things.	Fine, grainy texture makes picture look old.	Grainy strokes suggest a rustic, homespun look.
PATTERN	Repeating swirls of the stars dominate earth and man-made forms.	Tight, repeating curves give the waves motion; smooth curves of sails and clothing seem calm.	Repeating ovals and curves suggest crowding and quiet.
PERSPECTIVE	Vertical spire and geometric buildings appear to be behind the trees and in front of the hills.	Size and gray hues make one ship seem distant; tilt of sail makes the closer ship lean to the left.	Limited perspective gives a sense of crowding; book adds a sense of space.

DESCRIBING PICTURES AND MUSIC

THINKING SKILL: Verbal classification

CONTENT OBJECTIVE: Students will use class relationships diagram to classify art and music terminology.

DISCUSSION: TECHNIQUE—Use a transparency of the class relationships diagram to record students' discussion of terms commonly associated with art and/or music.

DIALOGUE—Encourage students to discuss the similarities and differences in the meanings of the same term when used to describe a work of art or a work of music. For example: **Composition** refers to the way a work is put together. Composition in art refers to how shapes, lines, and colors are placed in the picture. Composition in music refers to the piece itself. (The verb "compose" refers to the process of creating it.)

Rhythm is underlying repetition that gives unity or movement to a work. In art, rhythm is achieved by repeating shapes, lines, textures, and colors. In music, rhythm is the beat.

Pattern refers to a collection of the same elements that gives order to a work. In art, pattern is achieved by repeating or gradually changing shapes, lines, textures, and colors. In music, pattern may refer to either the beat or to a repeating series of notes and phrases.

What is the effect of rhythm in music? (To hold the work together, to establish and hold an effect, and to associate with other music, feelings, objects, or sounds.) **What is the effect of rhythm in a picture? How is the effect similar to its expression in music?**

Repeat this line of questioning for other shared terms. Encourage students to suggest explanations for the use of the same terms in music and in art. Identify additional terms which could describe only pictures, only music, or both (for example: curve, line, order, style, tone, regular, and irregular). Discuss how the effect of a musical element produces a similar effect in art.

RESULT—Some terms apply only to music; others apply only to art. Some terms apply to both and have slightly similar and slightly different meanings in each discipline.

WRITING EXTENSION

• **Select one term that is used to describe both pictures and music. How is its effect similar and different in pictures and in music?**

THINKING ABOUT THINKING

• **How did using the diagram help you understand the effect rhythm, pattern, or composition has in paintings and in music?**
• **How might it be confusing to use the same words to describe elements of pictures and elements of music? How can that confusion be prevented?**
• **Why do people use the same terms to describe a picture or a musical work?**
• **What do the shared terms suggest about creating effects in pictures and in music?**
• **How is a sense of sadness suggested in music? How is it suggested in a picture?**
• **How are the words we use to describe sadness in music and in art alike?**

SIMILAR ENRICHMENT LESSONS

• To depict relationships between various works of an artist or composer.
• To describe the styles, media, historical era, significance of several artists or composers.

DESCRIBING PICTURES AND MUSIC

DIRECTIONS: The following terms can be used to describe pictures, musical compositions, or both. Write each term in the region of the diagram where it fits.

color, composition, harmony, melody, pattern, rhythm, shape, texture

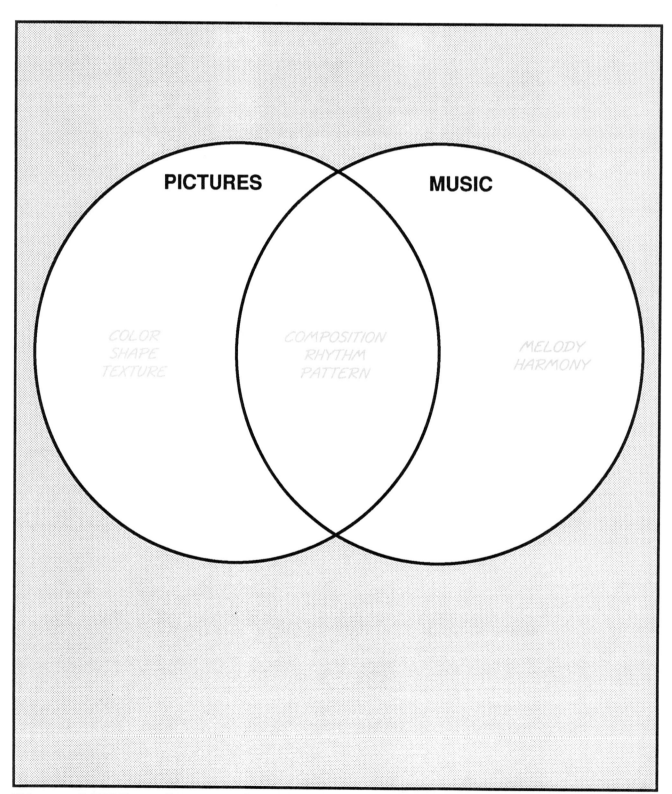

PICTURES

MUSIC

COLOR
SHAPE
TEXTURE

COMPOSITION
RHYTHM
PATTERN

MELODY
HARMONY

CHAPTER 8 – PERSONAL PROBLEM SOLVING

	SHORT- AND LONG-TERM GOALS (Branching Diagram, Compare and Contrast Diagram)	
TIME MANAGEMENT: HOW WELL DO I USE MY TIME? (Matrix Chart, Transitive Order Graph)		TIME MANAGEMENT: PLANNING MY TIME (Matrix Chart)
	EFFECTS OF PROLONGED TELEVISION WATCHING (Central Idea Graph)	
WHAT MAKES A GOOD LEADER? (Central Idea Graph, Matrix Chart)		REDUCING LUNCHROOM WASTE (Central Idea Graph)
	STEPS IN PLANNING A BUDGET (Flowchart)	
WEIGHT OF BUBBLE GUM (Transitive Order Graph)		CALORIES IN FOOD (Interval Graph)
	HOW DO I LEARN IT WELL? (Flowchart)	
DO I REALLY KNOW IT? (Flowchart)		THINK/PAIR/SHARE (Flowchart)

SHORT- AND LONG-TERM GOALS

THINKING SKILL: Compare and contrast, planning

CONTENT OBJECTIVE: Students will use branching diagrams to classify examples of these types of goals and to identify their own. They will use a compare and contrast diagram to identify similarities and differences between short- and long-term goals.

DISCUSSION: TECHNIQUE—Draw a large branching diagram on the chalkboard. Use it to record responses as students discuss examples of short- and long-term goals and to identify and classify their own goals. Use a transparency of the compare and contrast diagram to record how short-term and long-term goals are alike and how they are different.

DIALOGUE—Discuss the difference between short-term and long-term goals. **Short-term goals** are those actions which can usually be done with less time, effort, and planning. They give us an immediate sense of having finished the task and being satisfied with it. **Long-term goals** usually require more effort, time, and planning, but are usually of greater value and personal significance. They usually require more reflection to decide whether the goal has been satisfied. Students often do not understand this distinction and, therefore, fail to set long-term goals in favor of short-term satisfaction. Identify short-term and long-term goals commonly held by students in your class.

Short-term goals are often a step toward a long-term objective. Use the following diagram to project the long-term goal for each short-term goal in this lesson.

Clean my room ⟶ Know where to find what I need
Meet someone new ⟶ Have more good friends
Study for a Friday test ⟶ Get better grades
Exercise 20 minutes a day ⟶ Be in better physical condition

Encourage students to identify the long-term goal for which their short-term goal is a step. Similarly, identify the short-term goals which may be necessary to fulfill a long-term goal.

Why is it important to know the difference between short- and long-term goals? How does knowing the difference help you understand how much time and effort you must spend in order to achieve them? How does knowing the difference in time, effort, and satisfaction influence which you might decide to do first (your priorities)?

RESULT—Understanding the difference between short- and long-term goals helps us identify the types of goals we set and understand what may be required to satisfy them.

WRITING EXTENSION
- **Describe how short- and long-term goals are alike and how they are different.**
- **Compare your own short- or long-term goals with those of a friend, a hero, a family member, or a fictional character.**

THINKING ABOUT THINKING
- **How did using the diagram help you understand short- and long-term goals more clearly? How did listing them help you understand the difference between them.**
- **Suggest another decision in which you think that using this graph would be helpful.**

SIMILAR PERSONAL PROBLEM SOLVING LESSONS
- To compare or contrast desirable or undesirable habits or alternatives.
- To compare or contrast choices, responsibilities, privileges, and courses of action.

SHORT- AND LONG-TERM GOALS

DIRECTIONS: Short-term goals are actions which can usually be done with less time, effort, and planning, and give immediate satisfaction. Long-term goals usually take more time, effort, and planning, but usually mean more in the long run. Which of the following goals are short-term and which are long-term? On the top branching diagram, sort this list. On the bottom diagram list some of your own short- and long-term goals.

Clean my room	Exercise 20 minutes every night
Get better grades	Have more good friends
Improve my physical condition	Know where to find what I need
Meet someone new	Study for a test

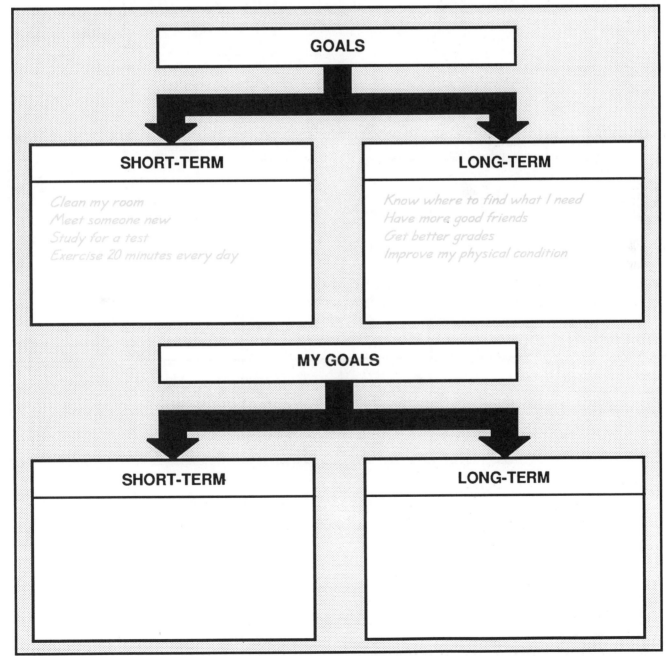

GOALS

SHORT-TERM

Clean my room
Meet someone new
Study for a test
Exercise 20 minutes every day

LONG-TERM

Know where to find what I need
Have more good friends
Get better grades
Improve my physical condition

MY GOALS

SHORT-TERM

LONG-TERM

SHORT-TERM AND LONG-TERM GOALS

DIRECTIONS: Think about how the short- and long-term goals on the branching diagrams are alike and how they are different. Write your answers on the compare and contrast diagram.

SHORT-TERM GOALS		LONG-TERM GOALS

HOW ALIKE?

Both require effort and action

Both are desired

Both are attainable

Both give satisfaction

HOW DIFFERENT?

WITH REGARD TO

SHORT-TERM		LONG-TERM
Usually require less effort	AMOUNT OF EFFORT	*Usually require more effort*
Usually require less time	AMOUNT OF TIME	*Usually require more time*
Usually have a quick, but less significant, reward	REWARD	*Usually have a slower, but more significant, reward*
Usually require less planning	PLANNING	*Usually require more planning*
Usually less lasting and less valuable	LASTING VALUE	*Usually more lasting and more valuable*

TIME MANAGEMENT: HOW WELL DO I USE MY TIME?

THINKING SKILL: Planning, prioritizing

CONTENT OBJECTIVE: Students will use a matrix chart to identify how efficiently they currently use their time, then rank these examples of time use on a transitive order graph. *NOTE: These two lessons on time management (examining and planning time usage) should be taught sequentially. The lessons on distinguishing short- and long-term goals and examining the effects of prolonged television viewing are also relevant to this series.*

DISCUSSION: TECHNIQUE—This is the first of two lessons on time management involving the following steps:

1. examining the effectiveness of one's current time use;
2. recording current time use, deciding whether the time spent on each kind of activity is appropriate, proposing and evaluating a new schedule for proposed changes, and examining the personal benefits of being responsible for one's time.

DIALOGUE—This exercise helps students understand their own time-use priorities. Upper elementary students begin to make additional decisions over personal aspects of their lives. As students approach adolescence, it becomes increasingly important that they gradually release the misconception that something or someone else is responsible for their choices, including their time use. Discussion for this lesson should emphasize why and how one manages one's time.

Think about times when things didn't work out because you didn't have enough time to do them well. What explains why the time wasn't there? (Habits; didn't judge the time adequately; travel, preparation, or use of equipment or tools took longer than expected; interruption; a more attractive opportunity came along; started too late; physical condition, i.e., hungry, tired, sick). **What conditions might you change to prevent that from happening again? What might you remember that would help you manage a similar situation better in the future?**

Think about some situations in which you were wasting time. What conditions or thoughts led you to do that? (Habits; encouraged by friends; impulse; didn't like what you were doing and found something else more appealing; didn't have a good idea of something better to do; poor planning.) **What might you do to prevent that situation from happening in the future?**

The idea of "wasting time" carries with it a sense of criticism. All of us waste time to some extent. Wasting time can come about because time that might have been spent more productively is spent on something that is less valuable. However, it can also occur when we spend time on something that doesn't work out for reasons that we could not anticipate or control. Therefore, wasting time doesn't necessarily mean that the individual is misguided or negligent. The purpose of the discussion is to help students become aware of the value of choosing the use of their time and selecting strategies for managing it more effectively. Avoid negative, self-blaming comments; stress the personal satisfaction that comes from feeling confident and responsible about one's ability to manage time.

Students may also confuse "wasting time" with appropriate relaxation, resting, "taking a break," or activities, such as exercise or hobbies, which allow us to return to serious tasks rejuvenated and productive. Time is wasted by unnecessary steps, unnecessary repetition, spending time fretting over past dissatisfactions, mistakes, or unrelated conditions that reduce our effectiveness in doing what is important.

Think about occasions when plans didn't work out because you didn't do things at the right time so you could do them well. What explains why the time wasn't right? (Wrong time of day; worked on an assignment after it was due; felt physically tired; had to work after experiencing something unpleasant or stressful; hungry; places from which you needed to buy supplies were closed; people you needed to talk to weren't available.

What can you do to prevent that from happening in the future? What does your use of time suggest about what you think is important? Could you use your time in more appropriate and beneficial ways? Are you spending enough time at activities which support your physical, social, and intellectual growth?

Special attention should be paid to the adequacy of study time, reading time, exercise, and social activities. Think/Pair/Share discussion of time priorities brings positive peer examples to light. Students may recognize that those whom they admire for school or sports performance place a premium on the time spent to develop their special skills.

Help students realize that the completed transitive order graph represents their own current priorities. Listing examples of best and worst time use allows students to identify a few activities that can be expanded or eliminated one at a time. They will not be overwhelmed by trying to make too many changes at once. It may be beneficial to discuss how priorities change as people change. Students may discover that their priorities are different from those of younger students and of older siblings.

RESULT—As thinking people, we can understand, plan, and revise any aspect of our lives which we choose to change. We do not have to leave to chance, to unexamined habits, or to the wrong people a decision as important as how we spend our time. We can decide to spend our own time more effectively by examining the consequences of our time use. We can plan how to be a more responsible and productive person.

WRITING EXTENSION
- **Describe how you prefer to use your time.**

THINKING ABOUT THINKING
- **How did using the transitive order graph help you realize which ways of using your time are really important to you? How did using it help you understand how much of your time is spent inefficiently?**
- **How did you decide which tasks are a more important use of your time?**
- **How did listing your priorities on the graphs help you understand your time use more clearly than you did before this exercise?**
- **Suggest another decision which you could make more effectively by prioritizing information on a graph.**
- **Design another diagram that would help you make plans and choices.**

SIMILAR PERSONAL PROBLEM SOLVING LESSONS
- To rank alternatives or goals in decision making.
- To prioritize the goals of changing time or money use.
- To compare costs of consumer goods by brand or retail store.
- To plan a wardrobe by color, type of clothes, and season.

TIME MANAGEMENT: HOW DID I USE MY TIME?

DIRECTIONS: Think about things that you have done in the past week. What things did you do that worked well and were a good use of your time? Give an example of something you did that worked well because the time had been planned in advance. Give an example of your having just the right amount of time to do the task. Give an example of doing a project or job at just the right time (not too soon or too late).

What things did you do that did not work well and were not a good use of your time? What didn't work out because you didn't have enough time? Did you sometimes, for one reason or another, end up wasting time? Did some activities not work out well because it wasn't the right time to do it or because you had not planned for it?

WHY TIME WAS WELL USED

REASON	EXAMPLE
Task and time planned in advance	
Just enough time for the task	
Task performed at the right time (not too soon or too late)	

WHY TIME WAS NOT WELL USED

REASON	EXAMPLE
Not enough time to finish the task	
Wasted time	
Time not available when the task should be done	

TIME MANAGEMENT: GOOD OR POOR USES OF MY TIME

DIRECTIONS: Think about the things you did that were good uses of your time. List the good activities, beginning with the best, on the top transitive order graph.

Think about the things you did that were poor uses of your time. List those activities from the bottom upward, with the most wasteful at the bottom of the second transitive order graph.

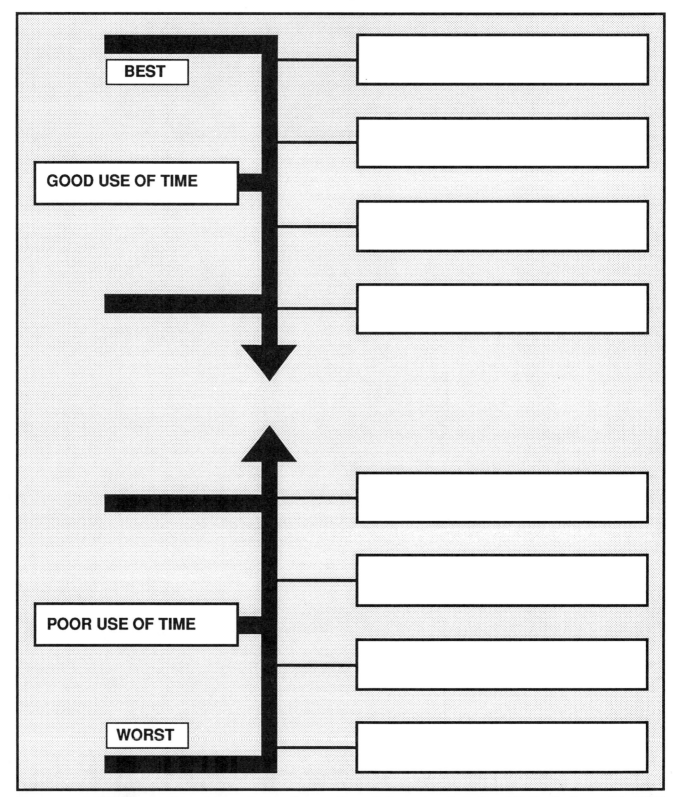

BEST

GOOD USE OF TIME

POOR USE OF TIME

WORST

TIME MANAGEMENT: PLANNING MY TIME

THINKING SKILL: Planning, prioritizing

CONTENT OBJECTIVE: Students will use a matrix chart to identify how they are currently using their time and to plan how they would prefer to use their time. *NOTE: These two lessons on time management (examining time use and planning time) should be taught sequentially. The lessons on distinguishing short- and long-term goals and examining the effects of prolonged television viewing are relevant to this series and may also be taught with this lesson.*

DISCUSSION: TECHNIQUE—This is the first of two lessons on time management involving the following steps:

1. examining the effectiveness of one's current time use;
2. recording current time use, deciding whether the time spent on each kind of activity is appropriate, proposing and evaluating a new schedule for proposed changes, and examining the personal benefits of being responsible for one's time.

Students use a time-diary matrix to record their use of after-school time for one week. By recording the number of hours they spend weekly on various types of activities on a time-analysis matrix, students will decide whether the time spent on each type of activity is about right, too much, or too little. Students will then use a time-planning matrix to propose the total number of hours they prefer to spend on each type of activity. Finally, students will use a new copy of the time-diary to make a new schedule based on the proposed changes. This lesson is best introduced on Monday. On the following Monday, students will discuss observations or surprises which they discovered in the way they used their time.

DIALOGUE—Discussing individual student's time totals may not be as useful as identifying trends and priorities within the class. Help students identify the five major categories in which they spend their non-school waking hours. Ask students to identify the five activities at which they spend the most time. Continue to poll the class, adding new categories or tally marks as necessary. Ask students to determine which types of activities are the biggest "time hogs."

As with managing money, we can't take charge of how we spend our time until we understand how we are currently using it and identify how we prefer to use this important resource. What types of activities do people in this class spend most of their time doing? Are these important activities? How might you change what you do now to have time for more important activities?

Which activities must you do at a given time? (Youngsters in this age group frequently have some parameters around which they must plan their daily schedule. Such activities might include: classes, mealtimes, bedtimes, regular family activities, day-care provisions, or required chores.)

How much of your time is spent on activities that you actually choose? (Students are usually surprised to find out how much of their time is not accounted for by set guidelines. Because some family commitments require students to do certain things at a given time, students may fall into the expectation that other people control most of their time. They do not realize that they have a choice about many blocks of time during weekends or on weekdays after school.)

Students may also not exercise choice by habit, by allowing friends to do it for them, or by impulsive decisions. Not deciding how to use one's time is also a choice people make.

After students determine the amount of time spent at various activities, which activities are set by others, and which ones they choose, they are ready to prioritize new choices.

Are you spending enough time at activities which support your physical, social, and intellectual growth? (Special attention should be paid to the adequacy of study time, reading time, exercise, and supervised social activities.)

When students have revised the amount of time they need to spend at various tasks, have proposed a new schedule, and have tried it for a few days, discuss with them how well their new plan is working.

How workable is the new schedule? What activities were scheduled too tightly? Could you follow the schedule comfortably? What things did you do that you could not have done if you hadn't planned your time? How did you feel about planning and managing your time? Did your family know that you were managing your own time? What was their reaction to your taking responsibility for planning your time use?

Encourage students to relate their personal time management to requirements of holding a productive job. Examine students' current level of understanding of how managers plan time for jobs. Encourage students to relate the need to plan their own time with their success in school now and on the job later.

RESULT—If we know how a resource is being used, we can examine whether it is being spent wisely. We can decide and plan to spend our time at what we believe to be important. If a person does not plan his own time well, he will probably work for someone who will.

WRITING EXTENSION
• **Why is it important for you to decide how to use your time?**

THINKING ABOUT THINKING
• **How did using the time-analysis matrix help you understand how you were using your time and how you can change it? How did using it help you understand how much time you have control over?**
• **How did you decide what was a more important use of your time?**
• **How did looking at your time use objectively on the graphs help you understand your habits, priorities, and talents more clearly than you did before this exercise?**
• **Design another diagram that would help you make plans and choices.**

SIMILAR PERSONAL PROBLEM SOLVING LESSONS
• To read schedules (bus, train, airplane, or class schedules).
• To record the effects of changing time or money use.
• To compare costs of consumer goods by brand or retail store.
• To plan a wardrobe by color, type of clothing, and season.
• To interpret sports data and tournament charts.
• To read charts for product comparison, statistics, newspaper summaries of issues.
• To read maps for information on attractions, campgrounds, lodging, etc.

TIME MANAGEMENT: PLANNING MY TIME

DIRECTIONS: To take charge of planning your own time, you must understand how you are currently using it and how you prefer to use it. You probably have some regular tasks around which you must plan your daily schedule. These regular tasks may include: classes, mealtimes, bedtimes, regular family activities, day-care provisions, and required chores. You will use a time diary to find out how much of your time you are spending at set tasks and how much of your time use you can decide for yourself.

Step 1. Keep a diary of how you spend your time after school on weekdays. Use the time diary matrix on the next page to record how you spend your time after school for one week. Write in each box what you did in that time slot. The diary is organized in half hour units. Try to estimate your time to the nearest fifteen-minute period. If an activity lasts forty-five minutes, mark half the next box with a line and draw an arrow to show that the activity lasted fifteen minutes into the next time period.

Step 2. When you have kept your time diary for one week, use the matrix below to summarize how your time was spent that week. Record the number of hours you spent each day on various activities after school. Add the daily totals to compute a weekly total. Total the number of hours you spent on each type of activity to compute a summary of your weekly time use.

TIME ANALYSIS						
ACTIVITY	**MON**	**TUE**	**WED**	**THUR**	**FRI**	**TOTAL**
Classes						
Studying						
Eating						
Sleeping						
Travel to school						
Travel to other places						
Exercise						
Talking with friends						
Dressing and grooming						
Reading						
Hobbies						
Watching television						
Shopping						
Household chores						
Nothing particular						
Other:						

TIME DIARY

TIME	MONDAY	TUESDAY	WEDNESDAY	THURSDAY	FRIDAY
2:30					
3:00					
3:30					
4:00					
4:30					
5:00					
5:30					
6:00					
6:30					
7:00					
7:30					
8:00					
8:30					
9:00					
9:30					
10:00					

REORGANIZING YOUR TIME

DIRECTIONS: Are you spending your time at activities which help you become as healthy as you want to be? Are you spending your time with people who bring out the best in you? Are you spending your time doing things that make your school work easier and more interesting to you? You have kept a diary of time use for after-school hours on each school day and now know how many hours each week you spend at various types of after-school activities.

For each type of activity, decide whether you are spending about the right amount of time, or whether you should spend more or less time at each task. Use the time planning matrix to record any changes you want to make in the total time you spend on various types of activities each week.

Use the time diary matrix to revise your schedule to show how you are going to change the time you spend at various activities each day.

TIME PLANNING MATRIX

ACTIVITY	NO CHANGE	DECREASE	INCREASE	NEW TOTAL
Classes				
Studying				
Eating				
Sleeping				
Travel to school				
Travel to other places				
Exercise				
Talking with friends				
Dressing and grooming				
Reading				
Hobbies				
Watching television				
Shopping				
Household chores				
Nothing particular				
Other:				

EFFECTS OF PROLONGED TELEVISION WATCHING

THINKING SKILL: Verbal classification, prioritizing, cause-effect

CONTENT OBJECTIVE: Students will use a central idea graph to identify consequences of prolonged television watching.

DISCUSSION: TECHNIQUE—Ask students to list as many consequences as possible and select the consequence that is the most significant for them. List chosen consequences on the chalkboard and mark each consequence with the number of students who also chose it as most significant. Record the six most frequently cited consequences on a transparency of the central idea graph.

DIALOGUE—Encourage students to draw inferences regarding the effect that prolonged television-watching may have on them personally. Ask them to identify other activities they may be missing while watching television.

You have identified some consequences of prolonged television viewing. Which is more significant in your mind: the undesirable direct results of watching too much television or the indirect results of missing other things? (This discussion is effective as a Think/Pair/Share activity, followed by a class discussion to summarize results.)

As you read the list of consequences, are there some types of consequences that are more obvious than others? (Health, recreational, social, educational.) **How could we find out whether the effects our class identified are true of other people your age? How much viewing is too much?**

Let's survey the class to find a class standard. Experts in this field recommend one hour per weekday and a total of four hours on the weekend. How does our class's standard compare with recommendations by experts on children's television? Why do you think that they are different? If you could only watch nine hours of television each week, how would you decide which programs to watch? (Review all the shows in the weekly television listings, decide which are most appealing, and circle only those which add up to the time limit? Review the shows you watch now and eliminate those you like least? Make a criteria list of what makes a television show worthwhile and review the weekly television listings for shows that are likely to match that? Decide which type of shows you like and select only from those? Start watching television and stop when you have reached the time limit?) **Which of these ways for planning your viewing will give you the best selection of shows?**

RESULT—By recognizing the effects of prolonged television viewing, one can decide whether its entertainment value is worth the consequences. We can judge whether what we are missing by long hours of viewing may be more important than the shows. We can decide how much viewing is appropriate and how we may alter our viewing habits.

WRITING EXTENSION
- **Describe the effects of prolonged television viewing.**
- **Describe how you would plan your television viewing.**

THINKING ABOUT THINKING
- **How did using the diagram help you understand the effects of prolonged television viewing?**

- Why is it important to understand as many consequences of a decision or activity as possible?
- How does knowing standards for selecting an activity help you make better decisions about it?
- What is the difference between a standard and a rule?
- To what extent did you accept the experts' standard? If you decided on more or fewer hours of television viewing, why did you think your standard was more appropriate in this case?
- How does planning a course of action affect the decisions you make? Why does it have an effect?
- Suggest another lesson in which depicting information on a graph would help you understand the consequences of an activity.
- Design another diagram to help you recognize consequences of an activity.

SIMILAR PERSONAL PROBLEM SOLVING LESSONS
- To illustrate the consequences of personal or class decision making.
- To illustrate the consequences of local, state, and federal government decision making.
- To illustrate factors leading to a personal or classroom conflict or issue.
- To illustrate factors leading to a local, state, or national conflict or issue.

EFFECTS OF PROLONGED TELEVISION WATCHING

DIRECTIONS: Think about how much time you spend watching television. What are the consequences of your spending this much time? Are there more important things that you could be doing instead?

In each box of the diagram, write one consequence of watching television several hours a day. Include activities that you cannot do because of the time spent viewing.

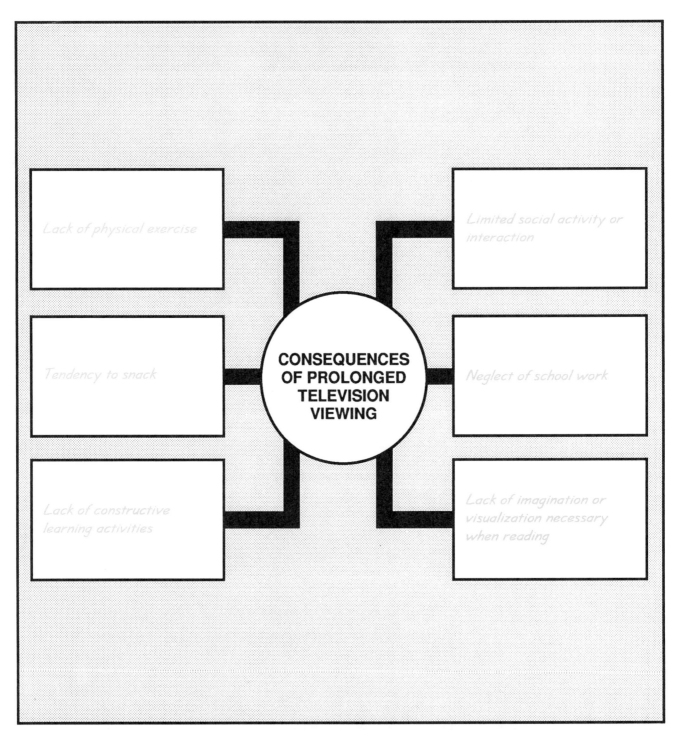

Lack of physical exercise

Limited social activity or interaction

Tendency to snack

CONSEQUENCES OF PROLONGED TELEVISION VIEWING

Neglect of school work

Lack of constructive learning activities

Lack of imagination or visualization necessary when reading

WHAT MAKES A GOOD LEADER?

THINKING SKILL: Identifying attributes, comparing

CONTENT OBJECTIVE: Students will use the central idea graph to identify qualities of an effective leader. Students will use a matrix chart to apply the qualities of an effective leader to compare individual leaders.

DISCUSSION: TECHNIQUE—Use a transparency of the central idea graph to record student responses as the class discusses characteristics of an effective leader. Encourage students to examine their own potential as leaders. Use a transparency of the matrix to record student comments as they compare school officers or government leaders.

DIALOGUE—Encourage students to identify leadership characteristics found in students who are running for class office or candidates for local or national government offices.

How does understanding the characteristics of an effective leader help you decide whether a person is likely to do well in an elected office? Why is it important to know what an office requires of a leader in order to decide whether a person is likely to do well in that position?

It is sometimes easier to see the characteristics of leadership in people we respect than it is to see it in ourselves. However, all of us demonstrate these abilities to some degree. Think about situations in which you have shown these qualities. How does understanding the characteristics of an effective leader help you appreciate your own leadership qualities? How does applying leadership characteristics to yourself help you see how you might serve as a leader?

How does understanding the characteristics of an effective leader help you appreciate the significance of a historical figure that we have been studying? Apply this analysis of leadership in a social studies lesson by examining a historical figure with regard to these characteristics. In each box, write examples of situations in which this person demonstrated leadership qualities.

This lesson may also be used to extend the Lincoln/Douglass lesson. Students may use the biographical information to describe Lincoln and Douglass in terms of confidence, communication skills, character, ability to work with others, knowledge/experience, and initiative.

Encourage students to think about community and school leaders in terms of their leadership characteristics. This technique leads to a stronger basis for opinions, more insight into the demands of leadership, and greater appreciation of contributions made by those who serve in leadership capacities. Students may use a blank central idea graph to describe a student leader or community official by identifying examples of situations in which that person has demonstrated leadership characteristics. These characteristics may also be applied to health and community service personnel (police, health career persons, librarians, and social service personnel).

RESULT—Choosing individuals for office should be based on the thorough examination of the leadership qualities, skills, and knowledge of the individual, not on specific statements or unexamined impressions. Understanding the characteristics of effective leadership allows us to make more informed choices and to evaluate an individual's ability as a leader.

WRITING EXTENSION

• Describe the characteristics of an effective leader.

• Compare the leadership characteristics of two officers, government officials, or historical figures.

THINKING ABOUT THINKING

- **How did using the graph help you understand leadership characteristics?**
- **How does identifying situations in which a leader has worked effectively help you understand the characteristics of leadership? Why is it important to identify specific situations in describing the characteristics of a person, character, or leader?**
- **How does comparing leaders or historical figures by listing their characteristics side-by-side allow you to understand how effectively they work?**
- **Design another graph that would help you describe an effective leader.**
- **Suggest another lesson in which the central idea graph would help you understand what you are learning.**
- **Suggest another lesson in which the matrix would help you understand what you are learning.**

SIMILAR PERSONAL PROBLEM SOLVING LESSONS

- To promote thorough examination of actions or outcomes by applying specific criteria.
- To illustrate qualities and achievements of historical figures, sports heroes, fictional characters, or officials and individuals who affect the lives of students.

© 1990 MIDWEST PUBLICATIONS • CRITICAL THINKING PRESS & SOFTWARE • P. O. Box 448, Pacific Grove, CA 93950

WHAT MAKES A GOOD LEADER?

DIRECTIONS: Read the passage carefully. In each box on the top graph, write why that particular characteristic of a good leader is important.

It is sometimes easier to see the characteristics of leadership in people we respect than it is to see it in ourselves. However, all of us demonstrate these abilities to some degree. Think about situations in which you have shown these qualities. In each box on the bottom graph, write examples of situations in which you have shown that leadership characteristic.

Whether an individual is an officer in a scout troop, a class representative, a person who takes responsibility in a church group or social club, or the President of the United States, a leader is a leader! Some leaders are recognized by being elected or appointed by other people. Some leaders are the people we seek out to get a job done, whether or not they have been elected or recognized as being responsible. The qualities of a good leader are the same, whatever the nature of the job.

A leader must have a great deal of confidence. A leader must trust that he or she generally makes good decisions and that, usually, these decisions work. People don't want a leader they can't count on. If a person doesn't believe in him- or herself, it isn't likely that others will have confidence in him or her either.

A leader must have good character because the leader sets the standard that others will follow. Good character includes honesty, openness, consistency, and dedication. A leader puts the goal and the welfare of those involved before personal gain or some favorite group.

A leader must be able to communicate ideas to others. The leader must be able to express ideas or solutions in ways that the other people understand. A sympathetic personality and good listening skills let other people know that the leader understands their needs and is prepared to take action to improve things.

A leader must be able to work well with the people who do the job. We have leaders because it takes more than one person to do a project in the community or in the school. A leader doesn't act by himself. The leader must respect the skills and contributions of all who participate in a project, remembering that it is the team that makes the goal possible.

A leader takes the initiative to get the job done. That individual does not wait for somebody else to do what's needed or blame others for its not being done. Leaders are self-starters whose example encourages others to be self-starters, too.

A leader should know enough about the project or position to do it well. If an individual must preside over a meeting, he or she should know how to do that. Experience is an important teacher. The leader should know what has and has not worked in the past, who can contribute the skills needed to do the job, and how people have been treated fairly in this kind of activity in the past.

WHAT MAKES A GOOD LEADER?

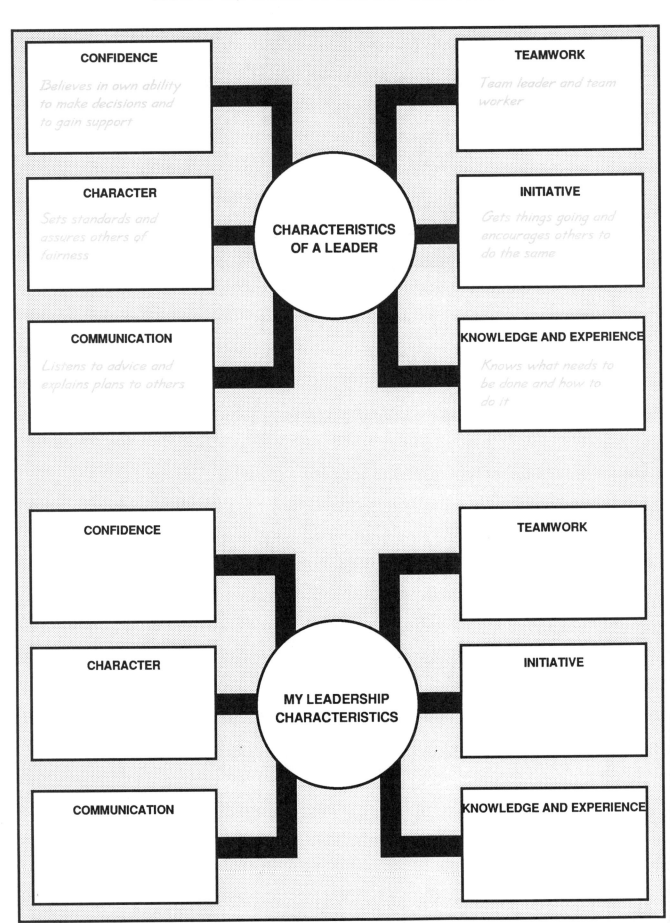

CONFIDENCE

Believes in own ability to make decisions and to gain support

TEAMWORK

Team leader and team worker

CHARACTER

Sets standards and assures others of fairness

CHARACTERISTICS OF A LEADER

INITIATIVE

Gets things going and encourages others to do the same

COMMUNICATION

Listens to advice and explains plans to others

KNOWLEDGE AND EXPERIENCE

Knows what needs to be done and how to do it

CONFIDENCE

TEAMWORK

CHARACTER

MY LEADERSHIP CHARACTERISTICS

INITIATIVE

COMMUNICATION

KNOWLEDGE AND EXPERIENCE

COMPARING LEADERS

DIRECTIONS: Write the names of three candidates, student leaders, or historical figures across the top of the matrix. In each box identify a situation in which that person has demonstrated that characteristic.

	NAME	NAME	NAME
CONFIDENCE			
GOOD CHARACTER TRAITS			
COMMUNICATION ABILITY			
TEAMWORK ABILITIES			
INITIATIVE			
KNOWLEDGE AND EXPERIENCE			

REDUCING LUNCHROOM WASTE

THINKING SKILL: Establishing causes, predicting consequences, evaluating solutions

CONTENT OBJECTIVE: Students will use the central idea graph to propose ways of reducing lunchroom waste. *NOTE: This lesson models practical problem solving processes which can be used for student consideration of problem situations within the school. Decide as a group whether lunchroom waste is a problem in your school. If it is not, use the three graphics to discuss the factors which explain an existing problem, its consequences, and alternative solutions.*

DISCUSSION: TECHNIQUE—Have students brainstorm causes for food waste in the lunchroom. List as many suggested causes as possible on the chalkboard. Poll the class, marking each cause with the number of students who agree with each suggestion. Record the six causes which the class selects as the most likely or most significant ones on a transparency of the central idea graph.

Repeat this process, asking students to identify the consequences of lunchroom waste. In each case, identify the school personnel and operations most affected by the waste, and the direct and indirect financial cost to the school.

Repeat the process again as students propose solutions to the problem of wasted food. Encourage them to be specific. (Sample answers provided on the graphs will not necessarily be the answers suggested by the class. Students may well arrive at different causes, effects, and solutions to the problem.)

DIALOGUE—This lesson simulates individual problem solving to resolve a school condition. Individual problem solving in this case involves generating causes and consequences for the purpose of suggesting possible solutions to the school staff. This lesson also alerts students that their own individual behavior, over which they have immediate control, may be contributing to the problem. Discuss with students the importance of identifying all causes which may contribute to a problem. Upper-elementary students tend to believe that once "a cause" has been identified, that is all that needs to be done.

In solving any problem, why is it important to identify as many causes as possible? Why is it important to evaluate whether a suggested cause is a likely one? What evidence do you have or must you find to know whether the cause is a likely one? Why is it important to evaluate whether a suggested cause is a significant one? Identify a cause that may be a likely, but not significant one. Why would you think about as many causes as possible, then limit your problem solving to a small number?

To evaluate the consequences of wasted food, examine the cost of the problem in terms of money and time. Examine how students may be affected, directly or indirectly, by the problem. Identify choices, materials, or activities that students may be missing because of the costliness of the food waste.

To evaluate solutions to the problem of wasted food, examine each suggestion's acceptability to all people involved: cafeteria staff, principal, teachers, students, janitorial staff, and parents.

What kind of information would you need in order to determine whether lunchroom waste is a problem in this school? What action might you take as a result of examining this situation? (Actions may include approaching the principal with the results of your discussion; deciding as a class and as individuals what you can do to reduce wasted food; conducting further research to estimate the extent of the problem.)

RESULT—Identifying causes, consequences, and potential solutions to a problem establishes a starting point for the solution. It is important to identify evidence of likelihood in discussing causes and consequences and to limit the factors to a manageable number.

WRITING EXTENSION

- Explain why it is important to identify causes, consequences, and possible solutions to a problem.
- Identify other school or individual problems that can be better understood using this process.

THINKING ABOUT THINKING

- How did using the diagram help you think of good ideas and select the most significant ones?
- What effect did listing the causes and consequences have on your awareness of the problem?
- Design another diagram that would help you identify or evaluate causes, consequences, and possible solutions.
- Suggest another problem in which using this graph would help you understand causes, consequences, and possible solutions.

SIMILAR PERSONAL PROBLEM SOLVING LESSONS

- To illustrate the consequences of personal or group decision making.
- To illustrate the consequences of local, state, and federal government decision making.
- To illustrate factors leading to a personal or group conflict or issue.
- To illustrate factors leading to a local, state, or national conflict or issue.

REDUCING LUNCHROOM WASTE

DIRECTIONS: Each day school cafeteria personnel must dispose of large quantities of food which students leave uneaten on their plates. Use the following central idea graphs to examine three questions related to this problem.

1. What explains the amount of food left uneaten on plates?
2. What are the consequences of wasting food?
3. What can be done to reduce lunchroom waste?

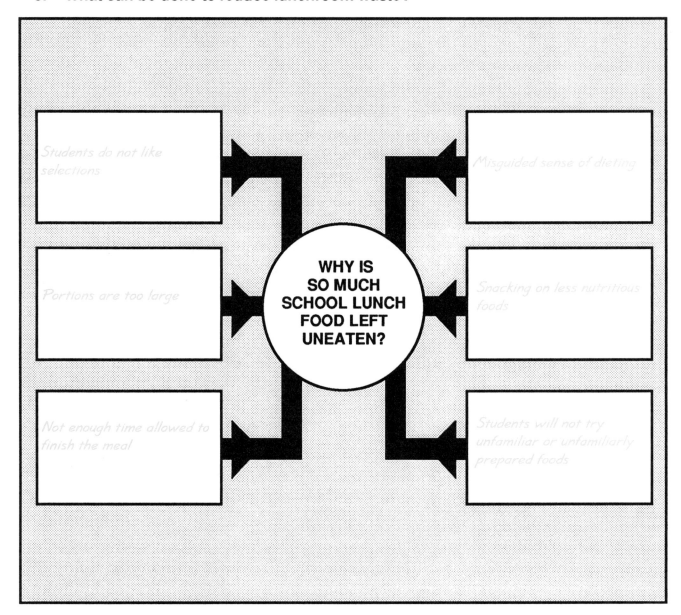

Students do not like selections

Misguided sense of dieting

WHY IS SO MUCH SCHOOL LUNCH FOOD LEFT UNEATEN?

Portions are too large

Snacking on less nutritious foods

Not enough time allowed to finish the meal

Students will not try unfamiliar or unfamiliarly prepared foods

ALTERNATIVE ANSWERS

- *Cold, overcooked, or underseasoned food*
- *Lack of choice —"all or none"*
- *Students in a hurry to play*
- *Students not hungry*
- *"Prepackaged" lunches*

REDUCING LUNCHROOM WASTE

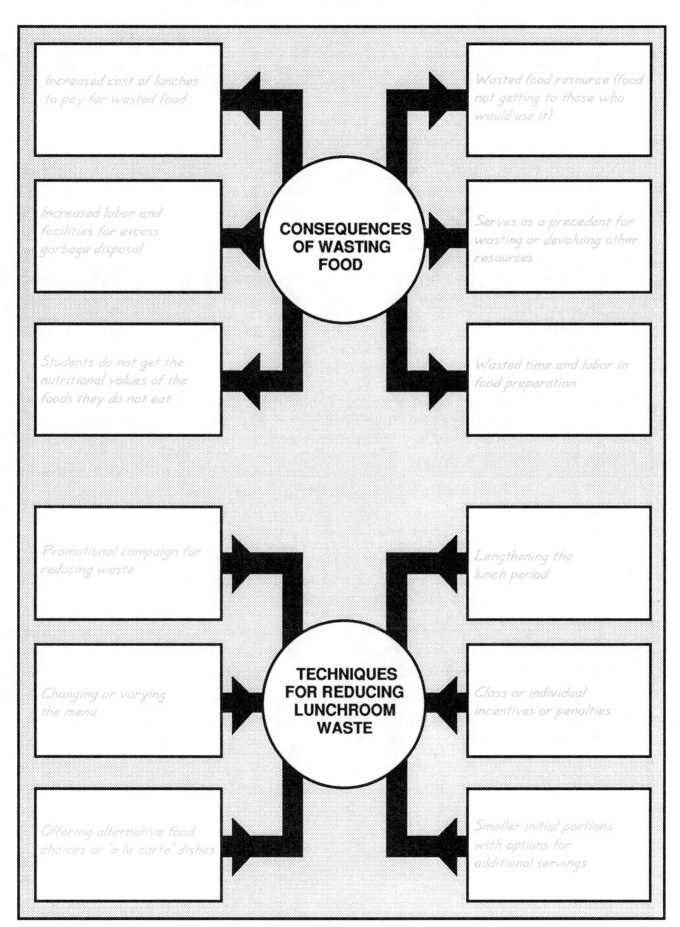

Increased cost of lunches to pay for wasted food

Increased labor and facilities for excess garbage disposal

Students do not get the nutritional values of the foods they do not eat

Wasted food resource (food not getting to those who would use it)

Serves as a precedent for wasting or devaluing other resources

Wasted time and labor in food preparation

CONSEQUENCES OF WASTING FOOD

Promotional campaign for reducing waste

Changing or varying the menu

Offering alternative food choices or "a la carte" dishes

Lengthening the lunch period

Class or individual incentives or penalties

Smaller initial portions with options for additional servings

TECHNIQUES FOR REDUCING LUNCHROOM WASTE

STEPS IN PLANNING A BUDGET

THINKING SKILL: Verbal sequences, prediction.

CONTENT OBJECTIVE: Students will use a flowchart to plan a personal budget. *NOTE: If some students do not get an allowance or are not paid for tasks, ask the class to define a "typical" allowance and use that as a basis for planning.*

DISCUSSION: TECHNIQUE—Use a transparency of the flowchart to record responses as students discuss the process of planning a budget.

DIALOGUE—Discussing individual student's expenditures may not be as useful as identifying trends and priorities within the class. Ask students to identify the five items on which they spend the most money. Randomly sample five students and ask them to identify the five items on which they spend the most money on a weekly basis. Write each item on the chalkboard and mark it each time it is identified by other students.

If these students are typical of our class, on what things do people in this class spend money? What does the way you use your money suggest about what you think is important? Are there other things you could do with your money that might be more appropriate or beneficial to you? How might you go about changing what you do now to have money for more important activities?

Discussion for this lesson should emphasize why and how one manages one's money. This helps students make informed decisions about their own money-use priorities. Youngsters in this age group usually have some regular, necessary purchases around which they should plan their budget. Students in upper-elementary grades can make more decisions over personal aspects of their lives. As they approach adolescence, it becomes increasingly important that they gradually release the misconception that someone or something else is responsible for their choices. This includes determining how to spend their money.

How much money do you typically spend for different things? Which are set purchases and which can you choose or change? How much of your money is spent on purchases about which you do not give much thought? (Not deciding how to use one's money is actually a choice.) **Are you spending enough money on items which support your physical, social, and intellectual growth?**

Think/Pair/Share discussions of individual budget plans allow positive peer examples to be brought to light. After students have examined desirable changes, determine what kinds of preferences students identify as a group.

How did you feel about planning and managing your money? Did your family know that you were managing your own money? What was their reaction to your taking responsibility for planning your budget?

Encourage students to relate their personal money management to requirements of holding a productive job. Examine students' current level of understanding of how managers spend money.

RESULT—If we know how a resource is being used, we can examine whether its being used wisely. We can decide and plan to spend our money on what we believe to be important. Thinking people should be able to understand, plan, and revise any aspect of their lives which they choose to change. They do not leave to chance, to unexamined habits, or to other people a decision as important as how to spend their money.

WRITING EXTENSION
- Describe how you choose to spend your money.
- Explain how this exercise affected the way you plan or budget your money?

THINKING ABOUT THINKING
- How did using the flowchart help you understand your budgeting decisions and how you can change them?
- How did using the flowchart help you understand how much of your money you have control over?
- How did you decide what was a more important use of your money?
- Suggest another decision which you could make more effectively by drawing your choices on a flowchart.
- Design another diagram that would help you make plans and choices.

SIMILAR PERSONAL PROBLEM SOLVING LESSONS
- To depict the process of personal decision making or time use, making a long-distance telephone call or operating a computer or video game.
- To plan personal projects, such as vacations, parties, and school or club activities.
- To illustrate cooking procedures, art activities, and school or traffic safety procedures.
- To depict directions for art projects, dance movements, or sports activities.
- To show deductive reasoning in games (Twenty Questions, Clue®, Master Mind®, or Bridge).
- To determine whether instructions or rules have been followed in similar lessons.

STEPS IN PLANNING A BUDGET

DIRECTIONS: Read the passage carefully to determine the decisions necessary for planning a budget.

Planning a budget involves answering a series of questions about what you **want** to do with your money and what you have **actually** been doing with it.

The basic question in budgeting is "What am I saving my money for?" Without a goal, you may continue to save money, but you are not likely to save regularly or to accumulate enough money for a large purchase. You may not have the motivation to reach your goal or a weekly plan to accomplish it. Therefore, consider whether what you want is more important than the things you have been buying. If you have a goal, decide how much you need to save and how soon you need to buy it.

A second question in creating a budget is "How am I currently spending my money?" If you don't know, then you are not likely to plan your spending and savings program systematically. Your motivation for saving may not be as strong, because you don't know how long it will take you to save for what you want. Therefore, make a list of everything you bought last week and add up your purchases.

If you know how you currently spend your money, then you can predict regular purchases and allow for unusual purchases without interfering with your savings plan. Therefore, write down exactly what you plan to do with your money next week.

Would you buy the same things next week? Those items that you would not buy again make up either unusual purchases that you don't expect to make again or things you have decided to do without. Remove those items from your list. The cost of those items that you would buy again next week form your basic purchasing plan.

Have you planned how much you will save each week toward your goal? If you have, put your savings aside and stick to your budget. Keep track of how well you are doing. If you have not planned how much you will save toward your goal, divide the amount of your savings goal by the number of weeks until you would like to reach your goal. This gives you the amount you need to save each week.

Do you have the amount of money you planned to save after you have made your routine purchases for the week? If not, you will have to decide if you want to do without some regular weekly purchases or increase the number of weeks you must save to reach your goal. If you reduce the amount of money you spend each week or increase the number of weeks you must save, you will then have enough money to save each week.

Put your savings aside and stick to your budget. Now just keep track of how well you are doing!

STEPS IN PLANNING A BUDGET

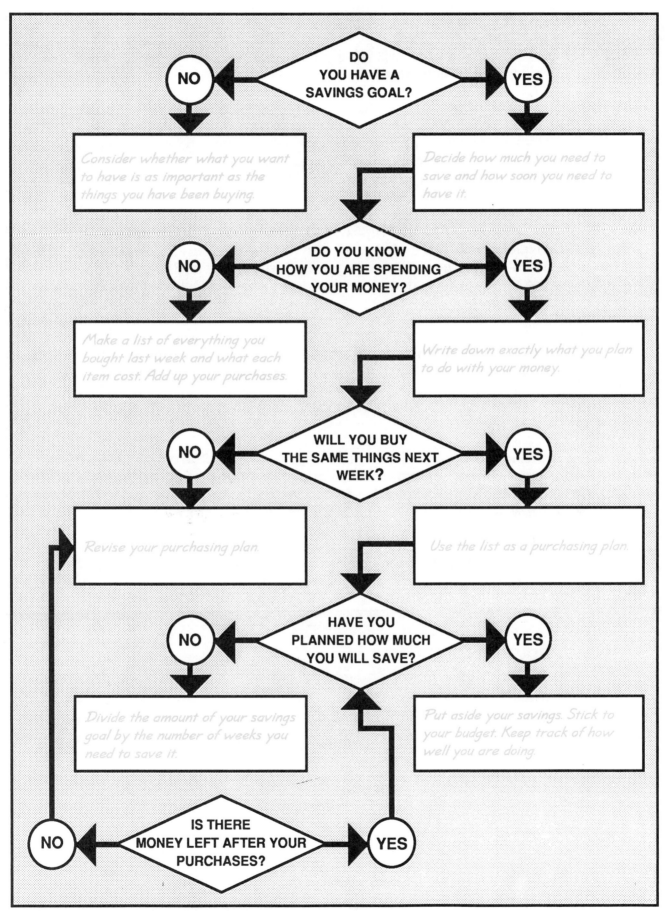

WEIGHT OF BUBBLE GUM

THINKING SKILL: Depicting values, estimating

CONTENT OBJECTIVE: Students will use a transitive order graph to identify which bubble gum gives them the most weight per unit.

DISCUSSION: TECHNIQUE—Use a transparency of the transitive order graph to record responses as students compare the weight per unit of pieces of bubble gum.

DIALOGUE—Remind students that the exact weight is not necessary; only the correct order of weight is significant. Students may wish to write the weight next to each brand name to help keep track of the order. The key concept in this lesson involves unit price.

If one piece of each brand of bubble gum costs the same, which brand gives you the most bubble gum for your money? How does knowing how much bubble gum you are getting in each piece help you understand which is the best buy? How do you find out whether all these brands cost the same for each piece? (If each piece of bubble gum does not cost the same, guide students through the process of computing the cost per gram.)

What factors other than unit price are important in your selection of bubble gum? (Taste; length of time that the flavor lasts; availability; bubble-blowing capability; whether it has baseball cards.) **What factors would not be important in your selection of bubble gum?** (How it is advertised; whether other people like it; whether the package is cute.)

Extend this lesson by explaining the grocery store practice of unit pricing (price per pound, ounce, pint, etc.).

How does knowing the price per pound of cereal help us decide which brand of cereal is the better buy? How does knowing the price per pound of cereal help us decide which size box of the same brand of cereal is the better buy? What other purchases do you make in which knowing the unit price would be helpful?

RESULT—Knowing the unit price helps us make more cost-effective purchases. Determining the significant factors in making choices helps us make better decisions.

WRITING EXTENSION
- **Explain how knowing the unit price of an item helps you get more for your money.**

THINKING ABOUT THINKING
- **How did using the graph help you understand and remember which brands of bubble gum give you the best value per piece?**
- **Design another graph that would help you describe the relative value of products.**
- **Suggest another situation in which using this graph would help you make better decisions.**

SIMILAR PERSONAL PROBLEM SOLVING LESSONS
- To compare price and weight in comparison shopping.
- To prioritize actions, items, or alternative choices.

WEIGHT OF BUBBLE GUM

DIRECTIONS: Read the passage carefully to determine the weight of various brands of bubble gum. Write each weight beside the brand name to help you compare their relative weights. Use the transitive order graph to record the brands in order, from the most to least weight per piece. Some weights are exact, but others can only be estimated from the data in the passage.

A consumer magazine for children compared the weight of a single piece of six popular brands of bubble gum. If a stick of each of these brands sells for the same price, the consumer gets a different amount of gum for the same price. The more the stick of gum weighs, the better value you are getting, and the less likely you are to need two pieces to blow a bubble.

Bubble Yum®, at 6.2 grams, is nearly three and one-half times the weight of Trident®. A stick of Carefree® or Orbit® weighs 2.8 grams. Compared to Carefree®, a stick of Chewels® weighs only 0.3 grams more, but a stick of Soft 'n Sugarfree® weighs about a gram more.

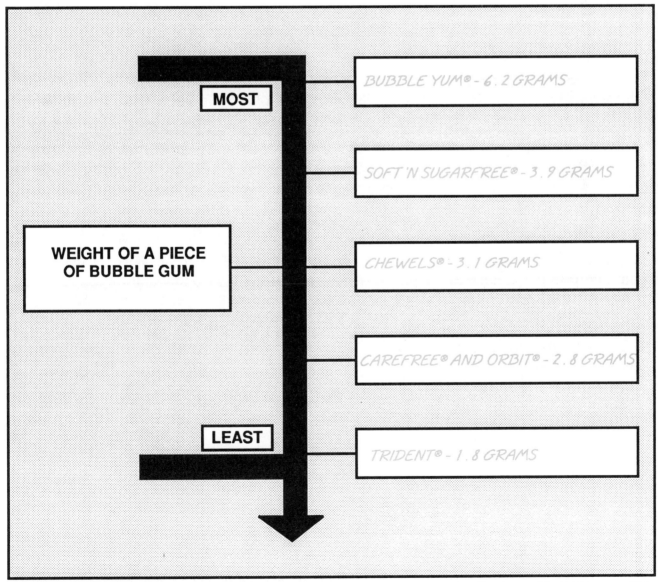

MOST

BUBBLE YUM® - 6.2 GRAMS

SOFT 'N SUGARFREE® - 3.9 GRAMS

WEIGHT OF A PIECE OF BUBBLE GUM

CHEWELS® - 3.1 GRAMS

CAREFREE® AND ORBIT® - 2.8 GRAMS

LEAST

TRIDENT® - 1.8 GRAMS

CALORIES IN FOODS

THINKING SKILL: Comparing values, estimating, predicting analogous values

CONTENT OBJECTIVE: Students will use an interval graph to depict the caloric value of various foods.

DISCUSSION: TECHNIQUE—Use a transparency of the interval graph to record the caloric values of different foods. If your students have not discussed calories, explain the concept that a calorie is a measurement of heat or energy produced by food. The following approximate caloric values may be helpful in establishing a frame of reference.

- One slice of bread = 75 calories.
- One tablespoon of butter (the serving needed to butter a slice of bread) = 100 calories.
- Eight ounces of whole milk (one glass) = 160 calories.
- One egg = 80 calories.
- One teaspoon of sugar = 16 calories.
- One tablespoon of jelly = 50 calories.

DIALOGUE—Encourage students to draw inferences suggested by the graphic representation and to identify trends or surprises in the relative caloric value of foods. When students know the calorie content and the nutritional value of their food choices, they have better principles for food selection.

What types or classes of foods are found on this list? (Entrees [main dish foods], drinks, desserts, snacks, vegetables, or fruit.) **Which foods belong in each class?** (If students seem uncertain about food classes, use a branching diagram to organize the foods under each type. Add other foods to each of these categories and look up their caloric value.)

Many upper elementary and middle-school students are concerned about their weight and make poor food choices in an effort to lose or gain weight. As they discuss the caloric values of foods in this lesson, emphasize the nutritional value of various foods and the importance of a balanced diet, in addition to caloric content.

Why do different foods have different numbers of calories? What characteristics do high-calorie foods have in common? What characteristics do low-calorie foods have in common? If you wanted to limit the number of calories you eat, which foods shown on the graph might you avoid? If you wanted to lose weight, which main dishes might you choose? Which drinks? Which desserts? Which snacks? (Vegetables or fruits may also be snacks.)

If you wanted to increase the number of calories you eat, which main dishes would add calories and other good nutrients to your meal? Which drinks? Which vegetables or fruits? Which desserts? Which snacks?

Which of your guesses were more than one hundred calories (high or low) from the actual caloric value? Why was your estimate off? (Did not realize the number of calories compared to other foods; did not realize that food preparation could add calories; was accustomed to buying fast food, regardless of the number of calories; did not really want to know; never thought about it before.) **How does knowing a few items in each calorie range help you estimate the number of calories in other foods more accurately?**

If students have studied the concept of "calorie" in science, it may be helpful to distinguish between calories of energy in physics and calories in foods. The scientific definition of "calorie" is "the quantity of energy necessary to raise the temperature of one gram of water by one degree Celsius (C) at constant atmospheric pressure." The word "calorie" in nutrition is actually 1000 calories, or one kilocalorie.

RESULT— Knowing the caloric content of the foods we eat and comparing their nutritional value gives us better principles for food selection. Our estimates of caloric value are often inaccurate; knowing some sample foods in each range of calories offers a basis for more informed estimates.

WRITING EXTENSION
- Explain why some foods have more calories than others.

THINKING ABOUT THINKING
- How did writing the foods on the interval graph help you "picture" the relative caloric value of foods?
- How does knowing a few sample values help you make better estimates?
- How does knowing why past estimates were off help you make better estimates in the future?
- Design another graph that would help you describe calorie decisions.

SIMILAR PERSONAL PROBLEM SOLVING LESSONS
- To describe cost ranges of items in a proposed budget.
- To depict speed, number, weight, and distances in sports statistics.

CALORIES IN FOODS

DIRECTIONS: See if you can guess about how many calories are in foods that students typically eat. Since it would be difficult to guess exactly, choose one of the following ranges of calories for each food. Write the calorie range in the calorie estimate column. Write each food in the appropriate range of calories on an interval graph.

A = 0–100 calories   D = 300–400 calories

B = 100–200 calories   E = 400–500 calories

C = 200–300 calories   F = 500–600 calories

FOOD	ESTIMATED CALORIES	FOOD	ESTIMATED CALORIES
APPLE	A	DOUGHNUT	B
BANANA	A	FRENCH FRIES (small order)	B
BANANA SPLIT	F	FRUIT ROLL (1/2 ounce)	A
CARROT	A	HOT FUDGE SUNDAE (1 scoop)	E
CEREAL (1 ounce, plain)	B	HAMBURGER (1/4 pound)	E
CHICKEN STRIPS (6)	C	HOT DOG	D
CHOCOLATE BAR (1 ounce)	B	ICE CREAM CONE (1 scoop)	D
CHOCOLATE CHIP COOKIE	A	PEACH	A
CHOCOLATE SHAKE (12 ounces)	D	PIZZA SLICE (1/12 large cheese)	E
COLA (12 ounces)	B	POPCORN (1 cup, unbuttered)	A
CORN CHIPS	B	SNACK CAKES (2)	C
DOUBLE CHEESEBURGER	F	TACO	B

CALORIES IN FOODS

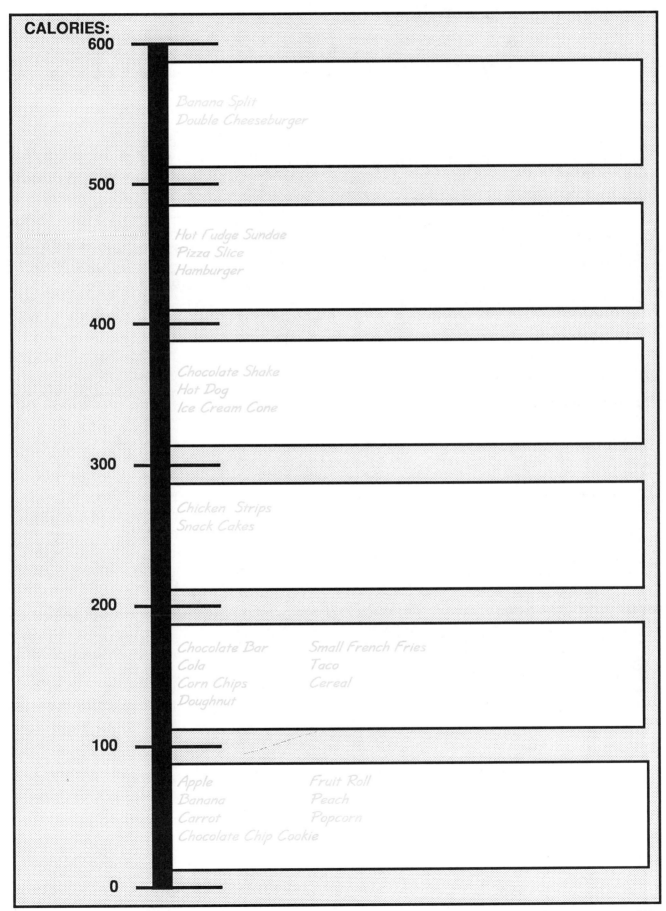

CALORIES:

600

Banana Split
Double Cheeseburger

500

Hot Fudge Sundae
Pizza Slice
Hamburger

400

Chocolate Shake
Hot Dog
Ice Cream Cone

300

Chicken Strips
Snack Cakes

200

Chocolate Bar   Small French Fries
Cola   Taco
Corn Chips   Cereal
Doughnut

100

Apple   Fruit Roll
Banana   Peach
Carrot   Popcorn
Chocolate Chip Cookie

0

HOW DO I LEARN IT WELL?

THINKING SKILL: Verbal sequences

CONTENT OBJECTIVE: Students will use a flowchart to identify the steps in learning a new skill or operation. *NOTE: This process is the student's metacognitive response to the use of the Hunter model. It guides students' monitoring of their own learning and can be used to teach procedures in any discipline.*

DISCUSSION: TECHNIQUE—Use a transparency of the flowchart to record responses as students report the steps in learning a new skill or operation. Use the steps to review a recent lesson involving a mathematics operation. Use these steps to design bulletin board displays to remind students of their part in the teaching/learning process.

    This lesson introduces students to the application of the six steps for effective teaching attributed to Madeline Hunter. The purpose of this lesson is to enable students to manage their own learning by monitoring their thinking at each step of the teacher's explanation of a new process. The student should clarify any unclear step and seek appropriate assistance.

    The lesson may be taught either directly or inductively. The student directions illustrate direct instruction. Students read about a process, record it on the left flowchart, then recall these steps in learning a recent mathematics operation. To introduce the lesson inductively, ask students to think about how they learned a recent mathematics operation and to write phrases on each line of the flowchart recording what they remember about learning the process. This experience prepares the student to apply the principles presented in the lesson.

    DIALOGUE—Encourage students to identify why it is important to seek appropriate help when any step in the process is not clear.

Step 1 (Anticipatory set)

Why is it important to identify examples of when you have learned something like this before? (To save time; to tie the new process to something that you already know how to do; to reduce anxiety or confusion about the new lesson.) **Why might you have trouble remembering when you learned to do something that was like this?** (Did not understand what the teacher was referring to; was absent for a previous lesson; forgot the previous lesson.) **What can you ask your teacher to do to help you understand the example?** (To remind you again of the process or terms; to give another example; to talk to you later about a missed lesson.)

Step 2 (Statement of objective)

Why is it important to clarify what your teacher is going to teach? (If you think you are going to learn to do one thing, and your teacher is going to teach something else, you are likely to be confused at the beginning of the lesson.) **Why might you be unclear about what your teacher is about to teach?** (You might not understand the terms.) **What can you ask your teacher to do to help you understand the objective?** (Clarify unfamiliar terms.)

Step 3 (Explanation/modeling)

Why is it important to follow what your teacher is explaining? (If you misunderstand the steps, the order of the steps, or why you do the steps, you will not be able to do the process correctly. When your teacher models a process, you have the opportunity to hear how someone else thinks through the problem.) **Why might you be unclear about what your teacher is explaining?** (The explanation could be long and complicated; your train of thought could have been interrupted; one step wasn't clear to you, so everything after that seems uncertain to you; you became confused or anxious and missed the rest of the process.) **What can you ask your teacher to do that would help you understand the explanation?** (Ask for clarification when the process is being explained.)

Step 4   (Guided practice)

Why is it important to practice the process correctly and immediately and to make sure that you understand it properly? (So that you do not practice incorrectly and establish wrong habits; so that you do not do your homework incorrectly; for your personal confidence.) **Why might you be unclear about how to do the process?** (You may have thought that you understood your teacher's explanation or example, but found that you did not when you tried to do the work by yourself.) **What can you ask your teacher to do to help you learn to do the process correctly?** (Ask to see the steps again; ask your teacher to check your work to see where you started making mistakes; ask your teacher to listen while you explain what you thought was the way to do it.)

Step 5   (Independent practice)

Why is it important to practice the process on your own? (For speed, personal confidence, and accuracy. When you are tested, you will be able to do the process well and quickly.) **Why might you make errors or take too much time to do the process?** (May not really understand what the process means; may not be remembering it correctly; may be fearful of making mistakes and make errors because of tension or confusion.) **What can you ask your teacher to do to help you do the process more accurately and quickly?** (Ask for another explanation; ask if there are shortcuts; ask to see the process pictured or mapped; ask for additional practice.)

Step 6   (Application)

Why is it important to know when you will do this again? (If you think the process is important, and know when and how you are going to use it again, then you may remember it better. You will anticipate using the process and feel more confident of doing it well.) **Why might you be unclear about when you will use the process again?** (If you are not certain of what the process really means, you may not see its future use.) **What can you ask your teacher to do to help you predict when you will use it again?** (Ask for other examples; explain why the process is important; relate it to other lessons.)

RESULT—Learning is more efficient and effective if one knows what to do to learn the process. Knowing why the steps in an explanation are important, what might lead to confusion, and what to do to clarify the objective puts the learner in charge of the learning.

© 1990 MIDWEST PUBLICATIONS • CRITICAL THINKING PRESS & SOFTWARE • P. O. Box 448, Pacific Grove, CA 93950   331

WRITING EXTENSION

* **Describe the steps in learning a new skill or process easily.**

THINKING ABOUT THINKING

* **Why is it important to understand the steps for learning a new process?**
* **Why is it important to clarify your own learning?**
* **What advantages do you see in knowing the steps?**
* **What advantages do you see in predicting why you might be confused?**
* **What advantages do you see in knowing how to ask for help?**
* **Design another graphic organizer that will help you learn effectively.**
* **Suggest another situation in which a flowchart could help you learn more efficiently.**

SIMILAR PERSONAL PROBLEM SOLVING LESSONS

* To depict the steps in instructions, information retrieval, study skills procedures, and independent study.

HOW DO I LEARN TO DO IT?

DIRECTIONS: Complete the flowchart on the left to record why each of the steps in learning a new skill is important.

Think about the last mathematics operation that you learned. Complete the flowchart on the right to identify what you remember about learning each of the steps.

Experts who study how people teach and learn effectively identify six steps that make learning to do something new clear and easy. Many teachers follow these steps to explain a new mathematics operation, a science procedure, an art activity, or a sports play.

Whether or not your teacher follows these steps exactly, you can have the benefits of learning more efficiently if you know what to look for, why you might be confused, and what kind of help to ask for.

Step 1:   Identify when you have learned something like this before. Connecting new learning to something you already know makes it easier and less confusing to learn the new skill. You are more confident that you will be able to do the new activity because you remember how well you can already do something similar.

Step 2:   Listen for the sentence or phrase that describes what you are about to learn. By understanding at the beginning what the lesson is about, you keep the purpose of the lesson in mind and connect the rest of the lesson to it. If you miss hearing the objective, you may almost follow the steps that the teacher is explaining, but not really understand what the process is for.

Step 3:   Be sure that you follow carefully the explanation or demonstration that the teacher shows you. If you misunderstand any step, you may not be able to do the process. Check yourself to be sure that you understand why, as well as how, each step in the process is done.

Step 4:   Did you practice the process enough while the teacher could help you? Although you think you understand how to do something at the time, you may later find out that you misunderstood or cannot remember how to do one of the steps.

Step 5:   Can you do the process accurately and quickly? Teachers assign the number of practice problems necessary for most students to do the task fast and well. Only you know whether you do the process quickly and accurately enough.

Step 6:   When will you use the process again? Expecting to use it helps you realize how well you understand it now and reminds you of the process when you are asked to use it again.

HOW DO I LEARN IT WELL?

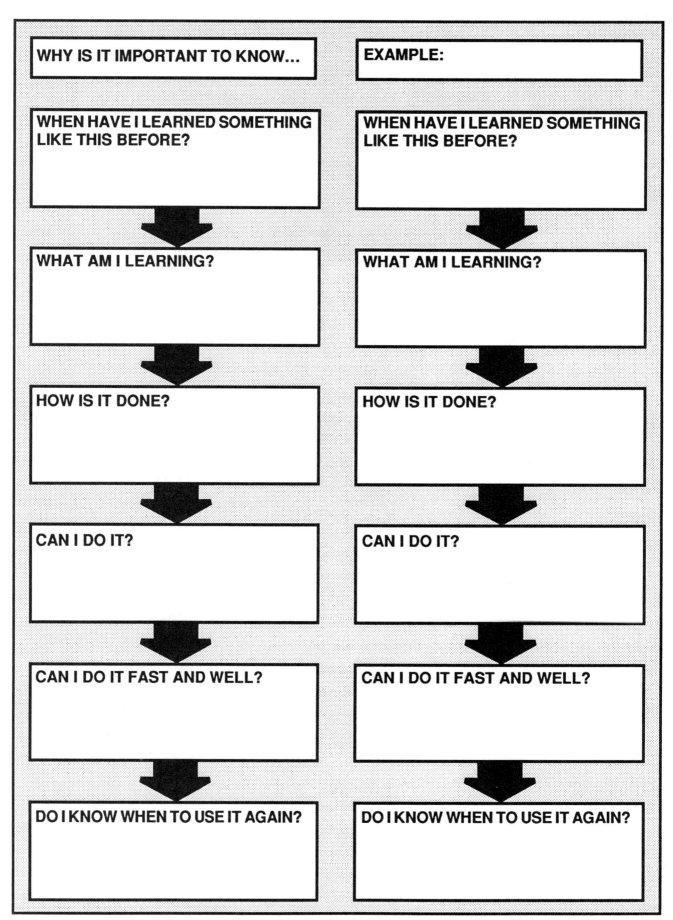

WHY IS IT IMPORTANT TO KNOW...	EXAMPLE:
WHEN HAVE I LEARNED SOMETHING LIKE THIS BEFORE?	WHEN HAVE I LEARNED SOMETHING LIKE THIS BEFORE?
WHAT AM I LEARNING?	WHAT AM I LEARNING?
HOW IS IT DONE?	HOW IS IT DONE?
CAN I DO IT?	CAN I DO IT?
CAN I DO IT FAST AND WELL?	CAN I DO IT FAST AND WELL?
DO I KNOW WHEN TO USE IT AGAIN?	DO I KNOW WHEN TO USE IT AGAIN?

DO I REALLY KNOW IT?

THINKING SKILL: Verbal sequences, verbal classification, identifying attributes

CONTENT OBJECTIVE: Students will use a flowchart to confirm their clear understanding of a concept. *NOTE: This process helps students "check" how well they understand key concepts and can be used to review such concepts in any discipline.*

DISCUSSION: TECHNIQUE—Use a transparency of the flowchart to record student responses as they review how clearly they understand key concepts. This process may be used to introduce significant concepts or to review concepts before a unit test. Design a bulletin board display of this process to remind students how to review for a test.

This lesson introduces students to the six steps of Hilda Taba's concept-development model. Usually, the Taba model is used by the teacher to explain a new concept effectively. The purpose of this lesson, however, is to teach students how to confirm their understanding of important ideas. It is the responsibility of the student to be certain that he or she understands a concept clearly. This review technique is an effective memory tool and promotes students' confidence in their ability to take tests.

The lesson may be taught either directly or inductively. The student directions illustrate direct instruction: students read the passage about the process, describe it on the left flowchart, then apply it to a concept they have recently learned. To conduct the lesson inductively, ask students to think about a recently-learned concept and to write phrases on the flowchart on the right to record what they remember about that idea. Then discuss why each question is helpful in understanding something.

DIALOGUE—Encourage students to identify why each step in the process is important in clarifying whether they truly understand an idea.

Step 1 **Why is it important to identify what kind of thing or idea this concept is?** (The category to which the concept belongs will be included in its definition. Accurately stating the category reduces confusion about the concept.)

Step 2 **Why is it important to be able to name some examples?** (Examples help you remember the concept.)

Step 3 **Why is it important to be able to identify some similar ideas?** (You usually learn new ideas by tying them to something that you already know well. A similar idea, even one not in the same field, becomes a "mental peg" on which to hang the new concept.)

Step 4 **Why is it important to be able to identify concepts that are different?** (If you do not understand an idea clearly, you may confuse it with something else. By recognizing ideas that are somewhat different and identifying why they are different, you can clearly distinguish this key idea from others.)

Step 5 **Why is it important to identify the important characteristics of the concept.** (Important characteristics will be included in a definition of the concept. If you do not know the important characteristics of a concept, then you really do not have a clear understanding of it and are likely to confuse it with other ideas.)

Step 6 **Why is it important to be able to define a key concept?** (A definition is the precise expression of what something is and how it is different from other things similar to it. A definition demonstrates how clearly you really understand a concept. When you combine the category in Step 1 with the significant characteristics in Step 5, you have formed a precise definition.)

RESULT—You can be sure that you know what something is if you can name what kind of thing it is, give some examples, identify some things that are similar to and different from it, name the significant characteristics, and write a full definition of it.

WRITING EXTENSION

• Describe the steps for checking how clearly you understand a concept.

THINKING ABOUT THINKING

• In what situations is it important to be sure you understand a concept?

• Why is it important for you to be confident about your understanding?

• Design another graphic organizer that will help you review a concept effectively.

• Suggest another situation in which using a flowchart could help you review a concept more efficiently.

SIMILAR PERSONAL PROBLEM SOLVING LESSONS

• To depict the steps in instructions, information retrieval, study skills procedures, and independent study.

DO I REALLY KNOW IT?

DIRECTIONS: Complete the left flowchart to explain why each step is important to be sure that you really understand what something is. Think about the example and answer each of the questions on the the flowchart on the right side.

Have you ever believed that you knew something well but found out on a test that you didn't really understand it as clearly as you thought? Would it help you to know what questions you could ask to "check out" how completely you understand what you are learning? The following six questions can help you do that.

1. **What kind of idea is it?**

   Name the category in which the concept fits. Be as specific as you can in naming the group to which the person, place, thing, or organism belongs. This step narrows your attention to the Idea you are trying to describe.

2. **Can I name some examples?**

   Name the best examples of this idea that you can think of. Examples help you remember the idea by images or memories. You can sometimes remember an example more easily than the idea it represents. You also use examples to explain the idea to someone else.

3. **What are some similar ideas?**

   Name something that is similar in some important way, perhaps from a different subject, that helps you remember the concept you are studying. Similarities connect what you are learning to what you already know.

4. **What are some different ideas?**

   Name something that is different from the concept you are studying, that you must not confuse with it. Identify how the difference will keep you from confusing the two concepts. Recognizing and knowing differences separates your new idea from other similar ones and helps you remember concepts clearly so that you don't forget it or misunderstand it.

5. **What are its important characteristics?**

   Name the qualities that make this concept what it is. If you really understand something, you can explain what makes it special and sets it apart from other things of this kind.

6. **Can I give a full definition?**

   Combine the category in Question 1 with the characteristics in Question 5 to create a complete definition. Naming the category and the characteristics that make it different from others describes the idea or thing and shows that you understand clearly what it is.

DO I REALLY KNOW IT?

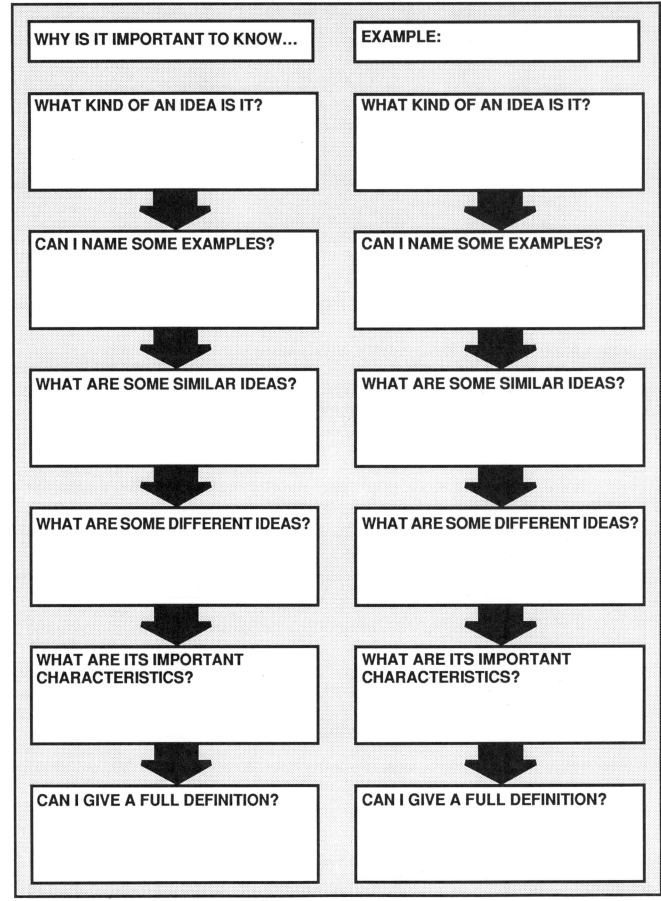

WHY IS IT IMPORTANT TO KNOW...

EXAMPLE:

WHAT KIND OF AN IDEA IS IT?

WHAT KIND OF AN IDEA IS IT?

CAN I NAME SOME EXAMPLES?

CAN I NAME SOME EXAMPLES?

WHAT ARE SOME SIMILAR IDEAS?

WHAT ARE SOME SIMILAR IDEAS?

WHAT ARE SOME DIFFERENT IDEAS?

WHAT ARE SOME DIFFERENT IDEAS?

WHAT ARE ITS IMPORTANT CHARACTERISTICS?

WHAT ARE ITS IMPORTANT CHARACTERISTICS?

CAN I GIVE A FULL DEFINITION?

CAN I GIVE A FULL DEFINITION?

THINK/PAIR/SHARE

DIRECTIONS: Think about the discussion your class just held. The following flowchart shows the steps in the Think/Pair/Share process used in the discussion. In each box of the diagram, explain how each step was useful in helping you and your partner understand and discuss the issue.

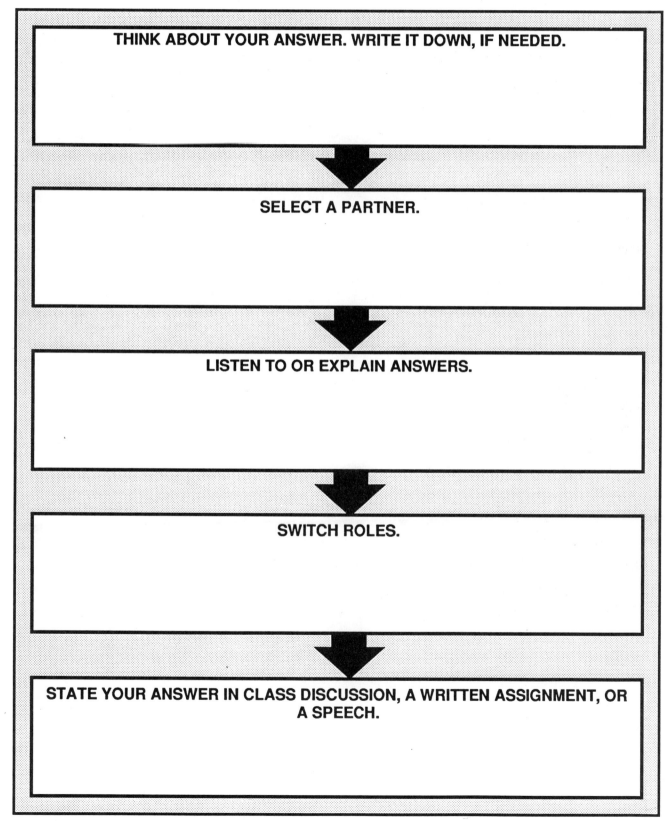

THINK ABOUT YOUR ANSWER. WRITE IT DOWN, IF NEEDED.

SELECT A PARTNER.

LISTEN TO OR EXPLAIN ANSWERS.

SWITCH ROLES.

STATE YOUR ANSWER IN CLASS DISCUSSION, A WRITTEN ASSIGNMENT, OR A SPEECH.

THINK/PAIR/SHARE

THINKING SKILL: Verbal sequences

CONTENT OBJECTIVE: Students will use a flowchart to confirm their understanding of a concept or process. *NOTE: This lesson introduces students to a popular, effective peer-coaching technique clarified in the research of Arthur Whimbey and John Lockhead. The purpose of this lesson is to demonstrate the effectiveness of improving students' understanding of important ideas by peer discussion.*

DISCUSSION: TECHNIQUE—Use a transparency of the flowchart to record responses as students discuss peer coaching as a study technique. Peer coaching may be used to introduce significant concepts or to review concepts before a unit test.

Since this lesson is best taught inductively, there is no background passage for students. To introduce the lesson, ask students to answer an evaluation question from their text material. Follow the directions on the flowchart. Conduct an appropriate discussion of the content issue. After the discussion, hand out the flowchart and ask students to identify how each step in the process was helpful.

Students may discuss the content issue informally or by a more structured listening technique. Informal discussion allows both students to understand how and why the partner describes an idea or carries out an operation in a particular way. Peer coaching allows the listener to point out errors, omissions, or misconceptions that the partner may express.

For a more structured listening exercise, the listener is limited to three types of questions: those which clarify the partner's idea; those which extend the partner's basic thought; and those which challenge the partner's interpretation or position. The listener may make no statements, but may only raise questions that will encourage the partner to reconsider, refine, modify, or extend his or her answer.

This lesson demonstrates the value of wait time and clarification before group discussion of significant ideas. It may also be used as a peer tutorial technique to allow students to reflect on, correct, or self-correct basic skills in mathematics, science, spelling, reading or any instruction that requires detailed directions.

DIALOGUE— Help students discuss why each step in the process is important.

Step 1:   **Why is it important to think through and/or write down your own thoughts before you answer complex questions? Why is it important to do this before you listen to other people's ideas?**

This step is an example of the use of wait time before class discussion of significant ideas. It allows students to reflect on and record their ideas before other comments alter or modify their thoughts. It allows less secure students to confirm that they had already thought of sound answers before other students explain similar ideas. It allows students to express their basic thoughts; the subsequent steps will allow them to express those ideas in the best choice of words at their command.

Step 2:   **Why is it important to try out your ideas with a partner before you discuss them in class?**

Rehearsing your answer helps you see its strong points more clearly. You clarify ideas so that you can express them better. You have the opportunity to test ideas with one person before speaking in front of the class. You are reassured by your partner about the value of your thoughts. You have an opportunity to change any part of your answer that seems inappropriate. Listening to how you explain your thoughts helps you clarify them.

Step 3: **Why is it important to listen carefully to a partner's explanation?**
Listening is the key to your being helpful to that person. You will learn new versions of his or her idea that may allow you to understand the subject differently. The active listening in this activity is useful in other personal and school situations.

What effect does being limited to certain types of questions have on the listener?
The listener must understand the idea from the partner's point of view and help the partner express the idea in the fullest possible way. The listener respects the value of the partner's thought and recognizes that all decisions about it are the partner's.

What effect does being asked certain types of questions about his or her idea have on the partner?
The partner realizes the value of his or her thoughts and is prompted to express them more effectively. The partner becomes confident in expressing his or her answer in class and often selects more descriptive or precise language.

Step 4: **Why is it important for the pair to switch roles?**
Both individuals gain from this experience and bring capabilities and insights to it.

Step 5: **Why is it important to use the thoughts, resulting from the Think/Pair/Share activity, immediately in class discussion or assignments?**
Application confirms the value of the thinking and the effectiveness of the technique. While students are still clear and enthusiastic about their ideas, it is important to put them to practical use.

RESULT—Discussing an idea or process with a partner clarifies or corrects it.

WRITING EXTENSION

• **Describe the steps to improving what you understand by partnership discussion.**

THINKING ABOUT THINKING

• **Why is it important to discuss what you understand with a partner? In what situations might Think/Pair/Share discussion be helpful?**
• **Why is it important to be confident about your understanding?**

SIMILAR PERSONAL PROBLEM SOLVING LESSONS

• To depict the steps in instructions, information retrieval, study skills procedures, and independent study.